Countering New(est) Terrorism

Hostage-Taking, Kidnapping, and Active Violence—Assessing, Negotiating, and Assaulting

Countering New(est) Terrorism

Hostage-Taking, Kidnapping, and Active Violence—Assessing, Negotiating, and Assaulting

Bruce Oliver Newsome and
W. James Stewart

CRC Press
Taylor & Francis Group
Boca Raton London New York

CRC Press is an imprint of the
Taylor & Francis Group, an **informa** business

CRC Press
Taylor & Francis Group
6000 Broken Sound Parkway NW, Suite 300
Boca Raton, FL 33487-2742

First issued in paperback 2020

ISBN-13: 978-1-138-50159-1 (hbk)
ISBN-13: 978-0-367-77897-2 (pbk)

Library of Congress Cataloging-in-Publication Data

Names: Newsome, Bruce Oliver, author. | Stewart, W. James (William James), author.
Title: Countering new(est) terrorism : hostage-taking, kidnapping, and active violence : assessing, negotiating, and assaulting / by Bruce O. Newsome and W. James Stewart.
Description: Boca Raton, FL : CRC Press, [2018] | Includes bibliographical references and index.
Identifiers: LCCN 2017028170| ISBN 9781138501591 (hardback : alk. paper) | ISBN 9781315144436 (ebook)
Subjects: LCSH: Terrorism. | Hostage negotiations. | Violence--Prevention. | Crisis management.
Classification: LCC HV6431 .N4929 2018 | DDC 363.325/16--dc23
LC record available at https://lccn.loc.gov/2017028170

Visit the Taylor & Francis Web site at
http://www.taylorandfrancis.com

and the CRC Press Web site at
http://www.crcpress.com

Contents

List of Figures

List of Figures

List of Tables

Acknowledgments

The authors thank the following officials, experts, and interns for information or advice (in alphabetical order):

- Sahra Agahi (University of California, Berkeley)
- Asad Q. Ahmed (Professor of Near Eastern Studies, University of California, Berkeley)
- Samar Amidi (University of California, Berkeley)
- Mitra Dastbaz (University of California, Berkeley)
- Arnaud Emery (Centre Lyonnais d'Études de Sécurité Internationale et de Défense [Lyon Center of International Security and Defense Studies], University Jean Moulin Lyon III, France)
- Jonathan Fisher (University of California, Berkeley)
- David O. Gonzales (former United States Marine Corps)
- Jeff Harp (former Assistant Special Agent in Charge, San Francisco Division and Hostage Rescue Team, Federal Bureau of Investigation)
- Ron Hassner (Professor of Political Science, University of California, Berkeley)
- Elsa Hugon (University Jean Moulin Lyon III, France)
- Douglas Hunt (former Supervisory Special Agent, Federal Bureau of Investigation)
- Neil Joeck (Research Scholar, Institute of International Studies, University of California, Berkeley)
- Andrew W. Krizaj (Crisis Negotiation Coordinator, San Francisco Division, Federal Bureau of Investigation)
- Nicole Le (University of California, Berkeley)
- John Lightfoot (former Assistant Special Agent in Charge, San Francisco Division, Federal Bureau of Investigation)

- Sayed Ammar Nakshawani (Professor of Shi'a Studies, Hartford Seminary, Connecticut)
- Gary Noesner (former Chief of the Crisis Negotiation Unit, Federal Bureau of Investigation, and author of *Stalling for Time: My Life as an FBI Hostage Negotiator*, 2011)
- Mike Pernick (Special Agent, Federal Bureau of Investigation)
- Hongmei Qu (University of California, Berkeley)
- Roy Ramm (Managing Director of Extra Yard; formerly Director of Negotiator Training, Metropolitan Police)
- Aditya Ranganathan (University of California, Berkeley)
- Saad Rehman (University of California, Berkeley)
- Sam Ridge (University of California, Berkeley)
- Mark A. Thundercloud (Crisis Negotiation Unit, Federal Bureau of Investigation)
- Calvin Tsang (University of California, Berkeley)
- Greg Walton (former Senior Team Leader, Special Weapons and Tactics, San Francisco Division, Federal Bureau of Investigation)
- Estelle Zielinski (Sciences Po—Institut d'études politiques de Paris)
- Darren Zook (Professor of International Relations, University of California, Berkeley)

Authors

Bruce Oliver Newsome, PhD, is a lecturer in international relations at the School of Global Studies at the University of California, Berkeley. Before teaching, he was a research policy scientist at the RAND Corporation in Santa Monica, California. He earned his undergraduate degree with honors in war studies from Kings College London, a master's degree in political science from the University of Pennsylvania, and a PhD in international studies from the University of Reading.

W. James Stewart is a graduate of the University of California, Berkeley, specializing in Middle Eastern studies including the Islamic State, Amman, Jordan, and Erbil, Iraq.

Disclosure

This research was not funded except by the authors themselves, for the public good. They received no restrictions or obligations or conditions on their access to the information or sources used in this research.

1

Introduction

Objectives

How should we analyze and assess new terrorist behaviors? What are the particular risks and challenges from new terrorism? Should we negotiate with terrorists? How should we negotiate with terrorists procedurally? To what should we aim during these crises? How should we end such crises? When should we use force against terrorists?

These are some of the questions answered in this book, using a review of the specialist literature, an unprecedented analysis of the large-*n* data, qualitative exploration of key cases, interviews with experienced officials, and real-world simulations of new terrorist crises.

More than 20 years ago, a few scholars identified the rise of what they categorized as "new terrorism," characterized mainly by increased lethality and religious motivations. This book takes an evidence-based approach to define and describe this new terrorism. Moreover, we show the acute adaptiveness and progressive developments of new terrorists, so that now, more than 20 years since new terrorism was identified, we should be thinking of the "newest terrorism" that has emerged in the last years, its form today, and its trends into the future.

New terrorists are increasingly risky. Terrorist hostage-takings, kidnappings, and active violence are increasingly frequent and deadly. Increasingly, these activities are used by terrorists as means to other ends—including, unfortunately, to lengthen publicity before mass killings.

This book seeks to improve our knowledge of new terrorist behaviors, and our skills in responding to new terrorist behaviors. Along the way, this book challenges some frequent myths about terrorist behaviors, such as incorrect characterizations of recent terrorist hostage-taking as being effectively the same as old terrorist hostage-taking (Dolnik and Fitzgerald, 2011, pp. 269–273).

Our new theories and data suggest that new terrorists are dramatically more ideological, murderous, and suicidal; they are generally less reconcilable, less trusting of official negotiators, less likely to release detainees, and more likely to kill detainees; they are less likely to demand ransoms, yet more likely to release hostages in cases in which they do demand ransom; they are more informed about the official side's policies, tactics, techniques, and procedures; they make use of new information and communication technologies to communicate with suppliers, controllers, surveyors, the public, and officials; they are more capable fighters—they kill more people even though they deploy fewer fighters per hostage; and they make use of freer societies to access easier targets, while holding more complex interpretations of legitimate targets and legitimate handling of hostages.

Given our new theories and data, we give more informed advice about how to navigate such crises, but we also challenge fashionable, wishful thinking that all terrorists are open to rational negotiation or de-radicalization, and the reductionist thinking that military responses always reflect badly on the official side (Cole, 2009, p. 238; Stern, 2010; Dolnik and Fitzgerald, 2011, p. 272; Powell, 2014, 2015). In this book, our evidence proves a category of hostage-taking that we call *irreconcilable hostage-taking*, in which the hostage-takers are intent on killing all the hostages eventually, whatever alternative is offered to them.

Most books on hostage-takings include only negotiations as official responses, but we include assessments, negotiations, and assaults in the full spectrum of potential responses. The intent of this book is to help the official counterterrorist side to assess, negotiate, and (if necessary) assault terrorist hostage-takers, kidnappers, and active shooters. For instance, we identify ways to manipulate the religious obligations and other obligations on terrorists not to harm detainees.

Scope

The focus of this book is on terrorist hostage-takings, kidnappings, and active violence. The scope of this book extends to official responses with terrorists generally. For instance, our advice on negotiating with terrorist hostage-takers, kidnappers, and active shooters is applicable to negotiating with other terrorists for other purposes, such as to make peace, or to discover demands. The implications also extend to nonterrorist hostage-takings, kidnappings, and active shootings.

This book is both descriptive and prescriptive. We describe terrorist behaviors, using our own extension of the most useful large-*n* dataset (Global Terrorism Database), qualitative exploration of key cases, and an unprecedented review of the doctrine issued by new terrorists themselves.

We prescribe useful, practical, and effective responses to these terrorist behaviors by applying our new descriptive knowledge, review of official practices, interviews with experienced officials, and real-world simulations of new terrorist crises.

Justifications

This book is interesting for anyone studying terrorism, violent crime, or negotiations. It is important to the improvement of our preparedness to deal with the increased frequency and deadliness of new terrorism, which is differentiated by changes in behaviors, capabilities, and intents.

This book effectively fills a gap in our knowledge and skills. It fills a gap in our knowledge because it compares old and new terrorist hostage-taking for the first time through large-*n* analysis. The large-*n* dataset used here, and in most analyses of terrorism in recent years, has previously lacked any differentiation of new versus old terrorism, which this book provides for the first time.

This book fills a gap in our skills because it prescribes responses to new terrorism in particular. Little literature focuses on responding to new terrorists particularly, and most of the latter fails to separate new and old terrorism practically.

This book is focused on terrorist behaviors, yet the skills, lessons, advice, and data in this book are relevant to crisis negotiation in general, not just terrorist crises in particular. Indeed, the increasing frequency of self-barricades, suicidal confrontations with police, and hostage-takings, and the increasing likelihood of terrorism, suggest that the skills, lessons, advice, and data should be generalized to police everywhere. Currently, most police are not especially trained for such crises, not even in America or Britain, where the risks are unusually high. These issues are illustrated well by the recent experiences and reflections of a police constable in the Metropolitan Police of London:

> As a newly qualified police officer, I arrived on scene at a two-storey house and was confronted by an extremely agitated man in an upstairs window. In one hand was a cigarette lighter, and in the other a knife held to the throat of his partner. He told me that no-one was taking him back to prison and any attempt by the Police to enter the building would be fatal. He cautioned that he had turned on all gas appliances in the house, and one flick of the lighter would cause a massive explosion. He asked for armed Police to attend and "end it all" and then I discovered that a negotiator was at least 30 minutes away.
>
> Police instructors are required to teach more legal topics and skills using less time and resources than ever before. As a result new officers are given little or no training regarding crisis interventions or hostage situations. I am forever grateful that personal interest had caused me to read various books on these matters. I employed techniques I had learned such as active listening, reflecting, stalling for time, monitoring for "suicide by cop" risk factors and more. Ultimately I moved the situation along to a peaceful resolution. The suspect released his partner and then presented himself to me for arrest.
>
> As global security issues evolve we are seeing changes in the scope and frequency of hostage incidents, especially involving terrorists and radicalized individuals. There has perhaps never been a time when a front line officer is more likely to confront a hostage/barricade situation, especially one with terrorist links. There exists a tremendous opportunity for the academic world to join with law enforcement and the security services to strengthen the knowledge of how to proceed in such circumstances.
>
> Front line officers are the first "eyes and ears" at practically every incident. Being able to identify risk factors, likely motives and intentions can greatly enhance the early situational awareness of specialized units who will ultimately take charge. It may also reduce the risk of a catastrophic failure due

to responding to the incident incorrectly. After all, there are no guarantees for when a fully trained negotiator will arrive on scene. Additionally, by developing an understanding of negotiation and communication an officer will no doubt increase their effectiveness in all manner of other situations.

Trained negotiators already have different approaches for talking to individuals with mental illnesses, suicidal intentions, gang members, ex-military etc. It seems natural and necessary that guiding principles for negotiating with the new terrorists are added to their "skills toolbox".

Finally, law enforcement institutions have a duty of care to protect their officers and the public. If knowledge and skills exist that could benefit both, we must share that wisdom with those who can use it for the greatest good.[1]

Preview

This book is organized into 13 chapters:

1. This introduction
2. Analyzing new terrorist behaviors
3. Assessing new terrorist risks
4. Should you negotiate?
5. Immediate management of the incident
6. Develop a relationship
7. Assess their psychology
8. Assess their motivations, intentions, and goals
9. Negotiating for ransoms
10. Negotiating for prisoners
11. Resolve the negotiation
12. Should the official side consider violence?
13. Assaulting

Chapter 2 reviews conceptualizations and assessments of terrorist active violence, hostage-takings, kidnappings, hijackings, barricades, and crises, before going on to review conceptualizations of terrorism—including political terrorism, religious terrorism, Jihadi terrorism, and new terrorism.

Chapter 3 describes the data and methods that we use to assess terrorism, the trends in terrorism risks since 1970, trends in terrorist hostage-taking risks in particular, and the particular challenges of new terrorism.

[1] This police constable chose to remain anonymous given recent directives from the Metropolitan Police toward anonymity when commenting on police work by current police officers. He was interviewed in August 2016.

Chapter 4 considers arguments about whether to negotiate with terrorists at all. In order to be most useful—in the applied, practical sense, we have reviewed the issue as a debate, and organized our review by nine affirmative or negative arguments, in sequential sections.

Chapter 5 reviews the processes of managing critical incidents in total, recommends a nine-step process, and explains the immediate four tasks or responses to the incident:

1. Isolate the local hostage-takers from any remote controllers
2. Assess the situation
3. Manage publicity
4. Manage time and contingencies

Chapter 6 explains the principles of developing a relationship with the hostage-takers (often described narrowly as "building rapport and trust"):

1. Employ active listening and empathy
2. Acknowledge skepticism
3. Appeal to morality, ethics, and religious laws
4. Consider trustworthy third-party intermediaries
5. Make minor bargains or trades
6. Provoke thought

Chapter 7 explains how to assess the other side's psychology by answering the following questions:

1. Are they rational?
2. Are they murderous?
3. Are they suicidal?

Chapter 8 teaches how to assess the other side's motivations, intentions, and goals:

1. Are they taking people in order to gain intelligence?
2. Are they seeking publicity?
3. Are they seeking ransoms?
4. Are they seeking to exchange prisoners?

Chapter 9 advises the reader on how to negotiate for the release of hostages or kidnapping victims in exchange for ransom. It explains how to understand and manipulate terrorists' motivations and legal and religious obligations given a demand for ransom, and reviews the arguments for and against paying for hostages.

Chapter 10 gives advice on how to negotiate for the release of hostages in exchange for prisoners, explains how to manipulate the hostage-takers given this demand, gives advice about how to manipulate international law and religious law in order to persuade the hostage-takers to grant special protections to certain categories of detainee (prisoner of war, noncombatant, female, child, able male, and low-value person), and reviews arguments about the justifiability of an exchange of hostages for prisoners.

Chapter 11 reviews the negotiator's objectives other than the release of hostages, the arguments over what makes a good deal, and the practical difficulties of implementing the deal.

Chapter 12 considers the arguments about whether the official side should consider using force, and when an assault should be triggered.

Chapter 13 considers the practical challenges of assaulting, and the principles, processes, and tactics of assaulting.

2

Analyzing New Terrorist Behaviors

In this chapter, we conceptualize and assess the following:

- New terrorist attacks
- Old terrorism, new terrorism, religious terrorism, and Jihadi terrorism

Terrorist Behaviors

Here we review terrorist attacks in the real world (not cyberspace, or idle threats), including active violence, hostage-takings, kidnappings, hijackings, barricades, crises, and any overlapping situations and terms.

Active Violence

Violence can be legitimate, such as when an officer shoots to death a resolute terrorist before he or she can detonate explosives in a crowded public place.

Here we are concerned with illegitimate terrorist violence. Most terrorist events start violently, so they often include or overlap what are normatively called *active shootings* in the English language. Unfortunately, the term *active shooting* is not always accurate, as the attacker might be using weapons other than firearms, such as knives or automobiles—increasingly so, among new terrorists. More literate terms would be *active attack* or *active violence*, although *active shooting* remains normative.

Given an increased frequency of active shootings, and increased attention, the term is now popular, while the issue has become more difficult for officials to handle:

> Of the many challenges local police departments and communities face, "active shooter" situations are among the most chaotic and disruptive. The term "active shooter" was once relatively unknown outside of law enforcement. That same term is now a headline somewhere in the U.S. on a near-weekly basis. The definition of such an attack is relatively straight forward—"an individual actively engaged in killing or attempting to kill people in a confined and populated area"—yet nothing about the real-time response to active shooter incidents is straight forward.
>
> The "active" part of the "active shooter" label refers to whether the shooting is believed to still be unfolding as law enforcement responds to the scene. Generally, responding officers will have little more information than an initial call for "shots fired," followed by additional calls suggesting a larger issue than an isolated shooting incident.
>
> **(Soufan Group, 2016)**

The U.S. Federal Bureau of Investigation (FBI) defines an active shooting as an active engagement in killing or attempting to kill people in a populated area. Isolating such active shootings (excluding weapons other than firearms, and excluding firearms used in organized crime, suicides, or accidents), the FBI reports a rising although volatile trend (Figure 2.1).

Such active shootings account for many times fewer events than other shootings in America (most of which are categorized as suicides or accidents, followed by organized crimes). In the two most recent years reported, the FBI counted 20 active shootings in 2014 and 20 events in 2015 (Figure 2.1). These 40 active shootings killed 92 American persons, whereas other shootings (including suicides and accidents) kill around 30,000 American persons per year.

Active shootings are so narrowly defined officially that they are not representative of all gun crimes (crimes using firearms), and they exclude gun crimes that

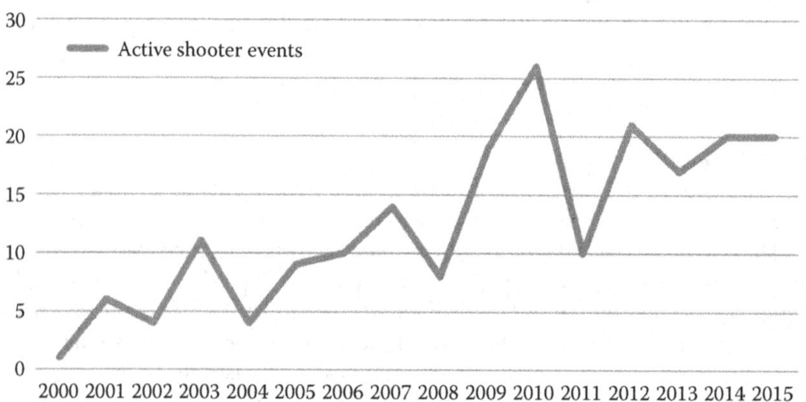

Figure 2.1 Active shooter events in the United States by year, 2000–2015. (Data source: FBI [United States, Federal Bureau of Investigation]. 2016a. "Active Shooter Incidents," FBI. Available at: https://www.fbi.gov/about/partnerships/office-of-partner-engagement/active-shooter-incidents.)

seem similar, such as ambushes of law enforcement officers, which average about 215 ambushes per year. More than 57,000 police officers are violently assaulted per year in America, of which only about a third were assaulted with firearms.

While active shootings account for a tiny fraction of all the crimes and deaths tracked by the FBI, terrorist active shootings are the deadliest crimes with firearms. In 2015, the deadliest terrorist attack and the deadliest active shooting for that year was the shooting to death of 14 people in San Bernardino, California, in December, by an American immigrant couple inspired by the Islamic State of Iraq and the Levant. In 2016, the deadliest terrorist attack and the deadliest active shooting in American history to date was the shooting to death of 49 people inside a nightclub in Orlando, Florida, in June, by an American man inspired by the same terrorist-insurgent organization.

In addition to terrorists, other criminals using firearms are murdering more people in America. In 2015, the murder rate in the United States rose by 10.8% compared to 2014, although this was still at a rate lower than peak rates in the 1990s. Of murders with a known primary weapon,[1] 71.5% involved firearms in 2015, compared to 67.7% in 2014. Most violent crime rates rose from 2014 to 2015, but the rise in the murder rate (by 10.8%) was greater than the rise in the overall violent crime rate (by 3.9%).

Active shootings are of concern outside of America also, even in countries with less freedom to access firearms, such as Britain. In 2013, a former member of the Metropolitan Police's firearms unit warned that "Firearms in the hands of criminals and those with malicious intent will always be an issue in a bustling city such as London and that is why we must rely on the ability of the police to tackle these persons" (Smith, 2013, p. 9). This was before a rash of terrorist active shootings occurred in Canadian, French, German, and American cities in 2014, 2015, and 2016, mostly inspired by the Islamic State of Iraq and Levant. Late in 2016, Britain's Assistant Commissioner for Counter-terrorism (Mark Rowley) launched a national campaign to encourage the public to inform the police of illegal weapons, and warned that almost half of all terrorist plots disrupted in Britain since 2013 involved an objective to obtain firearms (Flynn, 2016).

Hostage-Takings

Human beings can be detained legitimately, such as when an official authority imprisons a terrorist after a fair and just conviction. Such a person can be described as a detainee or a prisoner but is not rightly described as a hostage.

International law defines a hostage as "a person detained and under the threat of death, injury, or continued detention by an individual or group in order to compel a third party to do (or abstain from doing) any act as an explicit or implicit condition of the person's release" (United Nations, 1979a, Article 1).

---

[1] The FBI estimated 15,696 murders for 2015, and reported 13,455 murders by weapons for 2015 (FBI, 2016).

U.S. criminal law defines a hostage-taker as follows:

> Except as provided in subsection (b) of this section, whoever, whether inside or outside the United States, seizes or detains and threatens to kill, to injure, or to continue to detain another person in order to compel a third person or a governmental organization to do or abstain from doing any act as an explicit or implicit condition for the release of the person detained, or attempts or conspires to do so, shall be punished by imprisonment for any term of years or for life and, if the death of any person results, shall be punished by death or life imprisonment.
>
> **(U.S. Code, Title 18, Part I, Chapter 55, § 1203)**

Hostage-taking may overlap kidnappings and other abductions, although it implies the acquisition of hostages as collateral to another operation—such as a robbery or a hijacking that turns into a siege—or as a means to an end—such as ransom. Abduction implies taking someone against his or her will, without specified purposes (Humanitarian Practice Network, 2010, p. 229).

Kidnappings

Academic experts on terrorism have long differentiated hostage-taking from kidnapping, where the location of the latter but not the former is secret, such that moving hostages between secret locations creates a kidnap situation (Hudson, 1989, p. 332; Zartman, 1990, p. 167). Similarly, the Combating Terrorism Center at West Point, New York, found two main subcategories of hostage-taking:

- Kidnappings, where the detainers do not intend the location of the detainees to become known to the other side of the negotiations
- Hostage barricade situations, where the location is known (Loertscher and Milton, 2015)

Similarly, Al Qa'ida differentiates "secret kidnapping" from "public kidnapping," where the latter is effectively a hostage barricade. In secret kidnapping, "The target is kidnapped and taken to a safe location that is unknown to the authorities. Secret kidnapping is the least dangerous" (2004).

Since kidnapping and hostage-taking are legally and materially different, various terms are used to capture both, with their many nuances, such as *detentions* or *illegal detentions*.

Hijackings

A hijacking is an unlawful seizure. Terrorists have favored aircraft hijackings, for various material reasons, including predominant Western capitalist or national-state ownership, their great economic value, and their ease of use for containment of hostages (Newsome and Jarmon, 2016, Chapter 12).

Additionally, air hijackings have proven profitable from the terrorist's perspective, due to intensive public interest and news coverage, relative fragility of aircraft (at least when at high altitude), and considerable destructiveness when impacting the ground—indeed, the most lethal terrorist attacks in history involved the suicidal piloting of four hijacked airliners into the World

Trade Center in New York City, the Pentagon in Washington, DC, and a field in Pennsylvania on the way to Washington, DC, altogether resulting in more than 3000 dead, on September 11, 2001.

Air hijackers have enjoyed relatively high rates of negotiated escape. This profitability seems surprising given the tangibility of the crime. Air hijackings are well proscribed by early and many international laws, including

- Convention on Offenses and Certain Other Acts Committed On Board Aircraft, signed in Tokyo on September 14, 1963
- Convention for the Suppression of Unlawful Seizure of Aircraft, signed at The Hague on December 16, 1970
- Convention for the Suppression of Unlawful Acts Against the Safety of Civil Aviation, signed at Montreal on September 23, 1971

Hijackings and associated crimes, including hostage-taking, are well proscribed in domestic laws, too. Nevertheless, terrorists have escaped justice by negotiating free passage in return for release of hostages. For instance, in September 1970, the Popular Front for the Liberation of Palestine hijacked five airliners, each from different owners and airports. One hijacking was foiled and prosecuted in London, but the hijackers of the other four planes consolidated at an airfield in Jordan, released most of the hostages apart from a remainder of Jews and Americans, destroyed the planes with explosives, and escaped justice, and earned the release of four conspirators from jail, in return for the release of the remaining hostages.

Some hijackers escape justice judicially, not by negotiating during the hijacking, but by exploiting human rights laws after the event. In a particularly bizarre case, nine Afghan men were prosecuted for hijacking and false imprisonment under British law in December 2001, after they admittedly hijacked a plane in Afghanistan that ended up at Stansted airport near London in February 2000, where they were arrested. However, the Court of Appeal quashed their convictions in 2003 in order to permit their defense of duress (they claimed to be fleeing the Taliban regime), even though the Taliban regime had been overthrown in 2001. Additionally, in 2004, an immigration panel ruled that returning the men to Afghanistan would breach their human rights—this ruling forced the British government to grant temporary leave to remain. In 2006, the High Court ruled that the men could remain indefinitely under immigration laws (BBC, 2006).

Similarly, on December 23, 2016, two Libyan men armed with replica pistols and a hand grenade hijacked a Libyan state-owned passenger aircraft, with 118 people on board, and ordered it to fly to Malta, where they claimed asylum before surrendering, claiming that they supported the regime of Muammar Gaddafi that was overthrown in 2011 (al-Jazeera, 2016b).

Barricades

If the perpetrator has barricaded himself or herself alone, strictly speaking this crisis is a *self-barricade*. If hostages are involved, the crisis is best known as a *hostage barricade*. If the perpetrators are terrorists, then the term *hostage barricade terrorism* (HBT) can be used, which has been around for decades now.

These crimes are more frequently observed as nonterrorist behaviors, such as child abduction, restraining members of one's own family, or even threatening harm to oneself without any hostages, but, as we see in our statistical analysis later, hostage barricade terrorism is increasing in frequency and lethality.

Crises

Given the ambiguity about a hostage, particularly when the separation between a hostage and a self-barricader cannot be confirmed, American law enforcers have tended to talk about "crises" or "critical incidents," which do not necessarily include hostages—in fact, they do not imply anything except an abnormal issue, where an issue is a situation that needs to be resolved.

The FBI has led the American law enforcement community in studying "critical incidents" and training "critical incident negotiation," including through direct training by FBI agents of other law enforcers down to local jurisdictions. These training courses are usually known as "basic crisis negotiation training," and negotiators are often qualified or organized as a crisis negotiation team (CNT), which would routinely respond to any hostage-taking, kidnapping, threat of suicide, or self-barricade. The FBI's central negotiating team (Crisis Negotiation Unit [CNU]) is part of the Critical Incident Response Group (CIRG), which in turn is part of the FBI Academy, based at Quantico, Virginia.

What Is Terrorism?

In this section, we give a conceptual definition, provide an operational definition, and analyze some conceptualizations and data relating to political terrorism, terrorizing intents, violent intents, religious terrorism, Jihadi terrorism, and new terrorism.

Conceptual Definition

Terrorism is a highly contested concept. Consequently, it is difficult to study, legislate against, and cooperate against. In recent years, Western governments have adopted the terms *radicals* or *violent extremists* to avoid the controversies and accusations of prejudice. Some institutions, such as the World Bank, have chosen to use all three terms interchangeably (World Bank, 2016, p. 11). However, the term *violent extremist* literally is capturing many more types of violent actors than just terrorists.

Unfortunately, different persons, institutions, governments, and even departments within governments have different definitions of terrorism. Some terrorism scholars have been remarkably unambitious with their definitions. For instance, Walter Laqueur once wrote that "a comprehensive definition of terrorism...does not exist nor will it be found in the foreseeable future" (Laqueur, 1977, p. 5).

By contrast, Michael Stohl has noted "significant agreement that a definition of terrorism should include the following components: 'There is an **act** in which the perpetrator **intentionally** employs **violence** (or its threat) to instill **fear** (terror) in a **victim** and the **audience** of the act or threat'" (2012, p. 45).

We define *terrorism* as the use, threat, or support of violence with intent to terrorize.

Operational Definition

An *operational definition* is one that is useful for coding some event as either terrorist or not, such as when we want to count terrorist events replicably and transparently.

The disputes about how to define terrorism are normally disputes about how to account for each of the following four categorical things: actors; behaviors and activities; targets; and motivations, ideologies, and intents. Of these things, behaviors and targets are operationally easiest to observe; ideational things are most difficult to observe; the actors are somewhere in between (Newsome and Jarmon, 2016, Chapter 3).

By careful inductive and deductive arguments, Peter Sproat has provided the most complete behavioral and ideational definition of terrorism:

> [Terrorism is distinguished by] motive (political rather than private), intention (to instill fear rather than merely to destroy), and status (that allows certain legal violent activities of the state at home, which, if committed abroad, would qualify as terrorism to exist as legitimate punishment), while enabling particular arbitrary and/or indiscriminate actions to be labeled as domestic state terrorism. Thus, terrorism can be identified as the deliberate threat or use of violence for political purposes by either non-state actors or the state abroad, when such actions are intended to influence the victim(s) and/or target(s) wider than the immediate victim(s); or the use of such purposive violence by the state within its own borders when such actions either fail to allow the victim prior knowledge of the law and/or [fail to] distinguish between the innocence and guilt of the individual victim.
>
> **(Sproat, 1991, p. 21)**

This definition might seem so long as to be impossible to operationalize. We follow the operational definition used with the Global Terrorism Database (GTD), which covers events since 1970. (The GTD has been maintained since 2001 at the University of Maryland.) Conceptually, the GTD defines *terrorism* as "the threatened or actual use of illegal force and violence by a non-state actor to attain a political, economic, religious, or social goal through fear, coercion, or intimidation." Operationally, an event must fulfill the following criteria before admittance into the GTD:

1. Intentional ("the result of a conscious calculation on the part of a perpetrator")

2. Violent ("some level of violence or immediate threat of violence, including property violence")
3. Committed by subnational perpetrators
4. At least two of the following three criteria:
    a. "Aimed at attaining a political, economic, religious, or social goal"
    b. "Intention to coerce, intimidate, or convey some other message to a larger audience"
    c. Occurrence "outside the context of legitimate warfare" (START, 2016, p. 9)

In the United States, the FBI is the lead agency for countering terrorism, from prevention through investigation to arrest. The FBI defines *terrorism* as "the unlawful use of force or violence against persons or property to intimidate or coerce a government, the civilian population, or any segment thereof, in furtherance of political or social objectives." The FBI works within U.S. federal criminal code, of which Title 22, Section 2656f(d) defines terrorism as "premeditated, politically motivated violence perpetrated against noncombatant targets by subnational groups or clandestine agents, usually intended to influence an audience" (National Institute of Justice, 2017).

Political Terrorism

Traditionally, terrorism has been regarded as politically motivated violence. If terrorism means to influence constituencies and governments, it is political. In the 1970s, a decade when terrorism was globally salient for the first time, Paul Wilkinson, an early British-Israeli writer on terrorism, influentially defined *terrorism* as a form of political violence: "either the deliberate infliction or threat of infliction of physical damage for political ends" or "the systematic use of murder and destruction, and the threat of murder and destruction in order to terrorize individuals, groups, communities, or governments into conceding to the terrorists' political demands" (Wilkinson, 1977, pp. 30–31). Then the main dispute was about the legitimacy of political violence, otherwise the assertion of terrorism as political violence seemed stable. Terrorism as political violence remains popular. Reviewers of 73 definitions from 55 articles concluded that "terrorism is a politically motivated tactic involving the threat or use of force or violence in which the pursuit of publicity plays a significant role" (Weinberg et al., 2004, p. 789).

Defining terrorism by political motivations leaves several operational difficulties, such as judging the perpetrator's motivations and deciding how political the motivations must be before they become terrorist. Official authorities sometimes claim that their political opponents are terrorist in order to engender antiterrorist support instead of opposition to official repression. Some academics have tried to solve this conflation by condemning extreme ideologies while leaving nonextreme ideologies alone (Mockaitis, 2011, p. 17), but this does not help operationally (because we have no rule to differentiate extreme from nonextreme) and is open to manipulation by those who want to assert an opponent as either reasonable or unreasonable.

Dominic Bryan points out that defining *terrorism* by political motivations "is not very distinguishing. If we take the broadest definition of politics as being activities relating to relationships of power, then even acts of violence that relate simply to the person, such as armed robbery, assault or rape have, in the broadest sense, a political dimension" (2012, p. 21).

Terrorizing

Political motivations are necessary but not sufficient for terrorism. The intent to terrorize also is necessary. For Sproat, terrorist violence is certainly distinctly political, but although all terrorism is political violence, not all political violence is terrorism; the distinguishing characteristic of terrorism is its intent to terrorize (Sproat, 1991, p. 21).

Already by the 1980s, some authors had included the intent to terrorize as a fundamental part of their definitions. For some, terrorism's audience is more important than the victim (Stohl and Lopez, 1984, p. 8); they defined terrorism as a terrorizing form of "political violence" (Stohl and Lopez, 1984, p. 4), "the purposeful act or threat of violence to create fear and/or compliant behavior in a victim and/or audience of the act or threat" (Stohl and Lopez, 1984, p. 7), or "the use of threat of use of violence by an individual or a group, whether acting for or against the established authority when such action is designed to create extreme anxiety and/or fear inducing effects in a target group larger than the immediate victims with the purposes of coercing that group into acceding to the political demands of the perpetrators" (Wardlaw, 1989, p. 16). In the 1990s and 2000s, the intent to terrorize became a fundamental operational differentiator of terrorism from other political activities, but not a fundamental legal definition due to the difficulties of proving such intent in a court of law.

Subsequent conceptual definitions tended to emphasize the perpetrator's intent to terrorize more than the perpetrator's political motivations. Bruce Hoffman emphasized the political less and the terrorizing intent more:

> Distinguishing terrorism from other crime allows us to see that terrorism is political, violent, designed to have psychological repercussions, conducted by an organization with structure, perpetrated by non-state entity.
>
> **(1999, p. 43)**

> Terrorism is fundamentally the use (or threatened use) of violence in order to achieve psychological effects in a particular target audience.
>
> **(2001, p. 420)**

Later, Paul Wilkinson also chose to emphasize terrorism as a terrorizing form of political violence:

> Some commentators in the media, some politicians and members of the public continue to use "terrorism" as a synonym for political violence in general, when in reality it is a special form of violence. It is a deliberate act by a group or by a government regime to create a climate of extreme fear to intimidate a target social group or government of commercial organization with the aim of forcing it to change its behavior.
>
> **(2010, p. 129)**

> It is a special type of violence, not a synonym for political violence in general. It is the use and credible threat of extreme violence to create a climate of fear to intimidate a wider target than the immediate victims of the terrorist attacks.
>
> **(2012, pp. 11–12)**

For most authorities, terrorism must be terrorizing for political purposes:

> Terrorism [is] acts intended to inflict dramatic and deadly injury on civilians and to create an atmosphere of fear, generally in furtherance of a political or ideological objective.
>
> **(Humanitarian Practice Network, 2010, p. xix)**

For others, terrorism is certainly terrorizing but not necessarily political:

> Terrorism is a kind of violence intended to influence or modify the behavior of one or various audiences by arousing fear, sowing confusion, promoting the indiscriminate retaliations, stimulating admiration, and arousing emulation.
>
> **(Weinberg and Pedahzur, 2003, p. 3)**

Violent

Some theorists have continued to define *terrorism* as a form of political violence and have even operationally limited their scope to terrorist "murderers" (Juergensmeyer, 2001, p. 9).

However, not all political violence is terrorism; increasingly, not all terrorism is political or violent. (Some terrorists have been convicted for defacing websites or raising funds in support of designated terrorists.) In America, most terrorist prosecutions are for material support for terrorism, not violence, which is already well proscribed by laws that predate the new wave of terrorism. As terrorism started to include cyberactivism and other nonviolent activities and to be motivated more religiously than politically, defining *terrorism* as political violence seemed old-fashioned.

Religious Terrorism

In the 1990s, some analysts started to talk about a new wave of religious terrorism or *new terrorism*. Most explicitly, Bruce Hoffman (2001) identified a surge in religious terrorism during the 1990s. Mark Juergensmeyer identified the surge around the same time and defined *religious terrorism* as "public acts of violence ... for which religion has provided the motivation, the justification, and the world view" (2001, p. 7). David Rapoport (2004, p. 61) retrospectively dated religious terrorism back to the Islamic revolution in Iran in 1979, although Hoffman traced religious terrorism back to the ancient Israelite Zealots.

Religious terrorists tend to claim to defend a pure version of a major religion, but in practice they assert fringe interpretations, although the most persistent or influential have drawn attention to major concerns within the major religion (Juergensmeyer, 2001, pp. 218–221). Religious terrorists tend to have less realistic objectives, faith in unearthly punishments (such as hell) and rewards (such as heaven or paradise—*jannah* in Arabic), contempt for external norms and conventions, and contempt for those outside their particular religion (usually known as *apostates* in English, or as *infidels*—derived from an Arabic word that is commonly used by Muslim extremists).

Jihadi Terrorism

Terrorists can come from any religion, but the most frequent attackers and the deadliest terrorists per attack on average have been Muslim terrorists, at least as recorded in recent decades. At the same time, most of the victims of terrorism are Muslim. A material explanation is that Muslims tend to live with other Muslims, so are more likely to be victims of Muslim terrorism if only for proximity. An ideational explanation is that many Muslim terrorists are attacking other alleged sects of Islam that they regard as infidel (see Appendix A).

Even in countries where Muslims make up a minority in the general population and in that country's terrorists, Muslim terrorists tend to be deadlier per attack, on average. For instance, U.S. official statistics (managed by the FBI) indicate that most American terrorists are not Muslims, and most American terrorist attacks are not perpetrated by Muslims. In fact, most American terrorism is by rightwing activists, white supremacists, and animal rights activists: non-Muslim terrorists attack more frequently (Watson, 2002; Fitsanakis, 2016). This makes sense given American demographics: Muslims are a minority in America.

However, while American Muslims account for a minority of American terrorists, and only a minority of all American terrorist attacks, they tend to kill more people per attack, on average, and to cause more material costs. Since 2001, Muslim terrorists have been responsible for almost all of the deaths due to terrorism in America. In 2002 through 2015, 26 American Muslim terrorists killed 69 people (11 of the perpetrators also died), in 22 attacks inside American borders. In that period, 344 American Muslims were involved in violent extremism, of which 40% plotted against targets inside the United States, and another 10% plotted against targets still unknown (Kurzman, 2016).

Counting all active shootings (whether or not terrorist) in America, from 2002 through 2015, avowed Jihadi terrorists killed 45 other people, while non-Jihadi terrorists (the majority of active shooters) killed 48. The deadliest of these shootings, and the deadliest terrorist attack in America since September 11, 2001 (9/11), was in San Bernardino, California, on December 2, 2015, when a husband and wife, inspired by the Islamic State of Iraq and the Levant (ISIL), killed 14 people before they were shot to death by police (*New York Times*, 2015). This series does not count the deadliest shooting in America, and the deadliest terrorist attack since 9/11, by ISIL-inspired Omar Mateen, who killed 49 people in a nightclub in Orlando on June 12, 2016, before he was shot to death by police.

Muslim terrorists like to refer to themselves as *Mujahideen* (holy warriors) or *Jihadis* (religious strugglers, also derived from an Arabic word). They are known elsewhere as *Islamists*, although this term is prejudicial against Islam: the meaning (in this context) is "Islamist extremist" or "fundamentalist Muslim," who could be nonterrorist and nonviolent, although terrorist justifications are routinely based on fundamentalism. The term *Muslim terrorist* seems most literal in the English language but also more sensitive—not least because many Muslims deny that terrorists can be considered true Muslims. Each term is inaccurate and controversial.

We use the term *Jihadis* with awareness that the word has other meanings (such as the struggle for faith), on the grounds that it is used by terrorists themselves. Plenty of terrorists have asserted that the founders of Islam meant *Jihad* as a violent struggle, and that anybody who asserts otherwise is an apostate and a target for violent *Jihad* (Juergensmeyer, 2001, pp. 80–83). Even though their use conflates violent religious struggles (traditionally categorized by Islamic scholars as *Jihad as-sayf* or "struggle of the sword") with nonviolent forms of religious struggle (such as *Jihad al-nafs* or "struggle with one self"), we generally resist efforts to deny what terrorists call themselves, and we have not found another term that is less prejudicial or more accurate.

New Terrorism

As noted above, religious terrorism is often conflated with *new terrorism*, given a "new wave" of terrorism, or at least religious terrorism, in the 1990s. For some analysts, new terrorism and religious terrorism are the same, but even those who focus on religious terrorism observe that "the forces that combine to produce religious violence are particular to each moment of history," and that the new wave was driven by other trends of the same period, such as "antiglobalization," "ethno-religious nationalism," "the postcolonial erosion of confidence in Western-style politics and politicians," postmodern erosion of "traditional authorities" (Juergensmeyer, 2001, p. xii), "the devaluation of secular authority" (p. 15), and "a worldwide loosening of social control" (p. 119).

Some analysts have pointed out that "new terrorism" contains little that is categorically new, and have thus doubted that the term *new terrorism* is warranted, or have warned that the term is misleading, although it contains much that is relatively different in scale or emphasis than in earlier history (Spencer, 2014). However, in at least temporal terms, new terrorism is literally new, and thus the term is warranted in at least this literal sense, and some of the relative changes from the old to new periods are profound enough to introduce new terrorist behaviors, such as cyberterrorism.

In different readings, new terrorism is defined by many things: recency in time, religious motivations, new technologies, more networked

Table 2.1 Relative Differences between Old and New Terrorism, on 11 Dimensions, Presented as Absolute Poles of a Relative Scale

Dimension or Spectrum of Comparison	Old Terrorism	New Terrorism
Era	Circa pre-1990	Circa post-1990
Agenda	Negotiable political agenda	Irreconcilable religious agenda
Lethality	Low lethality attacks	High lethality attacks
Coordination of attacks	Single events	Multiple events
Discrimination of targets	Discriminate and limited	Indiscriminate and unlimited
Warning	Cooperative regime of warnings	No warning
Weapons	Conventional weapons	Dual-use items, cyber, unconventional weapons
Self-preservation	Capture-avoidance	Martyrdom
Finances	Large, traceable money flows	Privately held or transferred cash
Investigative geography	Local investigations	Global investigations
Organization structure	Tight hierarchies	Loose networks

organizational structures, and new methods and objectives. Few of these things are unprecedented, so new and old terrorism overlap on most dimensions, but the trends in each dimension are clear, so new terrorism is differentiated from old terrorism relatively, if not absolutely (Table 2.1). For instance, new terrorists are more lethal relative to old terrorists (Figure 3.2), for theoretical reasons already introduced above, such as the extremist religious motivations to kill infidels, and the increased availability of weapons.

For this book we code terrorism using the operational definition already used for the GTD, and we code new terrorism by religious motivations, meaning that groups with largely religious objectives or justifications are coded as new terrorist groups, which does not deny that they can have political or other objectives separate to their religious objectives. In the event of any ambiguity about a group's relatively religious objectives or nonreligious political objectives, we code primarily by their intents to maximize lethality, target infidels, and achieve the previous two objectives even at the expense of self-preservation. We code secular groups with earthly political goals as old terrorists, irrespective of when they occur.

3

Assessing New Terrorist Risks

In this chapter, we review the following:

- The data and methods we use in this book
- The history of terrorism risks
- The particular challenges of new terrorism

Data and Methods

In explaining the data and methods that we use in this study, we review the poor data used historically, the Global Terrorism Database from which we have developed our database, the need to code terrorist groups as either old terrorist or new terrorist, the dilemma about using historical data to extrapolate into future behavior, the dilemma about generalizing shallowly from broad analysis of the whole population of cases versus deep understanding of a few cases, and our use of real-world simulations to triangulate our analysis of real-world observations.

Poor Data

Understanding terrorism requires good intelligence or good theory, but good intelligence is usually kept out of the public domain or is politicized, while terrorism has not attracted many good theorists. Consequently, terrorism scholars tend toward highly subjective opinions, anonymous official sources, and conventional wisdoms and intuitions. One former intelligence officer, now an academic, has complained that "Lack of empirical data is the plague of overt psychological research on terrorists and leaves this field open to wild speculations" (Sageman, 2004, p. 80).

Early on, before terrorism studies became "popular" since 2001, two genuine social scientists found that research into terrorism is "not research-based in any rigorous sense; instead it is often too narrative, condemnatory, and prescriptive" (Schmid and Jongman, 1988, p. 179). One review found that only 3% of articles published from 1971 to 2003 used inferential analysis. The reviewers complained of "limited and questionable data" and rare use of "statistical analysis" (Suttmoeller et al., 2011, pp. 81–82). Another social scientist reviewed more than 60 published forecasts of terrorism, published from 2000 to 2010, and found little discernible theory or methods (Bakker, 2012).

Official forecasts of risks or security often mention terrorism but are not focused on terrorism. For instance, the U.S. National Intelligence Council's latest forecast (2012), with a horizon of 2030, included some forecasts of terrorism but was focused on other risks. Few think tanks forecast terrorism in any systematic way. In 2005, the RAND Center for Terrorism Risk Management Policy (since 2002, mostly in Arlington, Virginia) published a forecast of mostly Al Qa'ida terrorism up to the year 2020 (Chalk et al., 2005). In 2011, the Center for Strategic and International Studies (Washington, DC) published a forecast of Al Qa'ida terrorism up to 2025 (Nelson and Sanderson, 2011). Most of these forecasts were not accompanied by any description of methods sufficient to be replicated, and most were based on surveys of a handful of unspecified experts.

Global Terrorism Database

Fortunately, in the 2000s a superior dataset (Global Terrorism Database [GTD]) emerged, although no dataset is perfect. (For a review of the data publicly available, see Sheehan, 2012.) It was started in 1970 by the Pinkerton Group, before being taken over in 2001 by the University of Maryland, on contract to the U.S. Department of State. It started as an international terrorism database; it now lists the countries of the attacks and the nationalities of the victims, although rarely the nationality of the perpetrators. The GTD is unique because it now covers both international and domestic terrorist events. (See the operational definition in Chapter 2 to understand what the database recognizes as "terrorist." In 2005, GTD's data collection criteria changed: https://www.start.umd.edu/gtd.)

The GTD is a freely available dataset with global breadth and meaningful depth, with useful length back to 1970, including more than 170,000 incidents from more than 200 countries and territories. One peculiarity was the absence of any data for the year 1993, due to the loss of data before digitization, and various failures to recode, until a private solution was released (Acosta and Ramos, 2016), which we have incorporated, giving us a complete dataset for every year from 1970 to 2016 inclusive—47 years.

Still, the coding of events naturally lags months to years behind events and does not capture all events. Like any events-based database, the GTD understates the frequency and overstates the impact of the average event. It captures the more spectacular minority of all events, such as events that kill lots of people, while most terrorism kills no one and is not recorded anywhere except at local levels, such as politically motivated vandalism of infrastructure (see Leetaru, 2015).

We have used the GTD for our long-term analysis of terrorist hostage-taking. The GTD collects useful data on the types of terrorist behaviors, including hostage-taking, terrorist methods, which sometimes include details of the weapons and the number of attackers, the duration of events, the location of events, and the lethality of events. It does not categorize perpetrators as "new" or "old," so we added and coded these categories for ourselves.

New Terrorist Groups versus Old Terrorist Groups

The GTD includes observations of the perpetrators by affiliation with a terrorist group, although some of the groups are not identified, and even when groups are identified their nationality may be missing. Researchers at the Combating Terrorism Center at West Point found that "a significant number" of the hostage-takers in its own dataset (2001–2015) and the GTD (1970–2013) are not known, so it recommended additional effort to identify these unknown groups (Loertscher and Milton, 2015, p. 51).

None of these datasets differentiates terrorist groups as "old terrorist" or "new terrorist." We have added that differentiation, by coding religious groups as new terrorists, irrespective of when they occurred in the dataset's years (see the operational definitions in Chapter 2). Some groups choose names that make their motivations clear, such as references to "Islam" (indicating religious motivations) or to "Marx" (indicating nonreligious political motivations).

To help our coding of named groups, our primary and most authoritative sources were the Terrorism Research and Analysis Consortium (http://www.trackingterrorism.org/), followed by the U.S. National Counterterrorism Center (NCTC)—a department of the Office of the Director of National Intelligence, who reports directly to the President of the United States (https://www.nctc.gov/).

Many events in the Global Terrorism Database have been coded as having "unknown" perpetrators. This is problematic for our attempts to deepen the dataset by coding the perpetrators as either new or old terrorists. In the aggregate, likely most unknown perpetrators are new terrorists, because of the new terrorist's lower interest in political messaging, although we do not assume so. The likely motivations of unknown perpetrators can be inferred from the region where the event takes place, although we do not assume so—we note these inferences here only to help the reader to appreciate the likely distribution of new and old terrorists; we do not use any assumptions or inferences in our statistical analysis of the data by new and old terrorists. For example, the majority of events that occur in the Middle East and South Asia take place in Iraq, Afghanistan, and Pakistan. In these three countries, according to our coding of known perpetrators, new terrorism accounts for the vast majority of events where the perpetrators are known (98%, 99.7%, and 88%, respectively). The inverse is true in South America. Here, the majority of these events occur in Guatemala and Colombia, where 98% and 100% of the events with known perpetrators are carried out by old terrorists. These three regions collectively account for 65% of the events with "unknown" perpetrators (Table 3.1).

Table 3.1 Terrorist Hostage-Takings by Region (in Order of Total Events) and by Category of Perpetrator, for 1970 through 2016

Region	Total Events	Events by Old Terrorists	Events by New Terrorists	Events by Unknown Perpetrator
South Asia	3,084	1,109	1,019	956
Middle East	2,388	475	1,125	788
Sub-Saharan Africa	1,707	626	632	449
South America	1,523	1,214	5	304
Southeast Asia	684	290	271	123
Central America and Caribbean	623	343	4	276
Western Europe	318	218	21	79
Eastern Europe	147	105	5	37
North America	117	50	7	60
Russia and the Newly Independent States (NIS)	92	10	15	67
Central Asia	24	1	5	18
Australia and Oceania	14	9	0	5
East Asia	14	7	0	7

Source: Data from the authors' extension of the Global Terrorism Database.

Generalizability versus Depth

Large-*n* datasets (meaning datasets with relatively more cases), such as GTD, offer advantages and disadvantages compared to small-*n* datasets (relatively fewer cases, as illustrated by typical academic articles that study less than 10 terrorist attacks or groups).

With more cases, analysis of a large-*n* dataset can lead to conclusions that are more generalizable across all cases, whereas deep study of an individual case would better explain that one case but is not necessarily generalizable across all cases.

Deep analysis of a single case is more justifiable if the single case is particularly important or meaningful than the other cases. Broad analysis of all cases would be more useful if the vast majority of cases in the future follow the normal case of the past. However, large-*n* datasets, by being broadly generalizable, tend to be shallow, meaning that they offer less information about individual cases. These advantages and disadvantages cannot be resolved perfectly: large-*n* and small-*n* datasets are imperfectly competitive. A large-*n* dataset tends to simplify, while small-*n* approaches allow for deeper explanation of individual cases. Moreover, large-*n* datasets, including the GTD, are usually regarded as "longitudinal"—meaning that they cover a long period of time—but this can be misleading where the long-term trends are irrelevant to the most recent trends, particularly given dynamic or adaptive behaviors such as terrorism (Newsome, 2016, pp. 270–272; Newsome and Jarmon, 2016, p. 85).

For our study here, the GTD is useful for reaching generalizable conclusions about the sorts of weapons and methods that hostage-takers use, or the average duration of their hostage crises, or the like, but it is missing the depth that would help us understand why terrorists made choices to use a particular method, when to negotiate, what to demand, when to kill, and so on.

Consequently, in this study, we combined the GTD with some recent important cases and real-world simulations. This combination of large-*n* data with small-*n* depth is an example of methodological triangulation—seeking complementarity, or the best of both worlds, between the generalizability of large-*n* analysis and the deeper understanding of fewer cases (Newsome, 2016, pp. 231, 264).

Future versus Historical Behaviors

Compared to other pure risks, terrorism is an infrequent, dynamic, and uncertain behavior that does not reward trend analysts. Infrequent events are unreliable populations for statisticians, and terrorists are adaptive, so past behaviors are unreliable guides to future behaviors.

Long historical datasets (meaning datasets covering events over a long period of time, say from decades to years) can be misleading for analysts of any behavior, such as terrorism, that is highly adaptive, dynamic, or volatile. Long-term trends mean nothing today if the motivations or capabilities that were true in the past are no longer true today.

Take cyberterrorism as an obvious example: over the whole period covered by the GTD (since 1970), cyberterrorism would seem a trivial proportion of all terrorism, but we should not conclude that cyberterrorism will be a trivial proportion of future terrorism. Cyberterrorism is a relatively recent behavior, given the popular proliferation—around the 1990s—of information communication technologies that we associate with cyberspace, the Internet, cellular telephones, and other mobile electronic devices. To measure the frequency of cyberterrorism over the entire period since 1970 would be as foolish as to measure the frequency of automobile accidents since before automobiles were invented.

Similarly, the long-standing taboo against using chemical weapons and other commonly known "weapons of mass destruction" has broken down in the last decade or two, given more permissive environments and less restrained motivations, so the rarity of terrorist chemical attacks over previous decades is no longer evidence for future terrorist behavior.

In general, if terrorists have discovered, proliferated, or adopted some technology, method, or motivation that they will not give up, then the most recent period (in which this change has occurred) is most indicative of future trends, while the older period may have no relevance to the future (Newsome, 2016, p. 273). Consequently, we are more interested in new terrorism than old terrorism, and in the most recent trends in new terrorism, over recent years rather than decades. Moreover, we use real-world simulations to understand how terrorists are likely to adapt and respond to recent events or current conditions.

Unusually, we triangulate our analysis of large-*n* real-world data with three forms of qualitative sources:

1. Important cases
2. Interviews with official negotiators, counterterrorist specialists, and special operations forces
3. Real-world simulations

Simulations

Our simulations are not computer games; in fact, they are played in the real world, with real communications, such as telephones and e-mails, by real human participants. All roles are played by humans; no roles are simulated in the sense of automated; the humans themselves behave as they see fit, although constraints are imposed through the given situation and the given conditions. These simulations are technically "multisided"—meaning that not just one side but more are competing to achieve their objectives: terrorists, counterterrorists, journalists, victim families, and third-party intermediaries. The simulations are competitive, dynamic, and adaptive, because each side is interacting with every other, in real time.

Such "role-player simulations" are normative in official training of hostage-crisis negotiation, including at the Federal Bureau of Investigation (FBI), whose principal authorities recommend and forecast increased use:

> Also, highly realistic role-play scenarios (e.g., actual robbery setting, such as a bank, rather than classroom training), either conducted or closely controlled by experienced negotiators, would seem to improve the validity of this widely employed assessment method. Challenging, yet real-world scripted, practical exercises not only reinforce negotiation concepts, strategies, and techniques, but also significantly enhance a trainee's confidence level. Further, although practical problems are inherently artificial, if constructed properly, they can create a considerable degree of pressure and anxiety for the trainee. Anecdotally, many former negotiation students have commented that after dealing with realistic role-play scenarios in their training, real-world negotiated critical incidents were challenging but not overwhelming.
>
> Despite the fact that all barricaded hostage and crisis situations are unique, the basic emotions that drive them are universal and predictable. Effective negotiation of such events requires intensive and ongoing training of requisite skills in contexts as similar to the real incidents as possible. Therefore, we anticipate that carefully constructed role plays, incorporating the spectrum of potential emotions, will continue to be widely utilized in this capacity.
>
> **(Van Hasselt, Romano, and Vecchi, 2008, pp. 260–261)**

Simulations are valuable for researchers of behaviors, such as terrorism, that are practically or ethically impossible to observe directly and replicably. We cannot follow terrorists around, or put them under controlled conditions, for the purposes of academic research, without putting ourselves at considerable risk, or affecting our objectivity. Yet researchers of terrorism rarely simulate, partly because the method is considered exotic or technically challenging compared to the typical case studies. This is an unambitious attitude. Simulations can be used easily enough to study most behaviors. For instance, Bruce Oliver Newsome has used simulation to experiment with counterterrorist cooperation under different starting conditions, against a dynamic terrorist side, in which all participants were playing roles (Newsome, 2006).

Similarly, for this study, Newsome has designed simulations of terrorist hostage-taking, in which students of counterterrorism have played roles, on simulated terrorist and counterterrorist sides, while other students have played journalists, victim representatives, and intermediaries.

Two different simulations were used to produce data used in this study:

- One simulation was run in 2015, starting with a scripted hostage-taking event based on the crisis in Mumbai (2008), translated to a particular hotel complex in a particular major American city, in which the location, the weapons, the hostage-takers, and other material context were given, after which all sides were free to behave as they saw fit, with some physical or material decisions (such as the effectiveness of weapons) adjudicated by controllers.
- The second simulation was run in 2016, in which all sides were free to choose their own behaviors within the same American urban area (with a population of about 7 million), given the same objectives as in 2015.

In both simulations, the terrorist side was given the same group identity and five demands, which the role-players were free to choose between or prioritize:

1. U.S. admission of the group's grievances against the Iraqi and U.S. governments
2. U.S. withdrawal of support to the Iraqi Shia government
3. U.S. release of 10 colleagues from U.S. military detention
4. Monetary compensation for families of Jihadis killed by U.S. drone strikes in Yemen and Pakistan
5. Safe passage for the local hostage-takers to the group's home territory

Since terrorism is a particularly adaptive and dynamic behavior, modeling past events could be misleading, and the lessons could encourage counterterrorists to prepare to counter a past event that might never reoccur, similar to the stereotypical military's preparations to fight the last war. Our first simulation is realistic insofar as it models real events, but modeling past events is a choice against the modeling of future terrorists that may learn from, and adapt to, past events, including the attacks at Mumbai in 2008 and since 2008. Consequently, our second simulation (2016) allowed the role-players to develop their own starting position—including the target and the attack method, given the same objectives as in 2015, and given four fictional locals who had volunteered to act on the orders of a remote foreign terrorist group.

Each simulation included

- Two sets of rival journalists (two role-players each set), who could interview either side and report at any time by sending e-mails—representing news reports—to all actors
- Two role-players playing a state intermediary, which was in contact with both sides
- A role-player acting as the representative of the families of the hostages, who could speak with the official side and any journalist

In addition to role-players, the two sides were advised and observed by about a dozen real official negotiators, special weapons and tactics operators, intelligence analysts, and public affairs officers from the FBI and local police forces.

The players on each of the two main sides (official counterterrorist; terrorist) in each simulation were students of counterterrorism at the University of California–Berkeley in those years. In advance of the simulation, the students were trained—across 15 teaching weeks—in the motivations, methods, and capabilities of terrorists and counterterrorists. In the week of the simulation, they were assigned to read articles or chapters on terrorist hostage-taking (Zartman, 1990; Dolnik and Fitzgerald, 2011; Miller, 2011). At the end of each simulation, all participants were brought together for 30 minutes of debriefing or after-action review, after which they were given some days to write one to two pages of text on their lessons learned. They were specifically asked to summarize what they planned to achieve, what actually happened, and what they learned or would recommend, given the experience. Otherwise, they were at liberty to write anything in response to their experiences.

The second simulation (2016), in which both sides were given 2 weeks to plan for the attack before the execution of this attack during the 3 hours of the final class, proved to be the most motivational and most realistic:

> The hostage crisis simulation our class participated in this past week was one of the most interesting and hands-on experiences of my academic career. I had been anticipating this simulation since Week 1 of the class when I saw it on the class syllabus. In actuality, the simulation was nothing like what I had predicted it to be, but was much more intense and valuable. While neither side "won" in the simulation, the [terrorist] Ring's five demands were not met and [the official side] did not save the hostages, I believe all participants learned valuable lessons

in not only counter-terrorism, but also in teamwork, time management, and working under pressure.

(Thomas Sweeney)

The hostage crisis simulation was an extremely powerful and influential lesson; it was a demonstration of what it takes to combat terrorism "hands on." I was assigned to the terrorist side and I appreciated the fact that we were required to plan out our "attack," step by step. By having to find out what the logistics were of every detail required hours upon hours of planning. It allowed our side to dive into the minds and actions of real life terrorists and understand why they might choose certain actions and/or weapons, as opposed to others. To simply plan a simulated attack and give our all-inclusive details of each action we wanted to take took much thought and consideration; we spent at least 4 hours any given day of the 2 weeks before our simulation to prepare. We had many trials and errors ranging from location, to weapons, to our "terrorists," etc. To even pick a target was extremely challenging. Our group was able to realistically understand given the time frame, what the "terrorists" were and were not capable of achieving.

(Alexandra Zech)

After completing this simulation, it has become obvious how complicated and challenging these scenarios can be. Despite existing only as a simulation and capturing only a handful of the aspects that have to be managed, the crisis felt complex and overwhelming at times. While we were unable to reach a peaceful solution, I believe this was somewhat anticipated and inevitable given the nature of the terrorists' strategies.

(Vincent Strykers)

The hostage simulation for me tied together everything we have learned all semester. I think because I played the role of a terrorist, it forced me to look at the material from a new perspective. This was valuable because it meant taking a new look at the course-work, finding the areas in the real world that worked in the favor of being a terrorist, and the areas in which it proved to be difficult.

(Kylie McCaffrey)

What Is the Risk of Terrorism?

Terrorism is an ancient behavior; presumably it has been coincident with the entire history of human conflict. Here we briefly review terrorism since 1970, which is the year from which the Global Terrorism Database observes.

Terrorism is very infrequent compared to other crimes, conflicts, and natural events—some of which have been more costly than any terrorist event, but the risk of terrorism has been increasing over the long term—most acutely in the last couple decades. Risk is usually calculated as a combination (product) of frequency and returns (otherwise known as effects, outcomes, etc.) (Newsome, 2014). Both the frequency of terrorist events and the negative returns of these events have been increasing, meaning that the risk has been

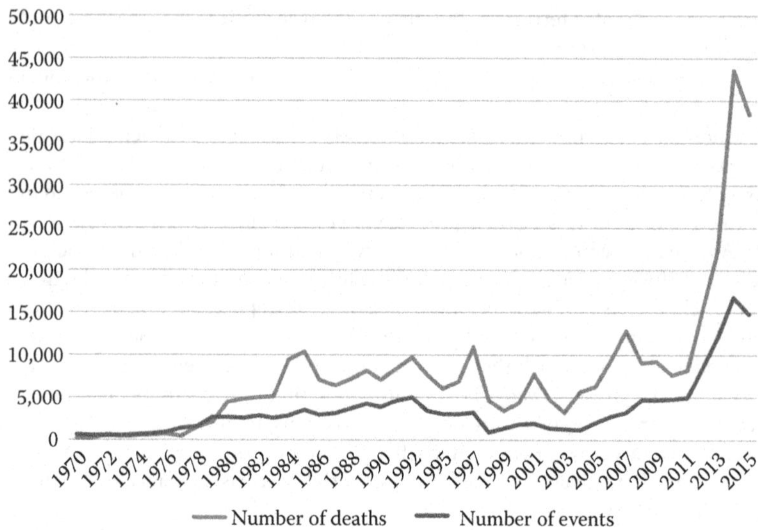

Figure 3.1 The lethality and frequency of terrorist events, by year, from 1970 through 2015. (Data from the authors' extension of the GTD.)

increasing by both of the dimensions of risk (Figure 3.1). New terrorists are riskier, if only because they kill more people (on average per attack; and in aggregate) (Figure 3.2).

1970s to 1990s

According to the Global Terrorism Database, only 500 attacks occurred globally per year from 1970 until the frequency started to grow in 1974, reaching about 2,700 in 1979. The frequency remained elevated but in slight decline for a few years before proceeding upward again, despite lesser steps back, until peaking at over 5,000 attacks in 1992. The frequency fell rapidly in the 1990s as governments countered terrorism more effectively while seeking settlements (the end of the Cold War helped to dampen the wider ideological conflicts). In 1998, terrorist attacks fell to a low not seen since the 1970s.

2000s

The frequency of terrorism remained low (relative to the previous decade) from 1992 through 2000. The attacks of September 11, 2001 (9/11) collectively amount to the deadliest single terrorist attack ever, with nearly 3,000 dead. Jihadi terrorists, mostly from Saudi Arabia, sponsored by Al Qa'ida (Arabic: *the base*) hijacked four airliners: they flew an airliner into each of the two towers of the World Trade Center, New York, causing fires that eventually caused each tower to collapse. They flew another airliner into the Pentagon—the headquarters of the U.S. Defense Department—in Washington, DC. The fourth airliner crashed into the ground in Pennsylvania during an attempt by passengers to gain control of the cockpit.

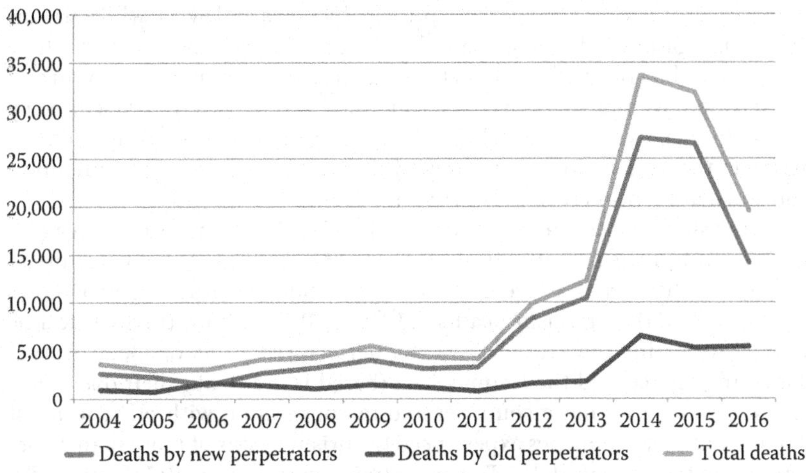

Figure 3.2 The lethality of terrorist events, by category of terrorist (old; new), by year, from 2004 to 2016. (Data from the authors' extension of the GTD.)

The U.S. "Global War on Terror" (officially from 9/11, 2001, to 2009) correlated with increased terrorism by frequency and average lethality (Figure 3.1), almost all of it outside of the United States, with the most rapid increases in countries subject to U.S. military interventions. In the early 2000s, the attack frequency remained steady—around 1,000 per year—although with increased lethality per average attack, until a dramatic rise from 2005 onward, as terrorism became mixed up in other conflicts, mainly in Iraq, Afghanistan, Pakistan, North Africa, East Africa, and latterly West Africa. Previously—compared to war, murder, and suicides—terrorism accounted for a relatively trivial proportion of violent deaths, but the Institute for Economics and Peace (2012, p. 37) concluded that "Terrorism has emerged as a significant source of conflict since 2001."

2010s

Terrorism frequency and lethality appeared to flatten from 2008 to 2010. The year 2011 was a year of optimism for counterterrorism, particularly for Americans. In December 2010, street-led revolutions started in North African countries, spreading to Middle Eastern Arab countries, becoming known as the "Arab Spring." These revolutions were seen to marginalize Al Qa'ida, because ordinary citizens were overthrowing harsh governments without the help of Al Qa'ida, which previously had claimed to represent ordinary Muslims in a campaign against pro-Western, un-Islamic regimes. On May 2, 2011, Usama bin Laden and some supporters were killed in a compound in Pakistan by U.S. special operators. On August 27, 2011, bin Laden's Libyan-born operations chief (Atiyah Abd al-Rahman) was killed in Pakistan.

However, the year of optimism (2011) was soon tarnished by realization that the Arab Spring had replaced secular stable states with religiously sectarian, unstable, or failing states, principally Libya and Syria, where Jihadis were congregating and basing themselves for operations elsewhere. Soon these same Jihadis had traveled overland to destabilize states as far away as Mali and South Sudan. Although Usama bin Laden was dead, Al Qa'ida survived, led by Egyptian-born Ayman al Zawahiri, who quickly proved, by publicly releasing messages that urged Muslims to congregate in Libya and Syria, that his ambition and command were no less than bin Laden's.

Terrorism increased in frequency in 2011, 2012, 2013, and 2014, with a 61% increase in terrorism deaths from 2012 (11,133) to 2013 (17,958). Terrorism deaths were five times as great in 2013 as in 2000 (Institute for Economics and Peace, 2014). Terrorism deaths fell from 2014 to 2015, the first decline since 2010, mainly due to effective counterterrorist focus on Boko Haram (based in Nigeria) and the Islamic State (based in Iraq), but their operations have expanded into more countries and in cooperation with other terrorist groups, and more countries experienced terrorism deaths of more than 25 per country, so the annual Global Terrorism Index worsened in 2015 (Institute for Economics and Peace, 2016).

The annual count of terrorist attacks decreased from 2015 to 2016, but while the frequency of secular political terrorist attacks reduced (by about 50%), they killed more people in 2016 than in 2015, while the frequency of religious terrorist attacks remained at practically the same record high in 2016 as in 2015, although they killed about 50% fewer people per attack. Terrorism decreased in Pakistan, Afghanistan, Syria, Yemen, and Nigeria, but increased in most other places—particularly, Iraq and the Western countries.

Islamic State

Al Qa'ida was surpassed, at least by 2014, by a new Jihadi group, whose earthly ambitions encouraged a new name of "Islamic State," once it had established territorial gains from Syria to Iraq. (It was known transitionally as the Islamic State of Iraq and al-Sham, which was abbreviated as ISIS; this was translated most accurately as the Islamic State of Iraq and the Levant, or ISIL; it is known derogatively by its Arabic acronym "Da'ish.")

ISIL has declared a worldwide caliphate (Islamic government). This ambition is materially beyond Al Qaida's ambition: Al Qa'ida wanted to stimulate a global war between its restrictive religious adherents and the infidel, but never led material aggrandizement on earth, except perhaps in Afghanistan in the 1990s. Otherwise, it postponed an earthly state until after it could persuade most Muslims of the superiority of its version of Islam. By contrast, ISIL prioritized the earthly state, and it attracted younger volunteers who were frustrated with al-Qa'ida's multi-generational patience.

For now, ISIL does not govern the world, but by 2014 it governed most of eastern Syria and northwestern Iraq, while groups from Egypt (Ansar Bait al-Maqdis) through Libya (Barka Province) to Algeria (Jund al-Khilafah) changed their names to match, and mature Jihadi groups pledged allegiance or alliance as far away as Somalia (al-Shabab), Nigeria (Boko Haram), Pakistan (Jundallah), and the Philippines (Abu Sayyaf). In 2016 and 2017, it lost territory in Syria and Iraq, but nevertheless increased its terrorism in Iraq.

Despite ISIL's territorial losses, wide consensus remained that ISIL is the greatest terrorist threat. Although the administration of Barack Obama (2009–2017) and the administration of Donald Trump (2017–2021) differed on strategy, they effectively agreed on risk, as illustrated by respective statements on the same day (December 7, 2016), when Obama released his last official statement on terrorism, including the verbal statement that "No foreign terrorist organization has successfully planned and executed an attack on our homeland, and it is not because they didn't try," while Trump said, "We will stop racing to topple foreign regimes that we know nothing about, that we shouldn't be involved with. Instead our focus must be on fighting terrorism and destroying ISIS" (Jaffe and Makamura, 2016; Dovere, 2016). Britain's foreign intelligence (MI6) chief said that ISIL remains the greatest threat to Britain (Faulconbridge, 2016).

Hostage-Taking Risk

Hostage-taking has been relatively successful operationally for terrorists. Some analysis from before the new wave of terrorism suggests that hostage-taking was successful for the terrorist side in about one-quarter of cases (27%). Certainly, in some cases, the terrorists were spectacularly successful, such as the early airline hijackings (in the 1970s), where terrorists killed passengers, blew up planes, and still escaped justice (Sandler and Scott, 1987).

The perpetration of hostage-takings has increased dramatically in frequency since 2011, by both old terrorists and new terrorists, but most dramatically by new terrorists (Figure 3.3). Even though secular and political terrorist attacks, including hostage-takings, decreased in 2015 and 2016 globally, the frequency of religious terrorist hostage-takings has risen, and the number of hostages taken nearly doubled; suicidal hostage-takings reached a record high; and seven of the

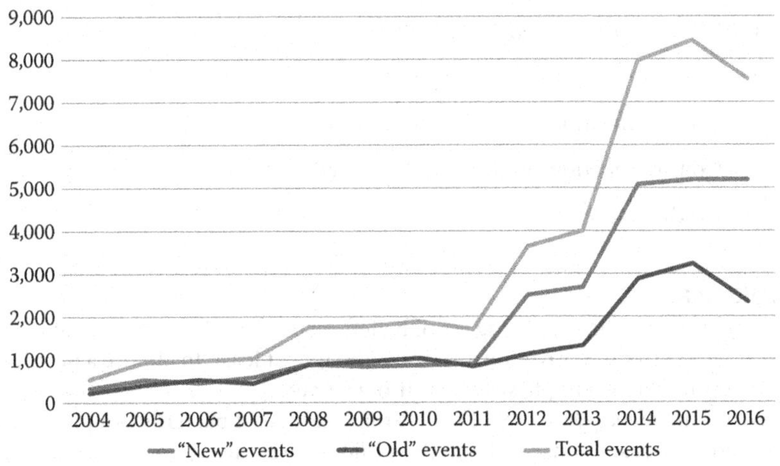

Figure 3.3 Frequency of hostage-takings by category of terrorist, 2004–2016. (Data from the authors' extension of the GTD.)

ten deadliest terror attacks were hostage-takings (>100 victims died in each). The Islamic State alone kidnapped more than 100 foreigners from 2012 through 2016, usually to behead them publicly (Cragin and Padilla, 2017).

What Is Particularly Challenging about New Terrorists?

As can be seen from Figure 3.2, new terrorism is riskier than old terrorism by both frequency and lethality. As can be seen from Figure 3.3, new terrorists are investing in more hostage-takings.

New terrorists are more challenging than old terrorists, for reasons that we categorize in 16 sections below:

1. Ideology
2. Murderousness
3. Suicidalism or willingness to die
4. Fighting capabilities
5. Mixed attack types and weapon types
6. More exotic weapons
7. More uncontrolled weapons
8. Irreconcilable objectives or intents
9. Informed and skeptical about official opponents
10. Surveillance
11. Communications with suppliers
12. Communications with controllers
13. Communications with the public
14. Communications with the official side
15. Communications with potential targets
16. Readier targets

Ideological

Terrorists tend to have a strong set of beliefs, commonly known as ideologies, that suggest strong motivations—strong enough, at least, to choose a peculiar behavior (terrorism) in pursuit of their objectives.

We define *ideology* as a set of beliefs that are at least partially not proven in any evidence-based sense—closer to opinions, prejudices, and biases, rather than facts.

While old terrorists are often characterized as more political in their objectives and ideologies, new terrorists are characterized as less political and more ideological in other dimensions—particularly religious ideology. For instance, Mark Juergensmeyer "conclude[d] that religious terrorism is seldom solely a tactic in a political strategy. It is also a symbolic statement aimed at providing a sense of empowerment to desperate communities" (2001, p. 11).

Here, we should clarify a common misunderstanding of ideology. An ideologue is not necessarily irrational. A *rational* person acts to optimize or at least maximize the benefits, and to avoid or minimize the costs, of their actions; rationality is sometimes used as a synonym for *reasonable*, which suggests persuadable, or open to evidence or argument, or able to learn.

Holding to an ideology does not necessarily prove irrationality. Generally, people live with all sorts of beliefs that are not strictly speaking proven or reasonable, if only for convenience, or under the constraints of imperfect information. A useful conceptual separation is to differentiate irrational ends (such as giving up freedom from prison in one's current life in order to kill an infidel in pursuit of an unproven afterlife) from rational means (such as choosing the most lethal weapon in order to kill an infidel). Terrorists seem to be generally rational in their means, even though new terrorists appear to the majority of us as generally irrational in their ends. This rationality in the pursuit of particular ends is often described as "procedural rationality" or "instrumental rationality." Rationality of means does not prove rationality of ends, or vice versa.

New terrorists are often categorized as particularly ideological, primarily because of high or extreme religiosity ("*extremism*"), where a certain set of religious beliefs is treated as superior to all other beliefs (for instance, Juergensmeyer, 2001). Beliefs in an afterlife or in heavenly reward (such as the Islamic paradise—usually known by the Arabic word of *Jannah*), or the superiority of God's pleasure, increase the chance of apparently irrational behaviors on earth, such as murder, knowing that murder will be punished by imprisonment or the death penalty on earth, prior to reward in heaven.

Such extreme religious ideologies drive increased murderousness, suicidalism, fighting capabilities, more willingness to develop new fighting capabilities, to mix them up, to try exotic weapons, to try uncontrolled weapons, and to declare irreconcilable objectives, as explained in the following sections.

Murderous

New terrorists have shown greater readiness to kill (Figure 3.2), presumably because religious ideologies drive contempt for infidels; the killing of infidels might even be justified as pleasing to God. Mark Juergensmeyer chose to treat terrorism operationally as synonymous with murder, and found that religious terrorism is characterized by "bloodshed executed in a deliberately intense and vivid way. It is as if these acts were designed to maximize the savage nature of their violence and meant purposely to elicit anger," akin to "exaggerated violence" or "performance violence" or "theater," or is "aimed at killing massive numbers of victims" (2001, pp. 9, 121–126).

Consider the violent Jihadi hostage-takings at the Dubrovka Theater in Moscow (2002), Beslan (2004), and Mumbai (2008), where the respective death tolls are officially at least: 170, including 40 attackers, in Moscow; 385, including 31 attackers, in Beslan; and 175, including 9 attackers, in Mumbai.

Indeed, in all of these situations, the hostage-takers killed early and behaved as if their ultimate objective was to kill as many as possible, where the hostage-taking was at least partly a means to postpone the crisis for attention, more than to provide opportunities for negotiation.

Not only are new terrorists differentiated by lethality, they are differentiated by their pursuit of particularly demonstrative forms of killing. For instance, one of Al Qa'ida's affiliates later wrote a prescription that allowed for hostages to be exchanged for something useful, but also prescribed maximum lethality and public terror if the exchange failed: "The policy of violence must also be followed such that if the demands are not met, the hostages should be liquidated in a terrifying manner, which will send fear into the hearts of the enemy and his supporters" (Naji, 2006, p. 78).

As shown in Table 3.2, three-fourths of hostages taken by old terrorists are released, while slightly more than a third of hostages taken by new terrorists are released. From frequencies, we can infer probabilities: old terrorists are likely to release hostages and can be expected to release three-quarters of their hostages on average, but new terrorists are unlikely to release hostages and can be expected to release only a third of their hostages on average.

Table 3.2 effectively understates the murderousness of new terrorists, because it does not show our further findings that new terrorists were responsible for fewer hostage-takings in our dataset (going back to 1970), yet took more hostages, killed more hostages, and released fewer hostages. As Table 3.3 shows, new terrorists kill more than twice as many hostages per event than old terrorists kill.

Of course, we should remember that most terrorist events result in no deaths, regardless of the motivations of the terrorists themselves. As Figure 3.4 shows, most terrorist hostage-takings, like most terrorist events in general, are not lethal—most are smaller or less deliberate acts than the spectacular events that dominate the news. Although most events are nonfatal, the figure illustrates our findings (as in Table 3.2 and Table 3.3) that a greater portion of new terrorist events are fatal, and that new terrorists kill more hostages per event, if any are killed at all.

New terrorists kill more hostages, even though new terrorists deploy more than six fewer hostage-takers per hostage (suggesting inferior capacity for killing) than old terrorists deploy, as shown in Table 3.4.

Table 3.2 Human Consequences of Terrorist Hostage-Takings, by Old and New Terrorists, for 1970 through 2016

Category of Terrorists	Number of Hostage-Takings	People Killed[a]	Number of Hostages	Hostages Released
New	3,109	15,636	39,918	13,688 (34.3%)
Old	4,457	6,526	33,107	24,687 (74.8%)

Source: Data from the authors' extension of the Global Terrorism Database.

[a] GTD does not specify the casualties, so we do not know whether those killed in any given event are hostages, bystanders, or responders.

Table 3.3 Rates of Lethality and Suicidalism, during Hostage-Taking Events, by New and Old Terrorists, for 1970 through 2016

Category of Terrorist	Number of Hostage-Takings in Which the Number of Casualties Is Known	People Killed/ Event[a]	Terrorist Deaths/ Event[a]	Explicit Suicides/Event
New	3,109	10.3 (1,511)	0.7 (2,852)	0.02 (3,109)
Old	4,457	5.1 (1,282)	0.4 (2,564)	0.0002 (4,457)
Unknown perpetrator	3,169	3.3 (887)	0.1 (2,130)	0.002 (3,169)

Source: Authors' extension of the Global Terrorism Database.

[a] Ratios are calculated by dividing the total number of killed by the number of events in which the number of casualties is known. In each cell, below each ratio, we have parenthesized the number of events in which the casualties are known.

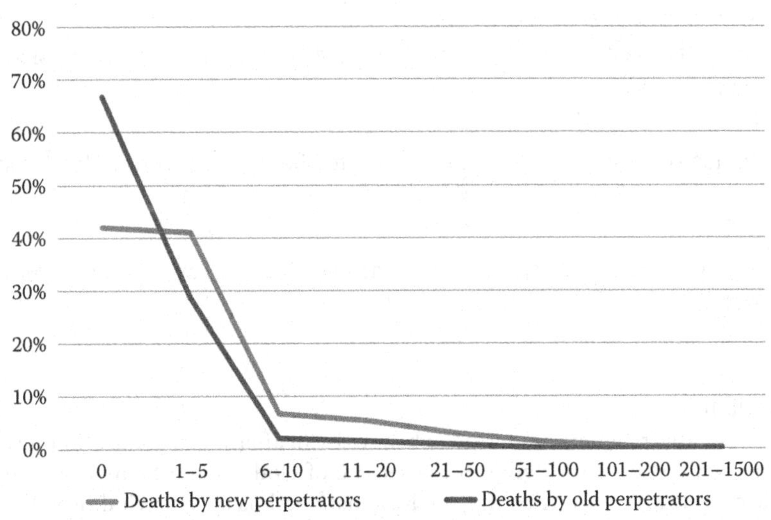

Figure 3.4 Proportion of hostage-takings ending in different counts of non-perpetrator deaths (deaths suffered by persons other than the hostage-takers), as a proportion of all events, by old or new terrorists, for the years 1970 through 2016. (Data from the authors' extension of the GTD.)

Table 3.4 Average Terrorists per Event, Hostages per Event, and Hostage-Takers per Hostage, for 1970 through 2015[a]

Category of Terrorist	Terrorist Hostage-Takers/Event	Hostages/Event	Hostage-Takers/ Hostage
New	41.7 (383 Events)	16.7 (2,348 Events)	8.3 (344 Events)
Old	29.4 (1,121 Events)	9.0 (3,644 Events)	13.9 (987 Events)
Total	32.5 (1,504 Events)	12.0 (5,992 Events)	11.1 (1,331 Events)

Source: Authors' extension of the Global Terrorism Database.

[a] In an effort to be as transparent as possible in our presentation of the data, the following tables present 10% and 25% truncated means for each of the averages in Table 3.5. We offer truncated means because some of the averages in Table 3.4 reflect a heavy-tailed distribution (distributions with large outliers). For instance, the number of terrorist hostage-takers per event—like any average—is skewed by a few outliers. The truncated means indicate that normally (ignoring the tails or outliers) the differences between new and old terrorists deployments are not as dramatic as the overall means would suggest, although new terrorists still deploy slightly fewer hostage-takers per event, deploy slightly fewer hostage-takers per hostage, and take slightly more hostages per event. To calculate our truncated means, we have removed the data in the top and bottom 10th and 25th percentiles of the data (exclusive) and calculated the mean of the remaining values.

Terrorists/Event	10% Truncated Mean	25% Truncated Mean
New	10.4	8.7
Old	10.8	8.7
Hostages/Event	10% Truncated Mean	25% Truncated Mean
New	4.5	2.4
Old	4.2	2.4
Average Terrorist/Hostage	10% Truncated Mean	25% Truncated Mean
New	4.5	4.1
Old	5.0	4.1

Suicidal

Theoretically, religious fighters who believe in an afterlife, or some other form of heavenly reward for dying in the service of God, should be more willing to accept death—as long as they believe that death is serving God or will be rewarded by God.

In the Islamic tradition, this form of virtuous suicide has come to be known by the Arabic of word of *Shaheed*, which is usually translated into English as *martyrdom* (itself derived from the Greek term for a "witness": *Martus*). The same concept exists in other traditions, such as the Christian tradition of *sacrifice*, which derives from the Latin word for something made holy (*sacrificium*). Indeed, the early Christians used the term *Martus* to describe each of the apostles as witness to the life of Jesus Christ, from which the term came to describe the witness to persecution under the Roman Empire, and thence sacrifice to the faith. All the monotheisms, and some of the polytheisms and spiritualisms, are founded on martyrs (Juergensmeyer, 2001, pp. 165–170; Lewis, 2013).

One historian proposed three necessary conditions for successful suicide attacks: "willing individuals [as perpetrators], organizations to train and use them, and a society willing to accept such acts in the name of a greater good." He described an "exponential increase in suicide bombing" since 2000 due to its perpetration by Jihadis (Lewis, 2013). Similarly, in November 2015, *The Economist* noted "the spread of a deadly style of attack that came to prominence in a Jihadist assault on Mumbai" in 2008. It identified suicidalism as the second characteristic of new terrorist hostage-taking (the first "characteristic" was the preference for firearms rather than explosives).

> A second characteristic of this style of attack is that the perpetrators have no expectation of coming out alive. Hostage-takers in the 1970s generally expected to be released as part of any deal to free their prisoners. In the Munich Olympics crisis of 1972, for instance, Palestinian terrorists demanded the release of more than 200 prisoners (as well as safe passage out of Germany) before a botched rescue attempt resulted in the deaths of all of their Israeli hostages. The advent of suicidal attackers, on the other hand, means there is less scope for negotiation. Often the main reason such attackers have for taking hostages is to complicate efforts by security forces to regain control of the site, since hostages may be killed in the crossfire.
>
> **(*The Economist*, 2015)**

As Table 3.3 summarizes, our analysis suggests that new terrorists are more willing to die or are more likely to be killed: more than twice as many new terrorists die per hostage-taking event than old terrorists die. Moreover, nearly all the explicit suicidal hostage-taking events are perpetrated by new terrorists (such events are undercounted due to the coding difficulties).

Although our data prove that more new terrorists than old terrorists die per hostage-taking, the majority of hostage-takings result in no observed perpetrator casualties. No terrorists were killed in 97% of events perpetrated by old terrorists, and 93% of events perpetrated by new terrorists, which suggests that hostage-taking is a low-risk choice for terrorists compared to different attack options. Still, Figure 3.5 supports our conclusion that new terrorists are more willing to die or are more likely to be killed during hostage-takings.

Fighting Capabilities

New terrorists are more capable fighters. They are motivated by their religious ideologies, murderousness, and suicidalism. In addition, new terrorists tend to consider their conflicts akin to wars, even though most academic conceptualizations tend to place terrorism as a nonstate conflict short of war. Religious terrorists tend to regard their wars as "divine" or "cosmic," in Mark Juergensmeyer's terms, for which the terrorists require all capabilities, whatever the terrorist

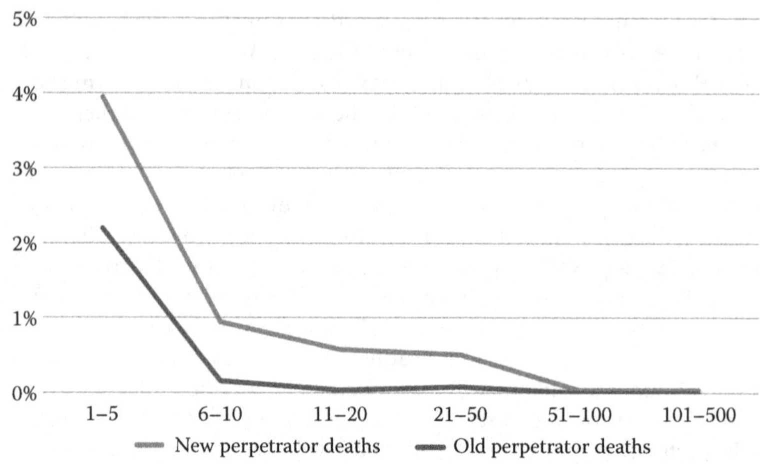

Figure 3.5 Proportion of hostage-takings with different levels of perpetrator (hostage-taker) casualties as a proportion of all hostage-takings, for the years 1970 through 2016, by old and new terrorists. Note: Most events show no casualties among the perpetrators. (Data from the authors' extension of the GTD.)

needs to defeat all enemies—superpowers included—and to create a new world. Such a cosmic war is usually considered eternal, until one religion or one God achieves dominance—"an all-or-nothing struggle against an enemy whom one assumes to be determined to destroy" (Juergensmeyer, 2001, p. 148).

Moreover, digital communications and the easier travel associated with globalization have led to wider diffusion of terrorist skills and knowledge, including of the infidel's capacities and procedures. Given the acceleration in political instability and state failure in the last couple of decades, new terrorists have more opportunities to acquire weapons and accessories (such as body armor or night-vision devices), and to prepare in ungoverned spaces. New terrorists can be expected to be better trained and equipped, causing concern for official personnel on police teams known as special weapons and tactics (SWAT).

> These same capabilities, unfortunately, can also aid the terrorists who will gladly pay the money for the enhancements if it furthers their cause. Many new pieces of equipment require hundreds of hours of training to become proficient in their use, but once properly trained, implementing some of these items places those who possess them in an incredibly advantageous position—a bad proposition for a SWAT team that lacks the equipment, going up against a terrorist who has the latest equipment and the training.
>
> **(Forest, 2007, p. 263)**

The superior capabilities of new terrorists as hostage-takers are proven by our findings, from our new dataset, that new terrorists deploy more hostage-takers per hostage-taking (suggesting superior capacity to defend themselves), and take more hostages per hostage-taking (suggesting superior capacity to hold hostages), as shown in Table 3.4.

Mixed Attack Methods and Mixed Weapon Types

Given new terrorists' interests in increased lethality, they are interested in using weapons that maximize lethality. Given religious contempt for their targets, or their desire to intimidate their targets, they are interested in particularly terrifying weapons.

One way to maximize lethality in the same attack is to mix methods, in pursuit of synergies between them, such as attacking a public space with explosives in order to force the survivors to flee through a bottleneck where firearms are most effective (firearms are dramatically more accurate and destructive at close range).

Our dataset shows that since the mid-2000s new terrorists have most increased the use of firearms and explosives, while old terrorists have most increased the use of incendiary devices (see Table 3.5).[1] The new terrorist's favor for firearms and explosives is evidence for new terrorist focus on increased lethality, while the old terrorist's favor for incendiary weapons is evidence for old terrorist focus on nonlethal damage to property and on lower risks to the perpetrator. Anecdotally, other analysts have observed the increasing use of firearms by new terrorists to maximize lethality since the mid-2000s (*The Economist*, 2015).

Since the mid-2000s, mixed-weapon attacks (that the Global Terrorism Database categorizes as "melees") also have increased, with the most dramatic acceleration in the last few years (see Figure 3.6 through Figure 3.10). GTD's category of "melee" is difficult to interpret, because the GTD includes the "melee" as a category of weapon—alongside firearms, explosives, and incendiary weapons—and sometimes regards the melee as a primary weapon type (see Figure 3.9), while coding the other weapons as secondary weapons. New terrorists theoretically prefer to mix firearms and suicidal explosives because of the increased lethality achieved with proximity in range and the complementarities or synergies between weapon types and attack methods, while old terrorists theoretically prefer to mix time-fuzed drop-off explosives and incendiary devices to maximize property damage. The new terrorist's intentions are indicated also by their interest in exotic weapons, as shown in the next section.

More Exotic Weapons

New terrorists have shown increasing interest in exotic weapons in pursuit of increased lethality or terror, including weapons that are legally and

[1] Here, we utilize only primary weapons—even if other weapon types are used in the same attack. We utilize five of the GTD's primary weapon types, which are—in order of declining frequency from 2004 to 2016: explosives, firearms, incendiary, melee or mixed weapons, and chemical. The other eight weapon types in the GTD are not reliably observed: biological, radiological, nuclear, and vehicle weapons are not observed as primary weapons in the GTD, even though other official sources show increasing frequency of biological and terrorist vehicle-ramming attacks; the other four categories are sabotage equipment, fake weapons, other, and unknown.

Table 3.5 The Number of Terrorist Attacks by the Four Main Weapon Types, as Categorized by the Global Terrorism Database, by New or Old Terrorist Perpetrators, for 2004 through 2015

	Firearms			Explosives			Incendiary			Melee		
Year	New	Old	All	New	Old	All	New	Old	All	New	Old	All
2004	109	69	381	164	128	678	9	9	30	9	1	15
2005	193	134	738	267	213	1,071	12	20	72	15	2	34
2006	153	159	973	244	280	1,512	10	27	95	18	12	60
2007	207	166	1,110	314	192	1,865	10	28	96	19	9	58
2008	259	254	1,313	426	394	2,729	39	83	263	25	34	105
2009	217	315	1,272	429	341	2,665	43	144	352	19	19	71
2010	212	322	1,371	438	392	2,706	23	151	274	30	45	99
2011	283	256	1,626	428	267	2,748	20	124	211	28	66	123
2012	802	392	2,481	1,493	563	5,412	86	76	251	13	25	53
2013	819	481	3,632	1,569	605	7,248	68	112	492	33	18	98
2014	1,515	1,055	4,988	2,662	1,123	9,483	100	242	629	70	85	218
2015	1,513	957	3,907	2,598	1,419	8,327	150	196	677	100	206	383

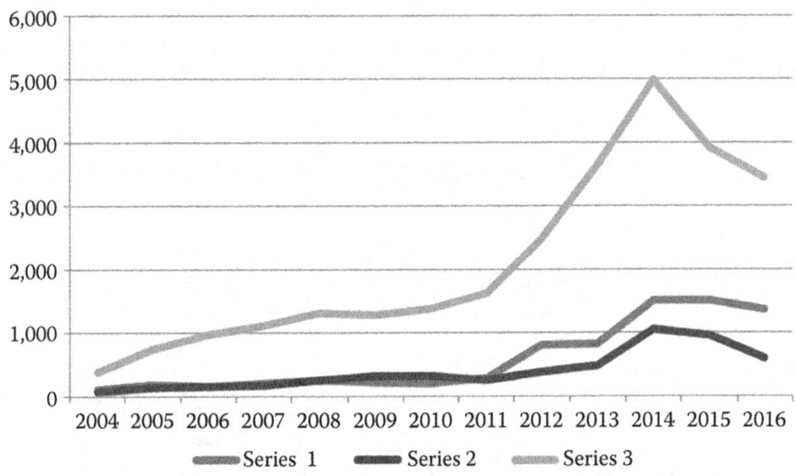

Figure 3.6 Number of terrorist attacks using firearms as the primary weapon type, by category of terrorist type, in the years 2004 through 2016.

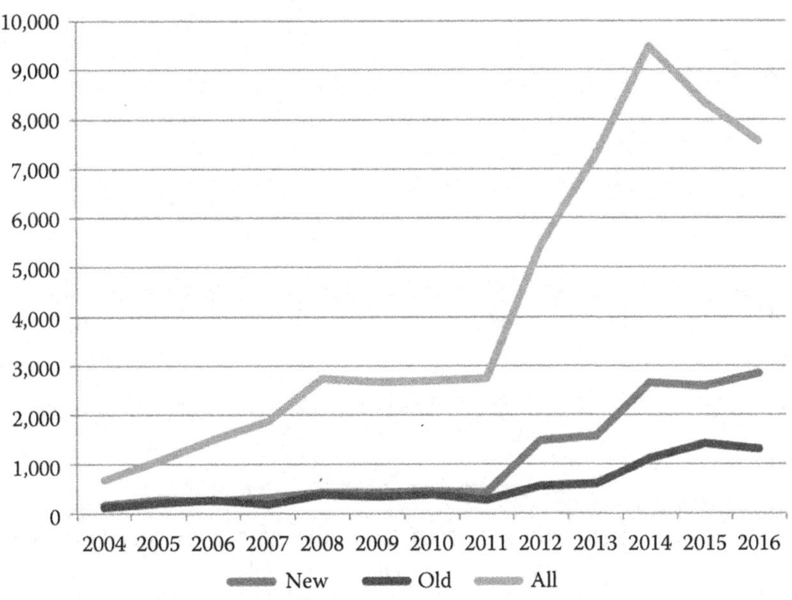

Figure 3.7 Terrorist attacks using explosives as the primary weapon, by category of terrorist type, in the years 2004 through 2016.

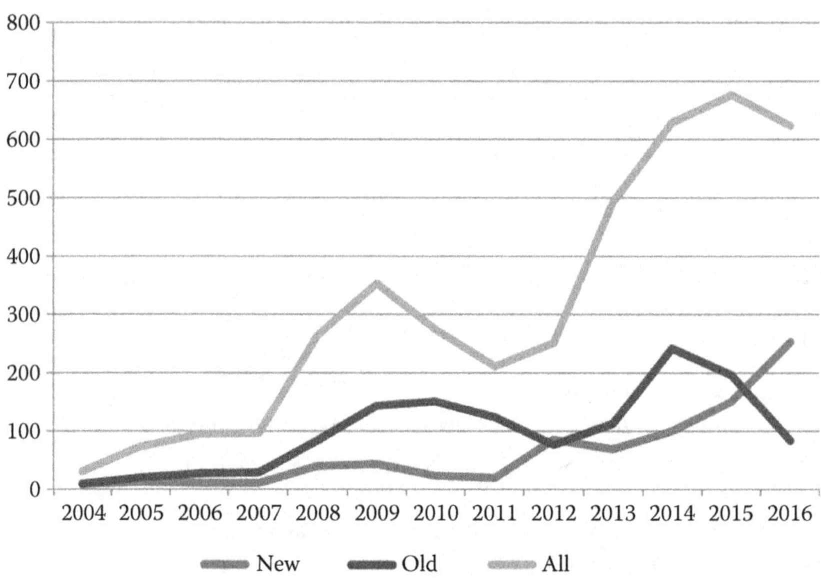

Figure 3.8 Terrorist attacks using incendiary devices as the primary weapon, by category of terrorist type, in the years 2004 through 2016.

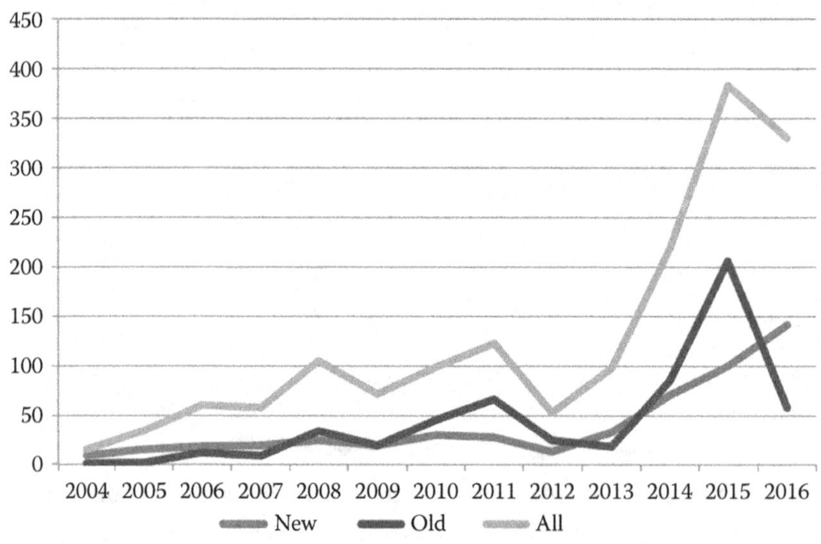

Figure 3.9 Terrorist attacks using melees as the primary weapon and attack type, by category of terrorist type, in the years 2004 through 2016.

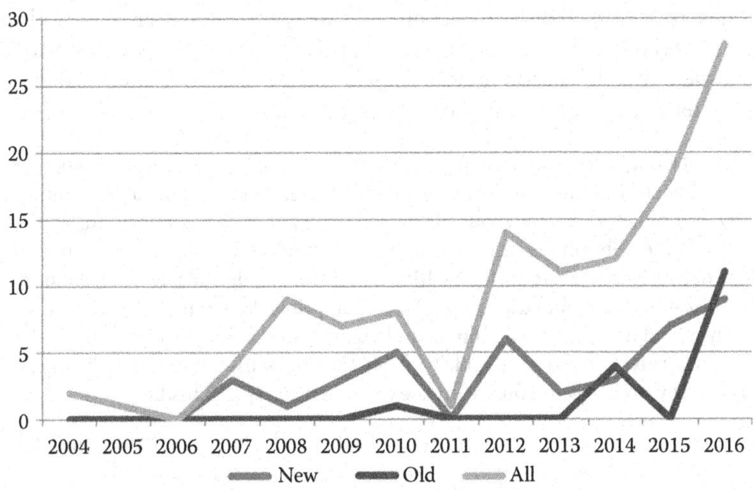

Figure 3.10 Terrorist events involving chemical weapons, for the years 2004 through 2016.

conventionally proscribed: chemical, biological, radiological, and nuclear weapons (CBNR), which are less accurately categorized as "weapons of mass destruction" (WMDs) (see Newsome and Jarmon, 2016, p. 167).

The GTD gathers reports on chemical weapons, showing a marked increase in terrorist use in the most recent decade of reporting (see Figure 3.10), which is probably underreported, because of the difficulties in coding chemical weapons and attributing the perpetrator. In some places, including Syria and Iraq, the use of chemical weapons has accelerated to unprecedented frequency, suggesting that the norms against use of WMDs of all types have collapsed, at least in that region. For instance, since 2014 through November 21, 2016, ISIL used chemical weapons at least 52 times in Iraq and Syria (mostly chlorine and sulfur mustard agents). This number surely is an undercount, and surely the true total would have been larger if not for the anti-ISIL coalition's strikes against sites suspected of manufacturing chemical weapons, and the capture of urban areas containing such sites (Schmitt, 2016).

More Uncontrolled Weapons

At the same time as new terrorists are seeking to increase lethality or terror with exotic weapons, they cannot put all their eggs in one basket. If they over-invest in such weapons, they increase their exposure to official controls and to the barriers to entry due to the skills required to utilize exotic weapons.

Thus, new terrorists encourage remoter or less skilled volunteers to take up less controlled weapons, including automobiles, sharpened blades, and corrosives, which are essentially impossible for officials to control without interrupting normal socioeconomic activities. While new terrorists would prefer their fighters to use the most lethal or terrifying weapons, where such weapons are controlled then uncontrolled weapons are better than nothing, from their perspective. For instance, in September 2014, ISIL's senior spokesman issued an exhortation for its followers to use whatever was available, in order of lethality, to wage Jihad in Western countries:

> The best thing you can do is to strive to your best and kill any disbeliever, whether he be French, American, or from any of their allies…If you are not able to find an IED or a bullet, then single out the disbelieving American, Frenchman, or any of their allies. Smash his head with a rock, or slaughter him with a knife, or run him over with your car, or throw him down from a high place, or choke him, or poison him. Do not lack. Do not be contemptible. Let your slogan be, "May I not be saved if the cross worshipper and taghūt [ruler ruling by man-made laws] patron survives. If you are unable to do so, then burn his home, car, or business. Or destroy his crops. If you are unable to do so, then spit in his face.
>
> **(Adnani, 2015)**

Automobiles

Blades and corrosives are easily accessible and deployable for most people, but offer less lethality than automobiles, since blades and corrosives must be used at proximate range against each person targeted, whereas an automobile can be driven into crowds. (This use of automobiles as kinetic weapons is often categorized as "vehicle ramming." It is categorically different than the historically dominant use of automobiles as carriers of chemical explosives—which are known normatively as vehicle-borne improvised explosive devices [VBIEDs].)

Unfortunately, the GTD does not yet observe automobiles as primary weapons, although it observes increasing use of vehicles as secondary weapons.

Vehicle Rammings, by Category of Perpetrator, for the Years 2004 through 2016, as Observed by the GTD

	New	Old	Unknown	All
2004	1	0	0	1
2005	0	0	0	0
2006	0	0	2	2
2007	1	0	0	1
2008	1	1	1	3
2009	0	0	2	2
2010	1	1	2	4
2011	1	3	0	4
2012	1	0	3	4
2013	0	1	1	2
2014	2	4	4	10
2015	6	27	1	34
2016	6	4	3	13

Anecdotally, journalists in Israel observed an increased frequency in the years from 2008 to 2011 (Lappin and Lefkovits, 2011), while the U.S. Department of Homeland Security issued warnings about increased terrorist use in June and December 2010, with a listing of example cases in America back to 2001, and warned that such use is a ready alternative to other weapons for "terrorists with limited access to explosives or weapons...[or] with minimal prior training or experience" (United States, Department of Homeland Security, 2010).

In October 2010, ISIL published its online magazine with an article urging its followers to use automobiles to attack crowds, preferably in wide pedestrianized areas, "in countries like Israel, the U.S., Britain, Canada, Australia, France, Germany, Denmark, Holland[,] and other countries where the government and public sentiment is in support of the Israeli occupation of Palestine, the American invasion of Afghanistan and Iraq[,] or countries that had a prominent role in the defamation of Muhammad." The writer urged drivers to carry firearms to continue the attack on foot after the vehicle is grounded, until "martyrdom." This advice started with the well-reported analogy of a four-wheel-drive "pickup truck"—modified with blades on its front—to a "lawn mower," mowing down "the enemies of Allah" (Ibrahim, 2010, p. 54).

Our observations through public media suggest that Jihadis have used automobiles with increasing frequency in developed countries recently, particularly against crowds gathered for politically or culturally symbolic events. Three particularly terrorizing events were perpetrated in the second half of 2016 by avowed followers of ISIL. First, in Nice, France, on Bastille Day (July 14, 2016), a Tunisian man drove a truck into crowds gathered on the waterfront to watch the fireworks, killing 84 and injuring 434 others, before he was shot to death. On November 28, 2016, a Somali refugee drove a car into pedestrians on the campus where he himself studied (Ohio State University), and wielded a knife, wounding 11, before being shot to death. On December 19, 2016, a Tunisian man hijacked a tractor-trailer, shot to death the Polish driver, and drove it into a Christmas market in Berlin, killing 12 and wounding 56. (He was shot to death in Milan, 4 days later.)

Blades

In the category of blades, primarily kitchen knives are used, although axes and screwdrivers have also been used. Blades are most accessible and deployable, and consequently more frequently used by terrorists than automobiles and corrosives.

Additionally, historical and religious texts contain descriptions of historical use of blades against enemies, if only for historical predominance before the invention of firearms and explosives. For instance, the Quran contains Medieval advice to "smite at their necks" in order to weaken enemies (perhaps because they were wearing body armor) prior to capturing them (Quran, 47:4). According to a consensus of Islamic scholars—from classical to modern, verse 47:4 provides conditions regarding the capture and release of enemy combatants, where combatants may be released gratuitously, upon a guarantee, or upon ransom. Given that the verse does not prescribe execution, scholars have interpreted this to imply that execution of captured combatants is prohibited in general. Other scholars cite the findings of classical jurists who have concluded that the execution of combatants is permissible under certain conditions[2] (Hamidullah, 1942, rule 439; Naqvi, 1974, pp. 33, 38; El-Dakkak, 1990, p. 109; Chaudhry, 2003; Al-Zuhili, 2005, p. 283; Munir, 2011, p. 89; Al-Dawoody, 2015, pp. 34–35). (In Chapter 10, we discuss the restricted circumstances in which Islamic law permits the execution of combatants.)

Although the Quran contains no prescription for beheading enemy combatants or captives, Jihadis have selectively interpreted this verse to justify beheading enemy combatants and captives (ISIL, 2014a). This helps to explain Jihadi showiness with blades in general, and beheading captives in particular.

In recent years, Jihadis have added to their classical tradition the justification that knives are more available. For instance, Al Qa'ida in the Arabian Peninsula urged killings with knives if other weapons were not available (Al-Najdi, 2006), and ISIL's English-language magazine has urged stabbings in Western countries, on the grounds that "One should not complicate the attacks by involving other parties, purchasing complex materials, or communicating with weak-hearted materials" (ISIL, 2014b, p. 44).

In our observations through public media, we have seen in recent years increased use of blades by avowed Jihadis in Australia, Belgium, Britain, China, Denmark, Egypt, France, Germany, Indonesia, Israel, Sweden, and the United States. For instance, on November 4, 2015, a young man, inspired by ISIL, stabbed four other students before he was shot to death on the campus of the University of California, Merced (Berman, 2015).

Large-*n* data show that Palestinian use of blades against Israelis surged in October 2015 (BBC, 2015). Further large-*n* evidence suggests that globally terrorists have used more blades every year since 2013. The GTD does not yet collect data on these weapons, except on knives (Figure 3.11) as used within a medley of attack types categorized as "melee" (Figure 3.9). This single measure clearly shows increased use of knives by all terrorists, particularly in recent years, presumably because of increased effectiveness of official controls on other weapons or the terrorist's increased focus on remote inspiration of amateurs.

Corrosive Chemicals

The third category of accessible weapon considered here includes corrosive chemicals, which effectively are being used as chemical weapons but are accessible generally as cleaning products. Sometimes corrosives are used in conjunction with other accessible weapons. For instance, on November 12, 2014, a Palestinian man injured seven Israelis in their car with acid and a screwdriver.

[2] Although verse 47:4 makes no mention of executing captured combatants, classical jurists such as al-Sarakhsi permit the execution of captured combatants "only if such punishment serves the public interest of Muslims" (Al-Dawoody, 2015, pp. 34–35). Other classical jurists and modern scholars agree that execution of captured combatants is permitted under certain conditions, which are discussed in Chapter 10.

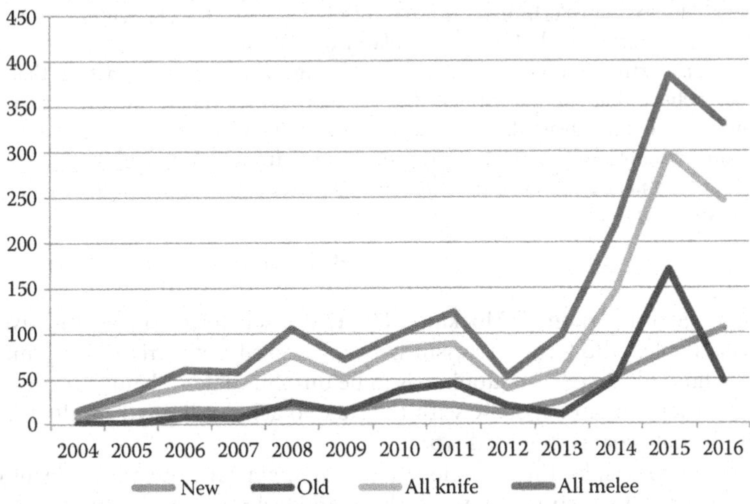

Figure 3.11 Terrorist use of knives in "melee attacks," for the years 2004 through 2016.

Irreconcilable Objectives or Intents

New terrorists, being more religiously ideological as their primary explanation, are less reconcilable than old terrorists, whose objectives are more political or material—and thus more "accommodate-able."

Decades ago, many analysts regarded politically ideological terrorists (political terrorists) as the most difficult with whom to negotiate, given their strong ideological commitment, bifurcation of right and wrong, strong loyalty to their group, hierarchy, planning, strategic competencies, and rationality (Stratton, 1978; Soskis and Van Zandt, 1986). However, the real observation should be that ideologues are difficult to negotiate, not that political ideologues in particular are difficult to negotiate. Political terrorists are normally categorized as old terrorists, since their political ideologies are normally secular or even explicitly atheist (as for Marxist terrorists), but their ideologies can be as intransigent as religious ideologies.

While ideologies differ, any ideology creates associated problems for the negotiator. Thus, ideologues are "the least likely to negotiate a resolution to a crisis," as their negotiation would likely be seen as a betrayal of their cause, whereas most criminals' "demands are quite logical (although often outrageous), and they are based in terms which can be met" (Combs, 1997, pp. 57–58). This message became stronger with the apparent growth in ideological fervor in the 1990s:

> Extremist criminals are also much more likely to be attack-oriented than defense-oriented. When a planned criminal act goes wrong, a typical criminal is much more likely to choose "flight" over "fight." The same cannot necessarily

> be said for extremist criminals, for some of whom a battle with law enforcement may be practically as desirable as the planned act itself...
>
> Many extremists adhere to ideologies so anti-government in nature that they believe that the government has virtually no legitimate authority over them at all. They insist that they have "constitutional" or "God-given" rights to do virtually anything without any interference from the government. When the government does try to interfere, anti-government extremists can become extraordinarily hostile.
>
> **(Anti-Defamation League, 2012, p. 5)**

Subsequently, Thomas Mockaitis (2011) defined terrorism as effectively irreconcilable: "the term terrorism is best reserved for extremist organizations whose ideology is so utopian as to be unachievable.... Unlike insurgent groups, they seldom negotiate with the state to achieve limited results when their ultimate goal is thwarted" (p. 17).

New terrorists, by their religious ideologies, appear most intransigent or irreconcilable. By their motivations, skills, and technologies, and the liberties of globalization, they are less interested in concession, and more capable of counternegotiating and of preparing hostage crises in which they hold more leverage over the other side.

These observations are consensual in the literature, although the explanations are varied. Theories of international conflict deduce that bargaining failures are most likely when the issues are indivisible, either side worries about the other side's commitment to honoring any agreement between them, and either side's imperfect information about the other side (Fearon, 1995). These conditions are strongest for religious terrorists.

Mark Juergensmeyer (2001) argued that religious terrorists have "cosmic" goals, such as to please God, which cannot be accommodated by apostates; they tend to defer control of all things to God, and to rationalize setbacks as holy tests; they value certain things as indivisible symbols that outsiders struggle to understand and thence to accommodate; they are certain about their righteousness and their enemy's impiety; "losing the struggle would be unthinkable"; they characterize their condition as a war, which "gives moral justification to acts of violence"; and they wage "cosmic wars" until the enemy is destroyed. "No compromise is deemed possible" (Juergensmeyer, 2001, pp. 148–162).

Monica Toft (2010) argued that belief in the afterlife gives religious fighters long time-horizons; she uses this theory to explain why civil wars in majority Muslim territories, and between Muslim sects, are more frequent and enduring.

Michael Horowitz (2009) argued that territory with religious value tends to be regarded as indivisible by the religious adherents: he uses his theory to explain why the Medieval Crusades lasted long after the costs exceeded the benefits, and to explain the lingering legacies of the Crusades in current disputes over the same territories (such as Jerusalem). This implies that religion motivates beyond where secular terrorists would give up. Ron Hassner (2010) agrees with the theory of "indivisibility," and goes further: he argued that the indivisibility of all religious goods (not just territory) leaves adherents with little wiggle room for bargaining.

Our analysis of the GTD gives empirical support for the theoretical expectation that new terrorists are less reconcilable. As shown in Table 3.6, new terrorist hostage-takings end in the release of the hostages 31% of the time, whereas old terrorist hostage-takings end in the release of the hostages 51% of the time; new terrorist hostage-takings end in the death of at least some hostages 60% of the time, while old terrorist hostage-takings end in at least some hostage-deaths less than 40% of the time.

Informed and Skeptical about Official Opponents

For one thing, new terrorists are better informed about the official side's policies, tactics, techniques, and procedures. Terrorists routinely use the Internet and e-mail to distribute official manuals on negotiating, which officials often post online for the public good anyway. New terrorists have studied past incidents and crisis negotiation team (CNT) manuals, and written their own manuals.

Relatedly, new terrorists are more skeptical of official negotiation. For instance, one of Al Qa'ida's manuals (2004) warns: "The enemy uses the best negotiator he has, who is normally very sly, and knowledgeable in human psychology. He is capable of planting fear in the abductors' hearts, in addition to discouraging them."

Surveillance

Terrorists make use of easier information and communication technologies to surveil their targets before the hostage-taking, to plan their attacks, to surveil their opponents during their hostage-takings, and to access news in real time—taking advantage of the rapid and exhaustive posting of news to the Internet or by distribution through social media. Consequently, some analysts have warned that new terrorists in particular are "unlikely to be tricked" by the official side (Dolnik and Fitzgerald, 2011, p. 268). For instance, at Beslan in Russia, on September 1, 2004, 33 Chechen-Ingush Jihadi separatists took more than 1,100 hostages in a school, over 3 days, during which they accessed the news in real time via broadcast radios and telephones, and were able to keep track of official Russian responses.

Communications with Suppliers

Materially, new terrorists have more access to information and communication technologies that enable them to communicate easier with potential suppliers of weapons, information, or other capacities. For instance, on July 22, 2016, in Munich, Germany, a German-Iranian man (Ali Sonboly), aged 18 years, with no official links to terrorism, obtained a pistol and ammunition illegally on the "dark net" or "dark web"[3]—a form of Internet accessible only

[3] A review in September 2016 found that most of the firearms for sale are American in manufacturer and vendor, but most of the destinations are European. Most of the firearms were pistols. Other items for sale include manuals on the manufacture of firearms and explosives. Given that participants protect themselves with anonymizing software, the review was incomplete (Paoli et al. 2017).

Table 3.6 Outcomes of Terrorist Hostage-Takings, by Old and New Terrorists, for 1970 through 2015

Category of Terrorist	Hostage-takings (count)	Unknown Outcomes	Known Outcomes						
			Total Known Outcomes	All Hostages Released	All Hostages Killed	Mixed: Released, Rescued, Killed	All Hostages Rescued	All Hostages Escaped	Failed Rescue Attempts
New	2,507	995	1,506	454 (30.2%)	631 (41.9%)	296 (19.7%)	90 (6.0%)	28 (1.9%)	7 (0.5%)
Old	4,121	2,011	2,107	1,090 (51.7%)	576 (27.3%)	256 (12.1%)	137 (6.5%)	46 (2.2%)	2 (0.1%)

Source: Data from the authors' extension of the Global Terrorism Database.

with special software, with which he shot nine people to death, and injured 35 others, before shooting himself.

Communications with Controllers and Recruits

Terrorists can use information and communication technologies to communicate with each other. The ease of communications today goes a long way to explain the dramatic rise in the frequency of terrorists acting alone (currently known in law enforcement communities as "lone wolves" if acting without foreign inspiration or "homegrown violent extremists" if acting remotely, with foreign inspiration but not direct material support). The frequency of these "singletons" has been increasing year after year since 2009; they are responsible for more than 70% of all Jihadi violence in Western Europe and the United States since 2010 through 2015. A primary explanation for their success is the difficulty of discovering a plotter who has no social support to alert the counterterrorist side (Davies, 2017).

Socialization can occur through cyber-space, without any real-world interaction. Terrorists can use information and communication technologies to communicate with each other. Official German analysis of 784 German residents who emigrated to join Jihadi groups in Syria or Iraq from 2012 through June 2016 found that they had been radicalized by friends (54%), mosques (48%), Internet contacts (44%), seminars (27%), organized distributors of the Koran (24%), and family (21%). During radicalization, friends became more important (63%), as did mosques (57%) (Heincke, 2017, p. 19).

The Islamic State's social media have attracted tens of thousands of foreign fighters from 2014 to 2016 (Milton, 2016). Of 38 plots or attacks in Europe from 2014 through October 2016, 19 (50%) received instruction online from ISIL members remotely. Of 38 terrorist plots or attacks inside the United States from March 2014 through February 2017 inspired by the Islamic State in Iraq and the Levant, at least 8 (21%) involved remote "virtual entrepreneurs" or "virtual plotters" using social media. They were involved in six separate cases involving support for travel to the Islamic State or other logistical activities. Analysts of these cases concluded:

> Social media, coupled with the ever-increasing availability of applications that offer encrypted messaging, has given virtual entrepreneurs the ability to both bypass Western counterterrorism measures and build close, trusting online relationships with recruits. As a result, virtual entrepreneurs have come to be seen by their followers as leadership figures from whom they can draw inspiration and take advice and instruction on how to act on their extreme beliefs.
>
> **(Hughes and Meleagrou-Hitchens, 2017, p. 6)**

Even "old terrorism" is shifting to social media. For instance, in February 2013 a Northern Irish woman (Christine Connor) used a fake name and photograph on a common social medium (Facebook) to declare a new dissident terrorist group ("United Struggle") opposed to the peace agreement in Northern Ireland. Remotely, she recruited two men to help her: an American man sent money, while an Englishman improvised explosive devices that she threw at police officers with intent to kill in two separate attacks in May 2013. The two men killed themselves after the arrest, before she was jailed in 2017 (Kearney, 2017).

Attackers can even take orders from remote controllers in other countries during the attack itself. For instance, the Jihadi terrorists who killed randomly before taking hostages in Mumbai, India, in 2008, used satellite telephones, mobile cellular telephones, and e-mail to exchange news and orders with controllers in Pakistan, over 3 days, until receiving suicidal orders at the end.

Communications with the Public

Information and communication technologies can be used to publicize the event from the inside. This was true before the new wave of terrorism, but mobile communication technologies in the era of new terrorism are more available and capable. Moreover, some observers have found that new terrorists are keener to reach a mass audience (Juergensmeyer, 2001, pp. 139–144).

Mobile communications are difficult for the official side to control; effectively new terrorists have the capacity to self-publicize their activities in the most gruesome ways. For instance, on July 2, 2016, six heavily armed terrorists loyal to ISIL seized the Holy Artisan Bakery in Dhaka, Bangladesh. They draped black cloths over security cameras to obscure the official side's view. While killing apparently non-Muslim hostages, the terrorists used hostages' cellphones to publicize the slayings on social media (Malik et al., 2016; Associated Press, 2016). Similarly, on July 26, 2016, two French men—one of whom had recruited the other over social media, both of whom posted on social media their loyalty to ISIL, took five hostages in a church in Rouen, Normandy, before filming the killing of a priest with a knife.

Communications with the Official Side

Terrorists can use information and communication technologies to contact the official side. For instance, in June 2016, over more than 3 hours, Omar Mateen killed 49 people in a nightclub in Orlando, Florida, during which he contacted the emergency telephone number (911) at least three times via his cellular telephone, stating his allegiance to ISIL, claiming falsely to have placed explosives in a vehicle outside and on his own person as deterrents to any police intervention, and threatening more attacks. Separately, still early in the crisis, he completed three calls (totaling 28 minutes) on his telephone with FBI crisis negotiators, during which he stated his allegiance and motivations, and falsely claimed to control a car bomb and a suicide vest as deterrents against any assault. He also placed at least one call to a private acquaintance (Zapotosky and Berman, 2016; Perez-Pena and Robles, 2016).

Communications with Potential Targets

Information and communication technologies can be used to attract targets. For instance, on July 22, 2016, in Munich, German-Iranian Ali Sonboly posted

Table 3.7 Sites of Terrorist Hostage-Takings, as Categorized by the Global Terrorism Database, by Category of Terrorist (New and Old), and by Human Outcomes, for 1970 through 2015

Target Type ↓	Number of Hostages Taken		Number of Attackers		Number of Hostages Released		Total Killed (Not Necessarily Hostages)		Number of Hostage-Takings	
Terrorist Category→	New	Old	New	Old	New	Old	New	Old	New	Old
Private citizens and property	20,644	8,924	5,908	9,633	5,977	4,293	5,771	2,113	1056	1,285
Business	3,919	5,914	1,919	3,674	2,688	5,079	1,008	377	205	728
Government (general)	1,724	4,493	419	7,391	414	3,250	899	602	256	698
Journalists and media	231	508	29	652	1,920	229	51	25	98	336
Police	2,426	893	3,514	7,289	960	1,178	1,057	580	281	212
Government (diplomatic)	395	1,996	107	1,883	255	2,996	57	66	68	150
Educational institution	2,647	2,929	485	180	1,339	399	706	22	82	107
Nongovernmental organization	341	216	100	61	231	126	44	6	87	41
Religious figures or institutions	933	529	217	424	98	1,348	236	338	79	84
Military	2,990	1,572	3,159	1,853	124	1,192	3,792	1,235	171	119
Transportation	254	2,530	186	759	90	1,362	52	140	15	65
Tourists	91	570	64	272	74	379	31	57	23	54

(*Continued*)

Table 3.7 (*Continued*) Sites of Terrorist Hostage-Takings, as Categorized by the Global Terrorism Database, by Category of Terrorist (New and Old), and by Human Outcomes, for 1970 through 2015

Target Type ↓	Number of Hostages Taken		Number of Attackers		Number of Hostages Released		Total Killed (Not Necessarily Hostages)		Number of Hostage-Takings	
Terrorist Category→	New	Old	New	Old	New	Old	New	Old	New	Old
Terrorists/nonstate militia	369	56	628	353	15	18	263	90	46	29
Violent political party	29	470	8	192	5	66	13	26	4	50
Telecommunication	1	37	0	214	1	21	0	1	2	42
Maritime	58	413	30	104	7	1,297	1	24	7	28
Unknown	2,085	157	0	167	62	27	29	8	8	21
Airports and aircraft	34	147	9	116	1,002	97	39	8	5	21
Utilities	36	152	58	281	36	74	8	75	3	18
Other	80	279	0	411	26	205	6	44	8	27
Food or water supply	4	27	0	104	2	1,000	0	24	2	5
Abortion related	2	0	3	0	0	0	0	0	1	0

Source: Authors' extension of the Global Terrorism Database.

a message, under a false identity, on an online social media site (Facebook) inviting the public for free food at a McDonald's restaurant, where he started his shootings, killing 9, and injuring another 35.

Readier Targets

Freer, more populous, and urbanized societies offer larger, more concentrated, and more confined subpopulations as potential hostages, such as in theaters, shopping malls, and schools. As shown in Table 3.7, new terrorists choose more public targets—theoretically in pursuit of higher lethality and terror—while old terrorists choose more politically useful or politically symbolic targets, such as embassies.

4

Should You Negotiate?

Negotiation is a dialogue toward an agreement. The Federal Bureau of Investigation's (FBI) Crisis Negotiation Unit (CNU) uses the Latin motto *Pax per Conloquium*, meaning "resolution through dialog." The current head (Mark Thundercloud) of this unit recognizes that negotiation is akin to communication and to crisis management:

> It's been my opinion for years that our unit was misnamed and should have been renamed the Crisis Communication Unit or something similar. Negotiation is a type of communication, but most of what we do involves de-escalation/crisis intervention techniques.
>
> True negotiation is a form of problem-solving and usually not too difficult, since both parties seek an agreement. That applies to terrorism cases, too. During kidnapping cases we employ crisis intervention and de-escalation techniques during interactions with families of victims, since they are usually in unfamiliar crisis states.
>
> **(Thundercloud, 2016)**

Others define negotiation as influence: "negotiation, ultimately, is the use of communication to exercise influence in order to change someone's thinking, behavior, and decision-making" (Dolnik and Fitzgerald, 2011, p. 268). This definition overlaps a particular practice in negotiations, known as "persuasive messages" or "influence tactics":

> We define the use of influence tactics as deliberate actions by one individual (e.g., police negotiator) directed at another individual (e.g., perpetrator) that seek to alter the attitudes and/or behaviors of the target in a way that would not have otherwise occurred.
>
> **(Rogan and Lanceley, 2010, p. 59)**

In this chapter we consider the arguments about whether to negotiate with terrorists at all (Figure 4.1). In order to be most useful—in the applied, practical

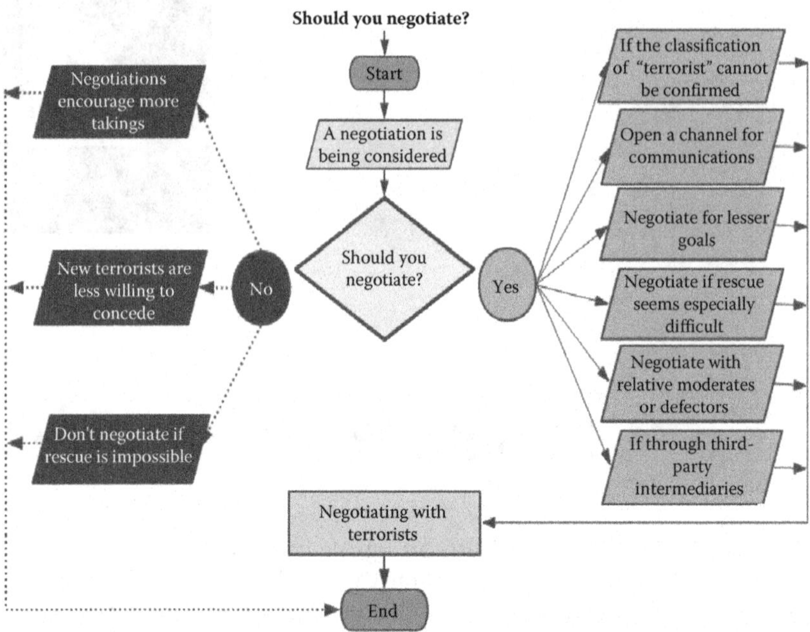

Figure 4.1 A flowchart considering the debates about whether to negotiate with terrorists.

sense, we have reviewed the issue as a debate, and organized our review by nine affirmative or negative arguments, in sequential sections:

1. Yes, if the classification of "terrorist" cannot be confirmed
2. No: negotiations encourage more takings
3. Yes: open a channel for communications
4. No: new terrorists are less willing to concede
5. Yes: negotiate for lesser goals
6. No: do not negotiate if rescue is impossible
7. Yes: negotiate if rescue seems especially difficult
8. Yes: negotiate with relative moderates or defectors
9. Yes, if through third-party intermediaries

Yes, If the Classification of "Terrorist" Cannot Be Confirmed

First, we need to acknowledge that in many hostage-takings, at least initially, the perpetrator cannot be confirmed as terrorist, in which case terrorism is effectively irrelevant to the officials who must make decisions about whether to negotiate. Such officials would not want to add to their burdens an additional consideration about whether or not the hostage-taker is terrorist—the officials want to work out how to engage with the hostage-taker as soon as possible. Additionally, officials keep their decision making simpler if they can avoid the semantic frame "terrorism," which implies more public and official alarm, and possibly also more constraints:

> I think it's worth pointing out that the word "terrorist" is often inflammatory and causes political leaders and the public to respond "no!" I think, though, in the middle of a crisis, the word itself and its political and strategic implications are a distraction. In fact, we often don't know during the incident if the subject is a terrorist or "just" a criminal. The police or FBI commander and personnel want to resolve the immediate situation—perhaps a hostage situation or barricaded subject—in a way that protects the public, the responders, and yes, even the subject(s).[1]

One principle for negotiating an end to conflict is to offer to decriminalize the other side in return for the other side's commitment to legitimate behaviors (such as nonviolent political expression). This commitment would allow negotiations without giving up the principle of no negotiations with terrorists. By application, the official side can continue to criminalize illegitimate actions, while decriminalizing the actor that gives up those illegitimate actions. This application even allows for the actor to be prosecuted for past illegitimate actions. However, practically, this application would fail if the actor is not incentivized to negotiate unless the prior actions too are decriminalized, which the other side cannot agree (perhaps in deference to the victims of those actions) (Kirkpatrick, 2017).

No: Negotiations Encourage More Takings

Intuitively and theoretically, negotiating with terrorists would encourage more terrorism, at least if the negotiations conceded to the terrorists something they wanted. Theoretically, this expectation is analogous to the basic theories about economic incentives, psychological rewards, and task fulfillment, which are well proven across many domains.

A causal relationship between negotiations and terrorism is difficult to prove with large-*n* datasets, given that negotiations are not necessarily revealed to the public domain, terrorists do not necessarily confirm their motivations, and the coding in large-*n* datasets tends to be remote. Anecdotally, many academics and officials observed that from 1968, when hostage barricade terrorism (HBT) began, initial government concessions seemed to encourage more HBT (Hudson, 1989, p. 326; Wardlaw, 1989, p. 157).

Philosophically, these commentators subsequently offered an essentially utilitarian argument against negotiating: the argument does not deny that negotiation might help the victim in the immediate case, but asserts that negotiating for this victim would encourage the perpetrators to take more victims,

[1] This statement was provided by a retired (as of 2016) counterterrorist agent and incident commander from the FBI, who chose to remain anonymous.

which ends up worse for society as a whole (Hudson, 1989, p. 323). Some have urged governments to declare that they will not negotiate with terrorists, and to publicize the expectation that sometimes "national security" comes before individuals, and that terrorism cannot be defeated: "Governments must realize themselves and must educate their publics to realize that there are no simple solutions to terrorism" (Wardlaw, 1989, p. 157).

In the 1980s and 1990s, governments normatively refused to negotiate, at least officially, although in the 2000s this norm broke down, as governments became desperate against increasingly effective terrorists and insurgents, as explained in the following sections.

Yes: Open a Channel for Communications

Negotiations as Communications

In practice, very few countries have adhered absolutely to their no-negotiations policy, even in the 1980s, when the norm was strongest (Hudson, 1989, p. 338). A policy of no-negotiation does not deter all potential hostage-takers; meanwhile government is constrained by its own policy, accruing victories to terrorists (Hudson, 1989, p. 322). The government's desire to avoid either causing risk to hostages, or a climb down from a no-concessions policy, boxes it in (Wardlaw, 1989, p. 155). "The fact remains, however, that politicians have painted themselves into a corner over terrorism by talking so loudly for so long about how they will deal a blow to terrorism, when in fact there is little that they can do to execute such action in the short term." This encourages the official side to view either military action or covert concession as its only viable options (Wardlaw, 1989, p. 159).

If the negotiations are reframed as something closer to communications, then negotiations-as-communications seem more frequent than an official policy of no-concession would suggest, and seem more legitimate: "It would appear that the most useful state response treads a difficult middle line...In other words, a government can indicate that it will respond firmly to terrorist acts and can demonstrate where it is feasible that it will not make concessions, but not put itself in the position of declaiming a policy which some day will have to be ignored" (Wardlaw, 1989, p. 158).

In the era of new terrorism, negotiations-as-communications remain strongly prescribed. For instance, academics Adam Dolnik and Keith Fitzgerald have written that "leaders do not actually mean that they will not negotiate. What they are really saying is that they will not make *deals* with terrorists, make *concessions* to terrorists, *compromise* with terrorists, or *reward* terrorists' behavior" (Dolnik and Fitzgerald, 2011, p. 267).

Similarly, Gary Noesner, former Chief of the Crisis Negotiation Unit at the FBI, urges clarification of negotiations-as-communications. His most succinct justification is that "Listening is the cheapest concession we can ever make" (Noesner, 2011, p. x).

> The problem arises from the misunderstanding of the term negotiate. Many embrace the false belief that negotiations are synonymous with capitulation or

acquiescence, and are therefore unacceptable. Correctly understood, negotiation is simply a dialogue between parties attempting to resolve a disagreement. While some may erroneously infer that negotiation means making substantive concessions, it does not. All agree that our government should not make substantive concessions which reward terrorists for their actions, including the release of prisoners. However, this tough stance does not require repeated public declaration that we will not negotiate, nor should we let this unequivocal phrase inhibit our willingness to open a channel of communications with terrorists in an attempt to save lives… The premise of negotiation is that by engaging in dialogue, we can better understand our adversaries and attempt to positively influence their behavior. Competent negotiation promotes a dialogue that helps defuse and de-escalate any incident, and almost always achieves better outcomes, even with terrorists. Mistaken belief that you cannot, or should not negotiate with terrorists often becomes a self-fulfilling prophecy, usually with lethal consequences. Terrorists are not immune to the influence of competent negotiations. Buying time through negotiation dialogue helps stabilize an incident, promotes better intelligence gathering, allows additional resources to be assembled, and better planning for any tactical action that may be required later. It can also achieve a peaceful outcome. When necessary, successful tactical intervention is best undertaken after significant planning and preparation, and as a last resort.

(Noesner, 2013)

Noesner asserts the value of opening communications as the opening step:

I feel as though rejecting the negotiation process because of any pre-conceived ideas we have about terrorist behavior is a flawed approach. It may be true that extremist jihadist terrorists may be willing to die and might in fact use the negotiation process to protract media attention before killing. While the outcome for a negotiated resolution in such incidents maybe low (only in these most extreme incidents by the way) there seems to be no good argument against attempting negotiations. One could say, "what do we lose" by engaging in dialogue? Despite what some may erroneously conclude, not all terrorists think and behave the same way and we should not view them all as reliably behaving the same way in every incident.

(Noesner, 2016)

Similarly, Roy Ramm, formerly Director of Negotiator Training at the Metropolitan Police in London, has stressed the legal and ethical virtues of negotiation:

We should always consider negotiation as our first response because, it is not the superiority of our weaponry or our numbers that sets us apart from terrorists is our belief in the rule of law. Negotiation is the practical application of that belief and a demonstration of the morality of a liberal democracy. In the face of terror's cruelest provocation, the threat to lives immediately before us, negotiation still offers the hostage takers the opportunity of a non-violent resolution and the protection of our courts and constitutions. This is a principle that is helpful in dealing with the media and post-incident enquiry. This is the moral basis of what we do.

(Ramm, 2016)

Official Communications

Negotiations-as-communications is helpful for public perceptions, particularly the victims' perceptions. A no-negotiations policy makes the state look passive, and leaves the hostages and their families isolated, hopeless, and resentful.

Even when the government participates, it can look self-restrained and vulnerable to private frustrations. Several governments have been criticized for mishandling communications with a hostage-taker and the victims' families. For instance, in April 2008, Somali pirates seized a French passenger yacht (*MY Le Ponant*) in the Gulf of Aden, with 30 crew members. A private adviser to one of the victim's families found that two agencies of the French government had created separate crisis negotiation teams (the Ministry of Foreign Affairs and the General Directorate for External Security [DGSE]). Although the teams set up a few meters apart in the same building, they refused to communicate with each other, and even papered over the windows of their respective rooms. Both teams could hear conversations on the boat through an open microphone connected to the boat's radio, left open surreptitiously by the boat's captain. Yet neither team had a Somali interpreter, although each assumed that the other did. Eventually, the private adviser proposed to recruit two Somalian immigrants from the streets. Two interpreters were recruited, briefed, and retained in the building until resolution of the crisis, for which they were paid in cash.[2] After payment of a ransom, the pirates released all the hostages, after which French special operations forces from Djibouti tracked the pirates to a village in Somalia, of whom six were captured, who were brought to France for trial.

The U.S. government has long practiced a policy of not conceding to terrorists, although at the same time it has participated in the crisis. For instance, U.S. agents have usually opened a criminal investigation. The FBI is the U.S. government's lead agency for counterterrorism and organized crime, but it does not make policy and is subject to other agencies or higher executives, through the Department of Justice and the Department of State to the National Security Council, the president's closest advisers, and the presidency itself. The Department of State's Bureau of Counterterrorism leads other agencies in pursuit of the safe recovery of hostages, to bring hostage-takers to justice, and to prevent future incidents. Its Hostage Policy Subgroup refines and implements U.S. policy.

Subject to policy, the FBI's crisis negotiators have been assisting families with their negotiations with kidnappers since the 1990s, without discriminating the kidnappers as terrorist or not. Agents have helped the victims and victims' families psychosocially, by privately briefing or advising the victims' families, or helping in the receipt, transportation, and health care of any released hostages. The capacities and constraints are articulated by the current leader of the Crisis Negotiation Unit (CNU):

[2] The private adviser who told this story chose to remain anonymous. She told her story to Arnaud Emery at the Centre lyonnais d'études de sécurité internationale et de defense (Lyon Center of International Security and Defense Studies), University Jean Moulin Lyon III.

> We're granted the authority to be the U.S. Government (USG) negotiators during hostage/barricade terror incidents when the USG is targeted, which is rare, but even then all decisions, especially regarding concessions, would be made by higher authorities in the USG.
>
> A criminal hostage/barricade situation, such as a trapped bank robber, is different. The on-scene commander(s), FBI or local police, would be the deciders.
>
> Regarding kidnappings, both terror and criminal, the decision-makers are family members, opting between things like ransom amounts, media releases, third-part intermediaries, etc. During kidnappings, negotiators and investigators provide input based on historical experiences, information about global regions and the suspected group responsible, among other things.
>
> **(Thundercloud, 2016)**

The FBI can legally negotiate (in the sense of communicate), despite the policy often articulated as "no negotiations with terrorists" (in the sense of no concessions), prompting calls for semantic change by a previous leader of the CNU:

> Despite the U.S. government's stated policy, FBI negotiators confronting terrorists holding hostages on a hijacked plane at JFK airport would indeed attempt to open a dialogue, not doing so would be reckless. Their efforts to secure the safe release of hostages in exchange for food for example would be appropriate, whereas releasing terrorists from jail would not. They understand the difference and so should our government decision makers. Our "no negotiation" rhetoric can cause confusion and uncertainty, even among our own officials who must manage these incidents.
>
> Government officials should avoid saying we will not negotiate with terrorists, and instead correctly and simply state when necessary what U.S. policy has always really been, that we will not make substantive concessions to terrorists. We should otherwise be quiet, as nothing more need be said.
>
> **(Noesner, 2013)**

In the process, higher actors in the U.S. government have sometimes negotiated with the terrorists in the sense of communicating with the terrorists, although officially it has not conceded anything. Over time, the government has communicated more with the terrorists on behalf of the victim's families, particularly after a surge in hostage-taking around 2010, and a surge in public criticism of apparent official passivity.

In 2014, the FBI publicized its Terrorism and Special Jurisdiction Program, within the Office for Victim Assistance. Upon a hostage-taking or kidnapping, it locates the victim's family, then dispatches an available victim specialist from the nearest of the FBI's 56 field offices. "The FBI uses an integrative approach to hostage cases that not only supports individuals and their families but also synchronizes the investigative and operational elements working to get the person back," said Carl Dickens, an operational psychologist in the program. The program helps to counsel the family, assists with emergency expenses, assesses the victim's responses, prepares for support of the victim after release, and notifies the family of legal proceedings (FBI, 2014, p. 28).

President Barack Obama's administration (2009–2017) used these capacities as evidence for a more virtuous official U.S. involvement in foreign taking of American hostages. However, the criticisms continued in 2015, such as by Barak Barfi, a former journalist involved with some of the victims of the Islamic State (often journalists, including Steve Sotloff, who was kidnapped in August 2013, and beheaded in September 2014). He directed his criticisms at the administration's policy and the practices of the government's agents or public servants. His criticisms of the administration's policy focused on passivity:

> In the last 10 months, the Islamic State has brutally executed four American hostages. As Americans died, their government was powerless to stop the slaying. For while European governments tirelessly toiled to secure the release of European hostages, President Barack Obama's administration's passive approach doomed their American cellmates...The White House did not do enough to rescue the four Americans. During Steve's imprisonment, it rarely worked with the hostages' families, kept them in the dark, and was essentially passive, rather than discussing ways to secure their release. And though the White House finally authorized an extraction attempt in late June 2014, it waited far too long to do so.
>
> **(Barfi, 2015)**

Barfi's criticisms of the government's practices blamed misplaced priorities:

> The U.S. government's principal channels with the four families largely consisted of mid-level officials from the Federal Bureau of Investigation and the State Department's Bureau of Consular Affairs. The FBI was useless. Its tasks were alternately to extract information and to comfort the family. It never shared intelligence. One European hostage, who was incarcerated with the Americans and subsequently released, told me he was shocked that the FBI seemed more interested in gathering evidence to prosecute the hostage-takers than it was in locating the Americans. Our lead agent misled me on several occasions, employing convoluted legalisms that would have impressed the greatest Talmudic scholars... The State Department was no better. When the mother of one of the hostages requested a senior point of contact at the White House, a State Department official rebuked her for going over her head. When Steve's father asked that I attend a government meeting, a consular official claimed the room was too small.
>
> **(Barfi, 2015)**

Public criticisms did encourage a change of policy: on June 24, 2015, President Obama announced an explicit change of policy, allowing families to negotiate private ransoms with official help, although the U.S. government would not make direct "concessions":

> I am reaffirming that the United States government will not make concessions, such as paying ransom, to terrorist groups holding American hostages...I

> firmly believe that the United States government paying ransom to terrorists risks endangering more Americans and funding the very terrorism that we're trying to stop. And so I firmly believe that our policy ultimately puts fewer Americans at risk. At the same time, we are clarifying that our policy does not prevent communication with hostage-takers—by our government, the families of hostages, or third parties who help these families. And, when appropriate, our government may assist these families and private efforts in those communications—in part, to ensure the safety of family members and to make sure that they're not defrauded.
>
> **(United States, White House, 2015)**

Obama revealed the creation of

- A Hostage Response Group under the National Security Council (NSC).
- A "Special Presidential Envoy for Hostage Affairs, who will be focused solely on leading our diplomatic efforts with other countries to bring our people home."
- A Hostage Recovery Fusion Cell at FBI headquarters in the capital, with officers from the Department of State, Department of Defense, Treasury, and Central Intelligence Agency.
- A family advocate: "Our new fusion cell will include a person dedicated to coordinating the support families get from the government. This coordinator will ensure that we communicate with families better, with one clear voice, and that families get information that is timely and accurate. Working with the intelligence community, we will be sharing more intelligence with families. And this coordinator will be the family's voice within government—making sure that when decisions are made about their loved ones, their concerns are front and center."
- "A new official in the intelligence community to be responsible for coordinating the collection, analysis and rapid dissemination of intelligence related to American hostages so we can act on that intelligence quickly." (United States, White House, 2015)

Lisa Monaco, Obama's counterterrorism adviser, clarified that the new policy and capacities allowed for official communications, and official facilitation of private communications, with the hostage-takers, even as it continued to prohibit the official payment of ransoms: "I want to take issue with the term 'facilitate', [the new system] will not facilitate ransom payments, it will give the families advice… No concessions does not mean no communications" (Roberts, 2015).

Anonymous U.S. officials claim that more than 70 American persons were released from hostage after the change in policy in June 2015, through about August 2016, when more than 12 remained to be released (Goldman, 2016).

The Obama administration's policy of communications without concessions has been challenged by political opponents, who point to the transfer of $400 million in cash by aircraft to Iran (designated by the United States as a state sponsor of terrorism since 1984), coincident in January 2016 with the implementation of a U.S.-Iranian agreement for Iran to limit its nuclear program, and with Iran's release of five Americans. Opponents have charged that the payment was a ransom. Officially, the administration asserts that the cash was the first installment in the resolution of a longer-term dispute about the United States freezing Iranian assets during the Iranian revolution in 1979, and the transfer was made in cash because the two countries have no banking relationship. The White House press secretary (John Earnest) said: "Let me be clear, the United States does not pay ransom for hostages." However, later, the State Department's spokesman admitted that it had delayed the transfer of the money until it was sure that the first three Americans had left Iran, although it still denied that this amounted to a "ransom" (Morello, 2016a; Shear, 2016). At the least, this dispute illustrates the political risks of navigating policies between no communications and no concessions.

No: New Terrorists Are Less Willing to Concede

While we should negotiate (in the sense of communicate) with all terrorists, we should not necessarily concede anything. Meanwhile, religious terrorists tend to make demands that are unacceptable to outsiders (the majority of people, given the exclusive in-groups that terrorists tend to form), while religious terrorists tend to assert inflexibility on their demands.

Without anything to concede, negotiations become more difficult, and may be described as ultimately pointless.

The literature provides strong consensus for these observations, although the explanations are varied, and the consensus has stimulated push-back against any assumption that new terrorists are absolutely averse to negotiations. For instance, Seth Cantey found some implicit openness to negotiation in some of the content of the magazines published by al-Qa'ida and ISIL, although those magazines are dominated by stark intransigence (Cantey, 2017). Some have observed that new terrorists are less negotiable (Dolnik and Fitzgerald, 2008, p. 15), while contradictorily suggesting practically no difference between old and new terrorists: "Contrary to public expectation, the 'new terrorist' hostage-takers are not delusional fanatics who claim to speak directly to God and who lack the capability to engage in rational conversation; they are highly politically aware, understand the principle of quid pro quo, and have a set of goals and expectations with regard to the outcome of the standoff" (Dolnik and Fitzgerald, 2011, p. 273). These particular authors offer as evidence some data from U.S. criminal hostage negotiations: CINT protocols worked in 95% of cases through 2000 (Dolnik and Fitzgerald, 2011, p. 269). However, this is a false analogy: nonterrorist hostage-takings are not analogous in motivations, hostage numbers, hostage-taker numbers, violence, or duration (see Chapter 3). Very few nonterrorist hostage-takers are murderous or suicidal; they usually arise after failed robberies or domestic violence. By one early analysis of terrorism during the acceleration of political-ideological terrorism, in 94% of HBT incidents, the perpetrators were willing to give up their lives, although in only 1% of cases were they determined to give up their lives (ITERATE data, in Corsi, 1981).

Dolnik and Fitzgerald suggested that new terrorists "understand the principle of quid pro quo," but Dolnik and Fitzgerald seem overly optimistic. Some Jihadis have taken hostages with intent to kill eventually: in these cases, hostage-taking was simply a means for attracting attention for a longer period of time before the final killings, and the hostage-takers had no intent to concede. Al Qa'ida itself refuted claims that hostage-taking must end with concessions: "History is full of facts proving the opposite. Many operations by the Mafia, or the Mujahideen were successful." Al Qa'ida drew attention to Shamil Basayev's operation against the Moscow theater in 2002, which ended in an official assault, without any concessions, after the long duration of the crisis, and its great death toll drew lots of attention, which Jihadis considered good for the cause (Al Qa'ida, 2004).

Dolnik and Fitzgerald noted fairly that hostage-taking is a signal by terrorists that they are open to negotiations. "In fact, the sole act of deliberate capture of hostages in the barricade scenario is in itself an expression of confidence on behalf of the terrorists that negotiating terms is possible" (Dolnik and Fitzgerald, 2011, p. 272). However, in response to recent failures of negotiation with Jihadi hostage-takers, some officials have urged shorter negotiation and quicker assault. For instance, the coroner for New South Wales in Australia criticized the delay before the police assaulted Man Haron Monis—an Iranian asylum-seeker, who took hostages in a café in Sidney in 2014, and killed one of them, 10 minutes before an assault in which he and another hostage were killed. An Australian negotiator pushed back, pointing out that "a rigid policy of non-negotiation and police aggression is potentially dangerous." However, "a rigid policy" is a straw man. He went on to state that "Attempts to negotiate with terrorists therefore appear to be worthwhile," but this is platitudinous (Roberts, 2017). Sometimes assault becomes more worthwhile than negotiation. Some Jihadis take hostages to draw out the crisis with no intent to negotiate, a previously unadmitted category of hostage-taking, which we term "irreconcilable hostage-taking," in which the hostage-takers are intent on killing hostages whatever anybody else does. In this case, the negotiation would be pointless, except to clarify the pointlessness or to buy time to prepare for an assault. The dilemmas of an assault are discussed in Chapter 12. The need to use force against an irreconcilable enemy is ignored by theorists who assume or observe that all new terrorists are negotiable—in fact, history already shows that not all terrorists are taking hostages with intent to negotiate for a peaceful outcome.

In any case, whether or not the terrorist is open to negotiation does not mean that the other side should negotiate, if it cannot accept or change the terrorist's demands.

We conclude that every hostage-taking deserves negotiation (at least in the sense of opening communications), at least in order to establish that a satisfactory solution would not be achievable by negotiation (as in the situations we categorize as "irreconcilable hostage-taking"), when negotiation should focus on other objectives, such as to help the preparations for assault, as described in Chapter 11.

Yes: Negotiate for Lesser Goals

Even if the official side cannot consider concession of the initial demands, it could offer minor concessions on the way to a resolution. Negotiating for lesser goals is taught by the FBI as a way to get to a resolution, or at least to prepare the other side for a resolution:

> These are all standard tactics of hostage negotiation: to minimize the consequences the perpetrator will face once the siege is over, and to assure him that he won't be hurt if he surrenders. The other essential part of the message is that harming someone will only make matters worse. Even so, there are times when playing it by the book won't get the job done, and when a more experienced negotiator might be more willing to improvise.
>
> **(Noesner, 2011, pp. 4–5)**

Even if the terrorists appear unwilling to concede, some commentators have advised the official side to communicate its own terms: "negotiation is inherent in the hostage situation. This is not to suggest that governments should cave in and ask terrorists to name their price. Rather, it means that since negotiation is implicit in the attempt to secure the hostage release, government should name its price and should seek to shift the agenda to a search for favorable terms" (Zartman, 1990, p. 165).

In hostage crises, prisoners tend to be exchanged on the condition that at least one of the hostage-takers' demands will be met to some extent (Zartman, 1990, p. 163, p. 173). Thus, officials should realistically expect to gain concessions from the opposing side if they agree to grant the opposing side concessions at least to a certain extent (Zartman, 1990, pp. 165–166).

This communication is productive if it encourages the other side to allow a concession that it had not previously considered: "Although statistics show clearly that giving in to terrorists' demands increases the likelihood of future incidents, meeting these demands through redefined formulas for lesser, acceptable terms of trade do not appear to have the same effect" (Zartman, 1990, pp. 175–176).

No: Don't Negotiate If Rescue Is Impossible

Some have urged pragmatism about whether to negotiate, essentially choosing on a case-by-case basis. This pragmatism leaves the practitioner with looser, more subjective guidelines than an absolute proscription on negotiating.

However, loose allowance, or waiting on a case-by-case basis, is not necessarily useful to the negotiator's preparations or even implementation. Helpfully, one analyst of old terrorism proscribed negotiating under two conditions:

1. If the victim cannot be rescued (perhaps because the victim's location will never be discovered or reached)
2. If the prevention of future imitative cases remains absolutely impossible

Under these two necessary conditions, negotiation would encourage more incidents, so it should be eschewed (Hudson, 1989, p. 323).

Yes: Negotiate If Rescue Seems Especially Difficult

By contrast, other commentators have urged more negotiation if the chances of a successful rescue or assault decline. This decline could occur because the hostage-takers become more militarily capable, the official forces become less military capable, or the terrorists have more time to prepare to defend themselves. In summary, the principle is that negotiation becomes unavoidable when the hostage-takers become unassailable (all other things equal).

The immediate reaction to the surge in terrorist hostage-taking in the 1960s was to negotiate, which encouraged more hostage-taking, so, by the mid-1970s, First World governments (we now know them as developed world governments) were preparing and using more military options. Their capabilities have generally remained high. However, by the mid-1980s, Second World (developing world) counterterrorist units had proven less successful—epitomized by the Egyptian assault on an Egypt Air Boeing 737, in which most passengers died, on November 23, 1985. While these governments had become less risk-averse, terrorists had learned better how to defend themselves, and to increase the risks to hostages, leading to a return to negotiating (Hudson, 1989, p. 327).

As soon as the 1980s, analysts warned that governments should negotiate in any HBT because the sites were usually highly exposed (usually airliners or embassies): such exposure raised the risks to the hostage-takers, and should raise their interests and opportunities for negotiations (Hudson, 1989, p. 232).

At the same time, the hostage-takers, given time, skills, and materials, can defend airliners and embassies easily, lowering the risks to themselves, and increasing their confidence in getting what they want from authorities. An airliner can be defended by wiring the passengers and exits with explosives, removing emergency chutes, hooding hostages, and keeping one terrorist capable of flying. Most hostage takers have survived; even when arrested, they were often soon released (Hudson, 1989, p. 333). These analysts reassured governments that in most HBT situations, governmental concessions would not encourage imitation, because terrorists realize that each situation is different (Hudson, 1989, p. 323).

These expectations hold for some new terrorists, too: certainly Al Qa'ida sought negotiation from "public kidnapping" if the hostage-takers are prepared to defend the situation:

> This is when hostages are publicly detained in a known location. The government surrounds the location and conducts negotiations...A target must be suitably chosen, to force the government to achieve your goals. Therefore, it is mandatory to make sure the kidnapped individuals are important and influential. [Then gather] enough information on the location and the people inside it.
>
> **(Al Qa'ida, 2004)**

Al Qa'ida identifies buildings, buses, road convoys, and airplanes as targets. "A connecting flight is a better option. Transit areas are more vulnerable where little inspection is provided" (Al Qa'ida, 2004).

In addition to considering the terrorist's acquisition of weapons that increase their defensive capacity, we should consider their deterrent capacity, such as a remote terrorist threat to attack somewhere more vulnerable if the official side should assault the hostage-takers locally. This deterrent capacity increases with certain weapons that are difficult to defend. By the 1980s, analysts already foresaw terrorist acquisition of weapons of mass destruction (WMDs), and considered negotiation more imperative in such an eventuality (Hudson, 1989, p. 324). This is a scenario that has increased in likelihood, given new terrorists' increasing interest in WMDs of all types, including nuclear weapons. If one were to follow the principle that one should be more open to negotiate with an enemy with more capabilities, one should be more willing to negotiate with an enemy with WMDs.

However, one should still assess whether the enemy has intent to negotiate. If the enemy has no such intent, (if they are "irreconcileable," as we explained earlier), the enemy would delay the inevitable use of WMDs, but would ultimately use them, so negotiations are pointless, except to gain time to prepare an assault—the only official solution is force, in order to reduce the enemy's capabilities.

Yes: Negotiate with Relative Moderates or Defectors

A proscription against negotiating with terrorists in general might include an allowance for negotiating with defectors or moderates.

Negotiation has utilitarian benefits. It damages the terrorist group when it acts as an incentive for defectors/splinters from the group. For instance, some have urged the United States to negotiate with those leaders from al-Nusra Front (based in Syria) who repudiate Jihadism and focus on fighting the regime of Bashar Assad, while the United States should sustain military actions against leaders who do not renounce their links with Al Qa'ida. In 2014, al-Nusra distanced itself from both Al Qa'ida and Islamic State of Iraq and the Levant, asserted its focus on the Assad regime, promised to refrain from attacking the West, sought removal from terrorist designation, and released peacekeepers whom it had kidnapped from their peacekeeping duties in the Golan (Watts, 2015).

Yes, If through Third-Party Intermediaries (TPIs)

Governments can use TPIs to escape their own prohibitions on negotiations with terrorists. Governments with a no-negotiation policy are more likely to use TPIs if the government can claim deniability.

For example, since the 1980s, both the Columbian and U.S. governments have used the International Committee of Red Cross as a TPI in negotiations with the FARC (Revolutionary Armed Forces of Colombia; *Fuerzas Armadas Revolucionarias de Colombia*)—a designated terrorist group based in Columbia, which has often detained domestic and foreign citizens for years at a time.

Since the 1990s, the FBI has been using TPIs regularly, although the family of the victim has the final say. Additionally, families might procure private security negotiators (many of whom are retired law enforcement negotiators), who in turn usually cooperate well with official negotiators.

A separate argument about TPIs is how to use TPIs to build rapport and trust, if the other side is too distrusting or hateful of the official side to negotiate directly. This is an issue of how to use TPIs—separate from the issue of whether to use TPIs, so we consider the separate issue in Chapter 6.

5

Immediate Management of the Incident

This chapter reviews the main processes of responding to critical incidents, before recommending a nine-step process.

The first four steps are essentially immediate responses to the incident, before or independent of any establishment of communications with the other side, which are described from Chapters 6 to 11. In this chapter, the first section reviews the main processes, before the following four sections go into detail on the initial or immediate four steps that we recommend in response to the incident, immediately and throughout:

1. Isolate the local hostage-takers from any remote controllers
2. Assess the situation
3. Manage publicity
4. Manage time and contingencies

Competing Processes of Managing Critical Incidents

Historical Practices

Wide consensus exists for the importance of specialized preparedness for responding to, and managing, hostage-takings, kidnappings, and active shootings.

> Communications need to be established with the hostage taker. There is a need for a negotiator element. Because the communication skills and conflict

> management skills used by a negotiator are different from those normally employed by patrol officers, it is important for departments to have trained negotiators...
>
> Overall control of the situation must be maintained. A command element is necessary. The designated commander needs to assume overall command. He or she is the final approving authority for operational decisions and is responsible for ensuring that the other elements function as they should...
>
> As soon as a strategy is developed and communications with the hostage taker are necessary, the team will be divided into their roles as primary negotiator, secondary negotiator, etc.
>
> **(McMains and Mullins, 2015, pp. 72–73, 85)**

Before the new wave of terrorism, an analyst suggested responding to terrorist hostage-takers in three steps:

1. "Diagnosis of the situation (or pre-negotiation)"
2. "Finding a mutually acceptable formula to frame the agreement"
3. "Implementing that formula with an agreement on details" (Zartman, 1990, p. 171)

Roy Ramm (formerly Director of Negotiator Training at the Metropolitan Police in London) has prescribed three steps:

1. Isolate ("isolate the hostage-takers from outside influences")
2. Communicate
3. Negotiate (Ramm, 2016)

A three-step process is intuitive and accessible because it generally begins with an orientation, passes through a middle phase of problem solving, and finally gets to the resolution of the crisis.

Various reviews of the processes suggest that successful processes generally proceed through establishing trust, building rapport, and using certain mutually reinforcing communication techniques. One review of official processes of negotiating hostage crises found that they normally varied between three and six steps (Baruch and Zarse, 2012). The "REACCT Model" prescribes six steps, whose first letters form the acronym:

1. Recognition of the situation's implications for official authorities and responsibilities
2. Engagement with the hostage-taker
3. Assessment of the hostage-taker
4. Controlling of the hostage-taker (such as by encouraging them to eschew violence or to calm down)
5. Contracting with the hostage-taker (including active listening)

6. Transference of responsibilities (McMains and Mullins, 2015, Chapter 3)

A separate review of official processes identified seven common "basic elements":

1. Isolate and contain the hostage-taker
2. Control the public, media, and emergency responders
3. Establish communication with the hostage-taker
4. Use socialized communication strategies, such as building rapport
5. Respond to demands and deadlines appropriately, especially to promote the safety of the hostages
6. Prepare for the handling of the hostage-taker's surrender, the release of the hostages, or a rescue attempt
7. Prepare for the psychological treatment of all involved (Grubb, 2010, p. 344)

Our Practical Prescriptions

Incorporating lessons from the processes above, we prescribe nine steps. All other things being equal, fewer steps are preferred, at least for simplicity of training and implementation, although new terrorist hostage-taking seems complex and challenging enough to us that we acknowledge nine steps. Negotiating with new terrorists is different, for material and ideational reasons. New terrorists tend to attack in larger, more capable groups, with more capacity for suicide and murder. New terrorists use new information and communications technologies that were not accessible even two decades ago, to surveil targets remotely (perhaps using online geographical mapping and imaging software), to communicate during their planning, and to purchase items or services of use to the attack. Consequently, the negotiator in new terrorist crises must be prepared for exceptional intentions, objectives, motivations, and ideologies; murder and suicide; and multiple actors and multiple channels.

We prescribe the following nine major steps (Figure 5.1), of which some have minor steps (Figure 5.2):

1. Isolate the local hostage-takers from any remote controllers
2. Assess the situation
    a. The number of hostage-takers
    b. The ultimate decision maker
    c. Their media of communications

Nine steps of the main process of negotiating critical incidents:
Step 1: Isolate the local hostage-takers from any remote controllers
Step 2: Assess the situation
Step 3: Manage publicity
Step 4: Manage time and contingencies
Step 5: Develop a relationship with the other side
Step 6: Assess their psychology
Step 7: Assess their motivations, intentions, and objectives
Step 8: Negotiate a resolution to the crisis
Step 9: Assault, if necessary

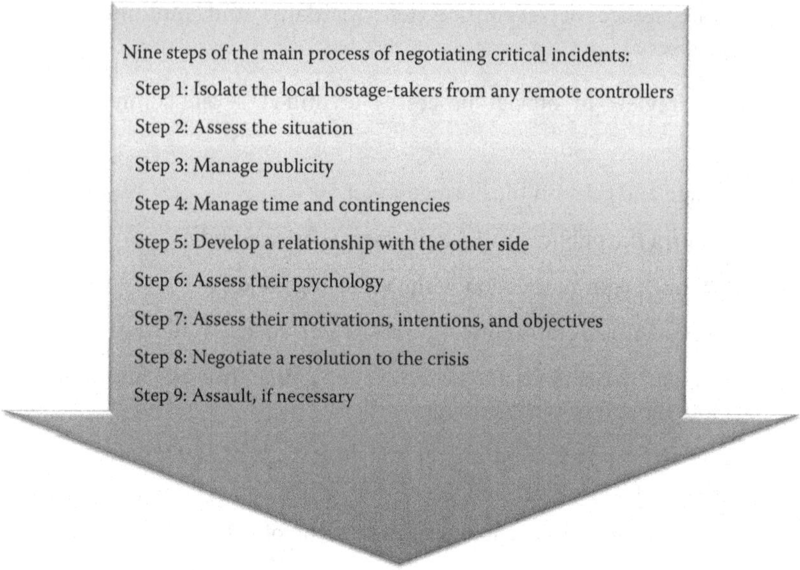

Figure 5.1 The major steps of our recommended process for negotiating critical incidents.

3. Manage publicity
4. Manage time and contingencies
5. Develop a relationship with the other side
    a. Actively listen and empathize
    b. Acknowledge skepticism
    c. Appeal to morality, ethics, or religious laws
    d. Involve trustworthy third-party intermediaries
    e. Make minor bargains or trades
        i. Grant subsistence
        ii. Grant publicity
    f. Provoke thoughtfulness on the other side
6. Assess their psychology
    a. Are they rational?
    b. Are they murderous?
    c. Are they suicidal?
7. Assess their motivations, intentions, and objectives
    a. Are they taking people in order to gain intelligence?
    b. Are they seeking publicity?

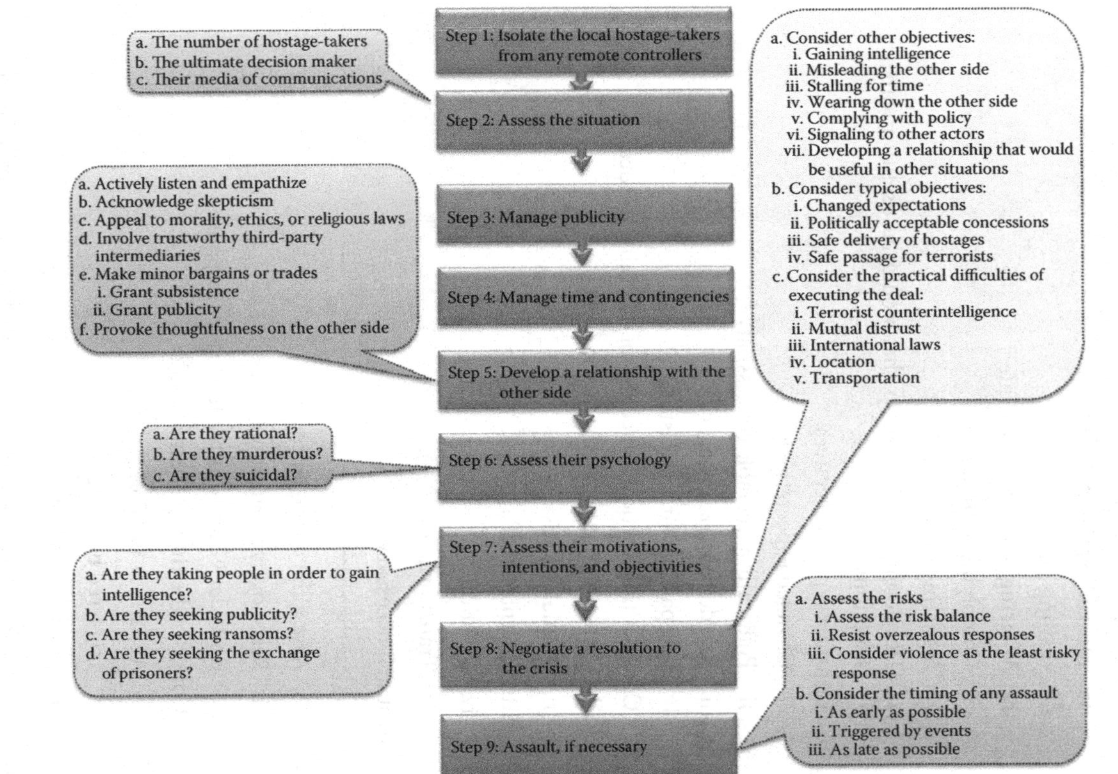
Step 1: Isolate the local hostage-takers from any remote controllers
a. The number of hostage-takers
b. The ultimate decision maker
c. Their media of communications
Step 2: Assess the situation
a. Consider other objectives:
i. Gaining intelligence
ii. Misleading the other side
iii. Stalling for time
iv. Wearing down the other side
v. Complying with policy
vi. Signaling to other actors
vii. Developing a relationship that would be useful in other situations
b. Consider typical objectives:
i. Changed expectations
ii. Politically acceptable concessions
iii. Safe delivery of hostages
iv. Safe passage for terrorists
c. Consider the practical difficulties of executing the deal:
i. Terrorist counterintelligence
ii. Mutual distrust
iii. International laws
iv. Location
v. Transportation
Step 3: Manage publicity
Step 4: Manage time and contingencies
Step 5: Develop a relationship with the other side
a. Actively listen and empathize
b. Acknowledge skepticism
c. Appeal to morality, ethics, or religious laws
d. Involve trustworthy third-party intermediaries
e. Make minor bargains or trades
i. Grant subsistence
ii. Grant publicity
f. Provoke thoughtfulness on the other side
Step 6: Assess their psychology
a. Are they rational?
b. Are they murderous?
c. Are they suicidal?
Step 7: Assess their motivations, intentions, and objectivities
a. Are they taking people in order to gain intelligence?
b. Are they seeking publicity?
c. Are they seeking ransoms?
d. Are they seeking the exchange of prisoners?
Step 8: Negotiate a resolution to the crisis
Step 9: Assault, if necessary
a. Assess the risks
i. Assess the risk balance
ii. Resist overzealous responses
iii. Consider violence as the least risky response
b. Consider the timing of any assault
i. As early as possible
ii. Triggered by events
iii. As late as possible

Figure 5.2 The major steps and some of the minor steps of our recommended process for negotiating critical incidents.

   c. Are they seeking ransoms?
   d. Are they seeking the exchange of prisoners?
8. Negotiate a resolution to the crisis
   a. Consider other objectives
      i. Gaining intelligence
      ii. Misleading the other side
      iii. Stalling for time
      iv. Wearing down the other side
      v. Complying with policy
      vi. Signaling to other actors
      vii. Developing a relationship that would be useful in other situations
   b. Consider typical objectives
      i. Changed expectations
      ii. Politically acceptable concessions
      iii. Safe delivery of hostages
      iv. Safe passage for terrorists
   c. Consider the practical difficulties of executing the deal
      i. Terrorist counterintelligence
      ii. Mutual distrust
      iii. International laws
      iv. Location
      v. Transportation
9. Assault, if necessary
   a. Assess the risks
      i. Assess the risk balance
      ii. Resist overzealous responses
      iii. Consider violence as the least risky response
   b. Consider the timing of any assault
      i. As early as possible
      ii. Triggered by events
      iii. As late as possible

We explicate each of these steps across several chapters, in order to break down their complexities into easier chunks for the reader. In the next sections of this chapter, we explicate the first four steps that we recommend as immediate responses to the incident, and throughout the crisis.

Isolate Local Hostage-Takers from Any Remote Controllers

Historical Practices

In old terrorist and nonterrorist hostage-taking, negotiators were consensually advised to separate hostage-takers from their remote controllers. This advice applies to new terrorists, too, although for some reason it has not been included in most of the prescribed processes that we reviewed above.

Roy Ramm has made "isolate" the first step of his three-step prescription:

> Negotiation communications should be conducted as securely possible. This means doing everything possible to isolate the hostage takers from outside influences. Negotiators have the greatest chance of success when the individual(s) with whom they are speaking are not directed, supported or encouraged by influences from outside the stronghold. This is equally important in maintaining the tactical advantage if an assault on the stronghold is planned.
>
> **(Ramm, 2016)**

Gary Noesner has emphasized the step, particularly as a lesson from his negotiations with the Davidians (led by David Koresh), in Waco, Texas, which had started in February 1993 after a failed raid by the Bureau of Alcohol, Tobacco, and Firearms, in which four agents and six Davidians were killed: "To gain control of the situation, we needed to control and limit all communication in and out." However, this proved technically difficult for much of the crisis, when Koresh used telephones to dictate his last testaments to journalists, and to wish his mother goodbye, while preparing his followers for mass suicide. In April 1993, weeks after the initial contact, a final assault was authorized, during which the Branch Davidians started a fire, after which Koresh and 79 others were found dead (Noesner, 2011, p. 99).

Other analysts have focused on the case of Mumbai in 2008 as evidence for the prescription to separate the hostage-takers from their remote controllers, who encourage killings and suicides as an endgame (Dolnik and Fitzgerald, 2011, p. 287). During the crisis in Mumbai (2008), the Indian authorities chose to listen in on remote communications rather than shut them down, to the benefit of intelligence collection, thereby allowing remote control to continue, while disallowing any use of the same channel by local negotiators who might wish to communicate with the local hostage-takers. Indian intercepts of verbal conversations via satellite telephones between the local hostage-takers and their remote controllers show that the remote controllers intended the hostage-takers to kill for as long as possible before being killed themselves. The remote controllers of the hostage-takers at the Jewish center explicitly ordered the killing of the last hostages before seeking death by confronting Indian soldiers. Only one of the 10 attackers was captured alive by the Indian authorities—Pakistani citizen Mohammed Ajmal Amir Kasab; he was captured wounded, even though he was under orders to martyr himself, and expected to do so; he was executed by hanging 4 years later.

Simulated Practices

Both of our real-world simulations (2015 and 2016) were designed with remote controllers, whose location was simulated as somewhere on the border between western Iraq and eastern Syria. The remote controllers had real-time control of hostage-takers homegrown in an American city, who (according to the fictional backstory) had volunteered through social media to the remote terrorist group. This design was chosen to mimic the foreign remote control of hostage-takers in incidents such as Beslan in 2004, Mumbai in 2008, and Paris in 2015. The homegrown hostage-takers were assumed never to have visited their remote controllers physically, but to have volunteered through social media. In both simulations, the given objectives were the same, including the escape of the homegrown hostage-takers to Iraq at the conclusion of their operation.

In both simulations, the students who were playing the remote controllers initially developed various creative ways of getting the hostage-takers out of the United States safely, but quickly gave up on such an unlikely objective, in favor of achieving other objectives through the martyrdom of the local hostage-takers, even though the suicidalism of the local hostage-takers was not certain.

In the second simulation (2016), the terrorist side prepared to isolate the four fictional homegrown American hostage-takers from official communications, and to ensure that the official side communicated with only the remote controllers. The terrorist side ordered the four American volunteers to leave all their personal electronic devices at home, and to take into the attack only one cellular telephone, purchased the day before to maintain communications with the remote controllers alone. The terrorist side ordered the volunteers to destroy all communications devices on the hijacked train, while warning the official side that any official attempt to contact the local hostage-takers would be punished with killings of hostages.

Similarly, in simulation (2016), the official side regretted the continuance of communications between the hostage-takers and their remote controllers, while remaining unable to communicate with the hostage-takers directly:

> In retrospect, we should have cut off communication between the hostage-takers and their handlers. This would have enabled us to communicate directly with the hostage-takers, who were much more likely to have developed psychological obstacles to executing the hostages and be less skillful negotiators than their leaders, especially while trying to keep all 41 hostages under control. Even though the Ring repeatedly threatened that the hostage-takers will detonate their vest bombs, their continuous communication with us signaled that they would rather reach a negotiated settlement than command the hostage-takers to blow themselves up.
>
> **(Kevin Chu)**

Our Practical Prescriptions

We prescribe "isolate" as the first step, because it protects subsequent steps from predictable problems, such as multiparty negotiations without transparency, and because it is a step that the official side can normally execute immediately. The official side should assess whether any remote controllers can be confirmed; even if this cannot be confirmed, the official side might take the precaution of jamming or cutting telephone and Internet communications from the site—except those under the official side's control.

Negotiations will be less controlled and less certain for the official side that is negotiating with the immediate hostage-takers that retain communications with any remote controllers. Additionally, remote controllers are likely to add more negative risks. Remote controllers do not share the local risks (such as official assault) and stresses (as simple as lack of sleep, water, or food) that the local hostage-takers cannot avoid. Consequently, the remote controllers would retain more resolve or intransigence, more tolerance of the local hostage-takers' suicidal and murderous intents, and more tolerance of harm to the hostages without the sympathies that proximate interpersonal interactions could generate, and without the local consequences.

By default, we recommend that the official side blocks or jams communications between the remote controllers and the local hostage-takers, probably by shutting down the local infrastructure supporting cellular communications or Internet communications.

We acknowledge the useful intelligence gathered by secretly listening on terrorist channels, but this intelligence is unlikely to be useful to the negotiator in time to influence the crisis, given the short duration of such a crisis (hours to days), although after the crisis the analysis is useful for drawing lessons and in the preparation of negotiators for future crises.

We allow only one other reason to allow remote controllers to continue to communicate with local hostage-takers (other than the advantage to the intelligence collector or future negotiator): if the official side has some direct leverage over the remote controllers, then the official side should allow the remote controllers to keep their channels open with the local hostage-takers, so that the official side can put pressure on the remote controllers directly in order to put pressure on the local hostage-takers indirectly. For instance, perhaps the official side can track the communications to the remote controllers' material location, which can be threatened with attack.

Assess the Situation

Historical Practices

Zartman (1990, p. 171) prescribed a first step that he described as "diagnose the situation." Diagnosing the situation is essentially a matter of intelligence collection and analysis. A later generation of negotiators prescribed immediate information gathering: "Information needs to be gathered. There is a need for an intelligence element that focuses on information about the incident, the people involved, and the tactical needs" (McMains and Mullins, 2015, p. 73).

An incident commander prescribed an immediate assessment of the incident as either terrorist or nonterrorist:

> At the onset of the crisis, the local commander must quickly determine if the situation is a terrorist strike or a civil crime, and in order to properly make this decision, the commander must be educated on the essence of terrorism and how it differs from other types of crimes.
>
> **(Forest, 2007, p. 261)**

Armed responders also emphasize the need for deliberative assessment before reaching any decisions, as articulated by the following former member of the U.S. Army's Delta Force:

> "Getting treed" is a metaphor for making decisions without context. Context is the reality of the situation around us. Without context, our minds have a tendency to take shortcuts and recognize patterns that aren't really there; we connect the dots without collecting the dots first. Overreacting, under reacting, and failing to do anything at all are all symptoms of "getting treed."...
>
> My common sense was telling me to take time to look, listen, and question everything. Common sense provides context, and context is common sense.... In combat, when leaders make decisions without context, the cost is mission failure, and all too often, the price is paid with the blood of their men.
>
> **(Blaber, 2008, p. 42)**

Simulated Practices

Likely, a hostage crisis starts without any warning to the official side—otherwise presumably the official side should have prevented it. Even given some warning of a hostage-taking, the warning might contain no information of use for understanding the particular hostage-taking event when it occurs, particularly if the terrorists are smart. Immediately, some physical or material information is likely to be apparent, such as the location of any dramatic abductions or attacks. However, beyond the most tangible immediate information, the negotiator should prepare to receive no remarkable information in the first hours.

This is illustrated by our second simulation (2016), which gave both sides the same 2 weeks for preparation before the simulated attack:

> Our preliminary investigations and effort to gather intelligence highlighted challenges inherent to intelligence collection. The lack of information we received at the beginning of the simulation forced us to make tactical decisions about where to investigate and replaced security measures with an element of guesswork. Significantly, we also faced issues of intentional red herrings on the part of the terrorists, who were able to distract our attention from the real target through contrived tweets about an attack at the [oil] refinery. We then used our resources to secure the refinery, rather than looking for suspicious activity elsewhere. Although the terrorists led us astray with their messaging, we had still arranged for surveillance on [municipal] trains and were surprised that we had not gathered any intelligence from this surveillance until the terrorist team told us that they had intentionally kept the target hidden from the four men carrying out the attack and had not let any of the men use the transit service leading

up to the attack. This demonstrates the challenges associated with new terrorism and the difficulty of confronting terrorist organizations that have international overseers and local agents who are not always fully aware of the plans for the attack that they are carrying out. This combination of actors makes detection of threats extremely difficult, as we witnessed in our simulation.

(Hannah Ousterman)

The value of assessing the other side is illustrated most strongly by our second simulation (2016), in which the official side forgot their initial intelligence—that four locals had volunteered to take hostages for a terrorist group located in the Middle East:

Zartman discusses the three-phase model of negotiations, and our error was in not spending adequate time in phase one, when we should have more completely assessed the situation at the beginning of the crisis before initiating negotiations.

(Zartman, 1990, p. 171)

When we received the first email from the terrorists during the 3-hour negotiation from the same account Mel had been using to talk to Abdul Aziz, we should have immediately recognized that we were working with terrorists on a high level, not the individuals in the train car. None of us made this connection, however, and this seriously hindered our ability to negotiate. Had we realized who we were actually talking to, we would have changed our strategy entirely and utilized language more appropriate for the high level negotiations with leaders of the Ismaeel Ring that were taking place. Our misunderstanding about who we were working with led us to focus on irrelevant issues, such as the needs of the four HTs [hostage-takers] and the physical condition of the 41 hostages in the train car. In the debrief, we discovered that the terrorist team had no intention of releasing hostages and was willing to kill the four HTs, who were little more than pawns in a larger operation.

(Hannah Ousterman)

Our single largest mistake that impacted us most severely was our confusion over our audience. We never found out whom exactly we were speaking to in our negotiation. We assumed that the number we gained over email was that of the terrorists in of [the train], since we believed that email to be linked to the four men in the network cell, not the Ismaeel Ring at large. We did ask whom we were speaking with and how they should like to be addressed, but we never asked if they were the ones onboard [the train]. This was completely our fault and changed the entire course of the simulation.

(Anastasia Selberis)

Another big flaw was not knowing whether the people we were negotiating with were the terrorists inside the train or the Ring leaders. Although we tried to

> figure out, the people on the phone were very arrogant and did not seem like they wanted to negotiate.
>
> **(Jason Tran)**

Our Practical Prescriptions

For this step, we prescribe an assessment of the immediate situation, such as the timing and location of the initial event, and estimates of the current material situation, such as the number of attackers, their weapons, the number of hostages, and the material structure of the space in which the attackers and hostages are contained.

We have separated the estimation of the attackers' motivations, intentions, and objectives as a later step, which we complete in Chapter 8.

In the sections that follow, we review three organizational dimensions of relevance to both the material situation and the negotiations:

1. The number of hostage-takers
2. The ultimate decision maker
3. Their media of communications

How Many People Are Involved?

The negotiator, and the personnel who might need to assault the hostage-takers, can benefit from knowing the size of the hostage-taking group. The number of any remote controllers is largely irrelevant to the size of the hostage-taking group, although in theory a remote group could threaten retaliation for any harm to its hostage-takers, if within its capacity.

The number of hostage-takers affects group psychology, the group's capacity to deter or defeat an assault, and the other side's confidence in the group's homogeneity in compliance with its own intents or decisions. In theory, a smaller group is likelier to act homogenously, in compliance with its plan or leader, without defections. This is useful to the negotiator who discovers some available leader or intent that is preferable to the other alternatives (Post, 2005; Arena and Arrigo, 2006, pp. 14–43).

A smaller group's homogeneity would be disadvantageous to a negotiator who wants to persuade the group of an alternative that has no sponsor or supporter within the group itself: "Small numbers of terrorists typically operate an atmosphere of groupthink that limits initiative and concessions, whereas large groups involve more complicated relations, including structuring devices such as hierarchy, rivalry, and camaraderie" (Zartman, 1990, p. 168).

Who Is the Ultimate Decision Maker?

One step toward understanding the group is to clarify the ultimate decision maker (Hudson, 1989, p. 335). As long as the group is compliant with an ultimate decision maker, the negotiator's intelligence task is simplified, since the negotiator needs to understand only the ultimate decision maker's psychology rather than every other group member's psychology, and needs to negotiate with only the ultimate decision maker.

For groups with multiple potential leaders, or competing leaders, or a leader with whom the other members are unreliably compliant, the negotiator shares an interest in asserting the leader with whom the negotiator prefers to negotiate.

What Media of Communications Are Available?

Traditionally the first prescription in a hostage crisis is to establish communications with the other side as soon as possible, at least to assess the other side's willingness to communicate (Hudson, 1989, p. 335; McMains and Mullins, 2015, p. 76).

This prescription became normative before the new wave of terrorism, when almost all communications were verbal—in person or via telephones that the official side controlled to all practical purposes. Yet today the negotiator must consider the many new media by which new terrorists communicate, few of which are within official control, unless the official side takes unusual measures (such as jamming all wireless signals) that usually have constitutional, social, and commercial implications.

New terrorists use these same technologies to enable remote control—sometimes from other countries—of the local hostage-takers. New terrorists have succeeded in using satellite phones, cellular phones, and e-mail to communicate with remote controllers. For instance, the killers and hostage-takers in Mumbai, India, in 2008, were controlled in real time via satellite telephones from Pakistan.

Sometimes, hostage-takers have ignored the official side, preferring to communicate directly with journalists or friendly intermediaries.

In the next two sections, we consider two broad categories of new media, which the negotiator must expect terrorists to use, sometimes directly to the public without the negotiator: digital media or "new media"; and telephone voice communications.

Digital Media

By digital media we mean e-mails, text messages between cellular telephones, messages posted online, and social media accessed through digital information and communication technologies.

Controlling the hostage-takers' channels and public media is more difficult in the era of new terrorism given the proliferation of information communication technologies, such as mobile telephones and wireless connectivity to the Internet. The negotiator should expect hostage-takers to carry information communication technologies, such as satellite phones, cellular phones, and computers or other electronic devices capable of e-mail or Internet access. For instance, during the occupation of a supermarket in Paris on January 9, 2015, in sympathy with the attackers on the Charlie Hebdo magazine offices, the hostage-taker talked directly with a television journalist via a cellular telephone.

Materially, new terrorists have access to communications that give them access to practically all information in the public domain. Terrorists have made more use of social media to receive public information and to manipulate public information. For instance, over 4 days from September 21, 2013, four armed men from al-Shabab killed 67 people and wounded 175 in the Westgate shopping mall in Nairobi, Kenya, while al-Shabab's press office sent hundreds of tweets from Somalia, with the primary intent of controlling the narrative and the audience—particularly in the immediate region (Mair, 2016).

Additionally, the victims, the victims' families, journalists, and anybody else with an interest can use these same technologies to attempt direct communications, surveillance, or reporting.

Anecdotal evidence and evidence from simulations suggest that new terrorists are more likely to communicate with outsiders by digital texts rather than voice. In simulation (2015), both sides preferred e-mail in the moment, and failed to graduate from e-mail to voice channels, even though they retrospectively wished they had progressed to voice, as illustrated by these participants. The terrorist side pushed for a telephone conversation most strongly, but the official side resisted, as it needed more time to deliberate and to respond—it feared that voice communications would lead to rash promises.

> [a student on the official side] The form of communication could have been improved by using a cellphone rather than an email account because some of the important emails were missed while we were trying to respond. We learned this too late in the simulation when hostages were already being killed and the tactical team was preparing to go in.
>
> **(Danielle Murray)**

> [another student on the official side] The use of emails was, according to me, a huge problem at communicating with the terrorists. It dehumanized the contact and made negotiations very difficult.
>
> **(Emilie Hannezo)**

> [a student on the terrorist side] The use of email as the mode of communication proved very ineffective, not only because it took too long to communicate demands and receive replies, but also because it made it extremely difficult to realize if the government negotiators were following through in good faith. Without this reassurance and ability to establish rapport with negotiators, it was difficult for us to gauge any real progress in the prisoner transfer, thus requiring us to stick with our firm deadlines to execute hostages.
>
> **(Andrew Grant)**

One explanation for the preference for e-mails over voice communications is generational, and another is self-interested deliberation. In the debriefing after the first simulation (2015), one student on the official side said that the millennial generation is more comfortable with text and e-mail messages than voice. Another suggested that they preferred iterated deliberation before responding to e-mails, whereas a voice communication implies immediate response each time that the other side stops talking.

One lesson is that official negotiators should be aware of a natural preference for deliberative communications by text over less controlled voice communications. Additionally, negotiators should learn to switch from text to voice communications when opportunities arise to speed up positive negotiations or to build rapport. This awareness and consideration can be trained.

However, another lesson is that the negotiator should train for communications via texts in case no opportunities for voice communications arise. Given the younger generations' preferences for text over voice communications, and increasing availability of text communications, negotiators should expect fewer opportunities for voice communications with the other side.

Finally, we note the millennial generation's exaggerated faith in social media for their internal communications. In each simulation, each side turned to social media to help the coordination of the members of a side. This worked well for coordinating meetings during the 2 weeks of preparations before the simulated terrorist attack in 2016, but not during the simulated attack itself:

> Hostage negotiation is extremely nerve-wracking and stressful. Even though we logically knew that the [municipal train] was not in actual danger, the act of negotiating, stalling for time, and trying to influence was extremely difficult to say the least. I think our biggest problem was a communication breakdown. Before the simulation began, our teammate Taylor suggested that communication would be key during the simulation to make sure everyone is on the same page. We all agreed to use an app called GroupMe, a group messaging app that allows us to quickly text one another with updated information to make sure we were all on the same page. Initially, I was going to be in charge of making sure that we were kept on track, but on the day of the simulation, it was hectic due to the attack on the [municipal train] and then my role turned into a secondary negotiator and an analyst in regards to analyzing the hostage list. Therefore, our internal communications broke down due to changing jobs during the simulation and the disorganization from the unexpected attack on the [municipal train] station.
>
> Another issue arising from the lack of communication using GroupMe was the fact that we did not receive the media messages from the terrorists when they send pictures of beating the hostages. This caused the HTs [hostage-takers] to believe that we were stalling for more time even though we genuinely did not know that they sent the media pictures.
>
> Finally, without GroupMe, people kept coming into the van, creating extra noise that made it hard for the negotiators to hear the demands and statements from the terrorists. This led to more inefficiency and probably led the terrorists to distrust us even more due to the repeat requests for clarification or for repeating a sentence. The FBI negotiator suggested that in the future, we as the negotiators should leave the van if we need more information rather than have people come into the van.
>
> **(Nicole Le)**

The obvious lesson from this humbling experience for this simulated official side is that officials should practice their immediate, proximate verbal communications and organization of physical space between themselves, while practicing their handling of information coming in from the other side via multiple types of media.

Telephone Voice Communications

Traditionally, negotiations have been conducted by voice, sometimes in person, normally (at least in recent 50 years or so) by telephone landlines. Indeed, official negotiators normally list a portable telephone landline among their required equipment, so that a telephone can be dispatched to the other side if the other side does not already have a telephone available.

Today, negotiators should expect all sides to be carrying cellular telephones—this is as true in the developing world as the developed world, if not more so, due to the relatively greater access to cellular communications over landlines. In some hostage-takings (such as Mumbai in 2008), the remote controllers provided the hostage-takers with satellite telephones to allow for voice communications. Where the attacker has no remote controller, the attacker is more likely to communicate with official authorities, as by Omar Mateen, while shooting to death dozens of people in a nightclub in Orlando in June 2016.

Suicidal or careless hostage-takers probably are less likely to care if these calls are observed by officials. Given public revelations over the last decade of official capacity to intercept electronic communications, future hostage-takers may eschew the carrying of telephones where they fear that the official side can access these same devices. During the crisis in Mumbai in 2008, Indian and British officials were able to intercept the voice communications by satellite telephones and to spy on the remote controllers in Pakistan via their computers. Public disclosure of these official capabilities must discourage future hostage-takers from exposing themselves similarly through their information communication technologies, unless they are suicidal.

Additionally, even if hostage-takers are carrying cellular telephones, they may prefer to use these phones for communication by texts rather than voice. As noted in the previous section, both sides may want to speak to each other but fail to achieve voice communications because of the greater allure or familiarity with other media.

Manage Publicity

Historical Practices

Official training in public affairs or public diplomacy during terrorism prescribes a balance between keeping the public informed (at least for the sake of an ideal free society), protecting privacy (even criminal identities might be protected by law until after a criminal conviction), and preventing public reporting that might help the criminals or harm a criminal prosecution (Combs, 1997; Nacos, 2009).

Moreover, public statements could undermine the negotiations. For instance, during the siege of the Davidians in April 1993, many agents from the FBI and the Bureau of Alcohol, Tobacco, and Firearms made offhand statements doubting Koresh's sincerity in his religion and his relationship with God. These statements delegitimized the rapport that the negotiation team was trying to build with Koresh in an effort to release more hostages:

> As governments and corporations have learned through the years, it's far better to have a designated press spokesperson stand before the media rather than the boss. When faced with a tough question, the spokesperson can reply that he or she doesn't have the information sought but will follow up later. This provides much-needed time to formulate and deliver the best answer to the question.
>
> **(Noesner, 2011, p. 112)**

Another of the involved agents recommends coordination between the different functional parts of the official side:

> It is a good idea to have the negotiation and tactical team leader review any press releases before they are distributed, or any announcements before they are made. If the subject has access to radio or television, nothing should be said that would disrupt the negotiation or tactical effort.
>
> **(Lanceley, 2003, p. 112)**

A further consideration in terrorist hostage-taking is whether to grant publicity to the terrorists in return for some advantage to the negotiations (Zartman, 1990, p. 175), which we review in Chapter 6 (on developing a relationship with the other side).

The public affairs officer and the negotiator should be prepared for the management of unofficial news reporters or journalists, and the hostage-takers' direct communications with such reporters.

In all cases, reporters cannot be ignored, otherwise they are more likely to speculate or to report on activities that the official side would rather keep secret, as remembered by an FBI negotiator:

> During an incident, reporters should be briefed as to what has transpired. No reporter is going to go back to his boss and say, "Yeah, boss, there is a hostage situation downtown, but the cops wouldn't talk to me, so I have no story."
>
> If law enforcement representatives do not talk to them, the media will air interviews with witnesses, families of the subject and victims, politicians, government officials, and released hostages. Reporters, broadcast and print, will go back to the office with a story, and they may as well have law enforcement's version of the incident.
>
> **(Lanceley, 2003, p. 110)**

Sometimes, hostage-takers have ignored the official side, preferring to communicate directly with journalists. This was true before the new wave of terrorism. For instance, in March 1977, the Hanafi Movement—a group of American Muslims who had split from the Nation of Islam in 1958—took

149 hostages and killed a journalist and a police officer across three buildings in Washington, DC. The crisis was resolved after 39 hours, without further violence, after negotiations through multiple channels—including clerics and public media. The U.S. law enforcement community drew the lessons that the hostage-takers' communications should be contained to channels that serve official interests, and that officials should have good relations with journalists (McMains and Mullins, 2015, p. 20):

> The media needs to be taken into consideration and an area established where they have access to information. They need frequent updates on what is happening, to the extent that the information does not compromise the tactics of the incident.
>
> **(McMains and Mullins, 2015, p. 73)**

Simulated Practices

Our lessons on this important part of the skill set are derived mostly from simulations. Before both simulations, the students had spent 1 week of readings and classes on public affairs/diplomacy, including a lecture from a public affairs officer in the local division of the FBI, who also participated as an official adviser in both simulations.

Our lessons are derived from particularly the second simulation (2016), which started in real time 2 weeks before the hostage crisis itself, rather than the first simulation (2015), which started with the hostage crisis. In the second simulation (2016), the official side mishandled the news media before the attack, having put out calls for help from the managers of hotels and oil refineries—targets based on misinformation from the other side:

> Information must be withheld on occasion in order to preserve the safety of not only the public, but also operations, agents, sources, and the perpetrators under investigation. During the week prior to the simulation [hostage-taking], we received a request for official comment on unfolding events by an investigative reporter named Emily. She discovered that our team had been requesting blueprints at high-end hotels in the area and were asking for suspicious behavior reports. At the time, we had been attempting to collect intelligence on unconfirmed threats, so we did not want to disclose any formal statement to the public at that time. So, we responded to the eager "Emily Reporter" that we were disappointed that she would tarnish our professional relationship, and she was reassigned. In retrospect, it is clear that the FBI asking hotels for blueprints would indefinitely leak to the media and the FBI would surely have to answer for it.
>
> **(Taylor Kennemore)**

The second of the fictional public affairs officers on the official side concluded that his side should have been more "secretive" before the hostage crisis:

> I realized the media plays an essential role, especially now that terrorists know how to use media as well. If we do not give the media what they want, then they can publish allegations or the terrorist's messages, which both will harm preventive measures and negotiations. I think we should have been more secretive before the attack. Therefore, the media would not be probing for questions beforehand and get frustrated with our typical response: "The investigation is ongoing." The way we treated the media prior to the simulation prompted unfavorable behaviors from the media.
>
> **(Jason Tran)**

The third of the actors playing a public affairs officer on that same side concluded that she should have been more forthcoming once the hostage crisis started:

> During the simulation, I continued my role as Public Affairs alongside Taylor and Jason. We began the simulation by releasing a press release assuring the public that the FBI would be doing everything in its power to secure the safety of everyone involved and that we would continue to update the public as soon as we could. After that, the simulation consisted of emails and interviews and press release. After the initial attack, I was called to do an interview with WNN. During the interview the reporters continually pressed to get more information and it was difficult to continue giving vague answers to their questions. I had some difficulty making judgment calls about what would be appropriate to tell the public and what was necessary for them to know. After we received the intelligence that Abu Hussein was one of the attackers taking hostages, I had a tough time deciding whether or not it would be helpful to release Abu Hussein's mugshot from when he was originally imprisoned. After consulting with Alice, I realized that the FBI has a responsibility to the public to continue to update them with as much knowledge as possible and that any little bit is worth it. Another difficulty I found working as public affairs was trying to make sure that the narrative the FBI was putting out was the narrative from which the public was receiving their information. The press was speaking with people in Syria and publishing the information without consulting the FBI. I believe that I failed in not keeping close enough contact with the press because the press released that the attackers were involved in a terrorist organization before the FBI had confirmed it. I felt as though I shuffled the interviews, press releases, and emails efficiently and I thoroughly enjoyed the simulation.
>
> **(Cierra Reimche)**

The first of these role-players also concluded that she could have been more proactive:

> In regards to my media role during the simulation [hostage-taking], I think we did a good job at responding swiftly to requests and not disclosing any information that would be detrimental to the operation, until the very end when I accidentally cc'd the terrorist group on an email demanding that the news network share their contact info for the terrorists. Overall, communication

> between team members was strong. I did feel, however, that we could have done a better job anticipating the requests of the media. I suspect that sending media contacts a vague statement before they even ask for one would be beneficial because it is almost certain that they will ask anyway, and it would give the FBI the leverage to ask the news to hold back on one part of the story because FBI had initiated contact and kindly provided information without being prompted.
>
> **(Taylor Kennemore)**

Meanwhile, the terrorist side realized the value of the news media before the attack:

> We prepared during our last meeting three press releases that expressed our demands and explained our grievances. Our goal was to raise awareness, to show that we were not "mad", but acting rationally in retaliation for violence committed by the United States. We addressed these press releases directly to the media and their publishing was a way to reach the public and rally them to our cause.
>
> **(Estelle Zielinski)**

However, the terrorist side was unprepared to deal with the other side or the news media:

> Furthermore, another outlet we could have used to our advantage was the media. I feel as if we were so focused on simply sending out press releases and talking to the negotiators that we put those in charge of media on the back-burner. Although it is reasonable that we did not trust Mel [the other side's fictional agent from the CIA] or the journalists to some degree, it would have been to our advantage to have our demands reiterated through the media. We want those watching the news to know why we were doing this. We did not want to be just the crazy people.
>
> **(Alexandra Zech)**

One of the principles for the official side is to craft a clear and consistent message, and utilize the event as a platform to project that message to as many people as possible (Nacos, 2009, p. 209). The terrorist side in the simulation (2016) attempted to make use of the same principle:

> Yet it was significantly more difficult than expected to ensure that we communicated such a clear and consistent message. Media misrepresentation of our demands, breakdown of channels of communication, and internal discord all lead to our message being convoluted and misunderstood.
>
> **(Collin Ting)**

The terrorist side invested more in the news media as their vehicles for signals, after losing trust in the official side's willingness to concede anything:

> After seizing the train and issuing our first press release, our men [simulated hostage-takers] were merely standing there with our hostages, leaving law enforcement no pressure to act quickly and accede to our demands. This proved to be a major strategic error and left us scrambling to impose some form of deadline for the hostage rescuers. We ultimately decided to resolve this by issuing a [dishonest] statement to the media that every 15 minutes of simulated time, we would kill a hostage...[In the second hour] Our team felt as though the [official side's] "negotiation" was merely meant to buy time for law enforcement to respond...Realizing this, we concluded that our only remaining tool was to utilize the media as a medium to manipulate public opinion. Thus we released numerous press statements and videos of hostages being beaten, in an effort to get the sympathy of the public.
>
> **(Collin Ting)**

Our Practical Prescriptions

Learning from the historical practices and simulated practices above, we summarize seven practical prescriptions:

1. Try to balance the public's rights and needs to be informed, the victims' and even perpetrators' rights to privacy, and the need to withhold information that might help the criminals or harm a criminal prosecution.
2. Do not release information into the public domain that would be useful to the terrorist side, unless its public utility is greater.
3. Do not ignore the news media—even if you are not at liberty to release information, acknowledge the news media.
4. Develop relationships with the news media before crises, on the promise of cooperation during crises.
5. Prepare to be more forthcoming once the crisis starts.
6. Create a clear and consistent message, and utilize the event as a platform to project that message to as many people as possible.
7. Do not release public statements that could undermine the negotiations.

Manage Time and Contingencies

Historical Practices

Planning for multiple contingencies (potential future scenarios) is a well-known principle in competitive endeavors generally, and in risk management particularly (Chapman and Ward, 2003, p. 54; Newsome, 2014, pp. 36–37), but it is not specified in any of the processes for managing critical incidents that we reviewed above.

The principle is simple: actors will be better prepared for, and quicker to react to, future situations that they have considered in advance, otherwise the official side wastes time working out how to respond and is generally left reactive rather than proactive.

Simulated Practices

The value of this principle is illustrated by the following quotes from participants on the official side of the simulation (2015):

- "Without a shared situational awareness among us we also failed to have any tangible contingency plan. Thus, we had no clear idea of what our bounds of their conduct were, and what would happen if they crossed these bounds" (Esben Mortensen).
- "Additionally, in the midst of the stress and the urgency, we forgot all the good ideas we had devised at first and started mostly reacting to the terrorists instead of making meaningful initiatives...a crucial element that we lacked was a contingency plan, that is, a set of predefined responses to a certain trigger. Not having this made us hesitant and we ended up waiting for the terrorists to kill many hostages before attacking the building" (Ingrid Munch).
- "When the realization of how quickly time was passing set in, we reacted hurriedly and panicky, hindering our organization and communication" (Reilly Ryan).

Our Practical Prescriptions

The official side must plan for various contingencies, including the different demands or responses that could come from the hostage-takers as reactions to official activities.

The official side must plan for contingencies that the other side controls or creates, such as a new demand, as well as for contingencies that the official side controls, such as a concession, or a choice to assault.

We seek to emphasize how more challenging, and more diverse, are the contingencies when dealing with new terrorists. New terrorist objectives are more diverse and fluid. Consequently, negotiators must plan for new terrorist hostage-takers who start out with no intent to negotiate, but may suddenly demand, for instance, money, as described in Chapter 9.

Within our recommended nine-step process of managing crises, we explained the first four in this chapter. In Chapter 6, we explain our recommended fifth step: develop a relationship with the other side.

6

Develop a Relationship

Negotiations of any type, from commercial business to hostage crisis, are easier to achieve if both sides have a prior relationship, or can develop one, particularly if the relationship develops some rapport or trust. Therefore, the negotiator should focus on developing this relationship, at least initially, rather than achieving some concession from the other side, which should become easier to achieve later, given development of the relationship.

In the following six sections, we review ways that we prescribe toward building such a relationship:

1. Actively listen and empathize
2. Acknowledge skepticism
3. Appeal to morality, ethics, or religious laws
4. Involve trustworthy third-party intermediaries
5. Make minor bargains or concessions
    a. Grant subsistence
    b. Grant publicity
6. Provoke thoughtfulness on the other side

Active Listening and Empathy

Historical Practices

In the Federal Bureau of Investigation's (FBI) training of negotiators, the FBI emphasizes interpersonal skills, such as empathy (relating to the other person, particularly emotionally) and "active listening" (acknowledging and sometimes repeating back what the other side said), as ways to build rapport and trust with the other side.

The FBI's "behavioral change stairway model" imagines climbing up a stairway that begins with empathy and leads to behavioral change.[1] Gary Noesner authored this model when chief of the Crisis Negotiation Unit at the FBI:

> Among negotiators, the process of trust-building is called the "behavioral stairway." You listen to show interest, then respond empathetically, which leads to rapport building, which then leads to influence…Being sincere and genuine are powerful tools to gain influence.
>
> **(Noesner, 2011, p. 12)**

However, Noesner admits that

> A large part of a negotiator's job is to establish trust, yet there are fundamental contradictions in that. In order to convince someone that despite all appearances to the contrary, everything will be okay, you have to project sincerity. You have to make him believe that what you are saying is honest and above-board. You have to address his primal need of safety and security by establishing a bond. And on rare occasions, you have to lie.
>
> **(2011, p. 3)**

In the 1970s and 1980s, American negotiators were taught to allow the subject to "ventilate" their anxieties and to stall for time in order to give more opportunity for de-escalation, while the negotiators should try to calm the subject and to establish some rapport (Lanceley, 2003, p. 19). Gary Noesner remembers being taught "that the key to successful negotiation was to discern the subject's motivation, goals, and emotional needs and to make use of the knowledge strategically. Once we understood the hostage taker's real purpose, we had a better chance of convincing him that killing the hostages would not serve that purpose and would only make an already bad situation worse" (Noesner, 2011, p. 34).

This process may start monadically, if the subject refuses to respond. This is known—in the American negotiations community, at least—as "'one-way dialogue,' where the goal is to address concerns that may not have been articulated, and answer questions that haven't been asked" (Noesner, 2011, p. 14).

> [W]hen I refer to one-way dialogue it is in the context of trying to open communications with a non-communicative individual. Instead of droning on endlessly asking them to pick up the phone and talk for example, the negotiator should start addressing their fears and concerns, and potential reluctance to

[1] Gary Noesner developed the model with a final step (top step) termed "behavioral change." Later, he modified the final step with the term "cooperation," given that law enforcers (unlike psychotherapists) properly aim for cooperation rather than long-term behavioral change. However, the FBI continues to use the original model, as developed by Noesner, with the final step termed "behavioral change." Sometimes, the model is reported with a final step termed "influence" (Vecchi et al., 2005; Noesner, 2016).

> talk, by stating that they are there to help and no one wants to hurt them, etc. We say that just because the individual is not responding (talking) does not mean they are not listening. A negotiator might say something like: "I know you must be concerned about all the police cars and cops you see outside. Let me assure you that we are only here because a neighbor heard some gunshots and we are concerned about your safety." Even though the individual has not articulated his fears, certain assumptions can be made about why he may not want to talk and what he may be concerned about, so go ahead and address them.
>
> **(Noesner, 2016)**

Noesner's successor (Mark Thundercloud) notes that nonresponsive subjects are probably expressive hostage-takers, not demonstrative hostage-takers:

> Generally, these are expressive situations where the subjects simply want the police to go away (and think they will if nothing is said) or are completely confused about their situations.
>
> Obviously, if the subject can't hear authorities for some reason is another issue, but an example is the Ruby Ridge, Idaho, incident when we knew the Weaver family was inside their cabin but refused to acknowledge our communications. As Noesner suggests, it was necessary to try different one-way dialogue angles to start the talks. It took almost a week before Randy Weaver finally said something to us that began two-way dialogue.
>
> **(Thundercloud, 2016)**

In the 1990s, Randall Rogan (a professor of communication) and Frederick Lanceley (a FBI negotiator) identified four key "triggers" for escalation or de-escalation in critical incidents, which they initially abbreviated with the acronym FIRE, corresponding with the capital letters in the following four triggers:

1. The subject's *F*ace (the subject's sensitive self-image)
2. The subject's *I*nstrumental demands
3. The subject's *R*elationship with the negotiator (usually based on trust and power)
4. The subject's level of *E*motional upset (Rogan and Lanceley, 2010, p. 35)

Having received criticism of the apparent aggressive acronym (FIRE), they changed to a prescriptive process for the negotiator, which they abbreviated with the acronym "SAFE":

1. Manage the hostage-taker's *S*ubstantive demands
2. Develop *A*ttunement or *A*ffiliation (relational closeness) with the subject
3. Allow the hostage-taker to save *F*ace
4. Manage the hostage-taker's *E*motions (Lanceley, 2003, pp. 35–37)

As active listening and empathizing, Lanceley emphasized the following:

1. *Emotion labeling*: Communicating observations of the subject's emotions, such as by saying simply, "You seem angry."
2. *Paraphrasing*: Asking clarifying questions founded on paraphrases of what the subject communicated, such as by asking, "Are you saying that you are angry?"
3. *Reflecting or mirroring*: Repeating the subject's most recent word or clause as a question, such as by asking, "It made you angry?"
4. *Open-ended questions*: Asking directed questions that must be answered substantively, not with a "yes" or "no" alone, such as by asking, "Who made you angry?"
5. *Minimal encouragers*: Releasing sounds or words that indicate the listener is still present, while the subject is still communicating, such as by saying, "okay."
6. *Silence*: Maintaining silence immediately before and after communicating an important point, such as when the official side needs to make clear that a demand cannot be met.
7. *"I" message*: Explaining one's own emotion as an effect due to the subject's behavior, such as by saying, "I feel worried when you don't pick up the telephone when I call" (Lanceley, 2003, pp. 203–204).

Rogan and Lanceley later conceptualized two levels of negotiation: first, effectively active listening and empathy; and second, influence:

> In reflecting on what we know about negotiation, it can be useful to divide our understanding into two levels. One level of understanding is focused on the interpersonal factors that fuel crisis negotiation and how changes in these factors allow an interaction to begin, unfold, and resolve. The need to develop affiliation, reduce crisis intensity, and respond to the perpetrator's "face" issues are among the factors that have been shown to play a role in the progress of negotiation and its success...The second level of understanding centers on the cues and responses that underlie and give rise to the patterns found at the strategic level. The focus here is toward the interconnections among messages, the responses typically elicited by certain cues, and the way in which these cue-response sequences build to move a negotiation down a particular path.
>
> **(Rogan and Lanceley, 2010, p. 60)**

Michael McMains (formerly chief psychologist for police department of San Antonio, Texas) and Wayman Mullins emphasize the SAFE approach:

> They suggest that in any police negotiation, it is important to track and deal with the Substantive demands made by the subject, the Affiliation needs (liking and trust) involved in the relationship, need for the subject to save Face during the incident, and the need to attend to and manage the Emotions of the subject.

> By carefully tracking the statements made by the subject, negotiators can define which issues are leading to conflict and the dimensions that demand immediate attention—a strategizing tool that lets negotiators systematically review critical issues so that interventions can be designed to deal with the most pressing issue as defined by the subject.
>
> **(McMains and Mullins, 2015, pp. 45–46)**

Analysts of new terrorist hostage-taking have emphasized that, even with "new terrorists," "the same principles of negotiation such as active listening, focusing on understanding interests and alternatives, generating options, and the use of criteria are all still relevant" (Dolnik and Fitzgerald, 2011, p. 273). Dolnik and Fitzgerald add the following advice:

- "If negotiators want to maximize their ability to influence any particular individual, they must make an effort to understand what will be most persuasive *to him/her.*" Avoid "projection of one's own fears and biases, as opposed to an actual understanding of their motivations and strategic mindsets" (Dolnik and Fitzgerald, 2011, p. 271).
- Do not confuse "empathy and sympathy": "understanding" them is not the same as "agreeing" with them (Dolnik and Fitzgerald, 2011, p. 272).
- Do not ignore "the validity of some of their grievances and the conditions and personal perceptions that drove them to their extreme behavior" (Dolnik and Fitzgerald, 2011, p. 272).
- "This in turn gives the negotiator a chance to engage the other side on a more personal level, by asking about his or her *personal* experience with the alleged injustices and abuse. This then provides an opportunity for the negotiator to express empathy" (Dolnik and Fitzgerald, 2011, p. 288).

However, rapport and trust would remain impossible to achieve with resolutely hateful or distrustful opponents, whatever the negotiator's skills, in which case the official side should focus on other objectives, such as gaining intelligence. This is captured in the following procedural advice from Roy Ramm, formerly of the Metropolitan Police:

> One of the fundamental principles of negotiation is that the negotiators act with commitment and sincerity of purpose and try to build trust with the hostage takers but, a negotiated non-violent resolution is never the only contribution a negotiator can make or a measure of the success of negotiations.
>
> The effectiveness of negotiations in securing the release of the hostages and of a de-facto surrender must be continually assessed by the incident commander, who must have access to all available sources of intelligence and therefore be able to determine whether the lives of hostages are best protected by continued release and surrender negotiations or whether the negotiators are directed to a communications strategy intended to assist a tactical intervention.

> Negotiators should never assume that all hostage takers intended to take hostages and therefore have a planned outcome. Even in terrorist incidents, it should never be assumed that the hostage taking was the terrorists' primary objective. It may be that action by law enforcement or simple accident of circumstance means that terrorists find themselves unintentionally holding hostages, perhaps even hostages of the same faith or religious persuasion as themselves. Whether a hostage taking was planned or "accidental" can have a fundamental impact on the negotiation tactics and the outcome of the incident.
>
> **(Ramm, 2016)**

Simulated Practices

In one of our simulations (2016), the terrorist representatives were so distrustful that they would not give personal names or acknowledge the end of a conversation, partially because the official side's clumsy communications suggested attempted manipulation, made worse by the official side's infiltration of armed responders into the hijacked train:

> As we saw from the simulation, once a variable of similar form, the infiltration of the SWAT team at the back of the train, scares the hostage-takers, any trust that once existed is destroyed and any attempt of regaining that trust is that much harder. Once the video of the SWAT team infiltrating the back of the train was leaked and the hostage-takers and their leaders were made aware, it was at this point that all negotiations became irrelevant. After the simulation had ended, I asked the actors playing as the leaders of the hostage-takers what they were thinking when they realized that the SWAT team had infiltrated the train and they replied that they had lost all interest in negotiations since they believed that the FBI team was not trying to meet any of their demands and actually focusing on how they were going to kill the hostage-takers. So, to the leaders, their main goal switched from getting the U.S. government to meet their demands to how many people could they get away with killing and how great of a spectacle could they make it.
>
> **(Jonathan Chow)**

One student on the terrorist side responded: "Dolnik [and Fitzgerald] recommend that the negotiators express empathy, ask questions and listen actively, but even if the other side did a very good job following his advice (especially on the phone), we knew that they tried to trick us" (Estelle Zielinski).

Moreover, in the same simulation, the terrorists turned the official strategy against itself:

> From the readings (Dolnik and Fitzgerald, p. 288), we knew that the other group would attempt to call us to speak more about our unrealistic demands. they used active listening to not only learn more about our emotional and psychological needs behind our demands, but also to buy more time and waste our time. However, we decided to use this technique against them. We would often have one member talking to their group simply to waste their time while we attempted to achieve our demands in other ways. This method proved effective

in keeping the opposing team from developing ideas to successfully save the hostages, but did not help us accomplish our demands.

(Thomas Sweeney)

We determined early on that it would be impossible to get any of our demands. Also, we knew through the FBI officials on our side that the other side would just negotiate as a time-wasting strategy, until they could devise with a tactical plan to rescue the hostages. With these in mind, our team went into the negotiation not expecting that anything would come from it. Therefore, the negotiation was easy because our "negotiation" was merely a time-wasting strategy to keep the other side more preoccupied, so all I had to do was keep the other negotiator talking.

(Katrina Oshima)

Our Practical Prescriptions

We accept the value of the following established interpersonal skills for negotiators:

1. Empathize (relate to the other person, particularly emotionally)
2. Actively listen (acknowledge and sometimes repeat back what the other side said)
3. Allow for the other side to ventilate feelings and thoughts safely
4. Build rapport
5. Build trust
6. Influence positively

We add, in the following four sections, some additional or finer skills that are not routinely acknowledged:

1. Avoid being perceived as patronizing or manipulative
2. Prepare to move from emotional to rational conversations
3. Prepare for resolute or diabolical terrorists who refuse a relationship
4. Maintain optimism

Avoid Being Perceived as Patronizing or Manipulative

Our first additional prescription is as follows: while developing a relationship, be mindful of the potential for the other side to perceive you as patronizing or manipulative.

Active listening and empathizing are not as easy or as powerful as often depicted in popular culture. In practice, active listening and empathizing are rare, deep interpersonal skills beyond our capacity to describe or prescribe in this document: our observations of official negotiators suggest that their active-listening and empathic skills are derived from some temperamental capacity, refined training, considerable routine practice (some official negotiators volunteer on suicide prevention telephone hotlines to maintain their skills between official crises), and humbling experiences. Very few people naturally acquire these skills to the level that would make an impact on resolute new terrorists.,

We have heard repeatedly, across many official training courses and the simulations referenced in this document, complaints from one side or another that the other side was manipulating or patronizing, while the other side passionately denied this perception and claimed that it was actively listening and empathizing throughout. One quote from a terrorist role-player in the second simulation (2016) will illustrate a typical recipient's complaint:

> On the other hand, negotiating became challenging when I started to attempt to gain concessions. It was clear from the very beginning, even without the forewarning of our FBI officials, that the other side had no intention of truly negotiating. At first, they merely said that they wanted to understand our grievances and us. Although I now know that they were advised to do that by their FBI official as a means of creating goodwill and rapport, it made me feel like they were being condescending, and although I was only acting in the simulation, it made me wonder if that strategy was actually effective in a real crisis negotiation. However, our negotiation may have been different from most, because we were informed about FBI crisis negotiation strategies and also because we were remote negotiators.
>
> **(Katrina Oshima)**

We advise trainers to teach negotiators to recognize unrealistic popular cultural and fashionable academic depictions, and to separate official prescriptions for active listening and empathizing from pernicious, unrealistic, simplistic depictions in popular culture (movies, television dramas, and books) and fashionable academic fields (such as conflict resolution and peace studies), which tend to suggest that every crisis can be resolved by talking about it or putting oneself in the other side's shoes. This simplicity takes the trainer or trainee away from the complexity of real conflicts, and neglects the conditionality of negotiating: the negotiator needs to be trained to diagnose and to adjust when active listening or empathizing is not working.

These observations of one side's negative perceptions of the other side's earnest active listening and empathizing are uncomfortable. We admit that our direct observations in official training courses and our simulations are of trainees or unpracticed students, while we have only indirect observations of experienced professionals in the field, who presumably are better at laying the foundations for a relationship through active listening and empathizing, before leveraging that relationship to deliver bad news or discuss surrender. However, our finding remains strong: that these skills do not come naturally to most, and must be trained and practiced by most, before they become effective in crises.

Thus, while we admit that proper implementation of active listening and empathizing are useful in most negotiations, we observe that the skills are rare. We worry about demotivating the trainer and trainee of these skills if we admit that sometimes the implementation may do more harm than good, such as by persuading the other side that the negotiator is insincere. However, we must admit so, on the merit of truthfulness, and in the hope of prompting the improvement of active listening and empathizing that is less likely to come across as manipulative or patronizing. Our central advice in this section is to train mindfulness of the potential to come across as manipulative or patronizing to the other side.

Prepare to Move from Emotional to Rational Conversations

The FBI teaches active listening and empathizing as useful largely for de-escalating, to allow for venting of emotions on the subject's side, and for gathering of information. These techniques are used throughout the communications with the subject.

When the subject is ready to surrender (which is almost always their safest option and thence presumably most rational option), they have reached a more rational state, when a more rational, less emotional, or more factual conversation can take place. Thus, more emotional interpersonal skills (such as active listening) should be emphasized at the start of the communications, but the official negotiator should be prepared to recognize when the subject is ready for a more rational conversation, and to move toward a more rational conversation, including perhaps bad news, such as the impossibility of meeting certain demands, on the way to a conversation that develops the subject's preference for surrender.

Such a switch normally would not appeal to a subject in crisis, so the negotiator should not switch too early. But if the official negotiator does not adjust to the subject's switch to a more rational conversation, then the negotiator may appear manipulative or patronizing in continuing to focus on emotions.

To be helpful, we advise such training to emphasize observant readiness for a switch from the emotional early stage of the communications to a more rational communication, whenever the subject is ready.

Prepare for Resolute or Diabolical Terrorists Who Refuse a Relationship

We have found that some new terrorists are too resolute or diabolical for anything to be resolved by simply listening or empathizing.

Nevertheless, those interpersonal skills must remain in every negotiator's skill set, and the negotiator should try these skills on the other side before concluding that they would not work, in which case the negotiator either tries to adjust or gives up the negotiation in favor of some other focus, such as intelligence gathering in preparation for an assault (see Chapter 11).

Maintain Optimism

If the negotiator realistically acknowledges that negotiations might not work with resolute or diabolical terrorists, the negotiator is being pragmatic, but we do not want such pragmatism to encourage unwarranted pessimism about the prospects of negotiation, or to encourage early termination of the negotiations. So long as the negotiator is negotiating, he or she should remain confident in the prospects, if only to maximize the chances of success in the negotiations. This confidence is a form of self-efficacy—one of the conventional emotional intelligences, although excessive self-efficacy can lead to rashness or foolhardiness.

The dilemma between pragmatism and optimism is illustrated in the following lessons written by a participant on the official side in the second simulation (2016):

> In order to guarantee peaceful discourse—active listening, mirroring the speaker's tone of voice and speech patterns, and getting to know the hostage-takers on a personal level are essential. Statements like "we understand your position and will help you if you clarify a couple extra things for us" establish guidelines for the rest of the conversation and produce more time for SWAT members to get into position. Regarding the debate between a "no concessions" hardline and always capitulating to terrorist demands—considering that the mere act of taking hostages presumes that the hostage-takers prefer not to die—I believe that the best policy is no policy at all. Situations constantly evolve; force should only be used as a last resort. For example, if terrorist demands are more theatrical than practical, we could utilize the media to broadcast their demands to the world and in return ask them for the release of a number of hostages. Adopting a humanist approach with jihadists establishes a level of mutual trust that would otherwise not be there, creating avenues for a stand-down. Aspiring martyrs can be talked off the ledge and persuaded to release hostages first before being granted their final wish. Hope is essential; without it, both sides lose the battle before it even begins.
>
> **(Jonathan Fisher)**

Our integrated advice in this section is:

1. Maintain self-efficacy in the principles of active listening and empathy
2. Remain wary of appearing manipulative or patronizing
3. Be ready to move from more emotional to more rational conversations
4. Be ready to give up on resolute or diabolical terrorists in favor of intelligence gathering in preparation for assault

Acknowledge Skepticism and Distrust

We add the prescription to acknowledge and to counter terrorist skepticism—particularly new terrorist skepticism, and most particularly Jihadi skepticism—of the official negotiator's trustworthiness.

Historical Practices

Our prescription is not found in historical counterterrorist practices but is endemic in terrorist practices and prescriptions, particularly those popular with or developed by Jihadi terrorists.

Modern interpretations of Islamic texts and laws imply that the enemies of Jihad are inherently untrustworthy. The Quran[2] includes a bloody warning against making peace with an untrustworthy enemy: "If they withdrew not from you nor give you guarantees of peace besides restraining their hands, seize them and slay them wherever ye get them. In their case, we have provided you with a clear argument against them" (Quran, 47:91). One influential Pakistani soldier-scholar has interpreted this Quranic warning as a warning against not just untrustworthy enemies but also infidels who do not share the same "divine" constraints: "In the initial stages of its realization, the Holy Quran made generous concessions to the adversaries to terminate the state of war and invited them to contribute in creating conditions of harmony and peace. The law of equality and reciprocity was observed in dealing with treaties and alliances. But, as the enemy went on rejecting one divine concession after another, it became necessary to adopt a harder line" (Malik, 1979, p. 35).

Furthermore, the Quran prescribes vengeance on those who break an agreement, and this perception is in the eye of any clerical pretender who claims to interpret events on God's behalf:

- "Those who break Allah's covenant after it is ratified, and who sunder what Allah has ordered to be joined, and do mischief on earth: these cause losses only to themselves" (Quran, 2:27).
- "But if they cease, Allah is oft-forgiving, most merciful" (Quran, 2:192).
- "But if they cease, let there be not hostility except to those who practice oppression" (Quran, 2:193).
- "If thou fearest treachery from any group, throw back their covenant to them so as to be on equal terms: for Allah loveth not the treacherous" (Quran, 8:58).
- "But if the enemy incline towards peace, do thou also incline towards peace, and trust in Allah: for He is the One that heareth and knoweth all things. Should they intend to deceive thee, verily Allah sufficeth thee" (Quran, 8:61–62).
- "As long as they stand true to you, stand ye true to them: for Allah doth love the righteous" (Quran, 9:7).

[2] All references to the Quran in our study are taken from: Ali (1934). The Holy Qur'an: Text, Translation, and Commentary, Lahore, Pakistan, available at: http://www.sacred-texts.com/isl/quran/index.htm. We are aware of alternative spellings of the term "Quran," such as "Koran" or "Qur'an." While "Koran" has been most familiar to Western audiences, this spelling is viewed as culturally offensive to some since it fails to reflect the correct way it is meant to be pronounced. Consequently, Western news sources have changed the spelling to "Qur'an" or "Quran" to reflect the correct Arabic pronunciation of it in an attempt to be culturally sensitive. Thus, the authors use the spelling "Quran" in this book given that it is culturally appropriate and relatively familiar to Western audiences. Source: http://ajrarchive.org/Article.asp?id=4239

One of Al Qa'ida's manuals (2004) warns: "The enemy uses the best negotiator he has, who is normally very sly, and knowledgeable in human psychology. He is capable of planting fear in the abductors' hearts, in addition to discouraging them." A manual adapted by Al Qa'ida for advising "lone wolf mujahideen" started with great emphasis on "security and safety, between negligence and paranoia," and went on to warn against Western officials who specialize in studying the ways of Jihad (Al-Adm, 2010).

Similarly, the Islamic State of Iraq and the Levant (ISIL) prepared a manual to train its recruits on its interpretations of Islam and warns against any deviants from its interpretation, including:

1. The "original disbeliever": anyone who has never followed Islam
2. The Muslim "disbeliever": anyone who "has committed a deed of disbelief"

Additionally, the manual warns against anyone who interprets Islam outside of ISIL's interpretation or who challenges the "intermediaries" (prophets and clerics) that ISIL recognizes. The manual lists the many ways in which a wayward Muslim nullifies his or her faith (these ways are listed as *nawaqid*—the plural of *naqid*, meaning nullification). The first *naqid* is to worship anything besides God as ISIL recognizes God. Indeed, ISIL's second *naqid* specifically warns against anyone "who places himself and God's intermediaries, calling on them and asking them for mediation, and trusting in them. This is disbelief by consensus."

The ISIL manual further warns against "hypocrisy": "when the outward is contrary to the inward, or showing something outwardly but concealing its opposite." The manual lists many examples of hypocrisy, including of "greater hypocrisy," of which the common sense is any challenge to God, his "messengers," or his laws, as interpreted by the manual (Binali, 2015, Section ix).

Similarly, ISIL's manual on *How to Survive in the West* starts with extensive warnings against the anti-Islamic and anti-ISIL bias in the Western "media," and promises guidance on how to live "a double life"—as essentially a true Jihadi (*mujahid*) pretending to be secular Western. The dominant subject of this manual is deception, where to deceive the outsider is glorious, and the Westerner is easily fooled given his or her naïve normative expectations, but the Jihadi must be wary of official agents who are skilled in deception and discovery (Islamic State of Iraq and Levant, 2015, pp. 5–6).

Our Practical Prescriptions

From these observations, we induce that probabilistically, Jihadis will be so distrusting of their enemies that they will never trust an official negotiator.

This probabilistic (not deterministic) theory puts the official side in a dilemma. The negotiator should be aware from the start of the possibility that the other side is distrustful. To counter the Jihadi's perception of the infidels' natural distrustfulness, the negotiator should remind the other side of historical instances where the official side has honored a peace agreement or any agreement with any enemy, and particularly with an enemy similar in ethnicity or religion to the hostage-takers.

From the start of the negotiations, the negotiator should be assessing whether the other side's distrust can be overcome. If the negotiator estimates that trust can be improved, the negotiations should continue toward a peaceful resolution. If not, the negotiator should move on to objectives other than the release of hostages (see Chapter 11).

Appeal to Morality, Ethics, or Religious Laws

Historical Practices

The official side should be clear about the actions that it would consider legitimate or illegitimate, consistently follow through on the promised consequences for illegitimate actions without appearing hypocritical (fair judicial detention and prosecution of illegitimate actions would qualify as legitimate), and consistently offer incentives to switch from illegitimate to legitimate actions (such as relieving a ban on the actor's organization in return for non-violent political expression) (Kirkpatrick, 2017). The official negotiator should expect a more moralistic dialogue with the religious terrorist than the nonreligious terrorist. Theorists of religious terrorism tend to propose that "religion provides the moral justification for killing and the images of cosmic warfare that impart a heady illusion of power" (Juergensmeyer, 2001, p. 11), and that terrorism depends on "the moral, ideological, and organizational support necessary for such acts" (p. 11).

Some analysts have prescribed official appeals to morality: "Since most terrorist movements use the rhetoric of liberation from oppression and inhumane treatment, the same language could be used to reiterate the innocence and suffering of the hostages, in order to appeal to the moral beliefs of the captors" (Dolnik and Fitzgerald, 2011, p. 270). However, these same analysts admit that "the advanced level of enemy dehumanization associated with religious sanction of their actions will almost certainly make the moral appeals on the terrorists' conscience unsuccessful" (Dolnik and Fitzgerald, 2011, p. 271).

Our Practical Prescriptions

In this section, we pursue the possibility that appeals to morality, ethics, or religious laws can be used by official negotiators to influence terrorists. We proceed in three sections as follows:

1. Proscriptions against aggressions
2. Proscriptions against breaking agreements
3. Any sectarian proscriptions or prescriptions

Proscription against Aggression

The negotiator should appeal to general religious proscriptions against aggression, while being prepared for the other side to characterize their aggression as self-defense, for which almost all religions allow explicitly. Mark Juergensmeyer found that the "cultures of violence" typical of religious terrorism include "the perception that their communities are already under attack—are being violated—and that their acts are therefore simply responses to the violence they have experienced" (2001, p. 12).

The Christian Bible and the Quran both contain proscriptions against aggression, but the negotiator should not be naïve about the religious terrorist's tendency to see all violence as defensive and provoked, in which case the proscription does not apply.

The Jihadi's false self-image of defensiveness is helped by the Quran's prescription for indiscriminate subterfuge: "When the forbidden months are past, then fight and slay the Pagans wherever ye find them, and seize them, beleaguer them, and lie in wait for them in every stratagem" (Quran, 9:5). Juergensmeyer found that "Islam is ambiguous about violence. Like all religions, Islam occasionally allows for force while stressing that the main spiritual goal is one of non-violence and peace...Muslim activists have often reasserted their belief in Islamic nonviolence before defending their use of force" (2001, p. 79).

If the official side estimates some room for negotiation, the official side cannot assume that a terrorist who is willing to negotiate is also not willing to deceive, or to execute violence on hostages even after releasing some.

Prescription to Keep Agreements

We suggest that the negotiator should appeal to general religious obligations to honor pledges and agreements—at least with those who keep agreements.

The Quran proscribes against violence given a peace treaty. For this reason, Al Qa'ida's manual includes this advice for negotiating: "It is essential for the brothers to abide by our religion and keep their word, as it is not allowed for them to kill any hostage after our demands and conditions have been met." The same manual includes this advice on the final exchange: "Abide by Muslim laws as your actions may become a *Da'wa* [call to join Islam]" (Al Qa'ida, 2004).

Sectarian Prescriptions and Proscriptions

If the terrorist is Jihadi, then the official side should try to confirm the sect with which the terrorist identifies, as the sect may have particular forms of morality, ethics, or law to which the negotiator can appeal for official advantage.

Islam has many sects, and these sects differ in many and subtle ways that we cannot summarize in the main text of this book. Instead, this book's Appendix A summarizes these sects, where the negotiator should look for any advantageous sectarian moral, ethic, or law, if any.

Officials should borrow from any sectarian interpretation that is most helpful to them, but they should avoid citing sources that the hostage-takers would interpret as incompatible with their own sect or interpretation. For instance, if officials are aware that the opposition claims to have a Sunni bias, then officials should avoid citing Shi'a scholars during negotiations. Similarly, if the official side is aware that the hostage takers are Shi'a, then they should avoid citing Sunni sources. If the religion or sectarian bias of the opposing side is unknown, then officials should avoid citing the sources from which religious interpretations have been borrowed during hostage negotiations. Such selection of sources and the communication of selected interpretations to uncertain, suspicious extremists will not be easy, suggesting that some negotiators should not even try, or should not try until they are especially trained in the scholarship. A particularly careless extremist might reveal an egregious misinterpretation of his or her own faith that any negotiator could exploit.

Third-Party Intermediaries

One way to build a relationship with unwilling opposing sides is to use a third-party intermediary (TPI). This is a separate issue than the question of whether to use TPIs to escape the official side's prohibitions on negotiating with terrorists, which we considered in Chapter 4.

Historical Practices

For decades, police and law enforcers have used TPIs to communicate with hostage-takers. These TPIs might interrupt the negotiator's attempt to develop a relationship with the other side, but might offer any of several advantages, which we categorize in two ways:

1. Procedural
2. Conclusive

The procedural advantages are those that help the negotiator immediately in the process of negotiation, such as by gaining time for the negotiator's own side to do other things.

The conclusive advantages are those that help the negotiator to resolve the crisis in favor of the negotiator's own side. For instance, in negotiating for a subject's surrender, the subject may feel that surrender to police amounts to total capitulation, while surrender to a TPI—particularly one of the same religion or ethnicity or nationality—is more allowable.

Positive or Neutral TPIs

However, unofficial TPIs are riskier than official negotiators in the senses that they are less officially controlled or accountable, are less specialized, or have prior negative relationships with the hostage-taker.

Retired FBI negotiator Gary Noesner remembers that "We had to be cautious in using intermediaries because the people most often in a position to help can be difficult to control. They frequently have their own agendas—a grievance, perhaps, or a desire to influence. Also, bringing them to the scene might expose them to danger." In one case, the police allowed a volunteer to speak with a distraught man who had taken hostage his wife on the grounds that she was having an affair. The volunteer claimed to be a friend of the hostage-taker, but on hearing his voice the hostage-taker became enraged and discharged his weapon: in fact, the volunteer was involved in the affair (Noesner, 2011, p. 159).

The same dilemmas are illustrated by an armed self-barricade in Markham Square, Chelsea, London, on May 6, 2008:

> [He demanded:] "I want to speak to my wife." But it was decided that this would not be allowed. The police negotiators, who decide how best to manage contact with the subject, would have made this decision based on many factors. For one, the prospect of talking to family and friends can sometimes be used as an incentive for the subject to surrender. For another, if contact is allowed it can sometimes escalate a volatile situation and any good work done by the negotiators can be lost in an instant. There is also the risk in cases where suicide is a potential threat that any conversation with a loved one could be a prelude to that suicide.
>
> **(Smith, 2013, p. 226)**

This armed self-barricader was shot to death by a police sniper 5 hours later.

We can conclude that TPIs should be neutral or seen positively by both sides, or at least lack any prior negative relationship with the other side.

Trustworthy TPIs

In some theories, the official side is more likely to get what it wants from a new terrorist via a TPI. The new terrorist's self-perception as "true believer" or "holy warrior" encourages a preference for suicidal glory over concessions to the enemy but is more likely to concede to a TPI than the intended enemy (Zartman, 1990, p. 185).

New terrorists, being less political and more culturally extreme than old terrorists, are more separated from traditional governments, so both sides should rely more on TPIs: "in situations involving the 'new terrorists,' where police negotiators are unlikely to be viewed as trustworthy counterparties (due to their affiliation), it may very well be the case that TPIs are sometimes preferable" (Dolnik and Fitzgerald, 2011, p. 283).

Nevertheless, Dolnik and Fitzgerald foresee that the first and second parties can engage in the same distrust, deception, and dishonesty indirectly as directly. For instance, TPIs allow the official "negotiator to stall for time by pointing to the difficulty of locating a key decision maker, or some other objective obstacle to meeting the terrorists' deadline." Such deception might encourage the terrorists to demand direct communications with decision makers, who then should point "out the need to be able to survive politically in order to ensure their implementation" (Dolnik and Fitzgerald, 2011, p. 284).

Culturally Literate TPIs

Materially, TPIs must be accessible to both sides. TPIs become more useful with their increased accessibility, perhaps due to geographical proximity, or a prior relationship, or their current availability given other commitments.

For practical reasons, TPIs are more useful if they speak the same languages as both sides.

For ideational reasons, TPIs are more useful if they are culturally similar or literate in the other's culture. For instance, theoretically, knowledgeable Muslim negotiators would be in the best of positions to negotiate with terrorists who claim to represent Muslim interests, given that they are less vulnerable to accusations of otherness than are non-Muslims, and they should be acculturated in Islamic ethics. Empirically, Jihadis tend to warn against trusting non-Muslims (Taliban, 2009; Al Qa'ida, 2004). Dolnik and Fitzgerald observe that "the 'new terrorists' tend to demand particular figures to serve as negotiators," such as people "whose general views on their grievance they are familiar with, and for people that have the authority to make decisions" (Dolnik and Fitzgerald, 2011, p. 283).

Governmental TPIs

Ostensibly neutral, majority Muslim, governmental TPIs have proven useful in negotiating between secular Western governments and Muslim extremists in several well-documented cases. For instance, the Iranian hostage crisis (1979) was resolved through the use of Algerian intermediaries, which resulted in the release of the final 52 American hostages to be returned alive.

In recent years, Qatar keeps appearing in the news as Western governments' TPI of choice. The exchange of United States Army Sergeant Bowe Bergdahl for five senior Afghani Taliban militants was negotiated by Qatari government intermediaries.

On January 11, 2016, the Canadian government announced that the Afghani Taliban had released a Canadian citizen (Colin Rutherford) after more than 5 years in detention. The Qatari government had mediated, but otherwise both governments refused to discuss Qatar's role (Boutilier, 2016). In May 2016, Spanish officials in Turkey received three Spanish journalists, who had been kidnapped in Syria in July 2015, probably by al-Nusra (*Jabhat an-Nusrah li-ahli ash-Sham*—"Front for the Victory of the People of the Levant"; latterly *Jabhat Fateh al-Sham*—"Front for the Conquest of the Levant"). Qatar said that it had helped, although all governments refused to explain the deal (Paul et al., 2016).

Farther south, the use of TPIs has resulted in reassuring outcomes in some cases, but contradictory outcomes in other cases. For instance, on June 1, 2015, Houthi rebels in Yemen released an American journalist (Casey L. Coombs, 33 years old) after about 2 weeks' detention, into Omani custody—Oman had apparently brokered the release, although no government would confirm this at the time (Hensley, 2015). Similarly, on September 21, 2015, Houthi rebels in Yemen released two American hostages (Scott Darden, 45 years old; Sam Farran, 54 years old), one Briton, and three Saudis. Oman had acted as the TPI and arranged for an aircraft to fly the hostages into Oman. The Americans had been detained since March (Rosenberg and Fahim, 2015). Yet on October 20, an American contractor was detained upon flying into Houthi-controlled Sanaa, perhaps accused of being a spy; by November 6 he was officially dead, without official explanation (Hensley, 2015). Happily, in June 2016, Yemeni government forces and Houthi rebels successfully negotiated for the release of prisoners through the use of a local Muslim tribe (Al-Jazeera, 2016a). A separate American hostage (Wallead Yusuf Pitts Luqman) was released in November 2016, after detention since April 2015, which was only publicized in October 2016. He was flown to Oman, presumably because Oman brokered (Morello, 2016b).

Nongovernmental TPIs

From most governmental perspectives, nongovernmental TPIs are riskier still. For instance, ISIL contacted the nongovernmental organization Doctors Without Borders with an e-mail address for transfer to the parents of an American detainee (Kayla Mueller), who had volunteered for the organization before her kidnapping in Syria in August 2013. The organization shared a smuggled letter from the victim to her parents, but withheld the e-mail address until it had secured the release of its employees 6 weeks later—it later explained that it did so for fear for their safety. Her death was confirmed in February 2015; the role of Doctors Without Borders was not revealed until August 2016. Kayla's father (Carl Mueller) told journalists: "They're a fabulous organization. They do wonderful work. But somewhere in a boardroom they decided to leave our daughter there to be tortured and raped." He also criticized the belated reaction of the Obama administration (Sidahmed, 2016).

Simulated Practices

Results from simulation suggest that new terrorists will be less trusting and less trustworthy than old terrorists, and more demanding of TPIs, given the increasing real-world use of TPIs.

In both simulations, the two sides were given immediate access to two types of intermediary: a role-player playing a fictional diplomat from Jordan; and a role-player playing a fictional operative ("Mel") working for the U.S. Central Intelligence Agency (CIA), who (both sides were told) had developed a relationship with the current terrorist side during earlier years when the United States and the terrorist side had shared a common enemy.

In the first simulation (2015), both sides perceived the other as restricted by their loyalties and objectives from negotiating usefully, while they perceived TPIs as noisy nodes for signals, or unnecessary intermediaries to direct communications. Consequently, both sides failed to use TPIs early or effectively, as illustrated here in a reflection written by somebody playing on the official side:

> Mel was contacted by the Jordanian official who briefly served as an intermediary, but we became nervous at the degrees of separation and essentially stopped communication with the official, instead choosing to directly deal with the leader of the group Abdul Aziz which proved to be a rash decision. Instead of using the potential contacts and power of the intermediary that Zartman outlines in his argument on negotiation, we got caught in dealing with the leader who was much more resolute in his demands.
>
> **(Reilly Ryan)**

In this same simulation (2015), the hostage-takers belatedly threatened to withdraw from direct negotiations with the official side, in favor of negotiating through a TPI: they justified this threat by referring to the real-world precedent set by the U.S. government in negotiating with the Afghani Taliban through Qatar since at least 2014.

A further example of the carelessness, if not disdain, with which the hostage-takers treated their TPIs is that the hostage-takers wanted to leave the mediator with most of the blame whenever negotiations would break down.

In the second simulation, the official side used Mel's channel belatedly toward the end of the 2 weeks before the hostage crisis, and not during the hostage crisis, due to the official side's clumsy attempt to use the channel as a vehicle for information gathering rather than rapport building:

> I believe that our biggest mistake was the misuse of Mel's email account. For the first week and a half of the simulation, our focus was entirely placed on preventing an attack, and this stopped us from thinking more critically about how to gather information about the terrorists that we would be negotiating with during the crisis. During the first phase of planning, we strategized about how to incorporate Mel, our CIA operative, and we did so under the assumption that Mel was intended as an infiltration tool, rather than a channel through which to build rapport leading up to the attack. The first email we sent to the terrorist team (The Ismaeel Ring) attempted to show Mel's connection to the Iraqi cause, rather than simply building a relationship between the parties. In our following email, we realized our mistake and attempted to backtrack and focus on the Ring's grievances, working with the information provided in the Dolnik reading about the essential need to build rapport with the HTs [hostage-takers] (Dolnik, 2011, p. 289). Unfortunately, this change in tactics confused the terrorist team and we lost almost all of their trust before the crisis had even begun. This hindered our ability to get the HTs to make good faith agreements in the negotiations.
>
> **(Hannah Ousterman)**

Meanwhile, the terrorist side started out suspicious of all other parties, including the official side, the journalists, and the intermediaries:

> In our simulation, we were given the assistance of a Jordanian and CIA asset to act as third party mediators. We were immediately skeptical of the CIA Asset, "Mel," and discounted him. However, the Jordanian contact provided us an opportunity to have a third party verify the monetary transfer or aid given. However, we quickly forgot about the Jordanian contact, when we felt that we could not trust them. The Jordanians reaching out to us spooked us and we rejected their offer. However, they actually could have been useful at confirming a monetary transfer that the FBI was working on.
>
> **(Kevin Fulgham)**

> We were also suspicious of the Jordan government and decided not to interact with them although they could interfere in our favor and meet at least some of our demands. I would think that having at least some of our demands achieved would have been better than nothing. However, my team was too suspicious of Jordanians...We did not trust Mel either because we knew that he was working for the CIA. The fact that we trusted no one surely did not help in the negotiation.
>
> **(Estelle Zielinski)**

Another argument against using TPIs is the delay caused by involving a third party:

> At the time, our focus was negotiating with the terrorist group over the phone. We tried to use third party intermediaries and Mel but the response time was not fast enough. Those assigned to negotiating through the third party intermediaries and Mel ended up helping with negotiating over the phone. Five people were standing around the phone—some just listening, others actually furthering the negotiations.
>
> **(Jason Tran)**

Our Practical Prescriptions

From our review of historical practices and the results of our real-world simulations, we conclude that negotiators should consider TPIs if

1. The other side rebuffs official efforts to develop a relationship.
2. The official side is short of capacity to negotiate for itself.
3. The official side temporarily needs to focus on other activities.
4. The other side is more likely to conclude (resolve) the crisis with a TPI.

The official side should prefer TPIs who

1. Are neutral or positively viewed by both sides, do not have prior negative relationships with the other side, and are not perceived as blameworthy for the other side's grievances
2. Are trustworthy to both sides, or can cooperate with the official side's deception of the other side without the other side realizing
3. Have proven capable in previous TPI roles
4. Are linguistically and culturally literate with both sides, or at least the other side
5. Are more accessible to the other, perhaps for geographical proximity or prior establishment of a channel
6. Have specialist capacities for crisis negotiation
7. Maintain a channel with the other side consistently and without contradiction

Minor Bargains or Trades

Historical Practices

Wide consensus exists on the principle of bargaining or trading with the other side for minor concessions in order to build trust or at least to develop a relationship:

> [W]e'd learn that part of effective resolution is pulling back from the end objective and focusing on how to establish a relationship with this guy, right now, at this moment.
>
> **(Noesner, 2011, p. 73)**

> The guiding focus was quid pro quo, "something for something." Consequently, principles of bargaining served as guidelines for early negotiating theorizing, training, and practice. The field was defined by terms like hostage, negotiate, and hostage incident. Currently, these ideas still apply to some of the incidents criminal justice negotiators deal with.
>
> **(McMains and Mullins, 2015, p. 12)**

Before the new wave of terrorism, negotiators conventionally sought to offer food, water, and medical aid to the hostage-takers or to the hostages through the hostage-takers. More controversial is the granting of publicity. We review these two categories of grant in the following sections.

Grant Subsistence

Negotiators have been advised for decades to lower tension by granting minor concessions (Hudson, 1989, p. 325), such as the supply of food, medical assistance, fuel, electricity, or even escape routes to the hostage-takers (Zartman, 1990, pp. 167, 180). Some of these concessions are so minor as to have no implications for policy or law. For instance, Gary Noesner refers to the opportunity, during a historical case in which a man abducted and barricaded his former romantic partner and his son in his home, to grant the man's request for clean clothes (Noesner, 2011, pp. 4–5).

However, new terrorists are less likely to allow for the subsistence of their hostages or even themselves. For instance, in the Beslan school siege (September 2004), the hostage-takers refused any food, water, and medical assistance, and claimed to participate in the same deprivations. In the same year, Al Qa'ida's manual warned hostage-takers to be wary that any food delivered by the other side is not poisoned or delivered by the other side's intelligence collectors or assaulters (Al Qa'ida, 2004).

Grant Publicity

One way to build rapport and to demonstrate trustworthiness is to offer publicity, although this is risky. For instance, in April 1993, during the official siege of the Davidians (led by David Koresh), in Waco, Texas, Gary Noesner decided to allow Koresh to tape-record his message about the Book of Revelations, as long as he made no mention of suicide. Noesner felt that the FBI team really had nothing to lose by broadcasting this tape on national radio, and much to gain: "If we allowed him to deliver a nationwide broadcast, then he and his followers would surrender peacefully. With a hand signal I encouraged Henry to pursue this is in more detail." Noesner offered agreement as a sign of good faith on the FBI's part, but Koresh reneged on his end of the deal by claiming that God told him not to come out of the compound yet. Ultimately, this led to more frustrations between the Hostage Rescue Team and the negotiators (Noesner, 2011, p. 99).

Granting publicity was prescribed during the days of old terrorism, on the grounds that publicity is easiest to grant, and that any demands can be whittled down under the added scrutiny of publicity (Zartman, 1990, p. 175). However, the official granting of publicity is controversial, not least because it rewards terrorism, glorifies terrorism in the act, and possibly encourages copycats. The official side will not be in a position to offer any grant unless superior officers agree, journalists or public affairs officers agree, and the terrorists agree.

Moreover, even if the terrorists are willing to release hostages, they may not need official help in gaining publicity. Hostage-taking almost always attracts publicity naturally: "It is the necessity to negotiate with terrorists, and to do so in the full glare of international media attention, which makes the siege/hostage situation such an important piece of terrorist theatre." Thus, hostage-taking receives more attention than its frequency deserves (Wardlaw, 1989, p. 147). This is increasingly true as new terrorists make use of new media.

New terrorists are less interested in trading publicity for hostages: as shown earlier, new terrorists are not necessarily seeking any additional publicity during the attack; rather they may be seeking natural publicity by maximizing the lethality or duration of the attack, without any intention to release hostages.

Simulated Practices

Our simulations add to the evidence that new terrorists are unlikely to be interested in minor concessions.

In the first simulation (2015), the official side offered medical supplies to save the wounded hostage-takers in exchange for release of the high-value hostages, but the hostage-takers dismissed the offer as not attractive enough. In the second simulation (2016), the official side offered medical support to the hostages, in response to terrorist claims to have harmed the hostages, but the terrorist side was only pretending to harm hostages and was suspicious that the official side would use medical supplies as some sort of vehicle for surveillance or assault.

Similarly, the terrorist role-players were not particularly interested in negotiating for publicity. For instance, in the first simulation (2015), before realizing any attack, the official negotiators planned to emphasize the current attention from news media and to downplay expectations for further publicity, but by the start of the attack (which, according to the script, killed innocent people before any hostages were taken, as was true in Mumbai in 2008), the terrorist side was satisfied with current publicity (which was modeled by unaffiliated students playing journalists) and was focused on other objectives (the release of fellow Jihadis from U.S. detention and financial compensation).

Similarly, in the second simulation (2016), the official side had prepared to grant publicity but mistakenly asked for other demands, while the terrorist side was satisfied with the publicity gained naturally through the natural interest of the four role-playing journalists:

> We deemed it worthwhile to stress the widespread attention to the hostage-takers' cause had already received. Assuming that publicity was a principle unstated goal the terrorists strove to achieve in their barricade hostage incident, we attempted to persuade the Ring that they had succeeded in broadcasting their goals to the American public and that killing hostages would only hurt their cause in the eyes of the public. The publicity argument was a successful starting point because it convinced the terrorists to continue speaking with us, but it was insufficient as the terrorists repeatedly asked us to prove our good faith by fulfilling their demands. We committed one of the gravest errors during our first phone call. After listening empathetically to their grievances and acknowledging them, we voluntarily addressed their demands. A cardinal rule of crisis negotiation is that negotiators should avoid asking subjects for demands, because it raises expectations and gives them too much power.
>
> **(Kevin Chu)**

This helps to explain the terrorist side's defection on an apparent agreement late in the simulation, to the genuine dismay of the official side:

> Although the U.S. team made a few critical errors, we also made some very good decisions and took the advice from FBI agents seriously, which helped us best manage the crisis. We were able to effectively reframe the terrorists' demands for the President to apologize for drone strikes in the Middle East by having the FBI media team release a tweet that expressed remorse that individuals felt the need to take violent action to show their discontent with U.S. policies. This was a part of our efforts to secure the release of two hostages and begin to establish good faith negotiations, however, when we released the tweet, the terrorists let the two hostages out of the train car and executed them on the spot. This decision on their part to flagrantly ignore the agreement led the [U.S.] team to make the decision to storm the train and end the negotiation.
>
> **(Hannah Ousterman)**

Our Practical Prescriptions

For the above review of the historical and simulated practices, we find that the negotiator should offer to grant subsistence to the terrorists under the following conditions:

1. The grant would develop the other side's relationship with the negotiator.
2. The grant would help to achieve critical concessions.
3. The grant would not violate policy or law.
4. The negotiator is authorized.
5. The grant would not encourage more terrorism.

6. The parties necessary to the practical implementation of the grant are willing, such as the journalists necessary to any publicity, or the officials who would be needed to carry sustenance to the point of delivery.

The negotiator should expect the following challenges:

1. New terrorists are less likely to be interested in sustenance, especially if suicidal.
2. New terrorists are less likely to be interested in publicity additional to what they can generate for themselves.
3. New terrorists are more likely to distrust the negotiator's motivations or to suspect the grant as a vehicle for some official subterfuge.
4. The recipients can use the grant to their own advantage, such as by using sustenance to lengthen the crisis without any intent to give anything in return, or to improve their relationship with the other side.
5. The recipients might renege on their commitments in exchange for the grant.

If the terrorists are not interested in any grant, the negotiator should still try to turn this refusal to advantage, while balancing the effort to develop a relationship with the other side:

1. If the other side refuses a grant of sustenance, the negotiator should encourage the hostage-takers to consider the negative publicity of their apparent carelessness with their own lives, if not their hostages' lives.
2. If the other side refuses a grant of publicity, the negotiator should warn of the increased likelihood of negative public reporting on subjects who refuse to communicate with journalists under agreeable conditions.

Further, the official side could consider secretly encouraging negative reporting, if this could be achieved without harming efforts to develop a relationship with the other side. (The question of whether to grant publicity is separate to the question of how to manage publicity, which we reviewed in the previous chapter.)

Provoke Thought

Historical Practices

During negotiation, the official negotiator should ask thought-provoking questions in order to build rapport and to slow down the other side.

We have induced this prescription from our findings. We have not seen it written explicitly in any official manual, or heard it said explicitly by any practitioner, although it seems to be part of their tacit skill set.

By definition, a negotiator who is skilled in empathy and active listening should be relatively mindful of what the other side is thinking, and of how to manipulate what the other side is thinking. Thought-provoking questions signal an effort to understand and to meet the other side's demands, and they encourage the other side to be more thoughtful, which suggests more consideration of the negotiator's messages, or at least occupies the other side's time away from harmful activities.

This mindfulness is proven by official concerns to draw the other side from thinking about certain negative ideas, intents, or emotions. For instance, good practice includes not drawing attention to the other side's own deadlines, which encourage anxieties and rash actions, as agreed by this former special weapons and tactics (SWAT) operator:

> The best way to deal with a deadline is to seemingly ignore it. That is, do not be pressured by a deadline and do not call attention to it. That tactic is to talk to the perpetrator or perpetrators through the deadline and not refer to it at all... Calling attention to a deadline may precipitate an action that otherwise might not be taken. The hostage-taker will want to prove that he has power by firing a shot, or hurting someone, or both.
>
> **(French, 2013)**

Simulated Practices

We have induced our prescription from observations of official training and our real-world simulations. The advantages and caveats are best articulated by a student who participated in a simulation (2015) on the terrorist side, who realized that the hostage-taker's fundamental trade-off in use of time is between three activities: "talk, think, or terminate" (Aditya Ranganathan). This trade-off is essentially the same for both sides:

- Talking—or at least taking the time to initiate or reply to communication—takes time away from thinking about the negotiations; it may prevent the hostage-takers from terminating their hostages if they are fully engaged in the communications.
- Thinking interrupts other activities and may have the virtue of encouraging reasoning away from terminating the negotiations or killing the other side.
- Terminating the hostages effectively ends all talking and thinking, given modern norms of military intervention once hostages are killed.

These are essentially the same dilemmas for both sides, where the official side chooses between talking with the other side, thinking of what to do, or giving up the negotiations in favor of a violent intervention.

The advantages of provoking thoughtfulness, given our caveat against provoking the other side's suspicions, are illustrated by the following contrasting communications by the official side, and the contrasting outcomes on the terrorist side, during a simulation (2015):

1. At one point, "Mel" (the role of a fictional CIA agent given a prior relationship with the other side) sent an e-mail that caused the hostage-takers to miss their own deadline for executions. The e-mail contained the following statement: "We are arranging a press conference to meet your first demand and have begun arranging the release of your men...the White House is working with the Pentagon in establishing flights with military escorts. This cannot happen overnight. We need to exercise reason. As a show of good faith, will you release the non-essential hostages?"
2. By contrast, a different e-mail from "Mel" contained this question: "Will you release the body of the slain hostage? The family has offered to pay $x for it." This was dismissed by the terrorist side as not a serious offer, but a deliberate distraction, which encouraged the terrorist side to reaffirm its deadline to kill.

Our Practical Prescriptions

During negotiation, the official negotiator should ask thought-provoking questions with the following purposes:

1. To help the negotiator to sense the other side's state
2. To suggest something positive to the other side
3. To encourage the other side to consider further some official suggestion
4. To distract or slow down the other side if the other side is thinking or acting contrary to the official side's interests
5. To signal engagement and to build rapport

We need to add two caveats:

1. While the negotiator should provoke thoughtfulness on positive things or at least things that distract the other side from negative things, the negotiator should not draw attention to negative emotions, intents, events, or activities.
2. A strategy of provoking thoughtfulness should not be perceived by the other side as intended simply to waste the other side's time, to distract, or to deceive.

7

Assess Their Psychology

Most processes of negotiation include a prescription to clarify the other side's psychology. This seems particularly challenging and consequential when the other side is a hostage-taker, kidnapper, or active shooter, since the other side has already chosen to behave in a counternormative way, so their psychology is likely to fall outside of normal experience. Some prescriptions explicitly expect the official side to manage the other side's psychology as peculiar. For instance, Michael McMains (formerly chief psychologist for the police department of San Antonio, Texas) and Wayman Mullins "developed principles that emphasized managing hostage incidents as though they were a crisis for the hostage-taker" (McMains and Mullins, 2015, p. 3).

We have broken down the clarification of psychology into three separate questions that the negotiators or their intelligence analysts should seek to answer, as explained in sequential sections below:

1. Are they rational?
2. Are they murderous?
3. Are they suicidal?

Are They Rational?

Historical Practices

Rationality loosely suggests reason. In more formal terms, it suggests logic or optimization (Newsome, 2016, pp. 179–192). Negotiating is generally held to be easier if both sides have the same understanding of what is rational. Rationality can serve as a common understanding across uncommon cultures and purposes. Rationality also suggests certainty relative to an irrational actor whose behaviors must be less predictable.

Most early literature on negotiating with hostage-takers focused on nonterrorist hostage-takers, most of whom appear to be mentally ill or psychologically abnormal in some way, and are characterized as most difficult for negotiators (Maher, 1979). An early typology of hostage-takers concluded that the least psychologically stable class (nicknamed "crazies" for short) was most difficult for negotiators, while profit-oriented "criminals" are easiest, and the ideologues[1] (typical of terrorists) are somewhere in between, being psychologically rational but unconventional in their norms, beliefs, and values (Hacker, 1976, pp. 12–17). A contemporaneous typology added revolting prisoners, in order to produce four types: emotionally disturbed hostage-takers (equivalent to "crazies"), criminals, revolting prisoners, and political ideologues (Hassel, 1975).

In the early 1980s, the Federal Bureau of Investigation (FBI) recognized eight necessary conditions for a resolvable crisis, in which the hostage-taker must be rational and psychologically stable enough to value his or her own life, recognize threats to life, and to communicate with the other side:

1. The hostage-taker must need to live.
2. The other side must threaten force.
3. The hostage-taker must issue demands.
4. The hostage-taker must perceive the negotiator as both willing to help and to harm the hostage-taker.
5. Time for negotiations must be available.
6. The hostage-taker and negotiator must have a reliable channel of communication.
7. Both the location and the communications must be contained.
8. The negotiator must be able to deal with the hostage-taker's decisions (McMains and Mullins, 2015, p. 147).

In the FBI's current training, the FBI parses its prescriptions by two categories of hostage-takers—instrumental and demonstrative (or expressive):

1. Instrumentalists take hostages as a means to an end. The instrumental hostage-taker is closer to the old terrorist hostage-taker. Given instrumental hostage-takers, the prescription is to bargain for tangible objectives (ultimately for peaceful surrender), to demand "give and take" from the other side, and to "make him work for everything he gets," with the objective of building rapport and trust.
2. Demonstrative hostage-takers do not necessarily have any end other than to demonstrate desperation or commitment. The

[1] This typologist nicknamed the ideologues "crusaders," but this is also a term used by Jihadis to label their enemies as symptomatic of the Medieval Christian crusaders against Muslim-ruled Jerusalem.

> demonstrative hostage-taker is closer to the new terrorist hostage-taker. The FBI's prescribed response is to focus on calming them down. Bargaining could frustrate them and escalate their demonstrativeness without building trust.

Some analysts have effectively differentiated between vengeful and nonvengeful hostage-takers, and have recommended against wasting time trying to negotiate with a vengeful hostage-taker, who needs to be detained or otherwise incapacitated before he or she can execute his or her vengeance violently (Goldaber, 1979).

Many analysts have concluded that ideological terrorists are most difficult for negotiators, due to their strong ideological commitment and the stark, simplified rationality derived from their ideologies (Stratton, 1978; Soskis and Van Zandt, 1986; Combs, 1997, p. 57).

Confusion arises over whether to regard ideologies as rational—given their starkness—or as irrational—given their tendencies toward fallacies, such as reductionism, faith, and *argumentum ad hominem*, and toward biases, such as the confirmation bias (for a review of fallacies and biases, see Newsome, 2016, pp. 179–192).

For some analysts of new terrorism, hostage-takers are always rational, even if aspects of their behavior are so abnormal to be misinterpreted as irrational. For instance, one frequently cited quote is that terrorists are "neither crazy nor amoral but rather are rationally seeking to achieve a set of objectives" (Richardson, 2006, p. 14). Dolnik and Fitzgerald have used the act of taking hostages as evidence for rationality: "A good crisis negotiator makes a clear distinction between the *human being* who, for some reason, has chosen to engage in an act of terrorism and the *act itself.* As detailed examination of historical cases shows, when terrorists embark on a mission to take hostages in a barricade setting they do so with specific—and rational—purposes in mind" (Dolnik and Fitzgerald, 2011, p. 272).

Barak Barfi, the former journalist who was involved with some of the American journalists detained by the Islamic State, blamed the FBI's approach for not recognizing the material rationality of a Jihadi demand for ransom:

> The FBI could have helped most when the Islamic State initiated contact with each of the families. Instead, it relied on hostage training manuals designed for dealing with psychopaths. That was the wrong approach. The hostage-takers did not have fractured egos that needed soothing. This was a pure money racket. Its ringleaders were not driven by ideology and displayed no psychological disorders.
>
> **(Barfi, 2015)**

The FBI responded that the Islamic State of Iraq and the Levant (ISIL) was not negotiating in good faith, and its demands were unrealistic, and that the FBI does not make decisions about participants or agreements.

Simulated Practices

Our simulations prove that terrorists face great challenges in preparing an attack in a sufficiently procedurally rational way to be successful as attackers, while (ironically) still appearing rational to the other side. In other words, terrorists can be purposeful, goal-oriented, strategic, and optimizers (all common tests of procedural rationality), but still appear irrational because of common flaws in their execution of a plan, signals, and communications.

In the first simulation (2015), the terrorist role-players were highly rational preparers of their attack:

> The planning of the attacks, the choice of weapons, the training of our men [the fictional hostage-takers] made me realize how complicated it is for terrorists to be successful. We had to take into account every parameter, to carefully design our plan and to think of every single detail. I realized that planning must take an enormous amount of time for terrorists and involves a consequent logistics organization.
>
> **(Estelle Zielinski)**

Indeed, hostage-taking may be evidence of irrational commitment, given the risks, as admitted by a role-player on that same terrorist side:

> I would like to note that in this planning, from the location to where the brothers would board the train, what cars they would take hostage, how each step would go down, every step had to be calculated. It felt as though one wrong step would unravel the whole thing. The line, "We only catch the dumb ones" we had heard from multiple FBI agents hung over my head. It was our job not to be the dumb ones. As a group we had to look at this vast web of constraints and figure out where the city was most vulnerable that we could take advantage of...Being the terrorist and identify all the risks that came with that showed me that the people who actual[ly] commit these acts are deeply attached to their causes. It is only a person who truly believes that the only way to make any difference through violence that will go all the way through with this attack.
>
> **(Kylie McCaffrey)**

After the first simulation (2015), the terrorist side realized that they should have communicated more clearly their justifications for why they were killing, whom they were killing, and the rationality of selection of victim. The hostage-takers failed to provide good-faith gestures as well as threats, and failed to give reassurance of who remained unharmed. Consequently, the official side sometimes wondered whether everybody was dead; the official side's uncertainties about the terrorist side led to a conclusion that the other side was unreliable, out of control, and thence untrustworthy.

In our second simulation (2016), the terrorist side appeared similarly irrational to the official side, even though it did not kill anyone until the end. The terrorist side was purposeful throughout: its troubles were due to its failure to plan its negotiating strategy, having invested so much time in planning the initial attack. Ironically, its investment in the initial attack was motivated to ensure that its hostage-takers were practically unassailable (they managed to hijack a train on an elevated track), but it was unprepared to negotiate after the attack:

> I feel that for the terrorist side (my team), we were not extremely prepared for the actual negotiation. We spent all of our hours planning the "attack," that we forgot to communicate who would do what and designate roles. We had a general sense of what to expect and from our readings we were able to conclude that they would try to keep us talking for as long as they could; however, we never collectively came together to discuss our game plan. When the negotiation started it was unclear what our first course of action should be. Towards the middle and end of the simulation, certain people took over certain tasks and roles and we all came together when bigger decisions needed to be made. With that said, I feel we needed to prepare more for the simulation and negotiating aspects of it. When the "FBI" called us to negotiate, our group did not know who was going to speak and then when someone did get on the phone, we kept having to mute it because either no one could reach an agreement on what to say or we simply did not know how to respond.
>
> **(Alexandra Zech)**

The terrorist side's internal uncertainty and disagreement appeared to the official side as evidence for irrationality. One of the problems for this terrorist side was unpreparedness for negotiations. A separate problem was over-suspiciousness:

> I think that we could have achieved better results in the negotiation. We did not have any of our demands met by the end of the simulation, although the blowing of the train leading to the killing of innocents could be considered to be a success for terrorists. We did not manage to negotiate successfully with the FBI. I think that we were too suspicious of them.
>
> **(Estelle Zielinski)**

As a sign that the Ismaeel Ring was serious, we released a series of videos showing us beating up hostages. We started with a female pro-Israel preacher. This turned out to be a mistake. Our public diplomacy experts told us that we lost the public appeal with that beating. Targeting vulnerable populations; women, children, elderly, will lose public appeal. Instead we should have started with the Special Forces operators and military general, as the first beating victims. It was our lack of communication with the team that led to this mistake. In our team, we did not designate someone to be in charge of timing our beatings. While several of members helped to suggest an order to potential victims, we did not have an executive decision about the order or timing of those beatings. Before the third beating, our team presented a public release to WNN, saying "a hostage will be beaten in five minutes, if you do not comply" yet within two minutes another hostage was beaten because of lack of communication and order hierarchy.

The lack of organizational communication structure proved to be a significant challenge for advancing our agenda. Within our team, we had two negotiators, who acted independently of the group, only involving the larger group when the FBI made efforts to comply with our demands of reparation for Yemen drone strike victims. Other parts of the team, included a press release agent, who targeted to the Blog news publication without involving the general consensus. Several other parts of the group formed a quasi-suggestions committee, but had not legitimate authority to make executive decisions. In designing our hostage attack, we forgot to focus on how we would organize our negotiation strategy. Directly before the simulation, one of the team members mentioned it would be beneficial to have a decision making process.

The segmented team parts made it hard to coordinate a reactive strategy to the FBI. Of the FBI's demands was the release of Louisianan Congressman and House Foreign Relations Committee Member. According to the FBI, they had his family putting pressure on for his release. At that time, we did not know that the FBI valued his life so much. Of our hostages, we evaluated he would be the second most valuable, behind the military general, and we planned to torture/abuse him in a very public manner to force the FBI to secede to our demands.

(Kevin Fulgham)

Our Practical Prescriptions

We have found already that new terrorists are more violent, more demonstrative, more vengeful, and more ideological than old terrorists—and thus we induce that new terrorists are likely to be more difficult than old terrorists as opponents in a negotiation.

We agree that the act of taking hostages is strategic, and that strategic decisions, rather than random behaviors, are rational in the procedural sense—more so if the hostage-takers actually optimize their choices for more effectiveness. However, procedural rationality is more of a cognitive skill than a psychological quality. The cognitive skills of optimization cannot necessarily indicate psychological rationality in the sense of psychological stability, which is what the negotiator wants. The negotiator would rather have a stable opponent than an optimizer.

Cognitively, the attacker probably needs to be procedurally rational in order to make the optimal choices between well-defended and undefended targets, between striking when the defenders are least expectant or most expectant, between striking when the potential hostage number is high rather than low, and so forth. However, this procedural rationality (optimization) does not necessarily prove psychological rationality (stability). Indeed, carrying through such a risky enterprise as taking hostages is good evidence of psychological instability, even if a successful attack is evidence of strategic thinking.

Terrorists are purposeful or strategic when they execute a planned hostage-taking, but this is a moot point if their psychology is unstable. Furthermore, their procedural rationality is of no use to the negotiator if their motivations, intentions, or objectives are not negotiable from the official side's perspective.

Moreover, terrorists may remain rational in the sense of being purposeful and strategic, but still appear irrational to the other side, when terrorists fail to communicate their rationality in their stressful and frictional execution of their plan, communications, and signals.

However, achieving a successful hostage-taking is evidence more of the cognitive skill of strategic thinking, or procedural rationality, rather than an objective rationality with which any optimizer would agree. So far as ideologues can be described as rational, they can be described as only instrumental rationalists, meaning that they attempt to optimize given their peculiar ends, which few other people could share or perhaps understand.

In both simulations, both sides tried to appear rational, having read academic and official advice to appear rational, but failed to achieve the appearance of rationality. This suggests that the prescriptions to appear rational and to assess the rationality of the other side are somewhat impractical.

More practical is to focus on tangible offers or trades that build a relationship whatever the perspectives of rationality.

Are They Murderous or Intent on Violence?

Historical Practices

Dolnik and Fitzgerald initially acknowledged that new terrorists are more violent:

> With the rise of the "new terrorism," barricade hostage incidents seem to have assumed a much less prominent role in the tactical repertoire of terrorist

> organizations. One of the main reasons behind this development has been the "new terrorists" increasing emphasis on lethality, which has led to the deflation of perceived benefits of casualty-less operations. In short, with the almost universal causal relationship between the number of fatalities and media attention, barricade hostage incidents in which no one dies have become less attractive. An even more crucial factor has been the changing nature of the "new terrorists" goals associated with the religious nature of their ideologies.
>
> As today's terrorists allegedly place less emphasis on politics in favor of religion, they presumably find themselves in less of a position to issue realistically accomplishable demands.
>
> **(Dolnik and Fitzgerald, 2008, p. 15)**

However, later, Dolnik and Fitzgerald made the strange claim that killing is never the primary objective of hostage-taking: "In fact, no terrorist *barricade* hostage crisis in history has *ever* been conducted with the primary aim of killing the hostages" (Dolnik and Fitzgerald, 2011, p. 272).

Their finding is factually incorrect. Killing is sometimes clearly the ultimate objective, even when it is not the initial primary objective (see Chapter 3). Hostages are sometimes held unharmed temporarily only to extend the publicity and the terror before the final acts of violence, which are likely to be scheduled for whenever the hostage-takers can no longer defend the situation against the other side. We categorize such hostage-taking as "irreconcilable hostage-taking," meaning that the hostage-takers are intent on killing the hostages eventually, whatever alternative is offered to them. This category should be conceptualized as one pole of a spectrum, with plenty of uncertain cases in between the poles (reconcilable; irreconcilable). The official side's challenge is to estimate where on that spectrum the current case lies, and whether that placement justifies continuing negotiation or immediate assault.

Irreconcilable hostage-taking is more likely for new terrorists. New terrorists are more likely to kill. The large-*n* data show that this is true within and without hostage crises. As Table 3.3 shows, new terrorists kill more than twice as many hostages per event than old terrorists kill. Murder of hostages is empirically more likely by new terrorists—by Sunni Jihadi terrorists in particular, and of American hostages in particular. Sunni Jihadis kill hostages at three times the rate of other hostage-takers (15% compared to 5%), and the rate goes up another three times when the hostages are American (47%) (Loertscher and Milton, 2015, p. 7).

Irreconcilable hostage-taking is clearest in the deadliest cases of hostage-taking, where taking hostages was instrumental toward mass killing. On 9/11, planes were hijacked with passengers as effective hostages, and were advised by the hijackers to comply in order to be safe, even though the hijackers' intents were to direct the planes into buildings, thereby killing everybody on board.

Since 9/11, terrorists have increasingly taken hostages as an initial step toward mass killing, not with intent to negotiate any other outcome than the deaths of the hostages. This is an important observation that does not seem to have been recognized in the literature. Following, we list the many highly lethal events in which the hostage-takers held hostages apparently just to delay the inevitable rather than with any apparent intent to negotiate for their release:

- In Beslan in Russia (2004), Jihadi separatists kept hundreds of hostages alive, but wired them with explosives in a crowded gymnasium, without releasing any negotiable demands. The attackers repeatedly provoked the official side before the official side assaulted; the remote controllers later blamed the official side for the high casualties.
- A Pakistani violent Jihadi group Hizb-ul-Mujahideen (HuM) has engaged in several kidnappings for the purposes of murder or recruiting, not with any known negotiation with any official side:
    - On December 14, 2005, an eighth-grade student, Liaquat Ali, was kidnapped and subsequently shot dead by members after he refused to join their ranks at Tanta in the Gandoh area of Doda district in Pakistan.
    - On July 27, 2006, members kidnapped 16-year-old Abdul Rashid Sheikh in an attempt to recruit him. On August 8, 2006, the army rescued Sheikh from captivity within the Thanala forests in the Doda district.
    - On March 21, 2008, 23-year-old Mohammad Shaffi was kidnapped from his house at the Bhakhna village in the Doda district before being shot to death by suspected members.
    - On May 16, 2008, a female militant by the name of Raja Begum was arrested in Gool, Ramban district. She and her husband were allegedly involved in the kidnapping and torture of three local boys in an attempt to force them to join the HuM group (South Asia Terrorism Portal, 2013a).
- A similar terrorist group, Tehreek-e-Taliban of Pakistan (TTP) has participated in kidnappings apparently to interrupt the victims' activities, without apparently negotiating for the victims' release:
    - On May 9, 2013, Ali Haidar Gilani, son of the former Prime Minister of Pakistan, Raza Ali Gilani, was kidnapped in Multan by Al Qa'ida militants. He was handed over to the TTP in January 2016; he was rescued in an unrelated security operation by Afghan forces on May 10, 2016 (Masood and Mashal, 2016).
    - On November 23, 2013, TTP militants abducted 11 teachers involved in a polio vaccination campaign for schoolchildren in Bara Tehsil, Khyber Agency. No demands were made, and the fate of the teachers remains unknown.
    - On April 14, 2014, a faction of TTP in Orakzai Agency, known as Orakzai Freedom Movement, and led by Hafiz Saeed, claimed to have abducted tribesmen from Tirah Valley for their involvement in "illegal" and "un-Islamic activities" on April 12, 2014.

A pamphlet, attributed to the Afghan Taliban, and distributed in parts of North Waziristan Agency on April 14, confirmed fighting between the TTP factions, which has killed a number of militants (South Asia Terrorism Portal, 2013a).

- Similarly, in Mumbai (2008), the purpose of taking hostages at the Jewish center was to lengthen the period of terrorist activity, with all the advantages for publicity and lethality, even though the prior attacks on the same day had been intended to kill randomly without intent to hold hostages. In the end, as we know from intercepted satellite telephone conversations, the remote controllers coached the hostage-takers on the correct moment to kill all hostages before the official assaulters could capture the hostage-takers themselves (Dolnik and Fitzgerald, 2011, pp. 286–287). The case of Mumbai (2008) was perpetrated by Lashkar-e-Taiba (Urdu: "Army of the Righteous"), a Jihadi group based in Pakistan.
- A similar Pakistani group is Lashkar-e-Jhangvi (Urdu: "Army of [Sunni cleric Haq Nawaz] Jhangvi"), which also has detained and barricaded victims without any apparent intent to negotiate their release: in April 2012, its operatives stopped a bus in Chilas with the intent to kill only Shi'a passengers; in August 2012, its operatives halted three buses near the city of Gilgit, on which they killed only Shi'a Muslims without any apparent desire to negotiate for the victims' release; in June 2013, its operatives self-barricaded inside a busy hospital in Quetta, seeking to kill wounded schoolgirls, who had survived a previous attack by the same group (Hunzai, 2013; Roggio, 2013; Tadros et al., 2013).
- In Nairobi in 2013, and in Paris in 2015, the Jihadi attackers self-barricaded inside crowded public spaces (a shopping mall in Nairobi in 2013; a supermarket in Paris in January 2015; a theater in Paris in November 2015) to keep their victims from escaping, and to keep rescuers out, until the hostage-takers or their accomplices had killed as many as possible, or attracted publicity for as long as possible.
- Similarly, in Mogadishu, Somalia, in June 2016, al-Shabaab's fighters targeted a hotel where two legislators were living, whom they killed, plus another 20 people, according to al-Shabaab's own statement. This incident was reported initially as a hostage situation, but al-Shabaab's premeditated intent was clearly murderous and suicidal (the attack started with a suicidal car bomb at the gates) (Hussein et al., 2016).
- On June 12, 2016, in Orlando, Florida, an American gunman, who claimed loyalty to ISIL, shot to death dozens of people within the first 16 minutes, before nominally taking hostages for the next 3 hours. This hostage crisis seems to have been created by his retreat

from armed police into the restrooms (toilets) at the rear of the club, where club-goers were hiding, some of them wounded. He made no attempt to kill more hostages until police blew a hole in the exterior wall to rescue them, at which point he started shooting on the escapees and was shot to death by police as he exited the same hole. He was responsible for 49 deaths by the end (Zapotosky and Berman, 2016; Perez-Pena and Robles, 2016).

- On June 13, 2016, near Paris in France, a French convicted terrorist who had already declared allegiance to ISIL, stabbed to death a police officer returning home, and barricaded himself in that home with the victim's wife and young son: after unsuccessful negotiations, police assaulters killed the perpetrator but found the wife dead, although the boy was unharmed (Perez-Pena and Robles, 2016; Rosemain and Carraud, 2016).
- On July 2, 2016, six heavily armed terrorists loyal to ISIL seized the Holy Artisan Bakery in Dhaka, Bangladesh. The assailants shouted "Allahu Akbar" as they raided the premises. Thereafter, the attackers asked all hostages to recite verses from the Quran. Those who could recite from the Quran were spared and given free meals, whereas those who could not were brutally shot or dismembered with machetes. The terrorists used hostages' cellphones to publicize the slayings on social media. The crisis ended when Bengali officials assaulted the terrorists and successfully rescued 13 hostages. The aftermath revealed the deaths of 20 hostages, 2 police officers, and 6 terrorists (Associated Press, 2016; Manik et al., 2016).
- On July 26, 2016, two men armed with knives took five hostages in a church in Rouen, France, before killing the priest on camera. Police shot the two men to death as they exited the church with three hostages. They had posted allegiance to ISIL, which later claimed responsibility.

Simulated Practices

In both our simulations, which established a terrorist group with new terrorist backstory, motivations, and objectives, the terrorist role-players always set out to be murderous, and did murder hostages.

Expectations of a raised risk to American hostages are triangulated by simulation (2016), when the lead negotiator on the terrorist side concluded that terrorists would not rationally intend to release hostages if the other side was represented by the United States:

> I can only assume that "real life" terrorist groups inform their men of the negotiation strategies of countries like the U.S. However, through this simulation, I realized that any informed terrorist group would not attempt a hostage negotiation

with a country like the U.S., because they would know that their demands would never be met. The only thing a terrorist group could hope to gain from a hostage situation is publicity. In such a case, they would intentionally end the negotiation, as we did, by killing all the hostages in an attempt to gain more publicity.

(Katrina Oshima)

Our Practical Prescriptions

We have found that new terrorists are more likely to be murderous and irreconcilable, and to take hostages just to lengthen the crisis before murder, rather than to exchange live hostages for anything. Sometimes, hostage-taking is simply a deliberate step toward murder, with no chance of negotiating a peaceful outcome.

American hostages run a relatively higher chance of being murdered by Jihadis. This is probably true for any Western hostages held by Jihadis, although the data are not differentiated enough by nationality of victim to be sure.

One explanation, proven by simulation, is the terrorist's expectation that America is unlikely to concede. However, we should remember that while this perception (that America would not make deals with terrorists) encourages harm to hostages in the short term, it should discourage intentional taking of American hostages for any sort of deal in the long term, even though it will not discourage the taking of hostages with intent to murder.

If the hostage-taker has already harmed hostages, or is intent on violence against the hostages, then the negotiator should expect a lower chance of successfully negotiating the release of these hostages than if the hostage-taker had taken hostages with some other intent, such as to exchange them unharmed for money.

Early in any attack, the murderous intent may be impossible to verify, since such attacks—in their initial violence, followed by the survival of some detainees—would look identical, whether or not the hostage-takers intend to kill everybody eventually or to release hostages in return for concessions.

Are They Suicidal?

Historical Practices

In theory and practice, a suicidal hostage-taker is less likely to resolve a crisis peacefully.

In the early 1980s, the FBI recognized the hostage-taker's desire to live, and fear of the other side's threat of force, as the first two of eight necessary conditions for a resolvable crisis (McMains and Mullins, 2015, p. 147).

Even before the acknowledged era of new terrorism, experts advised negotiators to clarify the hostage-taker's suicidal threshold (Zartman, 1990, p. 168). The threat of harm might dissuade a nonsuicidal hostage-taker. However, it is more likely to encourage the suicidal hostage-taker. If the hostage-takers are suicidal, the negotiator should be careful not to challenge their suicidal motivations, even while the negotiator challenges their goals: "Negotiations have to be careful not to challenge, dare, or incite terrorists to cross the [suicide] threshold in the process of bargaining" (Zartman, 1990, p. 168). The negotiator also should be careful not to appear to give the suicidal hostage-taker a choice between death at the hands of the official side or death at the hostage-taker's own hands: "Threats to the terrorists attack the opposing party directly, and...influence the location of the threshold of suicide" (Zartman, 1990, p. 170).

Dolnik and Fitzgerald extrapolated from old terrorist data to new terrorism: "To conclude, in most *hostage* cases, the outcome of dying a martyr's death represents the terrorists' fallback option, or 'plan B.' This means that as long as negotiators can maintain the perception that there is a chance of achieving something more attractive than this baseline position, negotiations are possible" (Dolnik and Fitzgerald, 2011, p. 282). These same analysts of new terrorism have warned negotiators "to make the distinction between the *willingness* to die and the unwavering *intention* to die" (Dolnik and Fitzgerald, 2011, p. 281). This seems a useful distinction, and implies that the negotiator should acknowledge the suicidal hostage-taker's willingness to die, while trying to encourage the hostage-taker's intention to live.

New terrorists are more suicidal than old terrorists. By one early analysis, old terrorists were suicidal in only 1% of HBT incidents; in 94% of the same cases, they were willing to give up their lives but preferred not to (ITERATE data, in Corsi, 1981). The Global Terrorism Database (GTD) does not allow us to know whether a hostage-taker is truly suicidal or not, but it does record how many hostage-takers die. As Table 3.3 shows, our extension of the GTD found that more than twice as many new terrorists die per hostage-taking than old terrorists die. At least one new terrorist dies in four times as many hostage-takings, proportionately, than any old terrorists die in hostage-takings: in new terrorist hostage-takings, the hostage-takers died in 6% of incidents, whereas hostage takers died in 1.5% of events perpetrated by old terrorists.

Simulated Practices

Given our theories and evidence, we induced probabilistically that new terrorists are more likely than old terrorists to be willing to die in the course of terrorism, and that remote controllers are more likely to encourage suicidalism in hostage-takers remotely than when they share the same risks locally.

In both simulations, even though the given objectives included safe passage of the local hostage-takers to Iraq, the terrorist role-players expected the local hostage-takers to die at the scene of the hostage-taking rather than release hostages or allow a bloodless rescue of hostages.

Our Practical Prescriptions

We have found that new terrorists are more likely than old terrorists to be suicidal, and that suicidal terrorists are less likely to resolve a crisis peacefully.

The negotiator should carefully assess the suicidalism of the hostage-takers.

If estimating them as suicidal, the negotiator should be careful to challenge their ends and means, without appearing to doubt their suicidal motivations or to threaten them with harm, short of confirmation of an irreconcilable hostage-taking. The negotiator should acknowledge the suicidal hostage-taker's willingness to die, while trying to encourage the hostage-taker's intention to live.

If estimating them as irreconcilably suicidal, the negotiator should switch to negotiating for intelligence and time in preparation for an assault.

If estimating them as nonsuicidal, a threat of harm is useful for deterring them from acting contrary to the official side's interests.

8

Assess Their Motivations, Intentions, and Goals

Those in negotiation of any type, from business deals to hostage crises, agree that an understanding of the other side's motivations, intentions, and objectives helps the negotiator. Zartman urged negotiators with terrorists to "discover their paramount preferred goals" (Zartman, 1990, p. 169).

Gary Noesner, formerly chief of the Crisis Negotiation Unit at the Federal Bureau of Investigation (FBI), remembers a formative experience with Frederick Lanceley, a pioneer negotiator at the FBI:

> Fred taught us that the key to successful negotiation was to discern the subject's motivation, goals, and emotional needs and to make use of the knowledge strategically. Once we understood the hostage taker's real purpose, we had a better chance of convincing him that killing the hostages would not serve that purpose and would only make an already bad situation worse.
>
> **(Noesner, 2011, p. 34)**

Dolnik and Fitzgerald warn against directly asking for demands, even though they prescribe using negotiations to understand the other side. Therefore, "negotiators should avoid asking the subject for demands, because it gives him or her too much power and raises expectations. The meticulously preplanned nature of 'new terrorist' incidents, as well as the involvement of hostage-takers who assume an overtly suicidal posture, is likely to make such an offer counterproductive" (Dolnik and Fitzgerald, 2011, p. 275).

We have broken down the clarification of motivations, intentions, and objectives into four separate questions that the negotiators or their intelligence analysts should seek to answer, as explained in the following sequential sections:

1. Are they taking people in order to gain intelligence?
2. Are they seeking publicity?

3. Are they seeking ransom?
4. Are they seeking to exchange prisoners?

Are They Taking People in Order to Gain Intelligence?

The terrorists may be detaining people in order to gain intelligence from them. Al Qa'ida's manual advises that kidnapping is one means toward gathering information useful for other operations, such as information on potential targets: "Information is collected in this method [surveillance of a site] by kidnapping an enemy individual, interrogating him, and torturing him" (Al Qa'ida, 1990, p. 54).

Similarly, the same manual warns sympathizers not to give up intelligence during detention: "In prison cells, do not talk to anyone you did not previously know. Some [prisoners] may be [enemy] agents or may have different orientations" (p. 128).

Are They Seeking Publicity?

Historical Practices

Before the new wave of terrorism, a common expectation was that terrorist demands "typically comprise publicity, ransom, and the release of government-held prisoners" (Zartman, 1990, p. 174).

New terrorists are more likely to take hostages without any demands, where the purpose of taking hostages is to lengthen the spectacle before killing, or to use the hostages as a means to another end—usually a deadly end, such as to fly planes into buildings (such as on September 11, 2001) or to force a hostage to get the terrorists through an access control (such as into the Charlie Hebdo magazine offices, on January 7, 2015).

At the same time, sometimes new terrorists ransom people for material profit, in which case they are likely to minimize the publicity, except as a channel to communicate with whatever audience might help them get what they want.

One of the five objectives written by Al Qa'ida (2004) is "bringing a specific case to light." Taken as a whole, the manual's five reasons for kidnapping are mostly political:

1. To encourage "the enemy to succumb to some demands"
2. To "create a political embarrassment between the government and the countries of the detainees"
3. "Obtaining important information from the detainees"
4. "Obtaining ransoms"
5. "Bringing a specific case to light"

In the same manual, Al Qa'ida praised the Moscow theater siege (2002) for "bringing a specific case to light"—Chechen separatism. This crisis ended in an official assault, without any concessions by either side, but the long duration of the crisis and its great death toll (more than 170 dead) drew a lot of attention, which Al Qa'ida considered good for the Jihadi cause, too (Al Qa'ida, 2004).

One of Al Qa'ida's affiliates later prescribed five objectives for taking or killing hostages:

1. The taking of hostages in order to cause the news media to publicize a statement (Naji, 2006, p. 96)
2. The killing of American hostages to cause a change of U.S. policy (p. 211)
3. The kidnapping of diplomats who are valuable enough to be released in exchange for the release of Jihadi prisoners (p. 78)
4. The kidnapping of a manager or an engineer from a petroleum company associated with a non-Muslim country in order to pressure the non-Muslim country to raise its petroleum price for the benefit of Muslim suppliers (p. 101)
5. The kidnapping of Arab Christian workers or Western reporters for the same purpose, if kidnapping Western workers is not feasible (p. 102)

As shown in Table 8.1, most terrorist hostage-takings are in locations known to the official side, suggesting that terrorists want the publicity in most hostage-takings. Table 8.1 shows practically no difference between the propensities of old terrorists and new terrorists to carry out hostage-takings in known locations.

Simulated Practices

In both simulations (2015 and 2016), the hostage-takers made the most of their demands just to generate publicity or to draw attention to grievances, not expecting their demands to be granted.

Our Practical Assessments

Our analysis and simulations suggest that terrorists will continue to hold most detainees in known locations. New terrorists are more likely to choose a known location to maximize publicity before escape, suicidalism, or murder, without intent to make any exchange.

Terrorists will continue to hold few detainees in undisclosed locations in order to ransom them for money or some other material profit, with intent to honor such an exchange.

Wherever an official side observes terrorists choosing a discoverable location, such as a shopping mall in daylight, the official side should assume that the terrorists are seeking publicity. If the attackers are new terrorists, the

Table 8.1 Hostage-Takings by Location (Known or Unknown), by Ransom (Demanded or Not Demanded), and by Category of Terrorist (New or Old), for 1970 through 2015

	Known Location, Ransom Demanded	Known Location, No Ransom Demanded	Unknown Location, Ransom Demanded	Unknown Location, No Ransom Demanded	Known Location; Ransom Demand Remains Unknown	Unknown Location; Ransom Demand Remains Unknown	Total
New	154 (6.1%)	1,840 (73.4%)	17 (0.7%)	147 (5.9%)	341 (13.6%)	8 (0.3%)	1,912 (100%)
Old	435 (10.6%)	3,018 (73.2%)	42 (1.0%)	185 (4.5%)	417 (10.1%)	24 (0.6%)	3,724 (100%)
Total	589 (8.9%)	4,858 (73.3%)	59 (0.9%)	332 (5.0%)	758 (11.4%)	32 (0.5%)	5,636 (100%)

Source: Global Terrorism Database.

official side should estimate that the purpose is likely to maximize publicity without intent to release hostages.

Wherever an official side estimates that the terrorist is trying to detain victims in an undiscoverable location, it should assume that the intent is to seek ransom rather than publicity.

Are They Seeking Ransom?

Historical Practices

As shown in Table 8.1, ransom is rarely demanded by either old or new terrorist hostage-takers. New terrorists are less likely than old terrorists to demand a ransom, at least in public. According to our extension of the GTD, new terrorists demand a ransom in somewhere between 6.8% (ignoring unknown cases) and 20.7% (counting unknown cases as if they are cases of a demand for ransom) of hostage-takings, while old terrorists demand a ransom in somewhere between 11.6% (ignoring unknown cases) and 21.3% (counting unknown cases) of hostage-takings.[1]

If any ransom had been demanded, new terrorists are more likely to release hostages. Table 8.2 shows that new terrorists have released, proportionately, twice as many hostages than old terrorists have released, in cases where a ransom was demanded, even though Table 3.3 showed that new terrorists

Table 8.2 Fates in Hostage-Takings with a Demand for Ransom, by Category of Terrorist (New or Old), for 1970 through 2015

Category of Terrorist Group	Hostages Released	Deaths, Cardinal Count (and Percentage of Total Hostages)[a]		Total Hostages, Including Unknown Fates
		Deaths Due to Event, Not Necessarily Hostages[a]	Low-End Estimate of Hostage Deaths[a]	
New	887 (54.2%)	137 (8.4%)	93 (5.7%)	1,636 (100%)
Old	702 (21.9%)	174 (5.4%)	153 (4.8%)	3,199 (100%)

Source: Global Terrorism Database.

[a] GTD does not keep information on specific victim casualties, so we cannot know whether those killed in any given event are hostages, bystanders, or responders. The low-end estimate of hostage deaths counts only deaths that occurred during hostage-takings that were not classified as terrorist "armed assaults," because this terrorist attack type is most likely to kill people other than hostages. Probably the number of hostages killed is far higher than our low-end estimate.

[1] Probably most of these unknown cases are cases of ransom but cannot be confirmed as cases of ransom because of the normative secrecy on both sides about the demands and particularly the payments, given the sensitivities about making concessions to terrorists.

Table 8.3 Fates in Hostage-Takings with No Demand for Ransom, by Category of Terrorist (New or Old), for 1970 through 2015

Category of Terrorist Group	Hostages Released	Deaths, Cardinal Count (and Percentage of Total Hostages)[a]		Total Hostages, Including Unknown Fates
		Deaths Due to Event, Not Necessarily Hostages[a]	Low-End Estimate of Hostage Deaths[a]	
New	9,923 (31.4%)	12,417 (38.4%)	6,152 (19.0%)	32,305 (100%)
Old	10,038 (36.8%)	5,137 (18.8%)	2,355 (8.7%)	27,292 (100%)

Source: Authors' extension of the Global Terrorism Database.

[a] GTD does not keep information on specific victim casualties, so we cannot know whether those killed in any given event are hostages, bystanders, or responders. The low-end estimate of hostage deaths counts only deaths that occurred during hostage-takings that were not classified as terrorist "armed assaults," because this terrorist attack type is most likely to kill people other than hostages. Probably the number of hostages killed is far higher than our low-end estimate.

released, proportionately, less than half as many hostages as old terrorists have released across all hostage-takings (whether or not a ransom was demanded).

While new terrorists are more likely than old terrorists to release hostages after a demand for ransom, they are less likely to release hostages if they have made no demand for ransom, as shown in Table 8.3.

In the minority of cases where ransoms are demanded, the detainees tend to be valuable or otherwise unusually newsworthy, so public perception is skewed toward events where ransoms are demanded and are reported. In some of these cases, the demands for ransom are nominal, not genuine.

As noted above, while new terrorists are likelier than old terrorists to take hostages with intent to kill them, new terrorists will sometimes exchange hostages for material gain. Consistent with theoretical expectations, new terrorists are less interested in political concessions. When new terrorists make demands in exchange for hostages, these demands are almost always for material profit.

From 2008 to July 2014, Al Qa'ida and direct affiliates took at least $125 million in revenue from kidnappings, of which $66 million was paid in 2013, according to estimates by the *New York Times*. The U.S. Treasury Department has cited ransom amounts that, taken together, put the total at around $165 million over the same period. In 2003, kidnappers received around $200,000 per hostage. By 2014, they were netting up to $10 million (Callimachi, 2014).

Some of the demands for money are made—and honored—by the most intractable violent Jihadi groups, including the Taliban and the overlapping Haqqani Network, which range across Afghanistan and Pakistan, even though the Taliban has formally forbidden ransoms since 2009 (in favor of exchanging prisoners). For instance,

- On March 27, 2008, Sean Langan, a British journalist, was kidnapped by members of the Haqqani Network when he arrived to interview a high-ranking Taliban member. A few weeks after ascertaining Langan was not a spy, the operatives negotiated for a ransom (amount unknown) for Langan and his interpreter, which was paid by Channel 4 News. Langan was freed 12 weeks later (Holmwood, 2008).
- In November 2008, David Rhode, a reporter for the *New York Times*, was invited to interview a senior Taliban commander before being kidnapped and later sold to Taliban operatives, now understood to be from the Haqqani Network. The kidnappers asked for a ransom of £25 m for Rhode's release. Rhode was able to escape captivity after jumping over a wall around the compound in which he was being held (Beaumont, 2009).
- On August 23, 2011, 16 miners were released after having been abducted on June 11 by Pakistani Tehreek-e-Taliban (TTP) operatives. An undisclosed ransom was demanded and paid to the kidnappers for their release (South Asia Terrorism Portal, 2013b).

The Islamic State has amazed observers as being brutal and fundamentalist, but the Islamic State of Iraq and the Levant (ISIL), too, has ransomed detainees—mostly religious outsiders of nationalities that are not prioritized for targeting or of too low a socioeconomic value to be worth taxing, but who are connected with other people prepared to pay ransoms. For instance, ISIL has warned Christians to convert to Islam, pay a tax as apostates, or face death. Most of the 1.2 million Christians in Syria fled. In February 2015, during a local territorial advance, ISIL kidnapped more than 200 Assyrian Christians from 12 villages in northeastern Syria. Thousands of other Assyrians fled from the area. ISIL demanded $18 million for their release. Assyrian groups (mostly in Sweden) paid an unknown number of millions of dollars for their release. The last 42 or 43 captives were released in February 2016 (BBC, 2016a).

Simulated Practices

In both simulations (2015 and 2016), the hostage-taking side was given the same five objectives, of which only one aimed for money, but in each simulation the hostage-taking side emphasized the demand for money, given their pessimism about gaining concessions on the given political demands or the release of comrades from U.S. detention.

In the second simulation (2016), in which the hostage-taking side was given the liberty to choose their own attack methods, it ended up negotiating for money alone, although it eventually gave up this demand under official advice that the United States would never pay for hostages, so it ordered the killing of hostages as an endgame.

In both cases, the demands for money were excessive and were intended more to punish the other side or maximize publicity than to make a profit. In the second simulation (2016), the hostage-takers initially demanded $2 billion for release of hostages—this mimics the real-world ISIL's demands for impossibly high amounts on the rare occasions it has asked for money publicly.

Our Practical Assessments

Ransom is rarely demanded by either old or new terrorist hostage-takers. New terrorists are less likely than old terrorists to demand a ransom—at least in public—but are more likely to release hostages, even though they are less likely to release hostages if they have made no demand for ransom.

New terrorists have ransomed particularly valuable persons, detainees initially detained incorrectly as spies, nationalities outside of targeted nationalities, or local persons with little local value for taxation but with wealthy foreign relatives or backers.

From these observations, we can induce a probabilistic theory that new terrorists are likelier to ransom detainees whose origins are local or who are not associated with a foreign government that has not intervened in the region (where intervention includes even remote nonmilitary aid), but which are associated with some wealthier interested party outside the region. New terrorists are unlikely to ransom detainees associated with a foreign government that has intervened in the region—they are more likely to kill such persons publicly; they may issue demands for impossibly high ransoms to extend the publicity and terror on their way to killing the poor victim eventually.

These theories are probabilistic, not deterministic. The behavior of new terrorists tends to be less reliable than old terrorists, and ISIL is the youngest, most brutal, and least reliable to date. These facts suggest that negotiation for the release of a detainee by ISIL to an extra-regional government is practically impossible.

Are They Seeking to Exchange Prisoners?

Historical Practices

Violent Jihadis seem likelier to consider the exchange of hostages for prisoners rather than for money. The same scholar of Islamic law who claimed no precedent from the time of the Prophet Mohammed for the payment of ransoms, nonetheless claimed to observe plenty of precedents for the exchange of prisoners:

> Of exchange, a special kind of ransom, there are many instances in the life of the Prophet: sometimes for one, at other [times] for more. In later times, it developed into a complicated institution involving the release of thousands of prisoners at a time. In certain treaties the value of the ransom of prisoners was fixed in definite sum of money.
>
> **(Hamidullah, 1942, Chapter 15, rule 453)**

We have some evidence that the violent Jihadi's default demand (if any) is for the release of Jihadi prisoners before money.

Pakistani and Indian violent Jihadi groups have practiced the exchange of hostages for prisoners for decades:

- In 1989, in India, an operative of the Al Umar Mujahideen terrorist group known as Mushtaq Ahmed Zargar kidnapped Rubaiyya Saeed, daughter of the former Home Minister of India (Mufti Mohammad Saeed). The terrorist group demanded the release of five of their detainees in return for Rubaiyya Saeed, and the Indian government complied (Revo, 2016).

- On October 20, 1994, in Pakistan, Ahmed Omar Saeed Sheikh and his peers of the Harkat-ul-Mujahideen terrorist group kidnapped four Western tourists: three Britons and one American. The group demanded the release of 10 militants held in Kashmir by the Indian government in exchange for the hostages' safe return. The hostages were freed by an official assault. One militant was killed in a shootout, and others, including Ahmed, were captured alive (Burns, 1994).

- On July 4, 1995, Harkat-ul-Mujahideen assisted a subsidiary Kashmiri militant group, *Al-Faran*, in kidnapping five Western tourists: two Britons, two Americans, and one Norwegian (*New York Times*, 1995a). The kidnappers demanded the release of Pakistani militant Maulana Masood Azhar along with 20 others imprisoned in India. One of the hostages from Norway was killed, and his body was found in August. The four remaining hostages were killed in December by the kidnappers, according to a captured rebel, after an ambush that killed four of the original hostage takers (*New York Times*, 1995b).

- On December 24, 1999, Harkat-ul-Mujahideen hijacked Indian Airlines Flight 814 and flew to several locations: Amritsar, Lahore, Dubai, and Kandahar. The terrorists insisted on the release of three militants (Mushtaq Ahmed Zargar, Ahmed Omar Saeed Sheikh, and Maulana Masood Azhar) in exchange for the hostages. The Taliban mediated negotiations between the group's hijackers and the Indian government. On December 31, the militants and the hostages were freed (Sharma, 2009).

- On January 23, 2002, American journalist Daniel Pearl was kidnapped by Harkat-ul-Mujahideen operatives. The group demanded the release of all Pakistani detainees from the U.S. base at Guantanamo Bay and resumption of a suspended U.S. shipment of F-16 fighter jets to the Pakistani government. Daniel Pearl was killed 9 days later; his body was discovered on May 16, 2002 (Pellegrini, 2002; Musharraf, 2006).

- On October 10, 2004, two Chinese engineers—working on a state-sanctioned dam in North Waziristan—were kidnapped by the Hakimullah Mehsud faction of the Pakistani Tehreek-e-Taliban. Abdullah Mehsud demanded the release from Pakistani detention of fellow Mehsud operatives. On October 15, Pakistani forces attempted a rescue, during which one of the two Chinese men and all of their abductors were killed, except for Abdullah Mehsud, who was in a different location (Craig and Khan, 2014).

- On March 26, 2010, the terrorist group known as the Asian Tigers kidnapped two former officials of Pakistan's Inter-Services Intelligence (ISI) and a British filmmaker (Asad Qureshi). The group demanded the release of three Afghan Taliban leaders (Mullah Abdul Ghani Baradar, Maulawi Kabir, and Mansour Dadullah). After the 10-day deadline had passed, one of the ISI officials, Khalid Khwaja, was killed, and a new demand was issued for the release of the group's previous three commanders and 120 jihadi militants held by Pakistan, and for a $10 million ransom in exchange for the release of Asad Qureshi (Yusufzai, 2010). Asad Qureshi was released after 6 months as a hostage, but it is unclear what was exchanged for his return (Sawer, 2010). The other ISI official, Sultan Amir Tarar, died of a supposed heart attack while in captivity in 2011. The group demanded $15,000 for return of Tarar's body (Walsh, 2011).
- On May 20, 2014, the Hakimullah Mehsud faction of the Pakistani Tehreek-e-Taliban kidnapped a Chinese tourist traveling from Lahore to Balochistan via the Khyber Pakhtunkhwa. By telephone, the group claimed responsibility and stated that the Chinese tourist was abducted to force Pakistani authorities to release TTP fighters in their custody (Sherazi, 2014). He was freed on August 22, 2015, during a Pakistani military operation (Shahabuddin et al., 2015).

In 2009, the Taliban switched from demands for money to demands for prisoners. The Taliban codified the change of policy in the 2009 edition of their *Layeha* (code of conduct):

> When you capture drivers, contractors, or soldiers, releasing them for money is prohibited. The provincial authority has the right to use him for a prisoner exchange...[if] the captured person is converted to Islam, then the [Imam] will exchange him if the captured person gives permission, but there should be a pledge that he will not convert back to the infidels.
>
> **(Taliban, 2009, Section 2.8)**

In the 2010 edition of its *Layeha*, the Taliban forbade ransoms but allowed prisoner exchanges:

> If a local soldier, policeman, an official or other responsible person with affiliations to the slave administration has been captured, it is at the discretion of the governor to release them in the case of prisoners exchange, as part of a goodwill gesture or in exchange of solid guaranties. Receiving money for the prisoner's release is forbidden
>
> **(Taliban, 2009, p. 107).**

On December 31, 2011, a spokesperson for the TTP criminalized "kidnapping for ransom" under Shariah law (South Asia Terrorism Portal, 2013b).

The Taliban has publicized the exchanges:

- In February 2009, the Taliban released seven citizens from the Pakistani Swat district in exchange for the release of three of its fighters (Roggio, 2009).
- On July 18, 2009, the Taliban released a video of captured United States Army soldier Sergeant Robert Bowdrie "Bowe" Bergdahl, who was kidnapped on June 30 (CNN, 2016). The Taliban initially demanded $1 million, the release of 21 Afghan prisoners, and the return of Aafia Siddiqui—a Pakistani scientist who was convicted for the attempted killing of U.S. soldiers in Pakistan (Yusufzai, 2010). The demand was reduced later to the return of six Afghan prisoners, and eventually five (Gannon, 2013). Bergdahl was finally released on May 31, 2014, in exchange for five detainees to be transferred from the U.S. base at Guantanamo Bay to Doha, Qatar. The five released Taliban affiliates have held high-ranking positions within the Taliban regime; Mullah Muhammad Fazl (Taliban army's chief of staff), Mullah Norullah Noori (senior Taliban military commander), Abdul Haq Wasiq (Taliban deputy minister of intelligence), Khairullah Khairkhwa (Taliban governor of the Herat province and former interior minister), and Mohammed Nabi (senior Taliban figure and security official) (Joscelyn, 2015; Pitt, 2015, pp. 28–37).
- A recent variation of the Taliban's demand for the release of prisoners is to threaten foreigners in order to deter the Afghan government from executing Jihadi prisoners. In August 2016, the Afghan Taliban released a video of an American woman (Caitlan Coleman), alongside her Canadian husband (Joshua Boyle), who had been kidnapped in 2012, warning that her captors were "willing to kill us, willing to kill women, to kill children [the couple had two children with them], to kill whomever in order to get these policies reversed or to take revenge" (Meek and Ross, 2016).

Al Qa'ida has also demanded prisoner exchanges:

- In September 2008, Al Qa'ida kidnapped the designated Afghan ambassador to Pakistan (Abdul Khaliq Farahi). Mediated by the Haqqani network, Al Qa'ida demanded the release of its comrades from Afghan detention. The Afghan government refused, so Al Qa'ida demanded $5 million, which was paid in 2010 (Rosenberg, 2014).
- In March 2012, Al Qa'ida's Yemeni affiliate called on the Yemeni government to release its fighters in exchange for 73 captured Yemeni soldiers (Roggio, 2012).
- In September 2015, Al Qa'ida gained five of its prominent militants from Iranian captivity in exchange for an Iranian diplomat who had been kidnapped by them in Yemen (Joscelyn, 2015).

The ISIL has demanded prisoner exchanges occasionally. In August 2014, the insurgent group demanded the release of its militants from Lebanon's Roumieh prison. The Lebanese government refused to negotiate, so the Islamic State of Iraq and al-Sham (ISIS) retaliated by executing soldiers captured from Hezbollah and the Lebanese national army (Cafarella, 2015, p. 7). ISIL's behavior toward Lebanon is in contrast to its behavior toward the Assyrian Christians that it kidnapped in February 2015, which it released up to February 2016 in exchange for money (BBC, 2016a).

However, in January 2015, ISIL proceeded in reverse, when it first demanded money for the release of two Japanese citizens, before showing the beheading of one of them, with a verbal statement by the other, saying that ISIL "no longer want money. So you don't need to worry about funding terrorists. They are just demanding the release of their imprisoned sister Sajida al-Rishawi." She had been detained since 2005 by Jordan for attempting to blow herself up in a hotel in Amman, where her husband was one of the suicide bombers who killed 57 people across three hotels. No exchange was made, so on February 1, 2015, ISIL released a video showing the second hostage's beheading (Shimbun, 2015a,b,c). Following our previous findings, we interpret ISIL's switch from money to a person as their objective as just a new way to extend the publicity.

Similarly, in April 2014, Boko Haram kidnapped 276 schoolgirls from Chibok in Nigeria—a kidnapping probably best known than any other due to the social media campaign known as "bring back our girls." According to videos and statements released by Boko Haram, it forced these girls to convert to Islam, and to marry its members in some cases, without any offer or demand for any exchanges, at least in 2014. Negotiations over some sort of exchange with the Nigerian government broke down at least three times in 2015, suggesting that Boko Haram derived more utility from keeping the girls than exchanging them. In March 2015, Boko Haram's leader (Abubakar Shekau) pledged allegiance to ISIL, prompting conflict within the group. Meanwhile, external military pressure rescued some of the girls. In September 2016, the Nigerian President appealed for help from the United Nations in negotiating for the release of the schoolgirls; a few days later, Boko Haram's leader offered the girls in exchange for "our brethren" (presumably members of Boko Haram in official detention). In October 2016, Boko Haram freed 21 more girls under a deal brokered by the Swiss government and the International Committee of the Red Cross. Contradictory reports suggest that some fighters were released back to Boko Haram. About 200 girls remain in captivity (Maclean and Akinwotu, 2016).

Simulated Practices

In our simulations, the terrorists' given objectives included the release of five comrades from U.S. detention at Guantanamo Bay, but the role-players did not estimate as likely that the United States would release prisoners, so never pursued their release, beyond including all five objectives in their initial press releases.

Our Practical Assessments

We have found that more traditional Jihadi groups are keener on exchanging prisoners than demanding ransoms, if they demand anything at all.

By contrast, more recent and diabolical groups seem to resort to a demand for an exchange of prisoners only for publicity, to terrorize affiliated outsiders, or in a desperate attempt to escape military consequences.

9

Negotiating for Ransoms

In this chapter, we focus on terrorist demands for a cash ransom in exchange for their detainees. A cash ransom is not the only material demand hostage-takers can make—they may demand the exchange of prisoners, which is described in Chapter 10.

In each of this chapter's two main sections, we give

1. A review of the arguments on whether you should agree to the exchange
2. Our advice on how to understand and manipulate their motivations and obligations

Should You Pay for Hostages?

If the terrorists demand payment for hostages, then the official side's next consideration is whether to pay (Figure 9.1). We review seven considerations in the following sequential sections:

1. No: Paying ransoms to terrorists just funds more terrorism.
2. No: In many countries, policy or law prohibits any payments to terrorists.
3. Yes: Prominent governments have already defected on their commitments not to pay.
4. Yes: Governments have used third-party intermediaries to escape their own prohibitions.
5. No: Payments do not always cause the release of the hostage as intended.

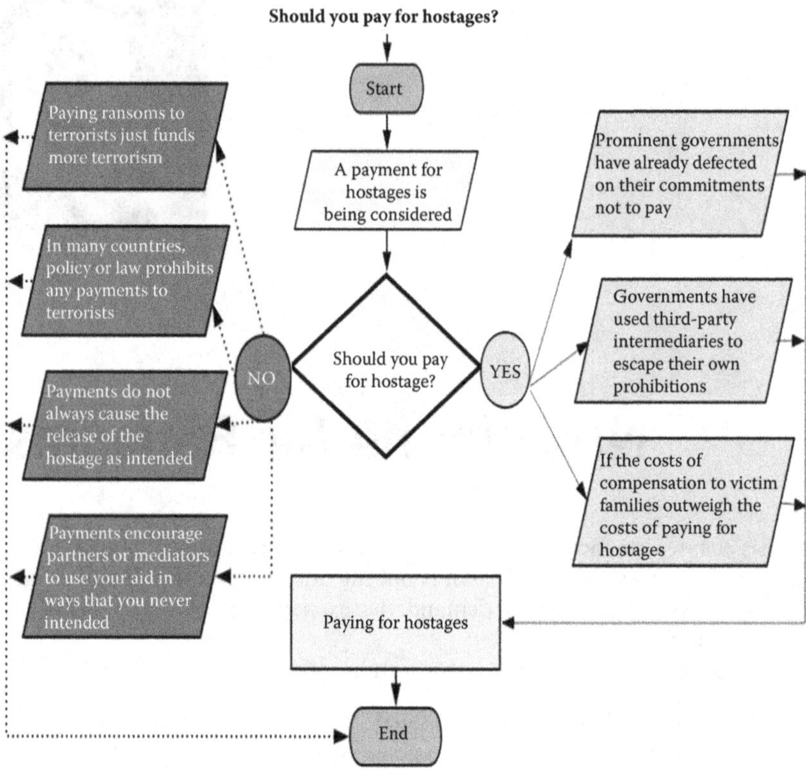

Figure 9.1 A flowchart considering the main debates about whether to pay for hostages.

6. No: Payments encourage your partners or mediators to use your aid in ways that you never intended.
7. Yes: If the costs of compensation to victim families outweigh the costs of paying for hostages.

No, Because Ransoms Fund More Terrorism

The arguments from Chapter 4, against concessions to terrorists on the grounds that such concessions encourage more terrorism, apply here. We have found some evidence in support of this expectation. For instance, in 2011, a year-long investigation (led by the U.S. military) concluded that a $2.16 billion transportation contract, which the U.S. government had funded in part to promote Afghan businesses, indirectly funded the Taliban in return for safe passage of convoys (DeYoung, 2011).

No, Given Policy or Law against It

Most developed countries have policies or laws against the resourcing of terrorists, which by extension prohibit the payments of ransoms to terrorists.

Some of these prohibitions are international:

- In 2013, the eight leading economies (G8) pledged not to pay ransoms to terrorists. This initiative was led by the United States and United Kingdom.
- On January 27, 2014, the UN Security Council adopted Resolution 2133, which called upon UN members not to pay ransoms.

The United States has its own domestic legal and political prohibitions against the payment of ransoms:

- The USA Patriot Act (October 26, 2001) prohibits any payment or assistance to terror groups that could boost their support, although no American has been prosecuted under this prohibition.
- The National Security Presidential Directive (also signed by President George W. Bush) of February 18, 2002, states that the U.S. government will not make substantive concessions, except for rare cases of ransoms for lure (i.e., to expose the takers to a tactical intervention).

On August 19, 2014, after the Islamic State released a video showing the beheading of James Foley (U.S. citizen, photojournalist), claiming retaliation for U.S. strikes in Iraq (which had started on August 8), the Department of State's deputy spokeswoman, Marie Harf, confirmed U.S. policy against paying ransoms: "We do not make concessions to terrorists. We do not pay ransoms. The United States government believes very strongly that paying ransom to terrorists gives them a tool in the form of financing that helps them propagate what they're doing. And so we believe very strongly that we don't do that, for that reason."

In August 2016, the Obama administration's press secretary (John Earnest) confirmed the policy, in response to accusations that U.S. transfer of cash to Iran in January 2016 was a ransom for four Americans released for Iranian detention, rather than official resolution of a longer-standing dispute about frozen assets: "Let me be clear, the United States does not pay ransom for hostages" (Shear, 2016).

However, the U.S. government does participate with third-party intermediates (TPIs) who pay ransoms, as explained below.

Yes, Given Many National Defections against Commitments Not to Pay

Even though the international commitments to avoid paying ransoms are strong, even the most legalist countries, including members of the G8, have paid ransoms. Unofficial reporting suggests that Austria, France, Italy, Spain, and Switzerland have paid for hostages in the last decade. Most expensively, France paid close to $60 million from 2010 to 2013 in exchange for five French nationals, albeit paid by a state-controlled French company rather than directly by the government. In March 2013, French President Francois Hollande declared that France would no longer pay for hostages, but in October four French nationals returned from captivity by Jihadis in Mali after a reported ransom of 20 million Euros, paid by a state-controlled company, using funds from France's secret service. Early in 2014, France secured the release of another four nationals, this time from Jihadis in Syria. In September 2014, Hollande repeated France's policy of not paying ransoms, but allowed for other countries "to help" France despite its policy, and uses these unnamed countries to explain the latest releases (RFI, 2013; Callimachi, 2014).

Given that so many prominent countries pay ransoms, leaving a minority of countries to refuse to pay any ransoms, the international commitments not to pay cannot be described as a norm, rather as an ideal. Without a norm, individual countries can easily defect on the ideal, and justify the payment of ransoms as in conformity with normative practice, albeit still in violation of international ideals.

Yes, If Using a Third-Party Intermediary

Even states with domestic laws against paying ransoms have facilitated the payment of ransoms through TPIs. Families or friends of the hostage may act effectively as TPIs, sometimes with official cooperation, or at least toleration. For instance, although U.S. law prohibits payment of ransoms to terrorists, the Federal Bureau of Investigation (FBI) has worked with families of victims to help their negotiations with the takers, even if the families choose to pay ransoms. The U.S. government has never prosecuted anyone for paying a ransom to terrorists. U.S. officials even cooperate in the process of paying a ransom. For instance, in 2012 the FBI provided intelligence to the family of Warren Weinstein, and vetted the Pakistani middleman, without officially approving the family's payment of $250,000 to Al Qa'ida (Entous and Barrett, 2015). However, in the latter case, the payment did not work as intended, as described in the following section.

In recent years, Western governments have increased the use of a few reliable TPIs. For instance, on August 24, 2014, Peter Theo Curtis (an American journalist, male, 45 years old) was released to the United Nations in Syria, 5 days after the Islamic State beheaded James Foley. Qatar brokered. A U.S. Department of States spokeswoman (Marie Harf) said Curtis's release followed a "direct request from the Curtis family itself to the Qatari government for its assistance." She declined to give further details, but stated: "The U.S. government does not make concessions to terrorists, which includes paying ransom. We did not do so in this case. We also do not support any third party paying ransom, and did not do so in this case. We are unequivocal in our opposition to paying ransom to terrorists."

Up to June 2015, the U.S. government's policy of criminalizing any payment of ransoms, by any party, essentially forced it to rely on private citizens or TPIs to pay ransoms in ways that did not violate policy. The U.S. use of TPIs has become easier given the looser policy that President Obama announced on June 24, 2015, allowing families to negotiate private ransoms. He clarified that U.S. "policy does not prevent communication with hostage-takers—by our government, the families of hostages, or third parties who help these families" (Roberts, 2015).

No, Because Ransom Payments Do Not Always Help

Sometimes a payment is made without causing the release of the hostage as intended. For instance, in 2012 the family of Warren Weinstein paid $250,000 for his release, after the FBI vetted the Pakistani middleman (without officially approving the payment), but the FBI warned that he might not be released, which proved correct. In January 2015, he was killed accidentally by a U.S. unmanned aerial vehicle attack on Al Qa'ida targets in a building in Pakistan, after which news of the payment emerged. White House Press Secretary Josh Earnest reasserted U.S. policy against such payments: "Unfortunately, this is a policy that's in place because ... paying ransom or offering a concession to a terrorist organization may result in the saving of one innocent life, but could put countless other innocent lives at greater risk" (Entous and Barrett, 2015).

Subsequently, a group contacted the U.S. government demanding money for return of his body. The United States refused, although Italy recovered the body of Giovanni Lo Porto, killed at the same time: Italy did not specify what it had done to obtain the body, but declined to comment on whether it had paid, which suggests that Italy did pay (Entous and Zampano, 2015).

One explanation for terrorist noncompliance with a ransom is that terrorists are unscrupulous and can be gratified to cause economic cost and psychological grief to the enemy at the same time.

Another explanation is that terrorists can be suspicious of cash payments. For instance, one of the documents captured when Usama bin Laden was killed on May 2, 2011, was a warning to Al Qa'ida's holders of an Afghan hostage that a "tracking chip" might be hidden in the suitcase used to deliver the cash. In separate documents, he warned of meetings with journalists who might be under surveillance, and even of going outside in clear weather due to possible surveillance (Strobel et al., 2016).

No, Because Ransoms Might Be Paid Out of Unintended Funds

The payment of ransoms by one government encourages other actors to pay ransoms, possibly with money provided by the first government for other purposes. For instance, from June to November 2010, Afghanistan paid $5 million to Al Qa'ida for release of the designated Afghan ambassador to Pakistan (Abdul Khaliq Farahi), who had been held since September 2008. Of the $5 million, $1 million came from a reserve built up from monthly Central Intelligence Agency cash payments to the Presidential Palace (Hamid Karszai), about $2 million came from the Pakistani government, and the rest came from Iran and Gulf state governments (Rosenberg, 2014).

Yes, Given the Costs of Compensation

Paying for hostages might be cheaper than paying compensation to hostages or their families for time spent in captivity, if the government is liable. In December 2015, the U.S. Congress and president passed a spending bill that included provision, to each hostage held at the U.S. Embassy in Tehran from 1979 to 1980, of up to $10,000 per day of captivity; some hostages were held for 444 days, for a value of $4,440,000 each hostage.

The family of Warren Weinstein, who was held by Al Qa'ida in Pakistan for 1,251 days from 2011 until killed by a U.S. air strike in January 2015, subsequently pointed out that his captivity would be worth up to $12,510,000 under the same rule, although the U.S. government rebuffed claims that it was liable under the same law. When the U.S. government acknowledged his death in April 2015, it promised an unspecified payment (O'Toole, 2016). In September 2016, the U.S. government agreed to pay nearly $3 million to the family of the Italian (Giovanni Lo Porto) who was killed at the same time but had not yet reached an agreement with the family of Weinstein (Miller and Jaffe, 2016).

Understanding and Manipulating Their Motivations and Obligations

New terrorist thinking and practice on ransoms are complex, so, in the following four sections, we review ideas for manipulating the ransom-seeking hostage-takers' motivations to official advantage:

1. For funds that the group will spend on further terrorist activities or associated bureaucratic activities
2. For subsistence and consumption of luxuries
3. For symbolic concession where more desirable concessions cannot be achieved
4. For religious duty or allowance

To Fund Terrorism

The Al Qa'ida [al.manual] (2004) listed "obtaining ransoms" as the fourth of the five objectives of hostage-taking and kidnappings. At least nominally, Al Qa'ida justifies these payments as funds for terrorism. For instance, from June to November 2010, Afghanistan paid $5 million to Al Qa'ida for release of the designated Afghan ambassador to Pakistan (Abdul Khaliq Farahi), after which Atiyah Abd al-Rahman wrote to Usama bin Laden: "God blessed us with a good amount of money this month." He promised that the money would be used for weapons and to compensate families of detained comrades (Rosenberg, 2014).

Other violent Jihadi groups, with more local aspirations, also claim to ransom to fund virtuous activities. For instance, since 2006, Pakistan has referred to Lashkar-e-Islam (*Urdu*: "Army of Islam")—already a designated terrorist group—as a "preeminent" militant and criminal group in Khyber Agency, in the Federally Administered Tribal Areas of Pakistan, and parts of Peshawar. It engages in drug trade, extortion, and kidnapping for ransom. Local drug smugglers, kidnappers, and extortionists aligned themselves with the group to come under its protection, but this caused it to lose legitimacy in the eyes of locals who previously tolerated the group to some degree. The group claims, "We are a force of Mujahiddeen. We have no criminals in our ranks and all the money generated from kidnappings is used for the noble cause of fighting social evils. This is allowed by Islam" (Nazir, 2011; Stanford University, 2012).

We conclude that the official side's best response to a hostage-taker that is seeking or claiming to seek funds to support terrorism is to characterize the hostage-taking as religiously or internationally unlawful, since such acts involve selfish profit seeking, and to target the publicity toward the terrorists' local community. Chapter 10 discusses how officials may draw from classical, early modern, and contemporary Islamic legal precepts to persuade Jihadi hostage-takers to release detainees, whereas international law may be used to persuade hostage-takers who might lack religious motivations.

Subsistence and Luxuries

Sometimes the motivation for material exchange is to finance basic subsistence or luxuries unrelated to the terrorist enterprise. For instance, the financing of basic subsistence seems likely only where the terrorists are poor for other reasons, or where their schemes for terrorism are abnormally expensive (normally the costs of terrorism are not barriers to entry).

Even where religious terrorists justify profit as a means to further terrorist ends (gaining money to spend on weapons, for instance), we have observed plenty of nominally pious terrorists who nonetheless spend money on secular luxuries, prostitutes, or just basic subsistence. Even where terrorists are well funded in developed countries, some have spent cash on items or services that seem incompatible with their religious claims, such as the hijackers who procured prostitutes and alcohol before 9/11. After 9/11, Anwar al-Awlaki was first arrested for soliciting prostitutes in 1996, and continued to procure prostitutes after 9/11, spending up to $400 a time for prostitutes until leaving the United States (his country of birth) in late 2002 in order to lead Al Qa'ida in the Arabian Peninsula (Yemen) until he was killed there in September 2011 (Cratty, 2013).

Some designated terrorist groups are explicitly Jihadi, but nonetheless, almost all their activities relate to profit making, as illustrated by the Abu Sayyaf Group and the Moro Islamic Liberation Front, both nominally committed to Muslim separatism from the Philippines, but with a long history of extortion and kidnapping for profit, dating back to the 1990s. They spend their profits on mostly their own consumption in underdeveloped areas of the Philippines, and remain relatively low-activity groups on the Jihadi scale. Effectively, such groups are thieves more than terrorists, without denying that they are certainly terrorist. They mix the most horrifying brutality with profit making from hostage-taking. For instance, on September 21, 2015, Abu Sayyaf kidnapped two Canadian men, a Norwegian man, and his Filipina girlfriend, for which Abu Sayyaf demanded huge ransoms. As its deadlines expired, Abu Sayyaf beheaded John Ridsdel in April 2016, and Robert Hall in June 2016, after Canada confirmed its policy against paying ransoms; in both cases, Abu Sayyaf released videos of the beheadings. Meanwhile, the kidnappers released the Filipina (Marites Flor). In September, they released the Norwegian (Kjartan Sekkingstad) and three Indonesian fishermen who had been kidnapped in July, after payments of at least $1 million (Butlangan, 2016). Abu Sayyaf has kidnapped at least 20 persons per year since 2014, when the group swore allegiance to ISIL. In the first 6 months of 2016, Abu Sayyaf earned at least $7.3 million from ransoms for 21 kidnappings (Gomez, 2016).

The official side's response should be to publicize the terrorists' self-enrichment and lack of piety, except where such publicity would interrupt current attempts to develop a relationship to the benefit of a current negotiation.

Symbolic Concession

The new terrorist's demand for material payments may be mostly symbolic, portrayed as an important concession by the other side, when the terrorist's true wants are impossible to fulfill. The financial demand can be seen as the terrorist side's valuation of its nonfinancial grievances or demands.

While the Islamic State treats local "apostate" communities as mass opportunities for material profit, it treats most detainees from outside the region as opportunities for demonstrating visceral violence. In most cases, the Islamic State has killed these detainees, without demanding anything before the killing, when it retrospectively blamed foreign policy. In a few strange cases, it demanded a ransom but conflated the demand with the foreign policy of the victim's home government. For instance, on January 20, 2015, ISIL posted video showing two Japanese citizens (Kenji Goto, a freelance journalist, and Haruna Yukawa, the chief executive officer of a private security firm, detained in August 2014), with the following statement:

> To the Japanese public, just as how your government has made the foolish decision to pay 200 million to fight the Islamic State, you now have 72 hours to pressure your government in making a wise decision by paying the 200 million to save the lives of your citizens. Otherwise this knife will become your nightmare.
>
> **(Shimbun, 2015b)**

This statement referred to a pledge of $200 million in nonmilitary assistance to Iraq by Japanese Prime Minister Shinzo Abe on January 18, 2015. On January 24, 2015, ISIL released a video showing the beheading of Yukawa, and a verbal statement by Goto, saying that ISIL "no longer wants money. So you don't need to worry about funding terrorists. They are just demanding the release of their imprisoned sister Sajida al-Rishawi [a terrorist convicted and imprisoned in Jordan]." On February 1, 2015, ISIL released a video showing Goto's beheading (Shimbun, 2015a,b,c).

The best explanation for ISIL's behavior toward this unfortunate detainee is that ISIL was seeking publicity, but uncertainly working out how to influence Japan politically, and gain money as a symbolic concession to ISIL's political grievances against Japan, even though its dominant intention was to kill the detainee on camera for publicity. Thus, ISIL killed the detainee on camera after failing to gain political concession or a ransom (Peritz and Walker, 2015).

Religious Duty or Allowance

Jihadi terrorists may perceive ransoming hostages as fulfilment of a religious duty, or at least as allowed under religious law, given the following quote from the Quran: "Therefore, when ye meet the unbelievers in fight, smite at their necks; at length, when ye have thoroughly subdued them, bind a bond firmly on them, then choose either generosity or ransom" (Quran, 47:4).

Islamic ethics and law are centered on the Quran, but include also the various other documents, interpretations, and historical events associated with the founding of the religion. Some interpreters of Islamic law suggest that ransom should be restricted to Muslim detainees held by non-Muslims:

> As regards Muslim subjects, it is the duty of the Muslim State to seek their release by giving money from the public treasury. The Qu'ran clearly [states] that a portion of the State income is to [be] allotted for freeing the necks, which is interpreted as aiding the prisoners and slaves to get themselves freed. There are clear Traditions [Hadith] of the Prophet also to the same effect recorded by Bukhari and others; for instance: "Manage to the release of the prisoner." As regards practice, I have not found any precedent of the time of the Prophet when ransom was paid for the release of Muslim prisoners. Exchange of prisoners will, however, be dealt with later. The Caliph Umar, however, ordered, "Every Muslim prisoner in the hands of non-Muslims must be relieved by means of the Muslim State treasury."
>
> **(Hamidullah, 1942, Chapter 15, rule 437)**

The same interpreter went on to suggest that Islamic law provides no obligations on the Muslim detainer of non-Muslims: "Muslim law leaves to the discretion of the commander to decide whether prisoners of war are to be (a) beheaded, (b) enslaved, (c) released [up]on paying ransom, (d) exchanged with Muslim prisoners, or (e) released gratis. We shall treat them separately" (Hamidullah, 1942, Chapter 15, rule 442).

Another Islamic scholar found historical examples of Muslim prisoners being exchanged for money or favor at the time of the creation of the religion, but still suggested no obligation: "The Holy Qur'an has legalised releasing prisoners of war on receipt of ransom in verse No. 4 of Surah 47... Release of prisoners on ransom, as already explained, also includes release in exchange. Several instances of the exchange of prisoners are found in the life of the Prophet; sometimes one for one, at others one for more." This scholar noted that the Quran allows for prisoners to be retained as slaves if they are not exchanged for favor or ransom. He noted that the Quran allows for the killing of prisoners in exceptional circumstances, which he did not specify (Chaudhry, 2003).

On the contrary, Muhammad Munir, scholar of Islamic law, cites the Quran, *hadith,* and specific jurists to argue that detainers are ethically and legally obliged to choose one of three options to terminate the captivity of prisoners of war: unconditional release, release upon a guarantee, or ransom. Munir (2011, p. 89) cites the Quran as follows to illustrate his thesis:

> Now when you meet [in war] those who are bent on
> denying the truth, smite their necks until you overcome them fully,

> and then tighten their bonds; but thereafter [set them free,]
> either by an act of grace or against ransom, so that the burden of
> war may be lifted: thus [shall it be].
>
> **(Quran, 47:4)**

Munir writes that the above verse "renders execution illegal and makes captivity a temporary affair that must lead to either unconditional or conditional freedom, or freedom bought with ransom" (Munir, 2011, pp. 89–90).

With Jihadi hostage-takers, the negotiator should try to persuade the other side to recognize the necessity of exchanging prisoners under religious, ethical, or legal obligations. While the scholarly consensus is against any Islamic ethical or legal obligation to ransom off detainees, the negotiator may deal with hostage-takers who are not as scholarly, and thus can be persuaded that they are under some obligation to the official side's advantage. Various studies theoretically and empirically support the conclusion that Jihadis are likelier to have cursory knowledge of the religion. This helps to explain the disproportionate migration of converts and Western-born Muslims into foreign Jihadi movements. Muslims with cursory knowledge of their religion are easier to manipulate by their Jihadi controllers (viciously) and by official negotiators (virtuously) (Barclay, 2011; Hassan, 2013; March and Revkin, 2015).

A negotiator might (probabilistically) succeed in persuading unscholarly Jihadis that their obligations are more peaceful and cooperative than they had initially believed. Having said that, some scholarly approaches to Islam, if so motivated, have been used to justify Jihad, as proven by terrorist leaders such as Usama bin Laden, who described himself as a Sheikh, scholar, and cleric of Islam.

10

Negotiating for Prisoners

While the previous chapter focused on cash ransoms, this chapter focuses on demands for the exchange of detainees.

This chapter informs officials of how to negotiate for the protection of detainees by taking advantage of international laws and religious laws, in ways most likely to sway the other side. International laws apply to any type of detainer. The chapter also aims to inform officials of how to negotiate with Jihadi extremists in particular (given their higher risks) using Islamic laws, standards of ethics prescribed by scholars of Islamic studies, and even standards articulated by violent Jihadis.

We caution officials against relying on domestic laws when negotiating for the release of prisoners with terrorists. First, terrorists tend to discriminate against certain nationalities and states, so references to domestic laws by the targeted state likely would be considered by terrorists as illegitimate, leaving the official side with no legal leverage unless the terrorists can be officially detained under criminal laws. Second, the use of domestic laws could exacerbate terrorist activity against representatives of the official jurisdiction. International and religious laws can be offered as higher than, or separate from, the domestic laws of any targeted state.

Jihadi terrorist groups might oppose international laws on grounds that they are biased toward Western standards of ethics and are diametrically opposed to Islamic standards of ethics. However, we show the many overlapping protections of detainees under both international and Islamic laws. For instance, officials will find that international laws that are agreed at the United Nations generally align with the international covenants of the Organization of Islamic Cooperation (OIC), which highlight human rights according to Islamic customs, and the Cairo Declaration on Human Rights in Islam (1990). Officials should also reference scholars of Islamic studies whose prescriptions align with their interests.

As in the last chapter, we proceed through two main sections:

1. A review of the arguments on whether you should exchange prisoners with terrorists
2. Our advice on how to understand and manipulate international and religious protections of prisoners

Should You Exchange Prisoners?

Even if the terrorist side seeks to exchange detainees, the official side may not want to cooperate. We acknowledge the same contrary argument as we acknowledged in Chapter 4 (any exchange encourages more hostage-taking or kidnappings). We also acknowledge the contrary argument that we acknowledged in Chapter 9 on paying ransoms (giving resources to terrorists just funds more terrorism). We do not repeat these contrary arguments here, except to acknowledge that they apply to both types of currency (ransoms and prisoners).

Historical Practices

Here we focus on the additional issue of precedents for the exchange of detainees. Even if the official side adopts a policy of not exchanging prisoners for hostages, the negotiator should expect the other side to bring up precedents, including three U.S. precedents from the 1980s alone:

- In 1979, U.S. President Jimmy Carter authorized the release of prisoners in exchange for American hostages held in Iran, which was concluded in January 1981.
- In 1985, U.S. President Ronald Reagan (who had been critical of Carter's handling of the crisis in 1980 before taking over in 1981) pressed Israel to release 756 Shi'a prisoners in exchange for the 146 surviving hostages on board TWA flight 847, of which 39 were American. (Greece had made a similar exchange already.)
- In the same year, his administration started to trade arms via Israel to Iran in exchange for American hostages. Israel was being paid for receiving arms that it was receiving nominally once, but was actually receiving twice. Some of the Israeli payments were diverted to support Nicaraguan insurgents known as "Contras," leading to the term "Iran-Contra affair" when disclosed in 1989.

At the time, the views of academic experts were critical of the Reagan administration, for the administration's defection from its own policy of not negotiating with terrorists, for negotiating through a designated state-sponsor of terrorism (Syria), and for being manipulated by the terrorists' clever use of the news media (Hudson, 1989, p. 322; Wardlaw, 1989, p. 153). "In the final analysis, the message conveyed to terrorist elements in the Middle East (and, in the longer term, elsewhere) was that the U.S. was a blustering giant, full of rhetoric, invective and brave statements of action, but incapable of or lacking the political will to take any real, effective action" (Wardlaw, 1989, p. 153). After the end of Reagan's administration, the exchanges of 1985 continued to be highlighted as an extreme example of concession to media-savvy hostage-takers, at a time when American news media were particularly interventionist against the policy of no-negotiation: "the most pernicious effect of the crisis was its validation of terrorism as a tactic" (Hoffman, 2006, p. 175).

More recently, in May 2014, the administration of U.S. President Barack Obama traded five members of the Afghani Taliban, detained at Guantanamo Bay for about 13 years, for United States Army Sergeant Bowe Bergdahl, who had been detained by the Haqqani Network since June 2009. Many Americans expressed concern about how this exchange would encourage more kidnappings, of whom one was Senator Ted Cruz (Republican from Texas), who said on ABC's *This Week*, on June 1, 2014: "What does this tell terrorists? That if you capture a U.S. soldier, you can trade that soldier for five terrorist prisoners?" A Taliban commander confirmed this expectation: he said that the swap has "made it more appealing for fighters to capture American soldiers and other high-value targets...It has encouraged our people. Now everybody will work hard to capture such an important bird" (Baker, 2014).

The United States is not alone in exchanging prisoners in recent years. Like the payment of ransoms for hostages by developed states that formally eschew the payments of ransoms (see Chapter 9), prisoners are exchanged by governments that formally eschew concessions to terrorists:

- Mali admitted in December 2014 that France cooperated in the release of four prisoners to Al Qa'ida in the Islamic Maghreb (AQIM) in exchange for the freedom of Frenchman Serge Lazarevic, who had been detained since 2011 (BBC, 2014).
- In March 2015, Iraq released five members of Al Qa'ida in exchange for an Iranian diplomat held by Al Qa'ida of the Arabian Peninsula (AQAP) (since July 2013) (Callimachi and Schmitt, 2015).
- On December 1, 2015, Qatar brokered the exchange of 13 Jihadis from Lebanese detention for 16 Lebanese soldiers and policemen held by the Nusra Front for 16 months previously—the Nusra Front had killed four detainees, one body of which it released in this exchange; nine Lebanese soldiers remained in the Nusra Front's custody (Perry and Bassam, 2015).
- In March 2016, after 2 years of intervention by a Saudi-led coalition in Yemen's latest civil war, which had killed more than 6,000 people and displaced millions by then, Saudi Arabia exchanged 109 Houthi rebels in return for nine Saudi soldiers (Al-Jazeera, 2016a).

Simulated Practices

In our real-world simulations (2015 and 2016), the hostage-takers referred to historical precedents, especially the trade for Bergdahl, in their attempts to persuade the U.S. side to concede to the release of 10 fictional comrades from U.S. detention.

Our Practical Prescriptions

We discourage officials from considering a prisoner swap. Precedents have encouraged routines in India, Pakistan, and Afghanistan, at least, and may have encouraged contradictory behavior by the more recent and diabolical groups. If any material exchange is to be considered, a ransom involves fewer detainees and seems more practical.

Understanding and Manipulating Their Motivations and Obligations

Officials should attempt to persuade extremists to release detainees by appealing to extremists' religious, moral, ethical, or legal obligations to do so. Even if the terrorists do not offer to exchange detainees, the official side should appeal to the new terrorist's legal, religious, moral, or ethical obligations to protect them.

Officials should characterize detainees as any or all of six categories of victims, in the following order of increasing complexity:

1. Low-value hostages
2. Able males
3. Children
4. Females
5. Noncombatants
6. Prisoners of war (POWs)

If officials fail to persuade extremists to recognize the detainees as falling into one category, then they should move on to the next category.

When negotiating with terrorists, officials should start with the legal, religious, moral, or ethical obligation that would be most advantageous to the official side—usually one that can be identified as developed or accepted by the other side (Figure 10.1).

International law applies to all groups, including nonstate actors such as terrorists, not just state actors. For religious law, we focus on Islamic and Jihadi obligations, given that Jihadi terrorism is riskiest. In conjunction with the following sections, the reader should remember Appendix A, which summarizes Islam's sects, some of which have competing religious, moral, ethical, or legal obligations by category of victim.

Low-Value Persons

Historical Practices

This book defines low-value hostages as anyone who is not a politician, ambassador, government agent, relative, or co-national of the targeted group.

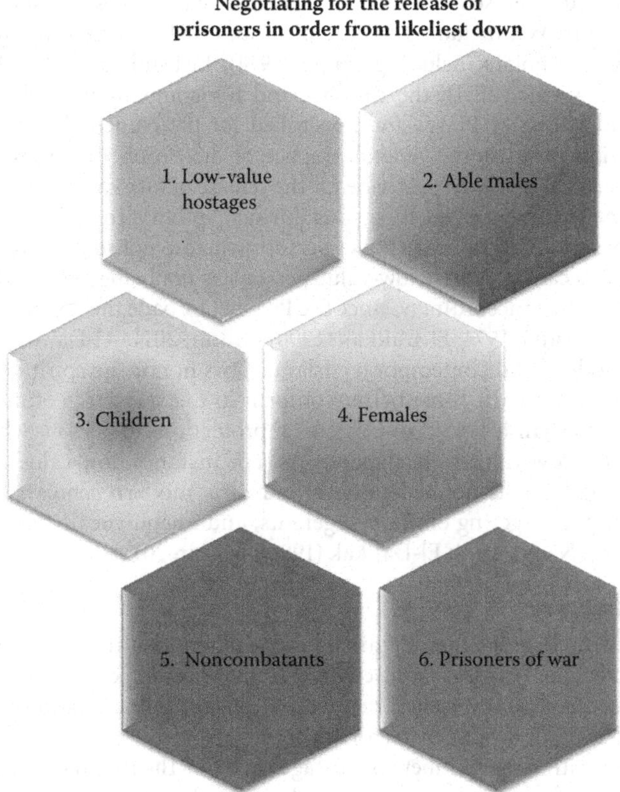

Figure 10.1 The six categories of hostages that can be beneficially categorized for their legal, religious, moral, or ethical protections, in order of increasing complexity.

International Law

International laws do not define "low-value persons"; however, they do protect all types of captives from violence, threats of violence, and discrimination. Officials should characterize low-value persons as falling into protected categories, such as POWs, civilians, women, and children, and they may refer to international laws related to the rights of the aforementioned categories. For instance, the UN Convention Relative to the Treatment of Prisoners of War protects persons of low value who are also POWs. The specifications concerning the rights of POWs according to this convention are detailed in the final section of this chapter—on POWs.

Islamic Law

Like international law, classical, early modern, and contemporary Islamic laws do not define "low-value persons." They do, however, grant protections to individuals who can be categorized as persons of low value, such as POWs, civilians, and children.

As specified in subsequent sections, classical Islamic laws prohibit the maltreatment of POWs, including torture or other cruel or degrading treatment. According to scholars including Naqvi (1974), El-Dakkak (1990), Al-Zuhili (2005), and Munir (2011), the Prophet and his companions prohibited the torture and killing of POWs and prescribed for their unconditional release. Thus, officials may use the general practice of the Prophet, and the juridical edicts of classical jurists to prescribe for the release of low-value POWs, and for the humane treatment of such persons during captivity. In addition, classical Islamic laws prohibit the targeting of persons who are not soldier-combatants. Thus, officials can categorize low-value persons as nonbelligerents and negotiate for their release accordingly, since the Prophet forbade the targeting of nonbelligerents (Naqvi, 1974; El-Dakkak (1990); Munir, 2011; Al-Dawoody, 2015).

Early modern and contemporary Islamic laws honor the spirit of classical Islamic precepts, while some better conform to the standards of modernity. Early modern Islamic laws provide general protections to persons who can be considered of low value to hostage-takers. For instance, low-value detainees can be categorized as nonbelligerents, and early modern scholars and clerics prohibit the targeting of nonbelligerents, and unequivocally prescribe for their release (Naqvi, 1974; El-Dakkak (1990); Munir, 2011).

Jihadi Practices

Terrorists tend to value their detainees to the extent that they are symbolic of the targeted side. Political representatives, ambassadors, or agents of the targeted government, or even their relatives, or at least their co-nationals, tend to be treated as of high value by terrorists.

In crises with large numbers of hostages (such as the illegal detention from 1979 to 1981 of Americans by Iran—a designated sponsor of terrorism), the hostage-takers have tended to separate the lower-value majority from the higher-value minority.

The Taliban (2010, p. 117) defined low-value persons as "common people," who are further characterized as persons who do not provide any means of support to their enemy combatants. Similarly, Al Qa'ida (2004) characterized persons who are not "influential" as those who are of lesser value to them. Both groups prohibit the targeting, kidnapping, or killing of low-value persons, since persons of lower value lack relative influence in the political or social affairs of the country in which they may be kidnapped.

Simulated Practices

In our real-world simulations, all sides were given the brief biographies of each of the notional hostages, including employment, rank, and relatives that would be considered of high value under our definition.

In the first simulation (2015), the hostage-takers recognized in advance that theoretically they should victimize any official representatives of the other side, the troublesome, or the most threatening hostages, although in this simulation the hostage-takers did not want to kill the high-value hostages first. Similarly, in the second simulation (2016), the terrorist side tried to leverage the high-value minority for official concessions.

Our Practical Prescriptions

Thus, officials should refer to historical precedents, some Jihadi precepts, and common sense as justifications for asking for the release of any hostage who can be categorized as of low value (Category 10.1).

However, this strategy may be counterproductive for the hostages who are left behind in an effective state of high value.

CATEGORY 10.1 Negotiating for the Release of Low-Value Hostages

INTERNATIONAL LAW

1. International laws protect all captives from violence, threats of violence, and discrimination. Refer to laws about the rights of POWs, civilians, females, and children, and attempt to categorize them as low-value hostages to negotiate for their safety and release.
2. All low-value persons who are POWs should be released if they are wounded, mentally or physically ill, or can no longer fight for any reason.
3. All low-value persons who are noncombatants are hostages, and they must be released since the taking of hostages is illegal in international law.
4. Hostages who are of low value to the official side will also be of low value to the detainers' side, so they should be released.
5. All low-value captives who are children (aged 18 or younger) must be released since it is illegal to detain children in international law.
6. All low-value hostages who are able males (aged 18 or older) capable of harming hostage-takers should be released.

CLASSICAL ISLAMIC PRESCRIPTIONS AND PROSCRIPTIONS

1. Classical Islamic practice does not account for "low-value hostages," but some classical legal precedents may be used to protect this category of captives.
2. For instance, only soldier-combatants were valid targets of interest. The targeting or capture of other persons who were not soldier-combatants was expressly forbidden (Munir, 2011, p. 94; El-Dakkak, 1990, p. 111; El Fadl, 1999, p. 149; Ibn Rushd, 1999, p. 458). Officials may characterize civilian captives as being of "low value" since they are not persons of interest who are susceptible to violence, war, or captivity.

EXTREMIST PRESCRIPTIONS AND PROSCRIPTIONS

1. Extremists define low-value persons as "common people" (civilians) (Taliban, 2010, p. 117), or those who are not "influential," such as public or government officials (Al Qa'ida, 2004).

2. Extremist groups stress the importance of *avoiding* lower-value targets. They emphasize utilizing their resources against persons of higher value, such as politicians or public officials. Al Qa'ida (2004) stresses the importance of targeting "important and influential persons," as does the Taliban (2010, p. 117).
3. Officials may characterize the hostages as persons of lower value since they may not have influence in political affairs, and to negotiate for their release.
4. The Taliban (2010, p. 117) characterizes "common people" (civilians) as persons of low value. Officials may characterize the hostages as "common people" or civilians who should be released since they have little power or influence in government affairs, and since extremist groups forbid targeting such types of people, anyway.
5. Officials might characterize types of hostages, such as women, children, and elderly persons as being of low value to detainers, and negotiate for the gradual release of each category of hostage.

EARLY MODERN ISLAMIC PRESCRIPTIONS AND PROSCRIPTIONS

1. Early modern law does not define low-value hostages; however, early modern legal precedents may be used to protect low-value targets.
2. The taking of captives who are not soldier-combatants is expressly forbidden. Thus, officials may characterize civilians as being of lower value and negotiate for their release since civilians are not to be taken captive.
3. Low-value hostages may not be harmed, killed, or exploited in any way while in captivity.
4. Low-value persons are to be fed and clothed.
5. Low-value persons have the right to communicate with their families until they are released.
6. Officials may remind detainers that captivity is regarded as a temporary condition by the most literal interpretation of the Quran (47:4)—by the decree and general practice of the Prophet, by the decree of his successors, by the decree of classical jurists and early modern jurists—and that the captives should therefore be released eventually if not expediently.

CONTEMPORARY ISLAMIC PRESCRIPTIONS AND PROSCRIPTIONS

1. Officials should attempt to categorize relevant POWs, civilians, women, children, and able males as low-value hostages and negotiate for their safety and release using Islamic laws and scholarly prescriptions.
2. Hostages who are of low value to the official side will also be of low value to the detainers' side, so they should be released.
3. All low-value captives who are hostages must be released since the taking of hostages is forbidden in Islam.

4. All low-value hostages who are females and not soldier-combatants should be released since it is forbidden to hold noncombatant female captives in Islam.
5. All low-value captives who have no beards or who have not reached maturity are children, and children are not to be held captive in Islam, so they should be released.
6. All low-value hostages who are able males can be threatening to hostage-takers, so they should be released.

Able Males

Historical Practices

Able males are males who have the capacity to harm or threaten detainers. Able males tend to be middle aged or younger.

International Law

International law does not define able males; thus, special protections concerning able males are not specified in any legal convention. However, international law protects broad categories of persons including civilians, children, and POWs. Officials can follow the prescriptions of international laws and attempt to categorize as many able-male detainees as possible as either civilians, children, or POWs. For instance, civilians who are taken against their will are classified as "hostages" in international law, and hostage taking is internationally illegal. Thus, officials might characterize all able-male detainees as hostages under international law and urge for their release.

Islamic Law

Classical, early modern, and contemporary Islamic laws do not define "able males"; however, each type of jurisprudence grants protections to other categories of captives, such as civilians, children, and POWs. Thus, officials may characterize able males as persons who are protected by Islamic laws such as civilians or children, or POWs.

Early modern and contemporary Islamic laws draw inspiration from the classical period. While no definition of "able males" exists in any Islamic legal doctrine, rights are afforded to other categories of males (and females) who are taken captive, such as civilians, children, and POWs. Officials may characterize young able males as falling under either of the aforementioned categories. Since the general consensus of early modern scholars and religious clerics lies against the targeting of civilians (Hamidullah, 1942; Naqvi, 1974; Chaudhry, 2003; Munir, 2011), officials can urge for the release of able males who are civilians.

Jihadi Practices

The Al Qa'ida manual explicitly targets able males because of their capacity for resistance:

> You must check the hostages and take possession of any weapon or listening device. Separate the young people from the old, the women and the children. The young people have more strength, hence their ability to resist is high. The security forces must be killed instantly. This prevents others from showing resistance.
>
> **(Al Qa'ida, 2004)**

Some sources suggest that officials should ask for the release of able males, as early as possible, as they are most threatening to the hostage-takers (Dolnik and Fitzgerald, 2011, p. 280).

Simulated Practices

In simulation (2015), the hostage-takers recognized that they should release strong or observant hostages early, before they can threaten the hostage-takers or gather intelligence, but contradictorily did not want to release anybody at all.

Our Practical Prescriptions

Officials should negotiate for the early release of able males, without explicitly drawing attention to their abilities (Category 10.2). Officials should rely on the hostage-takers' subconscious discomfort with able males who could threaten them, rather than draw attention to the potential for able males to threaten them, otherwise the hostage-takers could terminate the risks entirely by killing the able males immediately.

CATEGORY 10.2 Negotiating for the Release of Able Males

INTERNATIONAL LAW

1. Refer to international laws about the rights of POWs, civilians, and children, and attempt to categorize them as able males to negotiate for their safety and release.
2. Hostage takers should release young, able males who are over 18 because they are most threatening to them.
3. All young, able males who are under 18 are children, so they should be released. These can include able males who are adolescents and teenaged persons.

CLASSICAL ISLAMIC PRESCRIPTIONS AND PROSCRIPTIONS

1. Able male prisoners have been executed for crimes committed before their capture—that is, the soldier-combatants of Banu Quraydha were ordered to be executed by the decree of S'ad bin Mu'ad for betraying their alliance to the Prophet when they fought against him in battle (Munir, 2011, p. 91; Saleymeh, 2008, p. 538).

2. The common consensus among jurists is that no prisoner should be executed if it would harm the welfare of Muslims, or their governments (El-Dakkak, 1990, pp. 101, 109–110; El Fadl, 1999, p. 153).
3. Captured able male soldiers who fought against the Prophet during the Battle of Banu Quraydha were executed. The justification for their execution stems from the charge that the tribe betrayed their alliance with the Prophet by joining his enemies in battle against him (Munir, 2011, p. 91; Salaymeh, 2008, p. 538).

EXTREMIST PRESCRIPTIONS AND PROSCRIPTIONS

1. Extremist manuals do not explicitly define "able males," but some offer prescriptions as to how they should handle younger, more agile males during captivity.
2. Al Qa'ida (2004) describes younger persons as being threatening to hostage takers. Officials can persuade hostage takers to release younger persons to alleviate potential threats to the hostage takers.
3. Al Qa'ida forbids the involvement of "minors" in their activities. They imply "minors" are aged 14 or younger (2000, p. 17). Officials may characterize some young able males, such as adolescent teenagers, as minors, and negotiate for their release.
4. Extremist groups stress the importance of utilizing their resources against persons of higher value, such as politicians or public officials. Al Qa'ida (2004) stresses the importance of targeting "important and influential persons," as does the Taliban (2010, p. 116). Officials can characterize able males as persons of lesser value and negotiate for their release.
5. Officials may characterize able males as "common people" or noncombatant civilians who do not provide assistance to enemy combatants, and can negotiate for their release since extremist groups prohibit the targeting of such persons (Taliban, 2010, p. 117).

EARLY MODERN ISLAMIC PRESCRIPTIONS AND PROSCRIPTIONS

1. Early modern practice does not define able males; however, early modern Islamic legal precepts can be used to protect able males and to encourage their release.
2. Able males may be categorized as persons who are also civilians, and should therefore be released since the taking of civilians is forbidden.
3. Even if the prisoners are soldier-combatants, they are protected from violence, including execution.
4. If the prisoners are soldier-combatants, then they should be released unconditionally, released upon a guarantee (for exchange of prisoners, for instance), or released upon monetary ransom.

5. All able male POWs are not to be tortured, mutilated, or treated inhumanely in any fashion while in captivity.
6. Able males must be fed and clothed appropriately.
7. All captive able males must be granted the right to communicate to their families upon their capture.

CONTEMPORARY ISLAMIC PRESCRIPTIONS AND PROSCRIPTIONS

1. Islamic law does not define able males but often defines adult males, or persons allowable for combat, as males who have grown a beard or who have reached maturity. Young able males in Islam can range from persons who are aged 12 years to those who are middle aged.
2. All able males who are hostages should be released since the taking of hostages is forbidden in Islam.
3. All able male POWs should be released, even if desired concessions are not given to detainers.

Children

Historical Practices

Children generally enjoy special protections under international law and religious law. They are usually prohibited from combat, which helps to justify their normal status as victims or especially at-risk subjects, who should be threats, or of any high value to the hostage-takers.

International Law

The UN Convention on the Rights of the Child (UNCRC) grants special protections to children (UNCRC, 1989). The underlying principle of the convention implies that actors must behave in accordance with the best interests of children. The UNCRC defines "child" as "every human being below the age of eighteen years," unless the domestic laws of a country define "child" otherwise (Article 1).

The UNCRC protects children from violence, so officials can refer to its laws to protect children from harm while they are in captivity. Article 2 of the UNCRC prohibits all forms of discrimination against children, including those who are disabled (Article 23).

Article 6 of the convention grants every child the right to life.

Article 9 of the UNCRC states that children are never to be separated from their parent(s) or guardian(s) against their will, unless a state's judicial body determines that separation is necessary for the welfare of the child. If a child must be separated from his or her guardian, then the child must still be given the opportunity to communicate with the guardian(s) from which he or she is separated, unless continued contact would not be in the best interests of the child.

Article 11 prohibits all forms of trafficking of children.

Articles 12, 13, and 14 grant children the right to freedom of expression, thought, and religion.

Article 15 grants children the right to peacefully assemble in protest, unless such an assembly threatens the freedoms of others, or threatens national security in a democratic society.

Article 16 of the convention grants children the right to privacy. Articles 19, 34, 35, and 36 prohibit all forms of exploitation of children.

Article 20 demands that children who are exploited in any form must be taken from the environments in which they are exploited and be placed in the special care of responsible authorities.

Article 24 grants children the right to medical care that fulfills their needs, as well as hygienic quarters.

Article 37 prohibits the torture of children.

Article 38 prohibits the use of children under 15 years of age in armed combat.

Article 40 protects children who are accused of committing crimes, and grants them the right to privacy, legal defense, and fair judicial proceedings.

Religious Law

While Western laws tend to define "children" by age, Islamic definitions of "children" tend to be characterized as persons who have not reached puberty. The Prophet prohibited males aged 14 or younger from being used in combat. Most Islamic scholars indicate that male children tend to be aged 14 or less, whereas female children tend to be aged 8 or less (Islam, 2015). Some Islamic scholars note that the exact age range of childhood is disputed since children can reach puberty at different ages (Islam, 2015, p. 179). The Afghani Taliban defines "children" as "youngsters who have no beard," who "are not allowed to be taken for Jihad" because of their youth (Taliban, 2009, p. 10).

Officials may cite classical Islamic prescriptions to negotiate for the release of children characterized as those who had reached the age of maturity. According to the Prophet, children were never to be killed, even if children were used in combat by the Prophet's enemies. Children were not to be targeted or captured. If they were captured, then they could not be treated inhumanely or killed (Munir, 2011, p. 94; El-Dakkak, 1990, p. 111).

Negotiators can refer to contemporary Islamic laws and conventions that protect children. For instance, the OIC established the "Covenant on the Rights of the Child in Islam" (CRCI). Article 6.2 states that children must be guaranteed "the basics necessary for the survival and development of the child and for his/her protection from violence, abuse, exploitation, and deterioration of his/her living and health conditions" (OIC, 2004, p. 5).

Furthermore, Article 8.2 of the CRCI declares that "no child shall be separated from his/her parents against their will, and parents shall not have their guardianship revoked." The OIC's prescriptions apply to all children—not only to those born into Muslim families. By these standards, negotiators can ask for the release of all children from captivity, since all children have a right to live freely from "violence," "abuse," and "exploitation." Specifically, children must not be exploited for labor, sex trafficking, military combat, or any other interests of detainers.

Simulated Practices

Our real-world simulations included biographies of all notional hostages, which included the ages and genders of all hostages, but in neither simulation did the terrorist role-players make an issue of the age of any hostage.

Our Practical Prescriptions

Officials should ask for the release of all children, on the grounds that international laws and religious laws grant special protections to children, children are noncombatants, children are usually of no threat to hostage-takers, and children are usually of lower value than adults.

Officials can extend the number of children among the hostages by claiming that children are not just persons under a certain age, but any older persons who have not yet matured to offer the capacities typical of adults, such as physical strength or social influence.

The ambiguity of adulthood in Islamic law gives official negotiators the opportunity to negotiate for the release of children of greater age than would be considered children normally in Muslim societies: a useful opening demand would be for the release of all persons up to the normative age of adulthood in Western societies (18 years).

The negotiator should refer to precedents for the Jihadi release of children. For instance, at the school in Beslan in Russia (2004), on the second day of the siege, the hostage-takers (Chechen-Ingush Jihadi separatists) released 11 nursing mothers and 15 babies, even though they did not release hundreds of other female adults and children.

The negotiators may help themselves toward this objective if they characterize children as materially unrepresentative of the Jihadi's enemy, just as they should characterize noncombatants as protected in ways more familiar to Jihadis (see previous discussion). New terrorists often characterize their victims as not innocent, as taxpayers or voters for the government that has aggrieved the Jihadis. This suggests that the negotiator can take advantage of this characterization by asking for the release of children who neither pay taxes nor vote (Dolnik and Fitzgerald, 2011, p. 289).

Officials can attempt to ensure the safety of children by referring to laws during negotiations to dissuade hostage-takers from harming them (Category 10.3).

Officials may cite from the UNCRC to remind detainers to tolerate other rights granted to children as they remain in captivity.

Officials may cite both the UNCRC's Article 9 and the CRCI's Article 8.2 to persuade hostage-takers to release children altogether, on grounds that they have been unlawfully separated from their guardians. They may use these same articles to allow children in captivity to communicate with their families before they are released.

Officials can cite the UNCRC's Article 20 and the CRCI's Article 6.2 to protect children from any exploitation.

CATEGORY 10.3 Negotiating for the Release of Children

INTERNATIONAL LAW

1. Children are protected by international laws.
2. Children are all persons under 18 years of age.
3. Children are not to be detained or held hostage; they must be released immediately.
4. Children are protected from violence and all forms of exploitation.
5. Children are not to be used in combat.
6. Children are not to be forced into marriage.

CLASSICAL ISLAMIC PRESCRIPTIONS AND PROSCRIPTIONS

1. Children were characterized as those who had reached the age of maturity; however, the Prophet prohibited males aged 14 or younger from being used in combat.
2. Children were never to be killed, even if children were used in combat by the Prophet's enemies (Munir, 2011, p. 94; El-Dakkak, 1990, p. 111).
3. Children were not to be targeted or captured. If they were captured, then they could not be treated inhumanely or killed.

EXTREMIST PRESCRIPTIONS AND PROSCRIPTIONS

1. Extremists generally define children as persons who have not reached maturity (Taliban, 2010, p. 118; Islamic State of Iraq and the Levant [ISIL], 2014). However, the rights of children vary by different terrorist organizations.
2. It can be inferred that children are afforded the same protections as "common people," or civilians, since they are least likely to provide services to enemy combatants (Taliban, 2010, p. 117).
3. It can be inferred that children should be released from captivity since they are not to be targeted, anyway (Taliban, 2010, p. 117).
4. It can be inferred that children are of lesser value to detainers, so they should be released (Taliban, 2010, p. 116).
5. Children may not be used in combat (Taliban, 2010, p. 118).
6. Al Qa'ida prohibits the recruitment of persons who are 14 years or younger (2000, p. 17).
7. Al Qa'ida (2004) implies that children should be released.
8. It can be inferred that children are not to be killed, captured, or ransomed (Taliban, 2010, p. 117).
9. It can be inferred that children are to be protected from violence (Taliban, 2010, p. 120).
10. ISIL justifies the enslavement and sexual enslavement of children (ISIL, 2014a).
11. ISIL justifies the use of child soldiers, even if they have not reached maturity.

12. Children who are sold into slavery may not be sold separately from their parents (ISIL, 2014a). It can be inferred that children may not be separated from their parents.
13. Enslaved children or children held in captivity should be freed as this will ensure a fighter's place in paradise (ISIL, 2014a).

EARLY MODERN ISLAMIC PRESCRIPTIONS AND PROSCRIPTIONS

1. Children are persons who have not reached maturity.
2. Children are not to be targeted for any reason.
3. Children are not to be taken hostage.
4. Children are not to be separated from their parents.
5. Children are not to be exploited or abused in any fashion.

CONTEMPORARY ISLAMIC PRESCRIPTIONS AND PROSCRIPTIONS

1. Children are protected by contemporary Islamic laws.
2. Children are all persons who have not reached maturity.
3. Children are protected from violence and all forms of exploitation.
4. Children are not to be separated from their parents against their will.
5. Children are not to be held hostage, and they must be released immediately.
6. Children are not to be used in combat.
7. Children are not to be forced into marriage.

Females

Both international law and religious law recognize females as a category deserving of special protections and accommodations.

Historical Practices

International Law

If the hostage-takers are receptive to international law, officials should start with the UN Convention on the Elimination of All Forms of Discrimination Against Women[1] (United Nations, 1979b), which demands that women benefit equally as men, and that they be treated humanely. The convention prohibits all forms of discrimination, including violence like that of rape and human trafficking against women at all times. For instance, Article 6 of the convention prohibits "[human] traffic[king] of women, and exploitation or prostitution of women." Furthermore, officials can cite Article 16 of CEDAW, which prohibits forced marriages, and stresses the right of women to freely choose their spouses.

Similarly, Article 14 of the Geneva Convention Relative to the Treatment of Prisoners of War specifies that women must be granted the same protections as men, and must be accommodated according to the needs of their sex, which could be used to suggest that women need special accommodation.

[1] Available at: http://www.ohchr.org/Documents/ProfessionalInterest/cedaw.pdf

In addition, Part III, Section II, Chapter II, Article 25 specifies that male POWs must live separately from female POWs, and they must be accommodated according to their sex.

More gravely, the official side could attempt to ensure the safety of female captives by referring to the UN Convention on the Prevention and the Punishment of the Crime of Genocide (1948), which prohibits acts of intentional violence or discrimination against an identity group (genocide). Specifically, the systematic rape of females—whether in captivity or not—constitutes genocide (ICTR, 1998). Thus, any act of imprisonment of females with the intent to harm them, sexually enslave them, force them into marriages (which can lead to rape), or rape them can constitute the crime of genocide against female captives.

Officials should also consider referring to the UN Declaration on the Elimination of Violence Against Women (1993), which prohibits all forms of violence against women, and prohibits actors from claiming cultural, traditional, or religious rights as justifications for committing abuses against women (Articles 2, 3, and 4).

Religious Law

The official side can refer to contemporary Islamic laws and conventions that protect women, to negotiate for their release and to discourage inhumane treatment of female captives.

Officials may cite the Prophet, who is reported to have specified that females were not to be targeted or taken captive. Later classical jurists ruled that women were not to be targeted unless they were actively participating in hostilities. In the event that they were captured, they were not to be killed (El-Dakkak, 1990, p. 119; El Fadl, 1999, p. 159; Munir, 2011).

Officials should refer to classical Islamic and early modern Islamic scholars who proscribe against the targeting of sexual enslavement, and rape of females, including during times of war. Both Shi'a and Sunni clerics can be cited, depending on the denomination of the takers. An early modern Shi'a cleric, Ayatollah Ali-al Sistani (2010), flatly "prohibits the enslavement and rape [Arabic: *ightisab*] of women during warfare, and forbids sex with non-Muslim [captives]." His office further notes that rape "is a great sin, and the punishment is death, if proved".

Sunni cleric Omar Suleiman (2016) condemns the practice of enslavement of any kind by terrorist groups, stating that "reintroducing the institution of slavery is deviant in of itself" and that the act of rape "is considered one of the most grievous sins in Islam, it [is] considered *haram*...[and] warrants capital punishment." Saudi Arabian Sunni cleric, Sheikh Mohammad Saleh al-Munajjid (2009) also states that the punishment for those who rape is death. He further notes that those who rape while threatening the use of a weapon against their victim must face punishment according to the Quran (Al-Ma'idah, 5:33), which calls for either death, crucifixion, amputation of hands and feet, or exile.

The OIC proscribes against "all forms of discrimination, including violence against women" and "early and forced marriages," and it condemns "gender-based violence in all its manifestations, [es]specially domestic violence, trafficking in human beings, particularly women and girls, harmful traditional practices, and violence against migrant women" (OIC, 2008, pp. 5–6).

Jihadi Practices

Terrorist groups tend to exploit female captives by subjecting them to crimes against humanity such as rape, sexual slavery, or other forms of trafficking (Chan and Sengupta, 2016). In other cases, females, including children, have been forced to marry terrorist captors (Human Rights Watch, 2014).

New terrorists tend to be highly gendered, mostly for conservative religious reasons. (European communist terrorists have tended to stray most from gender norms, although their practices tend to be more hypocritical than their rhetoric.) Most terrorists, and more new terrorists, are male, who prefer to separate women and men—both in their terrorist activities and their hostages. For instance, during the siege of the theater in Moscow in 2002, the Chechen Jihadi hostage-takers progressively separated men and women, and separated Russians from non-Russians, where Russian males were most at risk (Dolnik and Fitzgerald, 2008, p. 77).

Many Jihadi manuals advise against targeting women, at least Muslim women. Al Qa'ida's manual on kidnapping refers to hostages with male pronouns, and urges hostage-takers to "Avoid looking at women." This suggests that they would be relieved to release women first. However, the same manual contains a warning against the advantages to the official collector of intelligence: "When releasing hostages such as women and children, be careful, as they may transfer information that might be helpful to the enemy" (al Qa'ida, 2004).

Moreover, the Islamic State (2014a) has publicized its rulings that non-Muslim female prisoners are the captor's personal properties that can be used as slaves, including sex slaves, and as gifts or items or exchange, without mention of release. Although its Point 27 states that a Jihadi would be rewarded by God for releasing an enslaved woman, apparently it means an enslaved woman held by the enemy.

Furthermore, the Islamic State has related that during the initial attack on the office of the magazine "Charlie Hebdo" in January 2015, the attackers (Chérif and Said Kouachi) were heard by their victims to say "we do not kill women" and "we do not kill civilians." When the brothers were cornered in their final refuge, French "police first thought the hostage was a woman, so they thought they could take advantage of the fact that the men 'do not kill women', However, they were saddened when they realized the hostage was a male" (Islamic State of Iraq and Levant, 2015, p. 56) This narrative can be interpreted in both positive and negative ways: positively, the narrative adds to the precedents for ISIL to proscribe harm to females; but negatively, the narrative suggests that future perpetrators could exploit the official side's expectations.

Meanwhile the Islamic State has justified the sexual enslavement and rape of non-Muslim and Muslim women (Callimachi, 2015; Silverman, 2015; Yehoshua et al., 2015).

A self-described female Jihadi has written a manual on the role of women in Jihad, which asserts some traditional roles, such as raising children, but obliges women to raise their children as Jihadis, and allows for women to fight in the Jihad, suggesting that the traditional separation of women as noncombatants will not apply in future hostage-takings (Sister Al, 2005).

Simulated Practices

Our real-world simulations specified all-male hostage-takers with about half as many female as male hostages, but in neither simulation (2015 or 2016) did the terrorist role-players discriminate women from men in any functional way.

Our Practical Prescriptions

The official side should attempt to draw the hostage-takers' attention to the strong international legal and religious legal prohibitions on discriminating against women and particularly against sexual violence against women (Category 10.4).

The official side should characterize female hostages as especially protected and unthreatening compared to able males. However, this strategy may be counterproductive in leaving males exposed.

The official side can exploit Jihadi precedents for not targeting females, although again this leaves males comparatively exposed.

CATEGORY 10.4 Negotiating for the Release of Females

INTERNATIONAL LAW

1. Females are protected by international laws.
2. All female captives are protected against violence, and all forms of exploitation, including rape and forced marriage.
3. All noncombatant females must be released.
4. All females require special accommodations according to their gender; they must be physically separated from men.
5. All female detainees must benefit equally as all men.
6. Detainers may not claim cultural or religious right to deny women of these protections.

CLASSICAL ISLAMIC PRESCRIPTIONS

1. Females were not to be targeted or taken captive, unless they were actively participating in hostilities. In the event that they were captured, they were not to be killed (El-Dakkak, 1990, p. 119; El Fadl, 1999, p. 159; Munir, 2011).

2. The women of the Banu Quraydha tribe were enslaved by the decree of S'ad bin Mu'ad as punishment for the tribe's male fighters who had reportedly betrayed their alliance with the Prophet by fighting against him in battle (Munir, 2011, p. 91).

EXTREMIST PRESCRIPTIONS AND PROSCRIPTIONS

1. The rights of females may vary by different Jihadi insurgent groups.
2. The rights of females are not mentioned by Al Qa'ida (2006) or the Taliban (2009, 2010).
3. The Taliban proscribes against targeting, capturing, and ransoming common people, which can include females who do not provide services to enemy combatants (Taliban, 2010, pp. 117, 120).
4. It can be inferred that females who do not support enemy combatant efforts are civilians, and they should therefore be released if they are captured.
5. It can be inferred that the rights granted to enemy soldiers are applied to female soldiers as well. Thus, captured female soldiers are not to be tortured or exposed to extreme temperatures (Taliban, 2010, p. 108).
6. If the female soldiers are Muslim, then they cannot be ransomed, and may instead be considered for unconditional release, release upon a guarantee, exchange for prisoners, or execution upon the jurisdiction of an appointed Imam or judge (Taliban, 2010, p. 107).
7. If the female soldiers are non-Muslim, then they may be considered for ransom, unconditional release, release upon a guarantee, prisoner exchange, or execution upon the jurisdiction of an appointed Imam or judge (Taliban, 2010, p. 108).
8. If a female captive is known to have supplied enemies with material support, then she may be killed in the process of being captured (Taliban, 2010, p. 108).
9. If a female is suspected to be involved in supplying enemies with material support, then she may be tried in court and sentenced to death if it is proved that she was involved supplying enemies with material support (Taliban, 2010, p. 107).
10. "Unbelieving women," specifically Christians, Jews, and polytheists, may be captured and taken as wives or slaves (ISIL, 2014a).
11. "Apostate" women (women who have renounced their faith) may not be taken as captives (ISIL, 2014a).
12. Females can be bought or sold as personal property and may be used as concubines (ISIL, 2014a).
13. Females may not be separated from their prepubescent children (ISIL, 2014a).
14. Females may not be sold if they become impregnated by their captor (ISIL, 2014a).
15. The release of female captives or slaves will be met with the reward of paradise (ISIL, 2014a).

EARLY MODERN ISLAMIC PRESCRIPTIONS

1. Females who are not soldier-combatants are not to be taken as captives; they must be released if they are held captive.
2. Females may not be killed, tortured, or abused; the sexual enslavement of women is expressly forbidden.
3. Females are to be fed, clothed, and separated from males in the event that they are captured.
4. Females are not to be separated from their children.

CONTEMPORARY ISLAMIC PRESCRIPTIONS AND PROSCRIPTIONS

1. Females are protected by contemporary Islamic laws.
2. Females are protected against violence and all forms of exploitation, including rape and forced marriage.
3. All females must benefit equally as men.
4. Females who are not soldier-combatants are not to be held in captivity.
5. Detainers do not have the religious right to deny women these protections since Islam forbids the capture and mistreatment of women, and they cannot claim cultural right since religious law (God's rule) is to be held above cultural norms (man's rule).

Noncombatants

Historical Practices

International Law

Rule 5 of Customary International Human Rights Law generally defines noncombatants as persons who do not fight in armed conflict, even if they serve armed forces that fight in armed conflict while they serve in a noncombatant role (ICRC, 2016). For instance, medical and religious personnel belonging to armed forces qualify as noncombatants since they do not fight in conflict as regular members of the armed forces.

Other types of noncombatants are civilians, who are afforded special protections under International Human Rights Law. The UN Geneva Convention (IV) Relative to the Treatment of Civilians further specifies all rights granted to civilians and noncombatants during all forms of armed conflict, including international wars.

Religious Law

Officials may also appeal to classical, early modern, and contemporary Islamic prescriptions to negotiate for the release of low-value persons.

Islamic scholars have tended to separate legitimate violence against combatants from illegitimate violence against noncombatants. Unfortunately, the prescription is confused by the ambiguity about what makes a noncombatant, at least compared to the understanding of "noncombatant" in the Western tradition. Consequently, the negotiator should be prepared to characterize noncombatants in more exclusive forms that are familiar to Jihadis. For instance, one Islamic scholar proscribes the following:

- All cruel ways of killing
- Decapitation of prisoners
- Fornication with captured women
- Mutilation (both men and beasts)
- Destruction of crops and cattle
- Killing noncombatant women, youths, servants, and slaves, even if serving combatant masters
- Killing noncombatant peasants, traders, merchants, and contractors
- Killing the old, the mentally deficient, the physically deformed, the blind, monks, and hermits (Hamidullah, 1942)

Negotiators should cite moderate interpretations from early modern Islamic scholars, or classical Islamic prescriptions that would be most helpful to the official side in negotiating for their release. Most usefully, scholars frequently proscribe against the killing of captured civilians. For instance, Dr. Shehzad Saleem warns, "Muslims who kill innocent civilians must know that they are violating the directives of Islam and committing a crime against humanity" (Saleem, 2002). Saleem substantiates his argument by citing the Quran:

> He who killed a human being without the latter
> being guilty of killing another or being guilty of spreading
> disorder in the land should be looked upon as if he
> had killed all mankind.
>
> **(Quran, 5:32)**

Additionally, Shi'a cleric Ayatollah Sayyid Ali al-Sistani (2015) cites the edicts of the Prophet Mohammad's progeny, who instructed fighters:

> To not indulge in acts of extremism, [to] not disrespect
> dead corpses, [to] not resort to deceit, [to] not kill an
> elder, [to] not kill a child, [to] not kill a woman, and [to]
> not cut down trees unless necessity dictates
> otherwise.
>
> **(al-Sistani, 2015, par. 2)**

Sistani extends the protection to non-Muslims:

> Never inflict harm on non-Muslims, regardless
> of their religion and sect. The non-Muslims [who live in

> predominately Muslim lands] are under the protection of the Muslims in those lands. Whosoever attacks non-Muslims is a betrayer and traitor. And rest assured that such an act of betrayal and treachery is one of the most repugnant acts in accordance to innate nature and the religion of God.
>
> **(al-Sistani, 2015, par. 7)**

Classical Islamic rulings proscribe against acts of extremism, including taking hostages or executing them (Munir, 2011; El-Dakkak, 1990, pp. 104–106, 108–112; El Fadl, 1999, p. 149). Persons who were considered civilians included noncombatant women, noncombatant male children aged 14 years or less, elderly, laborers, peasants, servants, slaves, and the mentally or physically wounded or diseased. Their targeting or capture was expressly forbidden (Munir, 2011; El-Dakkak, 1990, p. 119; El Fadl, 1999, p. 152).

Classical Islamic law allows for the capture of soldier combatants only, and prohibits the taking of all other types of persons as hostages (El-Dakkak, 1990, p. 111; El Fadl, 1999, p. 149; Ibn Rushd, 1999, p. 458; Munir, 2011, p. 94). In this sense, those who are not combatants, including government officials and those involved in supplying combatants, can be characterized as persons of lesser value to detainers, or as persons who are not to be captured or taken hostage under any circumstance.

Similarly, early modern (Hamidullah, 1942) and contemporary Islamic prescriptions as described in international Islamic legal treaties follow the general rule of detaining soldiers only while strictly prohibiting the kidnapping or killing of persons who are not soldiers.

Jihadi Practices

Since Jihadis claim to be in a perpetual state of war against their enemies, officials might draw from classical Islamic prescriptions regarding rules of war that were prescribed by the Prophet Mohammad as well as classical Islamic jurists.

A Jihadi manual that has been distributed widely since at least 2006 states that "you should know your target and refrain from killing innocent people, especially women, kids, and elders and you should take care of these types of people" (Khurasani, 2008, p. 10).

However, be aware that the Taliban (2010) separates noncombatants who offer services for the Taliban's opponents as "infidels," and prescribes capturing and killing them. These noncombatants include "contractors who transport and supply fuel and other equipment for the infidel government," "high and low-ranking employees of security companies," "interpreters," and "drivers involved in enemy supply" (Taliban, 2010, p. 107).

Our Practical Prescriptions

Officials should ask for release of noncombatants. This category can be extended to all civilians, particular females, children, or persons of diminished capacity. However, this strategy may leave behind military personnel or military veterans for greater targeting.

The negotiator can make use of both international law and religious law to demand special protections for noncombatants (Category 10.5).

Officials can use classical Islamic precepts to encourage the release of captives who serve enemy combatants, since such people were deemed as noncombatant persons whose capture is deemed unlawful by classical jurists and by the Prophet himself.

CATEGORY 10.5 Negotiating for the Release of Noncombatants (Hostages)

INTERNATIONAL LAW

1. Noncombatants are protected by international laws.
2. Persons not engaging in combat are noncombatants, including soldiers who surrender, are physically or mentally incapable of serving in combat, or cannot serve in combat for any other reason.
3. All captured noncombatants become "hostages," and it is illegal to detain hostages; therefore, all hostages must be released immediately.
4. Noncombatants are protected against violence.
5. Noncombatants have the right to legal defense and fair judicial proceedings.

CLASSICAL ISLAMIC PRESCRIPTIONS

1. The Quran (2:190) states, "Fight in the cause of Allah those who fight you; but do not transgress limits; for Allah loveth not transgressors"; (2:194) "If then anyone transgresses the prohibitions against you, transgress ye likewise, against him. But fear Allah! And know that Allah is with those who restrain themselves"; and (8:58) "Allah loveth not the treacherous."
2. Acts of extremism, including taking hostages or executing them, are forbidden (El-Dakkak, 1990, pp. 108–112; El Fadl, 1999, p. 149; Munir, 2011).
3. Persons who were considered civilians included noncombatant women, noncombatant male children aged 14 years or less, elderly, laborers, peasants, slaves, and the mentally or physically wounded or diseased. Their targeting or capture was expressly forbidden (El-Dakkak, 1990, p. 119; El Fadl, 1999, p. 152; Munir, 2011).
4. Only soldier combatants were permitted to be taken as captives; the Prophet prohibited the targeting of civilians. This prohibition is presumably extended to prohibit their capture as well (El Fadl, 1999, p. 149).

EXTREMIST PRESCRIPTIONS AND PROSCRIPTIONS

1. The definitions of "noncombatant" and "hostage" vary by extremist groups, and the rights of these persons differ accordingly. All

extremist groups claim that their codes of conduct are based on the Prophet Mohammad's conduct or Islamic law, though scholars of Islamic law and history often contest the validity of their claims by citing relevant *hadith*, which are historical reports of the Prophet's teachings and mannerisms, or specific legal rulings; whereas extremists tend to fail to cite credible and verifiable sources to validate their claims.

2. Al Qa'ida does not clearly define who "noncombatants" or "hostages" are, but they imply that any "servant" [of their enemies] can be kidnapped and taken as hostage. These "servants" presumably include soldiers and nonsoldiers who provide services to the detaining power's enemies in any fashion (Al Qa'ida, 2006, pp. 81–82). Al Qa'ida claims that the Prophet Mohammad permitted the practice of kidnapping servants affiliated with his enemies during the Battle of Badr, but they fail to cite a verifiable source from which they draw this assertion (Al Qa'ida, 2000, pp. 81–82).
3. Hostages may be tortured, beaten, and killed for the purpose of procuring intelligence because it is claimed that the Prophet authorized this practice, and that "religious scholars" permit this practice, though no specific source is cited to substantiate these claims (Al Qa'ida, 2000, p. 82).
4. Hostages may be killed if it is believed that they are withholding intelligence, or if it is believed that they may leak sensitive intelligence about the detainers to their enemies (Al Qa'ida, 2000, p. 82).
5. Hostages may be released in exchange for ransom, professional services, or intelligence, because it is believed that the Prophet Mohammad exchanged "most" prisoners for ransom, and released others for providing services to the Muslim community (Al Qa'ida, 2000, p. 82).
6. Hostages may not be killed after demands have been met (Al Qa'ida, 2004).
7. The Taliban (2010) does not explicitly define "noncombatants" or "civilians," but it refers to "common people." It is implied that such persons are those who do not support efforts of enemy combatants (Taliban, 2010, p. 117).
8. Common people cannot be intentionally targeted or killed (Taliban, 2010, p. 117); they must be protected by fighters (Taliban, 2010, p. 120).
9. Kidnapping [common] people for ransom for any reason is prohibited (Taliban, 2009, p. 118).

EARLY MODERN ISLAMIC PRESCRIPTIONS

1. Hostages are understood as civilians who do not participate in hostilities (i.e., those who are not soldier-combatants).
2. Extreme acts, like the taking of hostages for any reason, are expressly forbidden.

CONTEMPORARY ISLAMIC PRESCRIPTIONS

1. Nonbelligerents (noncombatants) are protected by contemporary Islamic laws.
2. Persons not engaging in combat are nonbelligerents, and this may include soldiers who surrender or lay down their arms, and soldiers who cannot fight for any reason.
3. All captured nonbelligerents become "hostages," and it is illegal to detain hostages; therefore, all hostages must be released immediately.
4. Nonbelligerents are protected against violence.
5. All accused nonbelligerents have the right to legal defense and fair judicial proceedings.

Prisoners of War

If the official side can persuade the terrorists to recognize the detainees as POWs, the official side can make use of extensive protections and rights in the negotiations. This category of detainee is extensively protected under international law, classical Islamic prescriptions, extremist prescriptions, early modern Islamic prescriptions, and contemporary Islamic prescriptions. As summarized in Category 10.6, international and Islamic law are largely in agreement about the most basic protections of prisoners.

CATEGORY 10.6 Negotiating for the Release of Prisoners of War

INTERNATIONAL LAW

1. POWs are protected by international laws.
2. They are protected against violence.
3. They have the right to communicate with external entities.
4. They have the right to basic necessities such as healthy food, weather-appropriate clothing, medical care, physical fitness, education, recreational activities, and paid labor.
5. They have the right to a hygienic environment.
6. They have the right to repatriation under certain conditions.
7. They have the right to legal defense and fair trial.
8. They have the right to self-governance.
9. They have a right to complain about the conditions in which they are held.

CLASSICAL ISLAMIC PRESCRIPTIONS

1. Quran (47:4) states: "Now when you meet [in war] those who are bent on denying the truth, smite their necks until you overcome them fully, and then tighten their bonds; but thereafter [set them free,] either by an act of grace or against ransom, so that the burden of war may be lifted, thus shall it be."

2. Only soldier-combatants were taken captive as POWs. Children, women, and elderly persons were forbidden from being targeted, especially if they did not take part in hostilities (El-Dakkak, 1990; Munir, 2011).
3. The Prophet released most POWs unconditionally, and ransomed others (Munir, 2011; El-Dakkak, 1990, p. 109).
4. The Prophet generally forbade killing POWs, with some exceptional circumstances (El-Dakkak, 1990, p. 110; Munir, 2011).
5. POWs were executed for crimes committed against the Prophet (such as persecution and physical torment, torture, or abuse like asphyxiation), crimes committed against Muslims (persecution), or for breaking an agreement (El-Dakkak, 1990, pp. 109–110; Munir, 2011).
6. The Quran (76:8) states: "And they feed, for the love of Allah, the indigent, the orphan and the captive."
7. The Prophet urged for the humane treatment of POWs, which included feeding them, clothing them, and prohibiting the use of torture or other kinds of violence against them (El-Dakkak, 1990; El Fadl, 1999, p. 149; Munir, 2011).

EXTREMIST PRESCRIPTIONS AND PROSCRIPTIONS

1. The rights of POWs vary by different *Mujahideen* standards of ethics.
2. Any persons who provide services to enemy combatants can be captured as POWs or killed during hostilities. These persons include but are not limited to soldiers (male or female), state police officers and government officials, contractors who supply materials to enemy combatants, employees of security companies, and interpreters who provide their services to enemy combatants (Taliban, 2010, p. 107).
3. The rights of POWs vary by POW type.
4. Only appointed Imams or judges have the authority to authorize the executions or punishments of POWs (Taliban, 2010, p. 107).
5. POWs who are Muslim enemy combatant soldiers, police, or state officials may be released unconditionally, exchanged, or released upon a guarantee. Muslim POWs may not be ransomed. Muslim POWs may be executed upon the jurisdiction of an appointed Imam or deputy (Taliban, 2010, p. 107).
6. Non-Muslim soldiers and state officials may be exchanged, released, ransomed, or executed upon the decree of an Imam or deputy (Taliban, 2010, p. 108).
7. POWs who are identified with certainty as supply contractors, interpreters, and officials of private security companies that provide services to enemy combatants may either be killed or given the death penalty upon capture. However, if there is any doubt as to whether they provide services to enemies, then they must not be killed, and may be released (Taliban, 2010, pp. 107–108).

8. In the absence of an Imam's or deputy's order, POWs must otherwise be treated humanely. They must not be tortured, killed, or mutilated for any reason (Taliban, 2010, p. 108).
9. POWs must not be exposed to starvation or harsh climatic conditions even if the detainers believe that the captives deserve death (Taliban, 2010, p. 108).
10. From the above prohibitions, it can be inferred that POWs must be fed, and they must be clothed according to the climatic conditions to which they may be exposed while in captivity.

EARLY MODERN ISLAMIC PRESCRIPTIONS

1. Only soldier-combatants may be captured as POWs.
2. POWs must not be killed or executed, including those who are non-Muslim.
3. POWs are not to be harmed, or threatened, or tortured for any reason.
4. POWs may be ransomed, released unconditionally, or released upon a guarantee.
5. Executions of POWs are permitted under exceptional circumstances, where the POW must be known to have committed exceptionally heinous crimes prior to capture that would warrant the death penalty upon his capture.
6. Persons such as contractors, suppliers, drivers, and interpreters are noncombatants, so targeting, capturing, or killing them is strictly prohibited.
7. POWs must be fed and clothed according to the climatic conditions to which they may be exposed while in captivity.
8. POWs are entitled to medical treatment.
9. POWs who are ill should be released.
10. POWs have the right to communicate to their families upon capture.

CONTEMPORARY ISLAMIC PRESCRIPTIONS

1. POWs are protected by contemporary international Islamic laws.
2. POWs are strictly belligerents (soldiers).
3. POWs have a right to medical treatment.
4. POWs have the right to communicate with their families upon capture and during captivity.
5. POWs must be protected against violence while in captivity.
6. POWs must not be killed or tortured.
7. POWs have the right to basic necessities, including food, clothing, and medical care.
8. They have a right to hygienic confinements.
9. It is obligatory for detainers to exchange POWs, or release POWs, even if concessions are not granted to them.

10. All POWs have the right to legal defense and fair judicial proceedings.
11. It is forbidden to discriminate against POWs on the basis of their identity (gender, religion, race, nationality, etc.).

Category 10.6 does not have room for the great complexities of protections for prisoners. The following sections explain

1. How POWs are defined in international law
2. How POWs are supposed to be treated in general
3. How POWs are supposed to be treated during their initial capture and handling
4. Prisoners' detention and conditions of confinement
5. Prisoners' rights to communications
6. Prisoners' rights to external access
7. Obligations to record and share information
8. The handling of wills, testaments, and deaths
9. The rights and handling of repatriations
10. The rights to sustenance
11. The clothing of prisoners
12. The hygiene of prisoners
13. Health, medical treatment, and recreation of prisoners
14. Religious freedoms of prisoners
15. Special treatments by rank
16. Rights to structured relations with the detaining power
17. Self-governance
18. Justice, fair discipline, and limited punishments
19. The treatment of escapees
20. Labor and work of prisoners
21. Prisoners' personal possessions and personal finances

Definitions

Several definitions of "prisoners of war" (POWs) exist and can be used to the advantage of officials. Following, we separate international law from religious law.

International Law

Generally, any armed person (combatant) who is captured and held by a party involved in armed conflict becomes a POW. Customary international law is more specific, as it grants "prisoner of war" status only to armed individuals or entities that act in accordance with the Geneva Convention on War (as agreed in 1949).[2] Thus, if any armed entity or individual involved in a conflict does not comply with the Geneva Convention, then they would not be afforded the protections of "prisoner of war" status should they be captured by enemy combatants (Henckaerts and Doswald-Beck, 2005, p. 384).

Customary international law defines "combatants" as "all members of the armed forces of a party to a conflict, except medical and religious personnel" (ICRC, 2016). International law also includes "dissident armed forces and other organized armed groups" within the category of "combatants." Such persons have the legal right to engage in armed conflict. Persons categorized within the definition of "combatants" or "prisoners of war" upon their capture enjoy special protections under the UN Geneva Conventions, where they may not face legal liability for engaging in combat only if their armed engagement is in compliance with the Geneva Conventions (Dörmann, 2003, p. 45; ICRC, 2016). Thus, international law indicates that only combatants are legitimate targets for capture.

Categorically, customary international law considers "unlawful combatants" as persons who are not protected under international humanitarian law. Unlawful combatants are persons who do not have the legal right to engage in combat. Persons who do not have the legal right to engage in combat include civilians and those who do not comply with the Geneva Conventions, namely, Geneva Convention III Article 4(2) (Dörmann, 2003, p. 47). Organizations that are internationally recognized as terrorist are considered "unlawful combatants" since their means of armed combat fail to satisfy the standards set by the Geneva Conventions.

Article 4 of the Geneva Convention Relative to the Treatment of Prisoners of War defines "prisoners of war" as "persons belonging to one of the following categories, who have fallen into the power of the enemy":

1. Members of armed forces, militias, or volunteer corps of an officially recognized state party to a conflict.
2. Other members of organized armed forces, militias, or volunteer corps belonging to organized resistance movements. In order for members of these entities to be considered as POWs in the event that they are captured, they must meet all of the following criteria (a–d):
   a. Have a commander who is responsible for his or her subordinates

[2] For the full text, see: http://www.un.org/en/preventgenocide/rwanda/text-images/Geneva_POW.pdf

    b. Clearly distinguish themselves from noncombatants[3]
    c. Carry arms openly
    d. Execute military operations in accordance with the Geneva Convention on war

3. Members of regular armed forces who claim loyalty to an entity that is not recognized by their captors.
4. Individuals who accompany armed forces, but do not execute military operations or engage in combat. These individuals include but are not limited to civilian members of aircraft crews, supply contractors, medical personnel, journalists, and members of labor units or services responsible for the welfare of the armed forces.
5. Members of civilian marine and aircraft crews belonging to parties to the conflict, who are not already protected by other legal UN conventions.
6. Individuals of a nonoccupied territory who spontaneously take up arms to defend themselves against invading forces but are not organized military units. These individuals must follow Geneva Convention Rules for War, and they must carry arms openly.

Article 41 specifies that all POW camps must post the entire text of the convention in the language that the POWs speak and understand, and it must be posted in areas where all POWs can access and read the document.

Islamic Law

Classical, early modern, and contemporary Islamic laws define combatants as armed persons who fight during hostilities (Naqvi, 1974; Hamidullah, 1942; Cairo Declaration on Human Rights, 1990; El-Dakkak, 1990; Munir, 2011). All three categories of Islamic jurisprudence strictly allow for the capture of soldier-combatants only, who then become POWs during captivity.

In the classical legal tradition, Naqvi specifies that "Islam does not permit Muslims to treat as belligerent persons who have not taken part in [the actual fighting of] the war" (1974, pp. 35–36). Naqvi cites the Quran (2:190) as stating, "And fight in the way of Allah against those who fight against you[.] [B]egin not hostilities. (Lo! Allah loveth not transgressors!)." The more widely accepted translation of this verse is slightly varied, although it encompasses the same point of targeting only enemy soldier-combatants: "Fight in the cause of Allah those who fight you, but do not transgress limits; for Allah loveth not transgressors" (Ali, 1934). Furthermore, Naqvi cites the Quran (60:8) to further substantiate the prohibition: "Allah forbiddeth not those who warred not against you on account of religion and drove

[3] For instance, members of organized forces can distinguish themselves from noncombatants by wearing uniforms that do not resemble civilian attire; personnel of these organized forces can wear or carry badges or medals that indicate they are affiliated with armed forces and not noncombatants.

you not out from your homes, that ye should show them kindness and deal justly with them. Lo! Allah loveth the just dealers" (1974, p. 36). Ali (1934) translates the same verse, "Allah forbids you not, with regard to those who fight you not for (your) faith nor drive you out from your homes, from dealing kindly and justly with them: For Allah loveth those who are just." In essence, the general consensus regarding the interpretation of the above verse lies with prohibiting the targeting or malicious treatment of those who are not taking direct part in hostilities.

Naqvi further specifies categories of persons who are considered noncombatants and are prohibited from being targets. According to Naqvi, classical Islamic legal tradition defines noncombatants as "women, minors, servants and slaves who accompany their masters, yet do not take part in actual fighting, the blind, monks, hermits, the very old, those physically incapable of fighting, the insane or delirious," and "persons engaged in worship alone, persons engaged in secular pursuits, and persons engaged in different trade and industry" (1974, pp. 31, 36). According to Naqvi, the Quran deems such categories of persons as lacking in fault since they have been unwillingly caught in the circumstances of war, and as those who cannot defend themselves. Their relationship to enemy soldier-combatants should thus be disregarded or forgiven. Naqvi cites the Quran (4:98), "Allah forgave the feeble among men, women, and children who are unable to devise a plan and are not shown a way" (1974, p. 36). Naqvi cites further edicts of the Prophet, who is reported to have said, "do not violate your promise, nor transgress upon vanquished people, nor mutilate the dead, nor kill the children, or those who are engaged in the service of places of worship" (1974, p. 36).

Early modern Islamic laws are influenced by classical Islamic law as they also permit the capture of only soldier-combatants. Hamidullah (1942) distinguishes combatants from noncombatants where the latter include women (who do not actively participate in hostilities), youths, servants, slaves—even if serving combatant masters, peasants, traders, merchants, contractors, the old, the mentally deficient, the physically deformed, the blind, monks, and hermits. Similarly, Munir (2011, pp. 93–94) specifies that noncombatants include women, children, and servants of any kind, including contractors, suppliers, or drivers. Furthermore, El-Dakkak, agree that only soldier-combatants who take part in hostilities may be treated as belligerents and taken as prisoners (pp. 111, 113). The authors specify that noncombatants who are protected from war and capture include workmen, traders, children, women, old people, the sick, and members of religious bodies (1990, pp. 112–113).

Contemporary Islamic law maintains the Islamic legal tradition by implying that only armed persons, or soldier-combatants, who are directly taking part in hostilities may be taken as POWs. Article 3 of the Cairo Declaration on Human Rights in Islam defines nonbelligerents (noncombatants) as including old men, women, and children, and specifies that they are protected from war operations and tactics, which include capture. Article 21 further prohibits the taking of hostages.

Jihadi Definitions

Terrorists' definitions of "combatant" tend to deviate from classical, early modern, and contemporary definitions, and they tend to breach fundamental Islamic laws pertaining to captives' treatment. Terrorists' characterizations and treatment of detainees can therefore be characterized as un-Islamic or heretical.

Whereas the general Islamic consensus defines combatants who are legitimate for capture as only persons who are actively engaging in warfare, such as soldiers, Jihadis justify capturing and/or killing persons who are not directly engaging in hostilities. For the Taliban (2010, p. 107), any person who provides services to enemy combatants can be captured as POWs, killed during hostilities, or executed after capture. Under this broad categorization, police officers, employees of security companies, supply contractors, drivers, and interpreters who provide their services to enemy combatants can be captured and even killed, despite the Prophet's explicit prohibition of targeting such persons who can be considered "servants" of enemy combatants.

The Taliban's 2010 edition of its *Layeha* generally discourages hostage-taking and delegates the responsibility for detention to its governors:

> If a local soldier, policeman, an official or other responsible person with affiliations to the slave administration has been captured, it is at the discretion of the governor to release them in the case of prisoners exchange, as part of a goodwill gesture or in exchange of solid guaranties. Receiving money for the prisoner's release is forbidden.
>
> **(Taliban, 2010, p. 107)**

Al Qa'ida (2004) justifies targeting any person who is "influential" to societies of their enemies, even if they are not soldier-combatants. In the past, Al Qa'ida has kidnapped defenseless persons not affiliated with armed forces, including *Wall Street Journal* reporter, Daniel Pearl, who was taken hostage on January 23, 2002, and brutally beheaded on February 21, 2002.

We have not found any guidelines that ISIL has published pertaining to the definition of POWs, or persons legitimate for capture, nor have we found any publications by ISIL that specify any protections made available to them. Our observations indicate that ISIL assigns collective punishment to persons affiliated with their enemies—whether civilian or soldier.

General Protections

International Law

The official negotiator should attempt to persuade the hostage-takers to characterize the hostages as POWs, and to extend the same protections as required under international law. For instance, the detention of POWs in accordance with international laws is burdensome, so the negotiator should try to persuade the detainer that the easiest option is to release prisoners.

Furthermore, given the burdens, the detainers should be persuaded that they are likely to violate one or another of the many legal articles, given that the detainers are already likely violating international law by engaging in terrorism, or because the sort of nonstate actors and unstable states that typically engage in terrorism are likely to lack the capacity for lawful detention.

Officials should emphasize that the detainers would face legal liability for any single violation, given that Common Article 3 of the Geneva Convention Relative to the Treatment of Prisoners of War subjects all parties (whether state actors or nonstate actors) to legal accountability should they violate any of the convention's provisions.

We should note that any negotiation strategy referring to international law can be undermined easily by references to the many developed states who have violated the Geneva Conventions, particularly the U.S. detention of prisoners at Guantanamo Bay, Cuba, and elsewhere, who were officially termed "illegal combatants" or "terrorists" rather than "prisoners of war," and were not afforded all conventional protections or treatments (United Nations, 2014; UNOHCHR, 2016).

Part II of the Geneva Convention Relative to the Treatment of Prisoners of War specifies other "General Protections of Prisoners of War."

Article 12 specifies that

- The "detaining power"[4] is ultimately responsible for the treatment of POWs.
- If the POWs are to be transferred, then they must be transferred by the detaining power to a party that has agreed to abide by the conditions of this convention.
- Once POWs are transferred, the new detaining power is responsible for their treatment.
- If the new detaining power fails to abide by the convention's provisions, then the POWs must be returned to their previous detaining power.

Article 14 specifies that

- All POWs are entitled to equal protections as granted by the convention.
- Women must be granted the same protections as men, and they must be accommodated according to the needs of their gender.
- Captors are not to restrict the rights of POWs.

Article 15 specifies that POWs have the right to free medical attention and free services that are necessary to maintain their health and well-being.

Article 16 reiterates the right for all POWs to be treated equally and humanely regardless of race, religious beliefs, nationality, political opinion,

[4] "The state [or entity] by which prisoners of war are held" (see Levie, 1961).

or any other distinction (including, presumably, although not specified at the time, sexual orientation or gender identity).

Article 41 specifies that all

- POW camps must post the entire text of the convention in the language that the POWs speak and understand, and it must be posted in areas where all POWs can access and read the document.
- The detaining power must also provide copies of all other publications relating to the conduct of POWs in a language that POWs can read and understand. Such additional types of publications include but are not limited to "regulations, orders, and notices."
- These additional publications must be posted in the same manner as the text of the convention is posted. Thus, additional publications relating to the conduct of POWs must be posted in a language that all POWs speak and understand, and copies must be made available for all POWs to access.
- Personnel of the POW camps must issue all orders and commands to POWs in a language that POWs understand.

Islamic Law

In addition to appealing to international law, the official negotiator can appeal to Islamic law, which often overlaps.

The classical Islamic tradition indicates that the relationship Muslim detainers should have with their prisoners must be one of guardianship and one that commands humane treatment regardless of the prisoners' religious affiliations. For instance, the Prophet is reported to have urged detainers to "always care for prisoners" (El-Dakkak, 1990, p. 110), and instructed his fighters to "recommend to one another that prisoners be well treated" (Munir, 2010, p. 486).

Moreover, the Prophet is reported to have treated Meccan soldiers detained after the Battle of Badr with profound consideration (Munir, 2010, pp. 471, 486), despite having faced persecution and humiliation himself by Meccan authorities. Officials should note that the detained captives of Badr were non-Muslim but were still afforded humane treatment and were released either unconditionally or upon ransom. Officials can cite this historical example to urge Jihadi detainers to release POWs and to treat them humanely regardless of their religious background, since this was the general practice of the Prophet.

Given the same history, some interpretations of Islamic law give special protections to POWs, similar to the Western tradition:

> According to Muslim law, a prisoner cannot be killed. Ibn Rushd even records a consensus of the Companions of the Prophet to the same effect. This does not preclude the trial and punishment of prisoners for crimes beyond the rights of belligerency. For this, we possess the high authority of the practice of the Prophet when two prisoners of the Battle of Badr were beheaded by his order.

> Muslim jurists clearly recognize that a prisoner cannot be held responsible for mere acts of belligerency.
>
> **(Hamidullah, 1942, Chapter 15, rule 440)**

Other Islamic scholars call for the release of POWs altogether even if the other side does not grant any concessions. For instance, Sunni cleric Dr. Khalid Zaheer writes that the Quran obliges believers "to not make prisoners of war as slaves but to free them with or without compensation" (Zaheer, 2004, par. 21). A Shi'a cleric, Imam Syed Fazil Hussain Mosavi, agrees that prisoners cannot be killed. He states that "fighters can either exchange prisoners of war, ransom them, or free them, but they are never to kill any prisoner, regardless if they are atheist or considered non-Muslim, and regardless if the opposing side grants desired concessions".

Similarly, early modern and contemporary Islamic traditions provide less detail when describing prisoner-detainer relations. Both traditions tend to be influenced by classical prescriptions. Thus, prisoner-detainer relations are mostly characterized by humane treatment regardless of the prisoners' religious affiliations (Cairo Declaration on Human Rights in Islam, Article 3, 17, 1990).

Jihadi Obligations

Jihadis rarely view detainees as prisoners who should benefit from the same protections as granted to POWs in the Islamic tradition, but as representatives of actors who have provoked, persecuted, or betrayed the Muslim community (*Ummah*). This view is reinforced by religious or ethnic prejudices. The negotiator should try to persuade the hostage-takers that the hostages deserve fair treatment as prisoners, but may not get past these Jihadi prejudices.

Munir has challenged the "Islamicity" of terrorist behavior. While Munir acknowledges that the Taliban in particular prescribes some conduct that is in accordance with fundamental Sharia[5] principles, he notes that the majority of their conduct has "no basis in Islamic law or international humanitarian law" (Munir, 2011, pp. 101–102). Munir observes that Jihadi terrorists arbitrarily choose to abide by a few Islamic principles to gain the support and trust of surrounding Muslim communities, although, in reality, most of their conduct illustrates deviance, and is regarded as a façade characteristic of perfidy.

To the official sides' benefit, Munir indicates that certain Quranic verses should not be interpreted as generalizable concepts applicable to the modern era;

---

[5] Sharia, also known as "Shariah," or "Shari'a," is generally understood to mean Islamic law. The term literally means "path" in Arabic, and its application encompasses guidance related to daily routines and religious obligations. Sharia is primarily influenced by the Quran and Sunna, or sayings and teachings of the Prophet; however, general consensus regarding how these must be interpreted is also taken into consideration. Mohammad A. Sergie notes that Sharia developed centuries after the Prophet's death in regions whose societies attempted to amalgamate their own distinct customs with Islamic precepts. These distinctions eventually led to diverging branches of Islamic traditions including the Sunni Hanbali, Maliki, Shafi'i, and Hanafi schools of thought as well as Shi'a schools including the Ja'fari branch. Source: http://www.cfr.org/religion/islam-governing-under-sharia/p8034

rather, they should be interpreted according to the context in which the verses are said to have been revealed to the Prophet centuries ago (Munir, 2011, p. 92).

Violence and Torture

International Law

Common Article 3 of the Geneva Convention Relative to the Treatment of Prisoners of War generally prohibits all parties from committing all types of violence against prisoners, including murder, mutilation, and cruel and unusual treatment such as torture.

Article 13 of the Convention specifies that

- POWs must "be treated humanely at all times."
- They must not be physically mutilated or subjected to medical or scientific experiments.
- They must also "be protected against acts of violence or intimidation, and against insults and public curiosity." Thus, POWs must be granted rights to privacy.

The only condition under which detaining powers are permitted to use force against detainees is specified by Article 42 of the convention, which justifies the use of force in "extreme" circumstances, such as if a detainee is actively using violence that is threatening the lives of others. Even under this circumstance, the detaining power must issue multiple warnings before using force. Article 42 regards the use of weapons against any POW as an "extreme" measure:

- Camp personnel must "always" warn all POWs (more than once) prior to using a weapon against them, except in extreme cases where the circumstances may require swifter action.
- The subjects of this protection include but are not limited to those who attempt to escape, those who are in the process of escaping, and those who had successfully escaped but are recaptured.

The use of violence against detainees in all other circumstances is prohibited by international law. Officials should consult the UN Convention Against the Use of Torture and Other Cruel, Inhuman, or Degrading Treatment or Punishment (UNCAT) to identify what constitutes "torture."[6] Officials should be mindful that Customary International Law, Rule 90,[7] prohibits all entities,

[6] "Torture" as defined by UNCAT (1984) is "any act by which severe pain or suffering, whether physical or mental, is intentionally inflicted on a person for such purposes as obtaining from him or a third person information or a confession, punishing him for an act he or a third person has committed or is suspected of having committed, or intimidating or coercing him or a third person, or for any reason based on discrimination of any kind, when such pain or suffering is inflicted by or at the instigation of or with the consent or acquiescence of a public official or other person acting in an official capacity. It does not include pain or suffering arising only from, inherent in or incidental to lawful sanctions."

[7] See: "Rule 90. Torture and Cruel, Inhuman or Degrading Treatment," available at: https://ihl-databases.icrc.org/customary-ihl/eng/docs/v1_rul_rule90.

state or nonstate, from committing torture and other cruel or unusual punishments against detainees in all circumstances, including circumstances in which detainees are known to have committed a crime, or are suspected to have committed a crime. Detaining powers are also prohibited from using torture as a means to gain intelligence from detainees (ICRC, 2016).

Islamic Law

Despite some disagreement among classical Islamic jurists in regard to the fate of POWs upon captivity, some argue that the general consensus among classical jurists prohibited the use of violence and torture against captured POWs, and they prohibited the killing of defenseless or wounded soldiers or POWs (El-Dakkak, 1990; Munir, 2011). Munir cites the Prophet who reportedly instructed his fighters to "slay no wounded person, pursue no fugitive, [and] execute no prisoner..." (2011, p. 90). Furthermore, El-Dakkak emphasize that "the Islamic rules governing war forbid Muslim warriors to torture their enemies or to subject them to treatment contrary to human dignity" (El-Dakkak, 1990, p. 104). These scholars cite Abu Bakr, the Prophet's father in-law and subsequent caliph, who is reported to have said, "such acts [of beheadings and torture] were committed by ignorant people before Islam existed; we refuse to be likened to them" (p. 105).

Some scholars of the classical tradition find that detainers were expressly forbidden from committing acts of violence or torture against POWs for any reason, including for the purpose of obtaining confessions (El-Dakkak, 1990, p. 104).

The execution of captured combatants is not explicitly permitted anywhere in the Quran. Thus, executing POWs is interpreted as being forbidden by a consensus of both classical jurists[8] and by the Prophet himself (Munir, 2011, pp. 89–92). One classical jurist in particular, Al Hasan bin Muhummad al-Tamimi (d. 656 AH/1258 CE) stated that "the Companions of the Prophet were unanimous on the prohibition of the killing of POWs (Munir, 2011, p. 90).

Additionally, Muhammad Munir cites the Quran (47:4) as illegalizing the killing of prisoners (Munir, 2011, pp. 89–90). Munir notes that the execution of certain POWs was permitted under exceptional and context-specific circumstances but was never explicitly established as a rule or legal precedent by the Prophet (Munir, 2011, p. 91). According to Munir, the Prophet authorized the execution of three to five persons in his lifetime, but all were executed for crimes that were committed before their captivity (pp. 92, 93). Most of these persons were executed because they had committed atrocities against persecuted Muslims before their captivity, whereas one was executed for breaking an agreement (p. 90, footnote 46). More specifically, Munir asserts that

[8] Munir reviewed multiple classical jurists and caliphs who prohibited the killing of POWs, including the following: Ali b. Abi Talib (40AH/661CE), Al-Hasan b. al-Hasan (d. 110AH/728CE), Hammad b. Abi Suliman (d. 120 AH 737 CE), Muhammad b. Sirirn (d. 110 AH/728 CE), Mujahid b. Jabr Mawla (d. 103 AH/721 CE), 'Abd al-Malik b. 'Abd al-'Aziz b. Jurayj (d. 150 AH/767 CE), 'Ata b. Abi Rabbah (d. 114 AH/732 CE) and Abu 'Ubayd b. Salam.

isolated incidences of executions in Islamic history should not be used as generalizable legal precedents, and executions should not be treated as "ordinary punishments," since such executions were authorized under exceptional circumstances (Munir, 2011, pp. 91–92).

On the contrary, one traditional Islamic scholar allowed for the local Muslim military commander to decide whether to behead prisoners at his own discretion (Hamidullah, 1942, Chapter 15, rule 442). Another Islamic scholar allowed for the killing of prisoners in exceptional circumstances, which he did not specify (Chaudhry, 2003).

Jihadi Obligations

Some Jihadis do proscribe violence against detainees. A well-distributed Jihadi manual includes the rules that the Jihadi "should not torture a captured enemy fighter…[or] kill or cut the body parts or burn them; the prisoners should be treated in a humane manner" (Khurasani, 2008, p. 10).

Furthermore, the Taliban's 2010 edition of its *Layeha* prohibits the maltreatment of hostages. The Taliban declares that, "Mujahids should not expose those detained by them to starvation, thirst, cold or heat even if they deserve death" (Taliban, 2010, p. 108; International Review of the Red Cross, 2011; Johnson and DuPee, 2012, p. 78).

On December 31, 2011, a spokesperson for the Pakistani Tehreek-e-Taliban (TTP) issued a statement on its behalf claiming that "all Mujahideen, local and foreigners, are informed that they should desist from killing and kidnapping for ransom innocent people and cooperate with this committee in curbing crimes. If any Mujahid is found involved in unjustified killings, crimes and other illegal activities, he will answer to Shura-i-Murakbah and will be punished in accordance with the Shariah law" (South Asia Terrorism Portal, 2013b).

Initial Capture and Handling

International Law

Part III, Section I of the Convention Relative to the Treatment of POWs specifies how POWs must be treated during the initial stages of their captivity.

Article 17 specifies that

- POWs must not be "physically or mentally" tortured as a means of retrieving information of any kind from them ("torture" as defined by the UN Convention Against Torture—see United Nations, 1984).
- POWs have a right to refuse to answer any questions, and should they refuse to answer, they must not be "insulted, threatened, or exposed to disadvantageous treatment of any kind."
- POWs who are unable to respond to questions due to psychological or other medical ailments must be transferred to medical services.
- Any questions asked of POWs must be asked in a language they understand.

Article 19 specifies that

- POWs must be evacuated immediately after their capture to camps located far enough away from combat zones so as to not endanger them.
- Prisoners must not be exposed to danger while they wait to be evacuated from a combat zone.
- POWs are allowed to remain in conflict zones only if they suffer ailments that would pose greater risks to their well-being if they were to be evacuated.

Article 20 specifies that

- POWs must be treated humanely while being evacuated.
- They must be given food, drinkable water, clothing, and medical attention.
- They must be granted conditions that are similar to those of their captors, and the detaining power must ensure the safety of POWs while they are being transferred or evacuated.
- The detaining power must keep a record of all POWs who are evacuated.
- If the POWs are to pass through transit camps, then their stay at the transit camp must be as brief as possible.

Islamic Law

Classical, early modern, and conventional Islamic laws specify how POWs are to be treated during their initial capture and how they are to be treated during captivity.

In general, classical Islamic precedents prohibit acts of perfidy, or deceit, which is commonly referred to as "treachery" in Islamic manuscripts, including the Quran. In particular, the Quran, the Prophet, and classical jurists and caliphs flatly prohibited fighters from deceiving enemy combatants, with some prescribing the punishment of execution for anyone, including Muslims, who engages in deceitful tactics of particular kinds against combatants in battle, and against POWs upon their capture. Such an example of deceit may involve promising to spare enemy combatants' lives if they surrendered, but reneging the promise by slaughtering them upon gaining their trust and their surrender (El-Dakkak, 1990, p. 107; Munir, 2011, p. 98). Caliph Ibn-Al-Khattab threatened to "cut the throat of anyone" who deceived enemy combatants in such a manner. Furthermore, the classical jurist Al-Shafi'i prohibited acts of perfidy to be committed against all types of combatants, regardless of their religious background. Muslim fighters were instructed to provide safe passage to captured soldiers and to "guarantee the safety of those who have surrendered and eschew the resort to perfidy for the purpose of killing [upon capturing them]." Acts of perfidy were not to be committed against POWs during their confinement, either. The Prophet's edict is regarded as a valid legal precedent among some classical jurists and caliphs for how POWs should be treated upon capture and during their confinement (El-Dakkak, 1990, p. 107).

Officials may use these prohibitions to persuade hostage-takers to not renege promises of releasing captives unconditionally or upon ransom, as such an act would constitute unlawful perfidy.

Detention and Conditions of Confinement

International Law

Part III, Section II, Chapter I of the Geneva Convention Relative to the Treatment of Prisoners of War specifies the conditions under which POWs are interred.

Article 21 states that

- Detaining powers have the right to confine POWs to spaces where they can be denied movement beyond designated perimeters.
- Prisoners may not be quartered in cramped spaces, except to monitor their health or if otherwise similarly necessary.
- POWs may be released under the condition of "parole, or on promise" (meaning that they will not take up arms against the detaining power). However, POWs must not be forced to accept freedom under these conditions.

Article 22 specifies that

- POWs must be held in confinements located on land.
- The confinement must be sanitary, and its conditions must not pose a threat to a prisoner's health. POWs are not to be held in penitentiaries, except upon their own discretion.
- If POWs are confined in unsanitary conditions, or in extreme cold or heat, then they must be transferred to a location that is more habitable.
- POWs must be detained in camps according to their "nationality, language, and customs," so long as they are not separated from the militias they were serving at the time of their capture, unless they consent to separation.

Article 23 states that

- POWs are not to be sent to or detained in areas that will expose them to munitions fire or military combat of any kind at any point in their captivity.
- POWs are not to be used as human shields.
- POWs are to be given the same protections as civilian populations insofar as they must be protected from aerial bombardments "and other hazards of war."

- Detaining powers must disclose the location of the camps where POWs of opposing countries are being held. POW camps must be labeled in a manner that clearly indicates (including to aircraft) that the location is a POW camp.

Part III, Section II, Chapter II of the Geneva Convention Relative to the Treatment of Prisoners of War specifies the conditions related to living quarters, food, and clothing granted to POWs.

Article 25 specifies that

- POWs must be exposed to the same habitable conditions as enjoyed by the military forces belonging to the detaining power.
- POWs must not be held in damp quarters, which would subject them to molds, colder temperatures, and other hazards to their health.
- Living spaces must be adequately heated and lighted, and POWs must be protected against fire hazards.
- Male POWs must live separately from female POWs, and they must be accommodated according to their sex.

Islamic Law

Early modern and contemporary Islamic prescriptions contain rules that directly relate to the detention and conditions of confinement in which POWs are to be held. As previously illustrated, POWs are protected against violence, and they must be held in hygienic confinements with access to medical care. In addition, POWs are to be fed and clothed according to the climatic conditions to which they may be exposed while in captivity (Cairo Declaration on Human Rights, 1990).

Communications

International Law

Part III, Section V of the Geneva Convention Relative to the Treatment of Prisoners of War specifies POWs' rights to communicate with entities beyond the confines of the POW camp in which they are held.

Article 69 specifies that

- Upon capturing POWs, the detaining power must inform all POWs and the powers on which they depend of POWs' rights.
- The detaining power must inform the aforementioned entities of how it will accommodate POWs' rights to communicate to parties beyond the POW camp.
- The detaining power must inform POWs and the powers upon which they depend of any changes it makes to conform with the rules of the present section.

Article 70 specifies the conditions under which POWs have the right to communicate with their families.

- POWs must be granted the right to communicate directly with their families immediately upon their capture, or within a week of their capture.
- POWs must be granted the right to communicate with their families if they are at a transit camp or any other camp, or if they are ill, or transferred to a hospital.
- All POWs must write to the Central Prisoners of War Agency as described in Article 123.
- In their communications with external entities, POWs have the right to disclose their state of health, captivity status, and location of captivity.
- All forms of communication to external entities must be sent immediately and must not be delayed for any reason.

Article 71 specifies that

- POWs have the right to send and receive correspondence.
- All POWs have the right to send at least two letters and four cards each month, not counting cards that must be sent upon their capture. The details that must be given on the cards should be in conformity with the model located at the annex of the convention.
- Limitations to POWs' correspondence may be established only if the protecting power is convinced that such limitations are meant to serve the interests of POWs. All other limitations may be imposed by only the power on which the POWs depend. If the detaining power wishes to impose limitations, then it must seek the agreement of the power on which the POWs depend.
- All forms of communication must be sent to external entities as quickly as possible, and they may not be delayed or denied correspondence for disciplinary reasons.
- All POWs who are unable to receive news frequently must be accommodated in a manner that will allow them to send and receive correspondence frequently, including in cases of urgency.
- All fees related to the correspondence may be charged to the POW's account, or paid by the POW directly.
- Parties to the conflict must allow POWs to communicate in their native languages, or in languages they best speak and understand.
- All mail belonging to POWs must be sealed and must have labels that describe its contents.
- All mail must include the address to which it must be sent.

Article 72 specifies that

- POWs have the right to receive packages containing food, drinks, clothing, medical supplies, religious paraphernalia, educational items, and any items of cultural or religious relevance. The detaining power will not be relieved of its obligations to provide POWs with such necessities even in the event that POWs receive them through other means.
- Any limitations to these shipments may be imposed by the protecting power, or by any organization that provides relief to POWs. Such limitations may only be imposed if they are in the best interests of POWs, or if extraordinary conditions make timely sending or receiving difficult.
- All conditions under which such packages can be sent to POWs must be agreed upon by the parties to the conflict.
- These agreements may not obstruct POWs' ability to receive relief supplies through mail.
- All medical supplies must be sent collectively in packages that must not contain anything other than medical equipment or medical supplies.
- All books must be sent in packages that must not contain anything other than books.
- All food must be sent in packaging that must not contain anything other than food.
- All clothing must be sent in packaging that must not contain anything other than clothing.

Article 73 specifies that

- Parties to a conflict must follow the rules regarding the shipment of relief supplies located at the annex of the convention, if they have not made special agreements regarding the shipment of relief supplies already.
- Any agreement made between parties to a conflict must not restrict the rights of POWs to access and use relief supplies.
- These agreements must not restrict the rights of the protecting power, the International Committee of the Red Cross, or any other organization that provides relief to POWs, or those that supervise the distribution of relief to POWs.

Article 74 specifies that

- All shipments that provide relief for POWs must be exempt from any kind of taxes, including taxes related to imports and customs.
- All mail sent to or from POWs will be exempt from postal fees.

- If relief packages cannot be sent through the post office due to weight restrictions or for any other reason, then the detaining power must pay for the transport of the packages.
- Unless parties to the conflict have made special agreements, all other costs related to the transport of mail must be charged to the accounts of the sender.
- High Contracting Parties[9] must make every effort to reduce the costs of correspondence sent to or from POWs as much as possible.

Article 75 of the convention specifies that

- The International Committee of the Red Cross or any other organization jointly approved by parties to a conflict may fulfill duties related to the shipment of medical supplies and other authorized items to POWs if military operations prevent the parties to a conflict from fulfilling such duties.
- These shipments may include correspondence, lists, and reports between the central information agency and the national information bureau.
- The shipments may also contain correspondence and reports in relation to POWs.
- Parties to the conflict are free to agree on other means of transport, provided that their alternative means are safe and mutually agreed upon.
- All parties to a conflict whose nationals benefit from the shipment of such material must divide costs of transport proportionally among themselves, unless they arrange for special agreements.

Article 76 of the convention specifies that

- All mail shipments must be confidential and shipped as quickly as possible.
- The dispatching state and the receiving state have only one opportunity each to censor the shipment.
- All shipments meant for POWs must be examined in the presence of the intended recipient or someone duly assigned by the POW, and the examination must not subject the items to deterioration, except in the case of written or printed matter.

[9] "High Contracting Parties" are international organizations or sovereign states that have agreed to abide by the terms of the convention; however, all Geneva Conventions are regarded as "customary law," where all actors, both state and nonstate, are subject to the provisions of these conventions, regardless of whether or not actors have officially signed an agreement to abide by their provisions.

- If any party to a conflict prohibits communications, either for military or political reasons, then the length of cessation of communications must be as short as possible.

In the context of hostage negotiations, officials may use Article 76 to their advantage by preventing communications between convicted terrorists who are in their captivity, and the leadership and other individuals belonging to their affiliated terrorist group, which can be regarded as a "Detaining Power." However, officials should be wary of terrorists who are aware of the laws of the convention and who are aware that they are protected by the convention. Those who are knowledgeable may exploit these provisions to their advantage by denying communications between POWs and the powers on which they depend. Officials should beware that the article does not specify the duration of time that cessation of communications may last, so officials may consider manipulating the time frame to their advantage.

Article 77 specifies that

- The detaining state must provide all the materials and facilities necessary to process all documents sent by the POW, especially powers of attorney and wills.
- The detaining power must also allow them to consult an attorney and take measures necessary for the authentication of their signatures.

Islamic Law

Although classical Islamic laws do not specify POWs' rights to communicate with their families, they do emphasize humane treatment of prisoners, which may be argued to include allowing them to communicate among each other. POWs should not be disbarred from social life during confinement, since isolation can be characterized as inhumane treatment given the psychological harms that may result from solitary confinement.

For reference, officials may cite the Prophet's prescription to "care for prisoners" and extend it to include communication rights.

Similarly, early modern and contemporary Islamic laws explicitly extend the Prophet's example of humane treatment toward POWs to grant communication rights to POWs. As previously illustrated, contemporary Islamic laws within the Cairo Declaration on Human Rights in Islam (1990) specify the detaining power's responsibility to organize "visits or reunions of the families separated by the circumstances of war" (Article 3). This protection indicates the right for POWs to communicate with their families.

Outside Access

International Law

Article 125 of the Geneva Convention Relative to the Treatment of Prisoners of War specifies that

- Representatives of religious organizations, relief societies, and other organizations assisting POWs should be given the necessary facilities to visit the prisoners, allocate relief supplies, and help organize prisoners' leisure time.
- These accommodations must adhere to measures that the detaining power deems essential to their own security.
- The detaining power can limit the number of societies and organizations that can operate within its territory given that the limitations do not prevent the societies or organizations from providing relief to all POWs.
- The International Committee of the Red Cross is granted special permissions, which must be respected at all times.
- Immediately after relief is given to the POWs, receipts must be signed by the prisoner's representative and forwarded to the relief society or organization that provided the aid, as well as to the administrative authorities responsible for the prisoners.

Part VI of the convention concerns general guidelines that entities may follow in order to verify that the provisions of the convention are being followed.

Article 126 specifies that

- Representatives of the protecting powers are permitted access to all areas occupied by POWs, including places where the prisoner is held or imprisoned, places of labor, and where transferred prisoners arrive and depart.
- Delegates of protecting powers have the right to interview the prisoners and their representatives without witnesses, using an interpreter if necessary.
- These representatives can choose where and when they visit, as frequently and for as long as they wish.
- The visits must not be prohibited unless it coincides with military necessity, which must only be an exceptional and temporary measure.
- The detaining power and the power on which the prisoners depend may decide whether compatriots of the prisoner may participate in these visits.
- These prerogatives also apply to delegates of the International Committee of the Red Cross, whose appointment should be approved by the detaining power.

Article 127 specifies that

- The High Contracting Parties should circulate the text of this convention throughout the population (including armed forces).

- Any military or other authorities who are responsible for POWs must have the text of the convention and be knowledgeable about its contents.

Article 128 specifies that

- Communication between High Contracting Parties will go through the Swiss Federal Council, and through the protecting powers during hostilities.
- They may adopt regulations relevant to applying the convention, and may communicate through official translations of this text.

Article 129 specifies that

- High Contracting Parties are responsible for penalizing persons who breach the convention by enacting relevant legislation. This includes people alleged to have committed the breach, and those responsible for ordering the act.
- The High Contracting Party must search for persons believed to be responsible for a breach, and bring them to court.
- If the party chooses, it can transfer these persons to another High Contracting Party for trial if they have "made out a *prima facie* case."
- High Contracting Parties must act to suppress actions that go against the provisions of the convention (excluding the grave breaches defined in Article 130). Safeguards should be in place to allow the accused an adequate trial and defense.

Article 130 specifies actions taken against POWs or their possessions that constitute "grave breaches" of the convention, which are prohibited. These actions include the following:

1. Willful killing of POWs
2. Torture or inhumane treatment (including biological experiments)
3. Intentionally causing serious injury to body or health
4. Forcing a POW to serve in the forces of the hostile power
5. Depriving the prisoner's rights to a fair and regular trial

Article 131 specifies that a High Contracting Party cannot absolve itself or another High Contracting Party of accountability in breaching these terms.

Article 132 specifies that an enquiry into alleged violations of the convention can be requested by any of the relevant parties to a conflict. The organization of these inquiries can be decided by the parties involved. If the parties do not agree, then they should nominate an umpire to decide for them. The parties must quickly end and suppress any violation as soon as it becomes apparent.

Information

International Law

Part V of the Geneva Convention Relative to the Treatment of Prisoners of War concerns rules regarding the establishment of databases that archive personal information of all POWs. These intelligence databases are referred to as "Information Bureaux."

Article 122 specifies that

- All parties involved in conflict must establish an Information Bureau of Prisoners of War. These information bureaus must be created in all cases of occupation or outbreak of conflict.
- Neutral and nonbelligerent powers involved in conflict must also establish information bureaus regarding POWs.
- All Prisoners of War Information Bureaus must have necessary accommodation, equipment, and staff to ensure that they function efficiently.
- All powers concerned may employ POWs at the bureau under the labor conditions provided in the present convention.
- The bureau must immediately forward the following information to the powers concerned, using the protecting powers as intermediaries, and it must also forward the information to the Central Agency as described in Article 123:
    - First name, surname, rank, army, regimental/personal/serial number, place and full date of birth
    - Indication of which power the prisoner depends on
    - The first name of the POW's father and maiden name of the mother
    - The name and address of the person to be informed
    - The address to where the prisoner's correspondence can be sent
- The information bureau should receive information relating to transfers, releases, repatriations, escapes, hospital admissions, and deaths from various departments and pass this information on to the POW's correspondent.
- Information regarding state of health of POWs who are seriously ill or seriously wounded should be supplied weekly if possible.
- The information bureau is responsible for replying to all inquiries regarding POWs, including those who have died in captivity.
- The bureau must also obtain any information concerning POWs that is not already in its possession.
- All written communications sent by the information bureau must be authenticated with an official seal.

- The bureau is responsible for also gathering all personal belongings of POWs who have been repatriated, released, escaped, or died in custody. These possessions include any currency that has not been converted to the currency of the detaining power, and any documents that may be of significance to the POW's family. These belongings must be sent in sealed packaging to the powers concerned, and all packages must clearly include the full identity of the person to whom the items belong, and a list of items that are contained in the package.

Article 123 specifies that

- A neutral country must have a Central Prisoners of War Information Agency, and the International Committee of the Red Cross can advise the relevant powers on how to organize the agency.
- The agency will collect all information about POWs and send it to the prisoner's country of origin, or the power on which the prisoner depends.
- The parties to the conflict must provide the necessary mechanisms or facilities through which the agency can transmit such information.
- High Contracting Parties should provide this agency with all the financial aid it may need.
- These provisions do not restrict humanitarian efforts of the International Committee of the Red Cross, or relief societies as specified in Article 125.

Article 124 specifies that

- Postage will be free for the national information bureaus and the central information agency.
- Similarly, telegraphic charges will not be applied, or will be significantly reduced.
- The exemptions provided in Article 74 similarly apply.

Wills, Testaments, and Deaths

International Law

Article 120 of the Geneva Convention Relative to the Treatment of Prisoners of War specifies that

- All wills of POWs must comply with the standards of validity established by the legislation of their country of origin. What constitutes legal validity must be communicated from the POWs' country of origin to the detaining power.

- Upon a POW's request or death, the will must immediately be sent to the protecting power, and "a certified copy" of the will must be given to the central agency.
- Death certificates that are formatted to match the sample located at the annex of the convention, or lists that are certified by a responsible officer of all POWs who have died as POWs must be sent to the Prisoners of War Information Bureau, established as per Article 122, as fast as possible.
- The family of the deceased POW must be informed as soon as possible. These certificates or lists must contain the following information, and they must be sent to the Prisoner of War Information Bureau in accordance with Article 122:
    - Identity of the POW
    - Date and place of death
    - Cause of death
    - Date and place of burial
    - Any necessary information required to identify the grave of the POW
- A medical examination of the body for the purpose of confirming death, establishing identity, and enabling a report must occur before the burial or cremation of the POW.
- It is the responsibility of the detaining authorities to ensure that POWs who die in captivity are buried honorably, in accordance to the religious rites to which they belong, if possible, and that their graves are maintained, respected, and marked.
- When possible, deceased POWs who depended on the same power must be buried in the same place.
- Individual graves must be used, except in unavoidable circumstances that would require the use of collective graves.
- Cremation is allowed only under circumstances where hygienically necessary or in compliance with the religion or expressed wish of the deceased.
- If the POW is cremated, the death certificate must state this decision and the reasons for it.
- The detaining power must establish a Graves Registration Service, which is responsible for recording all burial sites and grave details in order for the graves to be found.
- Lists of these details will be communicated to the power on which the deceased POWs depended.

- If POWs are buried or will be buried in a territory that is a party to the present convention, then the responsibility for maintaining these graves and recording additional transportation of the bodies must go to the power that controls the territory within which POWs are or will be buried.
- These provisions also apply to the ashes of cremated POWs, which must be kept by the Graves Registration Service until properly disposed of, according to the wishes of the home country.

Article 121 specifies that

- All incidents involving the deaths of or injuries to POWs that have been caused by or are suspected to have been caused by a sentry, another POW, or any other person must be investigated by the detaining power.
- The detaining power must investigate incidents where the cause of death is unknown.
- The detaining power must notify the protecting power in the event that an investigation into the death or serious injury of a POW is to take place. Such investigations must include statements from witnesses. The detaining power must establish a report that must include all statements taken from witnesses, and send the report to the third-party protecting power.
- In the event that the investigation indicates the culpability of one or more persons, the detaining power is responsible to take all measures to prosecute the said individuals.

Repatriation

International Law

Part IV, Section I of the Geneva Convention Relative to the Treatment of Prisoners of War concerns the conditions under which POWs may be repatriated or sent to a neutral power.

Article 109 specifies that

- Parties to a conflict are required to send seriously wounded or sick POWs back to their own countries, regardless of number or rank, after they have been cared for until they are fit to travel, in accordance with Article 110.
- During hostilities, parties to the conflict must make arrangements to accommodate sick and wounded POWs in neutral countries, with the cooperation of the neutral powers involved.
- Parties may also make agreements that aim for direct repatriation or internment in neutral countries of able-bodied POWs who have been in captivity for long periods of time.

- No POW who is eligible for repatriation may be repatriated without his or her consent during a conflict.

Article 110 specifies

- Three categories of POWs that must be repatriated to the power on which they depend:
    1. Those who are terminally ill, critically wounded, or whose physical or mental health has severely diminished.
    2. Those who are sick or wounded and are deemed by medical authorities as being unlikely to recover within a year, or those whose ailment(s) require(s) treatment that is beyond the ability of the camp to provide, or those whose mental or physical health have been greatly diminished.
    3. Those who have recovered from certain ailments, but whose mental and physical health remain severely deteriorated or permanently diminished.
- The following categories of POWs may be sent to a neutral country:
    1. Wounded or sick POWs whose recovery would be expedited within 1 year, or if treatment in the neutral country will expedite the recovery process of the POW, in general.
    2. POWs whose physical or mental health would severely deteriorate if they were to remain in captivity, but whose physical or mental health would improve if they were to be removed to a neutral power.
- The following categories of POWs who are sent to a neutral power may be repatriated to the power on which they depend:
    1. POWs whose health has declined to the point where they satisfy the conditions under which direct repatriation would be justified.
    2. POWs whose health remains in critical condition even after treatment.

Article 111 specifies that the detaining power, the power on which the POWs depend, and a mutually agreed neutral power must establish an agreement that will allow for POWs to be held in the neutral power's territory until the end of hostilities.

Article 112 specifies that

- Once hostilities occur, "Mixed Medical Commissions"[10] must be appointed to examine sick and wounded POWs.

[10] "Mixed Medical Commissions" consist of a group of medical authorities, such as doctors, who visit POW camps and must decide who among the POWs should be repatriated given their mental or physical health.

- POWs who are already deemed wounded or sick by the medical authorities of the detaining power are exempt from examination by Mixed Medical Commissions.
- The commissions must determine what should be done with POWs given their health, and such decisions must be made in accordance with the regulations in the annex of the convention.
- POWs who are determined to be gravely injured or sick by the medical authorities of the detaining power may be repatriated without being examined by a Mixed Medical Commission.

Article 113 specifies that

- POWs are entitled to examination by the Mixed Medical Commissions, as proposed by
    1. A physician or surgeon of the same nationality or of a nationality allied with the power on which POWs depend
    2. The POW's representative
    3. The power on which they depend
    4. By an organization giving assistance to POWs recognized by said power
- POWs who do not belong to these three categories may still be examined by Mixed Medical Commissions, but only after those belonging to the aforementioned categories have been examined.
- The physician or surgeon of the same nationality as the POWs, as well as the prisoners' representative, will be permitted to be present for any examination by the Mixed Medical Commission.

Article 114 specifies that POWs who have been hurt in accidents, excluding self-inflicted accidents, will have the benefit of this convention's provisions relating to repatriation or accommodation in a neutral country.

Article 115 specifies that no POW who has undergone disciplinary punishment and is eligible for repatriation or accommodation in a neutral country may be retained on the claim that they have not undergone punishment. If the detaining power consents, POWs detained "in connection with a judicial prosecution or conviction" and designated for repatriation or accommodation in a neutral country may undergo these measures before the end of the proceedings or completion of the punishment. Parties to the conflict will communicate the names of POWs who will be detained until the end of the proceedings or completion of the punishment.

Article 116 specifies that the detaining power and the power on which the POWs depend are responsible for all costs of repatriation or transportation to a neutral country.

Article 117 specifies that no person who has been repatriated may be used for active military service.

Islamic Law

Classical, early modern, and contemporary Islamic laws specify rights related to terminating the captivity of POWs. El-Dakkak (1990, p. 109) indicate that detainers are given only two alternatives in the Quran (47:4): unconditional release or release bought with ransom. According to Munir (2011, p. 89), the Quran (47:4) indicates that captivity of POWs is a "temporary affair that must lead to either unconditional or conditional freedom, or freedom bought with ransom"; execution is not mentioned and is interpreted as forbidden.

As discussed in Chapter 9, most early modern legal scholars follow the classical juridical tradition. They proscribe against the execution of POWs and instead prescribe up to three alternatives concerning the release of POWs: unconditional release, prisoner exchange, or release upon a monetary ransom (Hamidullah, 1942; Chaudhry, 2003).

Contemporary Islamic laws urge detainers, at the very least, to exchange POWs. For instance, Article 3 of the Cairo Declaration on Human Rights in Islam (1990) states that "it is the duty [of Muslims] to exchange prisoners of war and to arrange visits or reunions of the families separated by the circumstances of war." Thus, captivity is described as a temporary state in which POWs may be held according to contemporary Islamic laws.

Sustenance

International Law

In the Geneva Convention Relative to the Treatment of Prisoners of War, Part III, Section II, Chapter II, Article 26 specifies that

- POWs must be given daily food rations that must satisfy the nutritional needs of prisoners.
- Specifically, the rations must be sufficient in "quantity, quality, and variety" to prevent malnourishment and starvation of POWs.
- The regular diet of POWs must be recorded.
- POWs who are obliged to work must be given additional rations.
- All POWs must be supplied with sufficient drinking water that is safe for consumption.
- POWs are also allowed to be employed for the purpose of preparing meals.

Article 30 specifies that the dietary needs of POWs must be met to maintain their health.

Islamic Law

For some Islamic scholars, classical Islamic law prescribes the sustenance of prisoners:

> As regards the prisoners of Badr, the Prophet ordered: "Take heed of the recommendations to treat the prisoners fairly." The consequence was that many Muslim soldiers contented themselves with dates and fed the prisoners in their

> charge with bread. Abu Yusuf remarks that prisoners must be fed and well treated until a decision is reached regarding them...Prisoners are to be protected from heat and cold, and the like. If they have no clothes, these might be provided, as was the practice of the Prophet.
>
> **(Hamidullah, 1942, Chapter 15, rule 441)**

Classical Islamic precepts also instructed fighters to feed detained persons throughout their captivity. For instance, El-Dakkak (1990, p. 110) cite the Quran (76:8), "And they feed, for the love of Allah, the orphan, the indigent, and the captive"; the Prophet is reported to have said, "always care for prisoners." Similarly, a later Islamic scholar wrote that the Quran obliges captors to treat POWs kindly, with food and water, whatever their ultimate fate. "Before distribution, the Islamic government is responsible for their food, clothing, lodgement and in case of illness for their treatment" (Chaudhry, 2003, Chapter 2, rule 7). As discussed in Chapter 9, early modern Islamic scholars draw from classical Islamic jurisprudence when they proscribe against inhumane treatment of POWs during captivity. Hamidullah (1942) and Chaudhry (2003) follow the classical example of the Prophet's prohibitions of torture and prescriptions for the humane treatment of POWs. Whereas Hamidullah (1942) observed that execution of prisoners is generally prohibited, Chaudhry (2003) insists that POWs are entitled to food, drink, and medical care.

Similarly, contemporary Islamic laws described in Article 3 of the Cairo Declaration on Human Rights in Islam (1990) grant wounded and sick persons the right to medical treatment and grant POWs the right to shelter, food, drink, and clothing appropriate to the climatic conditions to which they may be exposed during captivity.

Clothing

International Law

Part III, Section II, Chapter II, Article 27 of the Geneva Convention Relative to the Treatment of Prisoners of War specifies that

- POWs have the right to be clothed according to the climatic conditions of their environment.
- They must be given "sufficient quantities" of clothing, shoes, and undergarments.
- POWs should be allowed to wear their own uniforms, if appropriate for weather conditions.
- It is the detaining power's responsibility to replace any threadbare clothing with new attire. POWs who work must be given clothing that is suitable for their work environment.

Islamic Law

Classical, early modern, and contemporary Islamic precepts grant POWs the right to have access to additional clothing during captivity. Drawing on the classical Islamic tradition, Munir (2010) writes that "POWs must be given clothing as the Prophet had provided the captives of Badr" (p. 486).

In addition, early modern precepts require that POWs be given "basic necessities" such as "food, drink, and clothing" (Munir, 2010, p. 492).

In contemporary Islamic tradition, Article 3 of the Cairo Declaration on Human Rights (1990) specifies that POWs "have the right to be fed, sheltered, and clothed."

Hygiene

International Law

Part III, Section II, Chapter II, Article 28 of the Geneva Convention Relative to the Treatment of Prisoners of War specifies that

- POWs must have access to canteens where they can ascertain necessities including food and personal hygiene products such as soap.
- Taxes of products made available through canteens must not be higher than other markets, and the profits from the taxes must be used to benefit POWs. If a camp is to be closed, then the profits procured from taxes must be given to an international organization that will use the funds to benefit POWs of the same nationality that contributed to the fund.

Part III, Section II, Chapter III, Article 29 specifies that

- The detaining power must ensure that POWs are interned in sanitary conditions, and it must take all measures to prevent the spread and outbreak of disease.
- POWs must have access to products that are meant to maintain personal hygiene, which must include female access to products that maintain feminine hygiene.
- Internment camps must have sufficient baths and showers; POWs must be provided with enough water and soap to maintain personal cleanliness, including for laundry and bathing.

Islamic Law

Classical, early modern, and contemporary Islamic laws prescribe hygienic practices. Classical Islamic laws command Muslims to practice good personal hygiene, so we can infer that the same practices should be afforded to those who remain under the authority of Muslims, including captives. For instance, the Prophet Mohammad regarded prisoners as being under the "care" of Muslim detainers (El-Dakkak, 1990, p. 110). "Caring" for prisoners involved feeding them, clothing them, and tending to ailments, so one should include the keeping of hygienic confinements.

Several verses in the Quran are dedicated to personal hygienic practices: the Quran (5:6) describes ritual purification or ablution, where Muslims are urged to cleanse areas of the body that are exposed to unsanitary matter or health hazards. The Quran (74:5) also commands, "and your garments do purify and uncleanliness do shun." The Prophet is reported to have prescribed specific guidelines for oral hygiene, bathing, and hygienic etiquette following urination and defecation (Cajee, 2012). Furthermore, classical Islamic figures including Mohammad Ibn al-Hassan forbade methods of torture, including mutilation, for ethical reasons and to prevent the spread of diseases (El-Dakkak, 1990, p. 104).

Classical and early modern jurists prohibited human contact with matter that was believed to be impure or vectors of disease. These include urine, feces, animal carrion, bodily fluids (including perspiration, blood, and semen), dogs, swine, and certain types of alcohol (Simon, 2010, p. 126). The general prescription for those who would come into contact with such hazards is to bathe (the Arabic term is *ghusul*). Officials may infer that prisoners under Jihadi captivity must be prevented from living in conditions that would expose them to vectors of disease, and that prisoners must be afforded the resources necessary for them to maintain personal hygiene, such as clean bathing water, washrooms, and utensils necessary for maintaining grooming and oral hygiene.

Contemporary Islamic prescriptions such as Article 17 of the Cairo Declaration on Human Rights state that "everyone shall have the right to live in a clean environment." This protection can be extended to POWs.

Health, Medical Treatment, and Recreation

International Law

Article 30 specifies that

- POW camps must have medical facilities where POWs must be treated for any health-related issues, including dental treatment, illnesses, injuries, or disabilities.
- The dietary needs of POWs also must be met.
- POWs are permitted to be interned in isolation wards only if they have mental illnesses, or if they are afflicted with contagious diseases that would cause an outbreak if they were not quarantined.
- If any POW suffers from health issues that are beyond the capacity of the camp's infirmary to treat, then they must be transferred to any other military or civilian medical facility that has the capacity to treat them as needed.
- Disabled POWs (the blind, for instance) must be granted special facilities in which they are to be treated and rehabilitated.
- Detaining powers must not obstruct or prevent POWs from receiving medical treatment.
- The detaining powers must provide POWs with records of their visitation to the infirmary, of the nature of the health condition, and of

the treatment received. Copies of these records must be forwarded to the Central Prisoners of War Agency.[11]

- All costs of treatment, including the maintenance of healthy POWs, must be covered by the detaining power.

Article 31 specifies that

- POWs have the right to regular medical check-ups at a rate of at least once per month.
- Each check-up must include a recording of the POW's weight. Medical personnel must record and monitor the overall "health, nutrition, and cleanliness of prisoners, and detect contagious diseases."
- Medical facilities must be equipped with the medical technologies necessary for monitoring the POWs' health and detecting diseases, including malaria, tuberculosis, and venereal diseases.

Article 32 specifies that

- The detaining power has the right to employ any noncombatant POW that is not a part of any military and is a medical practitioner or has experience in medical professions, to perform medical duties on other POWs. Medical practitioners include but are not limited to "physicians, surgeons, dentists, nurses or medical orderlies."
- If the detaining power uses qualified POWs to perform medical duties, then such POWs will still be considered as "prisoners of war," but must be granted the same rights and privileges as the detaining power's own medical personnel.
- POWs who are used for their medical expertise will be exempt from other forms of labor as specified in Article 49 of the convention.

Part III, Section II, Chapter IV discusses the rights of "retained"[12] medical personnel and religious clergy who are assisting POWs.

Article 33 specifies that

- Medical personnel and religious clergy who are retained by the detaining power for the purpose of assisting POWs will not be considered as "prisoners of war," but they must be granted all protections that POWs are given as described in this convention.
- Medical personnel and religious clerics must be granted access to all facilities relevant to their professions. Thus, medical personnel

[11] By international agreements, the Central Prisoners of War Agency is the International Committee of the Red Cross.

[12] "Retained" medical and clergy personnel are those who are not involved with any military but are voluntarily kept by the detaining power to provide their services to POWs. They are not considered POWs, but they are afforded the same protections as POWs in the event that they are captured by combatants.

must have access to all medical facilities to tend to POWs, while members of religious clergy must have access to all facilities designated for religious practice.

Medical personnel and religious clerics are to perform their duties within the limits of the military laws and regulations of the detaining power. The detaining power must accommodate the following rights granted to medical personnel and religious clerics (a–c):

a. Religious and medical personnel must be able to regularly visit POWs who are in labor facilities or hospitals located within or outside of the POW camp. The detaining power must provide transport services for this purpose.

b. Every POW camp must have a "senior medical officer" who is responsible for communicating with camp military authorities on all things related to the activities of retained medical personnel that are retained for their medical service. In the event that hostilities begin, all parties involved in the conflict must recognize the protections granted to medical personnel and behave with respect to their protections as specified in the present convention and Article 26 of the Geneva Convention for the Amelioration of the Wounded and Sick in Armed Forces in the Field of August 12, 1949.[13] Senior medical officers and religious clerics have the right to communicate with relevant personnel of the camp on all matters associated with their responsibilities. It is the detaining power's responsibility to provide necessary means of communication to allow camp personnel and the senior medical officer to exchange correspondence.

c. Medical and religious personnel are subject to camp rules and regulations of the detaining power. However, such personnel must not be forced to carry out other forms of labor other than that which are relevant to their expertise. Thus, medical personnel cannot be forced to perform duties unrelated to medical tasks, and members of religious clergy cannot be forced to perform duties unrelated to their religious duties. During conflict, all parties involved in the conflict must agree on how to provide relief for personnel who are retained for their services, and they

[13] Article 26 of the Geneva Convention, August 12, 1949: "The staff of National Red Cross Societies and that of other Voluntary Aid Societies, duly recognized and authorized by their Governments, who may be employed on the same duties as the personnel named in Article 24, are placed on the same footing as the personnel named in the said Article, provided that the staff of such societies are subject to military laws and regulations. Each High Contracting Party shall notify to the other, either in time of peace or at the commencement of or during hostilities, but in any case before actually employing them, the names of the societies which it has authorized, under its responsibility, to render assistance to the regular medical service of its armed forces." Available at: https://www.icrc.org/eng/assets/files/publications/icrc-002-0173.pdf

must behave in accordance to the agreed upon plan of relief. The detaining power will remain responsible for all POWs in its possession.

Article 38 of the Geneva Convention Relative to the Treatment of Prisoners of War specifies that

- Detaining powers must provide all POW camps with the necessary space and equipment for POWs to participate in "intellectual, educational, and recreational pursuits, sports and games."
- It is the detaining power's responsibility to provide opportunities for POWs to exercise and engage in outdoor activities in areas spacious enough to accommodate such activities.

Islamic Law

Classical, early modern, and contemporary Islamic regulations grant POWs the right to medical treatment. Munir (2010, p. 486) cites the Prophet's reported statement that followers should "recommend to one another that prisoners be well treated."

Early modern and contemporary Islamic prescriptions urge for POWs to have access to medical treatment. For instance, Article 3 of the Cairo Declaration on Human Rights states that "the wounded shall have the right to medical treatment."

Religious Freedoms

International Law

Part III, Section II, Chapter V of the Geneva Convention Relative to the Treatment of Prisoners of War grants POWs the right to engage in intellectual and physical activities.

Article 34 of the convention specifies that

- POWs have the right to practice their religious beliefs and customs freely, granted that they do not violate the regulations of the camp in which they are retained.
- These entitlements include the right to regularly attend religious services.
- It is the detaining power's responsibility to provide places of worship for POWs.

Article 35 specifies the rights of religious clerics who are captured by combatants:

- Religious clerics who are retained by a detaining power have the right to exercise their religious duties on or with POWs of the same religion.
- Religious clerics must be quartered with POWs with whom they can relate or communicate.

- They must be retained with POWs who belong to the same power on which they depend, or with POWs who speak the same language as they speak, or with POWs who practice the same religion as they do.
- The detaining power must provide religious clerics with transportation services that will allow for them to visit POWs situated outside of the camp, as mentioned in Article 33.
- Retained religious clerics have the right to communicate on matters related to their religious duties with religious personnel who are citizens of the country in which they are detained, as well as international religious organizations.

Article 36 specifies that

- POWs who are religious ministers have the right to administer religious duties to members of their community. Thus, such POWs must be treated in the same manner as official clerics retained by the detaining power.
- They must not be forced to perform duties other than those related to their religious profession.

Article 37 continues:

- If POWs lack access to official religious clerics of the same religion, or clerics who are POWs, then the POWs have a right to appoint a "qualified lay[person]" as a substitute for a religious cleric.
- The detaining power, the community of POWs of the same religion, and local religious authorities of the same religious creed must approve of the appointed layperson.
- If the layperson is approved, then he or she will be subject to all rules of the detaining power.

Islamic Law

Classical, early modern, and contemporary Islamic traditions prohibit forced conversions.

The Quran (2:256) states that "there shall be no compulsion in religion." From this Quranic precept, Munir (2010, p. 480) notes that the Prophet Mohammad prohibited fighters from coercing prisoners to convert to Islam. Rather, captives are reported to have willingly converted upon receiving humane treatment during captivity.

Munir notes that early modern Islamic precepts regard forced conversions as "absolutely not acceptable in Islam, and it is not a general rule followed by [contemporary] Muslims" (p. 480).

In addition, Article 10 of the Cairo Declaration on Human Rights in Islam (1990) specifies that "it is prohibited to exercise any form of compulsion on man, or to exploit his poverty or ignorance in order to convert him to another religion, or atheism." Thus, prisoners are afforded the right to religious freedom, and they must not be coerced to convert, or receive discriminatory treatment should they refuse to convert.

Rank

International Law

Part III, Section II, Chapter VI of the Geneva Convention Relative to the Treatment of Prisoners of War outlines rules for structuring POWs by rank and in relation to official authorities.

Article 39 specifies that

- The detaining power must designate a "commissioned officer" from its regular armed forces as the main authority of the POW camp (also known as "camp commander").
- This officer must be in possession of the convention, and he or she will be responsible for educating all provisions within this convention to all staff and guards of the POW camp.
- All personnel of POW camps will be responsible for behaving in accordance with the rights and regulations granted in the present convention.
- The governing authority (the detaining power) of camp personnel will ultimately be liable should its personnel breach any provisions within the convention.
- POWs are obliged to respect officers of the detaining power, such as by saluting them when appropriate.
- POWs who happen to be officers are not obliged to salute officers of lower ranks, but should salute officers of higher ranks, and they should salute the camp commander regardless of their own rank.

Article 40 specifies that all POWs have the right to wear badges that indicate their rank and/or nationality.

Part III, Section II, Chapter VII of the convention specifies the treatment of POWs according to their rank. Article 43 specifies that

- When conflict arises, all parties to the conflict must inform each other of the title and rank of types of individuals mentioned in Article 4 of this convention.
- Parties to the conflict must do this in order to ensure equal treatment of prisoners of equal ranks.
- All parties to a conflict must also inform each other of POWs who have been promoted to higher ranks.

Article 44 specifies that

- Officers and POWs of equal status must be treated with respect to their rank and age. Thus, POWs of the same rank and age must be treated equally.

- Other ranks of persons within the same armed forces can be used by the detaining power to provide service for camp officers. These other ranks must be able to communicate in the same language.
- The detaining power must keep record of the rank of camp officers and POWs of equal ranks.
- All persons who provide service for officers must not be forced to do other labor.

Article 45 specifies that all other camp officers and POWs of the same rank must be treated according to their rank and age.

Islamic Law

Classical Islamic tradition contains guidelines for the treatment of POWs according to their rank. Munir (2010, p. 486) writes of the Prophet's treatment of Thumamah bin Uthal, a captive who was the head of a rival tribe. The Prophet is reported to have provided food and milk to Uthal from his own home. In addition, Munir writes that the Prophet instructed fighters to "be kind to a dignified man who has lost his status," and that "if a noble man falls into your hands, treat him well" (p. 486). Munir argues that the Prophet's prescriptions and personal behavior serve as legal precedents for early modern and contemporary expectations regarding the treatment of POWs according to their rank.

Contemporary Islamic laws do not specify that POWs should be treated according to their rank. For instance, Article 3 of the Cairo Declaration on Human Rights in Islam (1990) specifies general rights granted to all POWs, but none that indicate special treatment according to rank.

Relations with the Detaining Power

International Law

Section VI, Chapter I of the Geneva Convention Relative to the Treatment of Prisoners of War specifies the rights of POWs in relation to the authorities of the detaining power. Article 78 specifies that

- POWs have the right to complain about the conditions in which they are held, and they have the right to request changes to be made to improve the conditions in which they are held.
- POWs must be afforded the opportunity to voice their opinion as to their state and conditions of captivity.
- Prisoners' representatives have the right to send reports about the conditions and needs of the POWs to the representatives of third-party protecting powers.
- The detaining power and its camp authorities have no right to punish POWs for issuing complaints, and they do not have the right to delay any reports or complaints, even if the reports or complaints are not substantiated with evidence.

Islamic Law

Our sources indicate that classical, early modern, and contemporary Islamic traditions do not mandate the relations that POWs are permitted to have with their detainers. However, officials can infer that Jihadi detainers must afford protections to POWs that are at least consistent with the theme of guardianship in the Prophet;s own prescriptions relative to prisoner-detainer relations.

Self-Governance

International Law

Section IV, Chapter II of the Geneva Convention Relative to the Treatment of Prisoners of War discusses the rights of POW representatives.

Article 79 specifies that

- POWs have the right to freely elect representatives every 6 months through casting confidential ballots, except in areas where POW camps have officers.
- In camps where officers or those of equal rank are present, the most senior officer or person of equal rank is to be recognized as the prisoners' representative.
- That officer is to be assisted by one or more advisors to be elected from among the POWs; the elected advisor or advisors are not to be officers themselves.
- The detaining power must approve of the representatives, and if they are not approved, then it must be made known to the third-party protecting powers why they were not approved.
- The prisoners' representative must share the same nationality, language, and customs as those they represent; thus, different sections of a camp will have different representatives in accordance with their language, nationality, or customs.

Article 80 specifies that

- Prisoners' representatives have a right to accommodate the physical, spiritual, and intellectual well-being of POWs.
- In the event that POWs decide to organize to create support groups, or to gather in peaceful assembly or protest, POWs' representatives must not be held responsible for any offenses that the POWs commit under their jurisdiction.
- If the prisoners decide to organize a system of mutual assistance, this organization must be within the prisoners' representative's jurisdiction.

Article 81 specifies that

- POWs' representatives are not required to do any other kind of work if additional work will make their current responsibilities as representatives too burdensome.

- Prisoners' representatives have the right to visit the premises of residing POWs to examine the well-being of the POWs in addition to the conditions in which they are held.
- The detaining power must provide all materials necessary, including transportation, to POW representatives so that they may execute these tasks and all other tasks related to their responsibilities.
- POWs have the right to freely converse with the representative about their conditions.
- The representative will be allowed to appoint assistants in order to complete their tasks.
- All facilities should be equipped with means for communication between the detaining authorities and the prisoners' representative.
- This accommodation should include the protecting powers, the International Committee of the Red Cross and their delegates, the Mixed Medical Commissions, and other assorted bodies.
- Prisoners' representatives of labor camps should be afforded the same opportunities as those who are representatives of the main camp.

Justice, Discipline, and Punishment

International Law

Section IV, Chapter III, Part I of the Geneva Convention Relative to the Treatment of Prisoners of War discusses the rules regarding punishment and disciplinary sanctions.

Article 82 specifies that

- POWs are subject to the laws, regulations, and orders of the armed forces of the detaining power; the detaining power is justified to take judicial or disciplinary measures against all who break those rules. However, the rules and regulations regarding disciplinary or judicial measures of the detaining power must be in compliance with the present convention.
- If the detaining power determines that an act committed by a POW is punishable, whereas the same act would not be punishable if it were committed by a member of its own forces, then the detaining power must enact disciplinary punishment in compliance with the provisions of the convention. All forms of punishment prohibited by the present convention are not allowed to be enacted against convicted POWs.

Article 83 specifies that

- Detaining powers should ensure that relevant authorities be as lenient as possible when deciding whether an offense committed by a POW should be tried judicially or disciplinarily.

- The detaining power should seek to enact disciplinary punishments rather than judicial punishments whenever possible.

Article 84 specifies that

- A POW should only be tried in a military court, unless laws in place in the civil code of the detaining powers allow for their own respective armed forces to be tried in civil court for a similar offense committed by the POW.
- A POW will not be tried in a court that does not offer the guarantees of independence and impartiality.
- POWs will also be afforded the rights of legal counsel and assistance for the sake of defense.

Article 85 specifies that POWs who have been prosecuted under the laws of the detaining power for acts committed prior to their capture are still protected by the rights of the convention, even if they are convicted.

Article 86 specifies that POWs cannot be punished for or charged with the same crime more than once.

Article 87 specifies that

- POWs must be tried and/or punished in the same manner that armed forces of the detaining power would be tried and punished for the same crimes that are allegedly committed by either type of individual. For instance, POWs cannot be sentenced by both military authorities and the courts of the detaining power for a particular act if a member of the detaining power's armed forces would not be subjected to similar treatment in the same circumstance.
- When contemplating all sentences to POWs, the courts or authorities of the detaining power must consider a lenient punishment or no punishment whenever possible, given that POWs are not citizens of the detaining power; they are held in its control due to extraordinary circumstances beyond POWs' will; and they are not necessarily bound by the regulations of the detaining power as a citizen of the detaining power would be.
- If the court of the detaining power reduces the penalty of the alleged violation, then the detaining power will not be required to apply the minimum sentence possible.
- The detaining power is forbidden to exercise the following kinds of punishment:
  - Collective punishment for individual violations
  - Torture as described in the UN Convention Against Torture (UNCAT) (UN, 1984)
  - Cruelty, as described in UNCAT
  - Imprisonment without daylight
  - Corporal punishment

- The detaining power may not deprive POWs of their rank, or prevent POWs from wearing and displaying any badges.

Article 88 specifies that

- Officers, noncommissioned officers, and persons who are POWs undergoing disciplinary or judicial punishment must not be subjected to treatment that is worse than treatment applied to armed forces of the detaining power of equivalent rank who have committed the same offense.
- POWs must not receive sentences that are more severe than sentences that members of the armed forces belonging to the detaining power would receive for the same offense. This applies to both male and female POWs.
- POWs who have served judicial or disciplinary punishments must not be treated differently than POWs who have not been served sanctions of any kind.

Section VI, Chapter III, Part II concerns the conditions under which disciplinary sanctions may be taken against POWs.

Article 89 specifies that

- The detaining power is prohibited from enacting punishments that are cruel, inhumane, or threaten the mental or physical health of POWs. Officials should refer to UNCAT to identify what constitutes cruel or inhumane punishment, according to international law.
- The only disciplinary punishments applicable to POWs are:
    - A fine not exceeding half of any earnings that a POW would receive in a period of no less than 30 days under Articles 60 and 62.
    - Removal of privileges that are not protected by the present convention. For instance, if POWs are given additional food rations for good behavior, then the detaining power may take away the surplus of food rations as punishment, but it cannot take away all food rations from POWs since such an act would constitute starvation, which is a form of cruelty and is prohibited by the present convention.
    - "Fatigue duties" must not exceed 2 hours each day; officers or POWs of equivalent ranks are exempt.
    - Confinement.

Article 90 specifies that

- The duration of a single punishment will not exceed 30 days.
- A period of confinement while waiting for the hearing of the offense will be deducted from the announced punishment sentenced to the POW.

- The 30 days provided cannot be extended even if the POW faces punishment for multiple offenses, regardless of the connection between them.
- The time between the pronouncement of the disciplinary punishment and its implementation cannot be longer than 1 month.
- If the POW is given an extended punishment that is 10 days or more, then a period of at least 3 days must pass between each punishment.

Article 95 specifies that

- POWs who are accused of an offense that is subject to disciplinary punishment cannot be kept in confinement while awaiting the trial unless a member of the armed forces of the detaining power is kept in the same manner in which the POW is being kept, or if it is necessary for the interests of the camp's order and discipline.
- The period of confinement spent by a POW while awaiting the outcome of his or her offense must be reduced to the minimum time possible and cannot exceed 14 days.
- Provisions laid out in Articles 97 and 98 will not apply to POWs who are in confinement who are awaiting the acquittal of offenses subject to disciplinary punishment.

Article 96 specifies that

- Acts that are considered offenses against discipline will be investigated immediately.
- All disciplinary punishment must be ordered by an officer who has disciplinary powers in his or her capacity as a "camp commander," or through a responsible officer who replaces him or her as a delegate with disciplinary powers. Powers cannot be delegated to a POW or be exercised by a POW. All courts and military authorities are expected to exercise jurisprudential matters competently and without prejudice.
- The accused must be given precise information about the offenses of which they are accused; they must be given the opportunity to defend themselves and explain the reasoning behind their conduct; they must be allowed to call witnesses; and, if necessary, they must be permitted to use the services of a qualified interpreter. All POWs must be permitted to exercise these rights before any disciplinary action is taken against them.
- All decisions regarding sentencing and punishments must be announced to the accused POW and to the prisoners' representatives in languages they understand. A record of these disciplinary punishments must be maintained by the camp commander and be available for inspection by the representatives of the protecting power.

Article 97 specifies that

- A POW cannot be transferred to a penitentiary establishment to receive disciplinary punishments.
- The premises on which disciplinary punishments are served must conform to the sanitary requirements that have been established in Article 25.
- POWs who are receiving punishment must be able to maintain a state of cleanliness, which is laid out in Article 29.
- Officers and persons who have equivalent status cannot be housed in the same facilities as noncommissioned officers.
- Female POWs who undergo disciplinary punishment must be confined in separate quarters from male POWs, and be under the immediate supervision of women.

Article 98 specifies that

- The rules of the convention will apply to POWs who have been placed in confinement, except where the provisions would be impossible to enforce due to the prisoner's confinement.
- Under no circumstances may a prisoner be deprived of the benefits outlined in Articles 78 and 126.
- A POW who is subjected to disciplinary punishment cannot be deprived of the privileges associated with his or her rank, and must also be allowed to exercise and be in open air for a minimum of 2 hours daily.
- Upon request, POWs must be allowed to attend daily medical inspections. They will receive required medical attention and be sent to the camp infirmary or a hospital if necessary.
- POWs will be allowed to read and write, and to send and receive letters. Packages and money sent by mail will be withheld from POWs until the completion of their punishment and will be entrusted to the prisoner's representative in the interim. Perishable items found in packages will be sent to the infirmary.

Chapter III, Section III concerns the conditions under which judicial proceedings involving POWs must take place.

Article 99 specifies that

- No POW may be tried or sentenced for acts that are not forbidden by the law of the detaining power or by international law at the time that the act was committed.
- POWs will not be morally or physically coerced in order to elicit an admission of guilt.

- No POW may be convicted without an opportunity to present a defense and without the assistance of a qualified advocate or counsel.

Article 100 specifies that

- POWs and the protecting powers will be informed as soon as possible of any offenses that are punishable by death under the laws of the detaining power. Other offenses cannot later be made punishable by death without agreement from the protecting power.
- A POW cannot be sentenced to the death penalty, unless, in accordance with Article 87, the court has taken into consideration that the POW is not a national of the detaining power and therefore not allegiant to it, but rather in its power as a result of circumstances beyond his own will, and still decides that death is the just punishment.

Article 101 specifies that if a POW is sentenced to the death penalty, the sentence will not be carried out for a period of at least 6 months from the date that the protecting power receives communication of the sentence, concurrent with Article 107.

Article 102 specifies that any sentence imposed on a POW can be valid only if pronounced by the same courts and in accordance with the same procedures imposed on members of the armed forces of the detaining power, and if the "provisions of the present Chapter have been observed."

Article 103 specifies that

- Judicial investigations relating to a POW will be conducted as quickly as possible, so that the trial can occur as soon as possible.
- POWs will not be confined while awaiting trial unless a member of the detaining power's military would be confined if accused of a similar offense, or if confinement is in the interest of national security.
- Confinement will not exceed a period of 3 months, and any time spent in confinement while awaiting trial will be deducted from any sentence that might be imposed later.
- Provisions of Articles 97 and 98 will apply to POWs in confinement while awaiting trial.

Article 104 specifies that

- In all cases in which the detaining power decides to prosecute a POW, it will notify the protecting power at least 3 weeks before the trial begins.
- The 3-week period begins on the day that the protecting power receives a notification containing the following information:

1. The POW's first and last names, rank, army, regimental, personal or serial number, date of birth, and profession/trade
2. Place of internment/confinement
3. Explanation of charges on which the POW will be arraigned, with applicable legal provisions
4. The court that will try the case, and the date and place where the trial will begin

- This information will also be provided to the POW's representative.
- If, at the opening of the trial, the court has received no evidence that the information was received at least 3 weeks previously by the protecting power, the POW, and the POW's representative, then the trial cannot continue.

Article 105 specifies that

- POWs are entitled to assistance by one fellow prisoner, to a legal defense by a qualified advocate/counsel of his or her choice, to call witnesses, and to the services of a competent interpreter, if necessary.
- The detaining power must advise the POW of these rights well before the trial is to take place.
- If the POW is unable to secure a legal advocate, then the protecting power will have at least 1 week to find the POW one.
- The detaining power will, upon request, provide the protecting power with a list of qualified advocates.
- If both the POW and the protecting power fail to choose an advocate, the detaining power will appoint one to defend the POW.
- The chosen or appointed advocate for the defense must be given at least 2 weeks before the trial to prepare a defense.
- The legal counsel may visit the POW freely, interview the POW privately, and confer with any witnesses for the defense, including other POWs.
- The advocate must be allowed to complete these duties until the term of appeal or petition expires.
- The details of the charges on which the POW will be arraigned and any documents that are communicated to the accused in accordance with the laws of the armed forces of the detaining power must be communicated to the POW in a language the POW understands, and "in good time" before the trial begins, and must also be communicated to the advocate for the POW.

- Representatives of the protecting power must be allowed to attend the trial, unless the trial is held privately in the interest of state security, in which case the detaining power must advise the protecting power of this.

Article 106 specifies that

- Every POW has the right to appeal or petition against any sentence he or she is given in the same manner that members of the armed forces of the detaining power have such a right.
- POWs have the right to demand an appeal for the purpose of changing the sentence, or reopening the trial.
- The POW must be fully informed of rights to appeal or petition and of the timeline to do so.

Article 107 specifies that

- Any judgement and sentence given to a POW must be immediately reported to the protecting power through a summary communication that must indicate whether the POW has the right to appeal with the aim of reversal of the sentence or reopening of the trial.
- If the sentence was not pronounced in the POW's presence, this communication must also be sent to the POW's representative as well as the POW, in a language understood by the POW.
- The detaining power must immediately communicate to the protecting power of a POW's decision to use or waive the right to appeal.
- If a POW is sentenced to the death penalty, the detaining power must send a detailed communication to the protecting power as soon as possible, at a mailing address previously made known to the detaining power.
- This communication must contain precise wording of the court's finding and sentence; a summarized report of the preliminary investigation and trial that emphasizes the elements of the prosecution and defense; and notification of the establishment where the sentence will be served, if applicable.

Article 108 specifies that

- After a conviction has become legally enforceable, sentences given to POWs will be served in the same establishments and conditions as members of the armed forces of the detaining power.
- These conditions must always conform to requirements of "health and humanity."
- Convicted female POWs will be held in separate facilities from men, and they must be under the supervision of women.

- POWs sentenced to penalties that deprive them of their liberty should have the benefits of the provisions of Articles 78 and 126.
- POWs should be entitled to receive and send correspondence, to receive at least one "relief parcel" each month, to regularly exercise in the open air, and to receive necessary medical care and desired spiritual assistance.
- They may be subjected to penalties only that are in accordance with the provisions of the third paragraph of Article 87.

Islamic Law

Classical, early modern and contemporary Islamic legal traditions all indicate that POWs have the right to defend themselves before judicial bodies upon charges of having committed any crime.

In the classical tradition, Munir (2011, p. 90) indicates that the common practice for dealing with prisoners who faced charges related to lesser crimes was as follows:

1. If the prisoner was guilty of committing the offense for the first time, then he or she was urged to repent, and a contractual agreement was formed where he or she would swear to never commit the offense again.
2. If it could not be proved that the prisoner was guilty of committing an offense, the prisoner was relieved of any kind of negative sanction.

More serious offenses that warranted executions involved those who were either charged with committing atrocities before their capture (Munir, 2011, p. 91), or those who breached an agreement. In cases that warranted executions, those who were sentenced to death were widely known to have committed the crime in question, and the nature of the crime was heinous enough to warrant execution. Detainers were expressly forbidden from committing acts of violence or torture against POWs for any reason, including for the purpose of obtaining confessions (El-Dakkak, 1990, p. 104).

Early modern and contemporary Islamic laws do not detail the specific judicial rights afforded to POWs should they be accused of committing offenses upon captivity. However, Article 19 of the Cairo Declaration on Human Rights in Islam (1990) specifies that accused persons have the right to a legal defense in the event that they are accused of committing a crime:

a. All individuals are equal before the law, without distinction between the ruler and the ruled.

b. The right to resort to justice is guaranteed to everyone.

c. Liability is in essence personal.

d. There shall be no crime or punishment except as provided for in the Shari'ah.

e. A defendant is innocent until his guilt is proven in a fair trial in which he shall be given all the guarantees of defence.

Escape

International Law

Article 91 of the Geneva Convention Relative to the Treatment of Prisoners of War specifies that

- POWs who successfully escape from camps have the right not to face punishment for having successfully escaped should they be recaptured.
- The escape of a POW is deemed to be a success when
  - A POW has joined the armed forces of the nation in power in which they depend or that of an allied power.
  - A POW left the region under the control of the "Detaining Power" or that of an ally of the original "Power."
  - A POW has joined a ship that is flying the flag of the power on which he or she depends, or a ship belonging to an allied power, or a ship that is in the waters of the territory of the detaining power, but not in the control of the detaining power.

Article 92 specifies that

- POWs who attempt to escape but fail and are recaptured will be liable to disciplinary punishment only for having attempted to escape, even if the POW has attempted to escape more than once.
- POWs who are captured after attempting to escape remain protected under the full provisions of the convention.
- A POW who has been recaptured must be sent to a military authority immediately.
- POWs who are punished due to an unsuccessful escape can be subjected to heightened surveillance. This surveillance cannot affect the health of the POWs, and they must be surveilled in a POW camp.

Article 93 specifies that

- The act of escape or attempted escape, regardless if the offense is repeated, must not be considered an aggravated crime if a POW faces trial by judicial proceedings for committing another crime while escaping successfully or attempting to escape. For instance, if a POW attempts to steal a naval vessel as a means to escape, and faces trial for both offenses of attempted theft of a naval vessel and of attempting to escape, the court will not consider the act of attempted escape as having caused further injury or aggravation to the detaining power as a means to increase the sentence against the POW.

- In accordance with Article 83, offenses that are committed by POWs with the intention to escape qualify for disciplinary punishment only. These offenses may include but are not limited to harm to public property, stealing items without the intention to enrich oneself, identity fraud, or wearing civilian clothing.
- Any offenses that involve violence or harm to another's life will qualify for harsher punishment.
- POWs who assist or encourage other POWs to escape are liable to receive disciplinary punishment only.

Article 94 specifies that if a POW escapes and is recaptured, the power on which he or she depends must be notified of the POW's attempted escape in the manner defined by Article 122.

Islamic Law

Classical, early modern, and contemporary Islamic practice do not specify rights afforded to POWs who successfully escape, or those who have attempted to escape. However, Munir (2011) cites the Prophet, who is reported to have said, "slay no wounded person, pursue no fugitive, execute no prisoner, and whosoever closes his door is safe" (p. 90). From this, officials can infer that escapees should not be pursued, and that attempted escapees should not be executed as punishment for attempting to escape.

Labor and Work

International Law

Part III, Section III of the Geneva Convention Relative to the Treatment of Prisoners of War concerns rules regarding the conditions under which prisoners can be utilized for labor.

Article 49 specifies that

- The detaining power may use prisoners for labor only if the prisoners are physically fit and capable of performing assigned duties.
- The detaining power must take into consideration the "age, sex, rank, and physical aptitude" of all POWs who are considered for labor.
- The detaining power should employ POWs with the intention to maintain their physical and mental health, rather than the intention to exploit them for labor.
- POWs who are "noncommissioned officers" must be considered for only supervisory roles. Other noncommissioned officers may ask to perform other tasks that are suitable for their rank and capabilities.

- POWs who are officers or of similar ranks may not be forced to work under any circumstances, and they should be provided work that is suitable to their rank and capabilities upon their request.

Article 50 specifies the categories of labor for which POWs are allowed to be utilized:

- In addition to labor related to camp administrative services, installation, or maintenance, POWs may be given work related to
    a. Agriculture.
    b. Any other form of labor that has no military character or purpose. POWs may also be used for extracting raw materials, except those related to metallurgy, machinery, or chemical industries.
    c. Transport services and maintenance of stores that serve no purpose to the military.
    d. Commercial business, including arts and crafts.
    e. Domestic service.
    f. Public utility services that serve no purpose to the military.
- POWs reserve the right to issue a complaint should any of the aforementioned provisions be violated. Refer to Article 78 for regulations regarding the complaint process.

Article 51 specifies that

- POWs must be employed in safe working conditions.
- The conditions in which POWs are employed must be equal to those available to the detaining power's own citizens.
- POWs must be provided food, clothing, and any equipment necessary for their labor.
- The detaining power must take into account the climatic conditions to which the workers and their labor environments are subject.
- Any national legislation passed by the detaining power that concerns the protection of employees and their right to work in a safe work environment, and regulations regarding labor practices, must also be applied to the context of the detaining power's use of POWs.
- POWs must be trained in their respective fields of labor, and they must be provided with relevant protections necessary to complete their duties. All training and protections given to POWs must be similar to training and protections given to employed citizens of the detaining power.
- POWs must not be exposed to risks to which the citizens of the detaining power would not be exposed given the same type of labor.

- The detaining power must not enact disciplinary measures that would make labor more difficult for POWs.

Article 52 specifies that

- No POW may be employed in forms of labor that are dangerous or unhealthy, unless they volunteer to work in such conditions.
- No POW must be employed in labor that would be humiliating if a member of the detaining power's forces were to be assigned to perform the same task.
- Any labor involving the removal of mines or other forms of explosives will be considered dangerous, and thus forbidden from assignment to POWs.

Article 53 specifies that

- The length of time that POWs are required to work must not exceed the length of time that ordinary citizens of the detaining power are required to work.
- The distance that POWs must travel to work must not be excessive.
- POWs are entitled to a break of at least 1 hour each day of labor, and they must be able to take their break during their period of labor each day.
- POWs have the right to a break that is as long as the break enjoyed by workers belonging to the detaining power.
- POWs are entitled to at least 24 consecutive hours (1 full day) off work each week.
- POWs who have worked for an entire year are entitled to 8 days of paid leave.
- The provisions of this convention also apply to POWs who are employed to complete individual tasks at the request of camp personnel, like that of "piece-work." For instance, camp personnel might ask a POW to complete a single task such as collecting fruit from a field. The amount of time a POW spends on this task must not be more than the amount of time a citizen of the detaining power would spend completing the same form of labor in a single workday. Thus, POWs who complete "piece-work" are entitled to the same workday period, as well as pay for their labor.

Article 54 specifies the rights of POWs who sustain injuries or who contract illnesses while at work, or as a result of their labor:

- Such POWs are entitled to medical care to the fullest extent their ailments require.

- It is the responsibility of the detaining power to provide such POWs with medical certifications necessary for the submission of claims to their country of nationality. The detaining power must provide copies of the certifications to the Central Prisoners of War Agency.

Article 55 specifies that

- POWs who work are entitled to fixed payment for their labor as specified under Article 62.
- They are entitled to monthly physical check-ups with the purpose of monitoring their fitness.
- Medical examinations must be appropriate to the type of labor. For instance, medical practitioners must be able to determine if a POW is physically fit to perform duties related to his or her type of work.
- If a POW feels incapable of working, then the POW must be sent to the camp's medical authorities to receive a professional opinion from a physician or surgeon. If medical authorities confirm that a POW is incapable of working, then the POW must be exempted from labor.

Article 56 specifies that

- All labor departments in which POWs are employed must be under the control of the POW camp's administrative body.
- The detaining power, all military authorities of the camp, and the camp commander are responsible for ensuring that all provisions of this convention are followed in all labor departments.
- The camp commander must keep records of all labor departments within his or her camp, and he or she must provide the records to any agency that provides relief to POWs of the camp, such as the protecting power or the International Committee of the Red Cross.

Article 57 specifies the rights of POWs who work for private entities:

- Any POW who works for private entities is protected under the provisions this convention, and he or she must be treated accordingly.
- The detaining power, military authorities, and the commander of the camp are responsible for the "maintenance, care, treatment, and work wages" of POWs who work for private entities.
- These POWs have the right to maintain contact with their representatives in the camp that they depend on.

Article 62 specifies that

- Detaining authorities must pay POWs fair working wages.
- The rate of pay must be fixed, and the amount of fixed pay must be determined by the detaining authorities.

- The pay rate must be "no less than one-fourth of one Swiss franc for one working day."
- The detaining power must communicate to the power on which POWs depend through an intermediary of the daily fixed pay rate that POWs will be given.
- The detaining power is responsible for providing working pay to all prisoners who perform any form of labor, including those who perform medical or religious duties.
- If a prisoner has a representative, and/or advisers, and/or assistants of any kind, then the working pay of the representative and advisers must be granted fixed pay, which will be funded by any profits procured from canteen services.
- The amount of pay given to these workers will be determined by the prisoner's representative, which must then be approved by the camp's commander.
- If the camp does not have a canteen fund, then the detaining power must give the prisoners a fair rate of pay.

Islamic Law

Classical, early modern, and contemporary Islamic laws do not explicitly grant employment rights to POWs.

Classical and early modern Islamic laws place the responsibility of sustaining POWs on the shoulders of the detaining power. However, some historical accounts portray the Prophet releasing POWs upon the condition that they would benefit the Muslim community by applying or providing skills related to their professions to Muslims. Thus, "ransom" in this sense is broadened to include other forms of material exchange, such as labor. For instance, Malami (1994, p. 47) and Ali (2015, p. 329) note that the Prophet released some prisoners taken from the Battle of Badr on the condition that they educated illiterate Muslims.

In contemporary Islamic law, Article 13 of the Cairo Declaration on Human Rights in Islam (1990) grants persons the right to employment. Although this legal prescription is not specific to POWs, officials may generalize it to include the protection of POWs, if possible.

Personal Possessions

International Law

Part III, Section I, Article 18 of the Geneva Convention Relative to the Treatment of Prisoners of War

- Outlines personal items that POWs have a right to possess at all times during captivity, which must not be taken from them by their captors. These items include identity documents, eating utensils, clothing, and items that have personal sentimental value to POWs—such as badges and decorative war medals.

- Money may not be taken from POWs without the consent of a ranking officer.
- Captors have the right to withhold items belonging to POWs for security purposes. These items include weapons, military equipment, military documents, and/or sums of money.
- All confiscated items must be returned to POWs at the end of their captivity.

Part III, Section IV discusses the right of POWs to have access to financial resources.

Article 58 specifies that

- The detaining power may limit the amount of money that prisoners can retain upon their capture. Any remaining funds may be confiscated from them.
- Camp authorities must keep record of the total funds of POWs, in addition to any funds that are confiscated from them. They must do this by creating accounts for POWs.
- None of the POWs' funds may be converted to any other currency without the consent of the POW.
- If POWs are allowed to purchase items and services outside of the camp without the use of cash, then the payments must be made by the prisoner or by the camp administrators, who must then place the charges to the accounts of the POWs. The detaining power must create rules regarding purchases.

Article 59 specifies that

- Any cash that is taken from POWs at the time of their capture must be reserved in the accounts that the detaining power is responsible for making on behalf of the POWs. This process must be in compliance with Article 64 of the convention.

Article 60 specifies that

- The detaining power must grant all POWs a fixed amount of pay each month.
- All funds granted to POWs must be converted into the currency of the detaining power.
- The detaining power must convert the following amount of pay from Swiss francs into its own currency, and give the funds to the relevant type of POW:
    1. Category I: Prisoners who rank below sergeant receive at least 8 Swiss francs.
    2. Category II: Sergeants, noncommissioned officers, or prisoners of equivalent ranks receive at least 12 Swiss francs.

3. Category III: Warrant officers and commissioned officers, or prisoners of equivalent ranks who are below the rank of major must receive at least 50 Swiss francs.
4. Category IV: Majors, lieutenant, colonels, or prisoners of equivalent rank must receive at least 60 Swiss francs.
5. Category V: General officers or prisoners of equivalent rank must receive at least 75 Swiss francs.

- Parties to the conflict can change the amount of pay given to the aforementioned categories of POWs through a special agreement.
- If the amount of pay listed above is more than the pay that armed personnel of the detaining power receive, then the detaining power must generate a contract with the power on which the POWs depend to modify the amount it must give to POWs.
- Until an agreement is reached about the amount of pay that must be granted to POWs, the detaining power must
  a. Credit the amounts listed above to the accounts of the relevant categories of prisoners
  b. Or temporarily reduce the amounts of pay listed above to amounts that are reasonable
- However, the amount granted to Category I prisoners must never be less than the amount given to armed forces of the same rank belonging to the detaining power.
- The detaining power must immediately provide its reasons for reducing POWs' pay to the power on which they depend.

Article 61 specifies that

- The detaining power must allow for the power on which the POWs depend to send POWs additional funds if the power on which they depend satisfies the following conditions:
  1. The sums sent must be sent to all POWs of the same category.
  2. The amounts sent to all POWs of the same category must be equal.
  3. The amounts sent must be sent to the individual accounts of all POWs within the same category.
  4. The process by which the funds are sent must be in accordance with Article 64.
- The detaining power will not be relieved of its obligations to provide pay to POWs under the provisions of the convention if the power on which the POWs depend sends additional funds to them.

Article 63 specifies that

- POWs must be allowed to receive any payments that are addressed to them individually or collectively.

- All POWs must be able to access their accounts, and they must be able to view their credit balances.
- POWs are subject to any financial restrictions that the detaining power views as necessary and imposes on them accordingly.
- POWs may accept payments from entities of other countries, and POWs may make payments to entities in other countries.
- Any payments made by POWs that are addressed to dependents must be given priority for processing.
- Should POWs send payments to their own country, the detaining power must send notification through a third-party protecting power to the power on which the POWs depend. The notification should include the name of the POW who is sending the funds, the recipient(s) of the payment, and the amount of funds to be paid expressed in the currency of the detaining power. The notification must be signed by the POW who is sending the funds, and also by the camp commander. The detaining power must record the payment into the accounts of the relevant POWs.

Article 64 specifies that

- The detaining power must establish individual accounts for each POW, which must include the POW's personal and financial information, plus
    1. Any amount of funds owed to and received by the POW from employment or from any other source
    2. Any amount of funds taken from the POW by the detaining power at the time of capture
    3. Any amount of sums that were taken from the POW and converted into the currency of the detaining power
    4. Any payments made to the POW in cash or in other forms, any payments made on behalf of the POW, any payments made at the request of a POW, and the amount of funds transferred under Article 63, paragraph 3

Article 65 specifies that

- The authenticity of all transactions and details in the account of a POW must be verified by the POW with his or her initials or signature, or with the signature of the POW's representative who will act on behalf of the POW.
- POWs must at all times have access to facilities where they can consult with camp personnel on matters related to their accounts, and facilities where POWs can obtain copies of any records related to their accounts. These facilities may be inspected by the

representatives of a third-party protecting power during their visit to the POW camp.

- If POWs are transferred, then their personal accounts must be transferred to the camp to which they are transferred.
- If POWs are to be transferred to a new detaining power, then all non-converted funds belonging to the POWs must be taken with them.
- All parties to the conflict may inform each other of the total number of accounts belonging to POWs.

Article 66 specifies that

- Once the captivity status of a POW has been terminated, either through repatriation or through release, the detaining power must issue documentation that includes all monies owed to the POW, and all monies owed by the POW. This documentation must be signed by an authorized officer of the detaining power.
- The detaining power must also maintain records of all POWs whose captivity status has been terminated by repatriation, release, escape, death, or any other means, and this documentation must show all monies owed to the POW and all monies owed by the POW.
- Such documents must be sent to the power on which the POWs depend through a third-party protecting power.
- Each sheet of paper comprising the documentation must be certified by an official of the detaining power.
- Once the status of captivity has been terminated for a POW, it is the responsibility of the power on which POWs depend to collect and distribute any monies owed by the detaining power to the POW.
- Any regulations mentioned in this article may be changed upon mutual agreement between parties to the conflict.

Article 67 specifies that

- Any pay issued to POWs in accordance with Article 60 will be made on behalf of the power on which they depend.
- These payments, as well as any payments made in accordance with Articles 63 and 68, will be discussed in agreements between the detaining power and the power on which the POWs depend at the end of hostilities.

Article 68 specifies the rights of POWs who seek compensation from the detaining power:

- Any POW who claims work-related injuries or disabilities must be referred to the power on which they depend through a third-party protecting power.

- The detaining power must follow the provisions of Article 54, and it must provide the POW with written documentation of the injury or disability, how the injury or disability was incurred by the POW, and any medical treatment the POW was given for the injury or disability. This document must be signed by a certified authority of the detaining power; any information pertaining to medical diagnoses and medical treatment must be signed by a certified medical authority of the detaining power.
- If a POW demands compensation for personal items that are either withheld by the detaining power or that are believed to be lost at the fault of the detaining power or personnel belonging to the detaining power, then the POW must be referred to the power on which he or she depends.
- Any supplies of necessities used by POWs while in captivity must be replenished by the detaining power.
- The detaining power must provide the POW with a written statement describing why any personal belongings of the POW have not been returned to the POW.
- The detaining power must send a copy of this statement to the Central Prisoners of War agency, which must then forward it to the power on which the POW depends.

11

Resolve the Negotiation

In this chapter we consider the end of any negotiation. The following sections review three questions:

1. What should be the negotiator's objectives other than a safe end to the crisis?
2. What is a good deal?
3. What are the practical difficulties for executing any deal?

What Should Be the Negotiator's Objectives Other Than a Safe End to the Crisis?

Historical Practices

The release of the hostages is not the only or even necessarily the primary objective for the official side during a negotiation with terrorists. Given the increased likelihood that newer terrorists have no objectives acceptable to the official side, and the increased unreliability of new terrorists, the negotiators may enter negotiations expecting no hostages to be released but still negotiating for other purposes.

Intelligence

Since the 1970s, official negotiators have been trained to stall for time in order to gather information of use to the tactical team (Lanceley, 2003, p. 19).

Experts from the era before the new wave of terrorism allowed for negotiations to proceed in order to gather intelligence that would be useful to the assaulters, such as the location of the hostage-takers and hostages, or their psychological state (Hudson, 1989, pp. 325, 335). In the law enforcement community, the intelligence relationship between negotiators and assaulters is obvious:

> The tactical team must have accurate, reliable, timely, and complete intelligence in order to perform their tasks. While the intelligence needs of the tactical team are no more important than the needs of the negotiating team, the tactical team needs more intelligence than the negotiating team. The negotiating team needs intelligence on the hostage taker and hostages and, in some cases, intelligence on the location.
>
> **(McMains and Mullins, 2015, pp. 113–114)**

Armed responders also appreciate the synergies of intelligence from official negotiators or released hostages who were in contact with the hostage-takers:

> Multisource usually means you have both signal intelligence (intercepted phone calls) and human intelligence (people actually on the ground). Both can be valuable on their own, but when you have them together, it usually means you have something credible. Credibility is everything when it comes to intelligence sources, so you have to know how reliable each of the sources is before you buy into the supposition the source is portraying.
>
> **(Blaber, 2008, p. 64)**

Similarly, another law enforcement officer emphasizes the chance of intelligence:

> Negotiators can compile useful intelligence for the tactical team while speaking to the subject. The tactical team can initiate actions to help the hostage negotiators establish and maintain contact with the suspect, such as using public address systems or breaking windows on the building.
>
> **(Cameron, 2014)**

Giving Time for Preparations

Analysts of old terrorist hostage-taking acknowledged that the negotiator can keep the hostage-takers engaged while other officials prepare for an assault, stall for time until the assaulters are ready, and gather intelligence from the negotiations that would be useful to the assaulters, such as the location of the hostage-takers and hostages, or their psychological state—all while trying to wear down the hostage-takers until they reconsider their objectives enough to negotiate a nonviolent outcome (Hudson, 1989, pp. 325, 335).

Similarly, analysts of new terrorist hostage-taking allow for stalling for time or lowering expectations:

> When handling demands in a hostage crisis, one of the things negotiators strive to achieve is the perceived position of an intermediary between the authorities and the hostage takers. If the demands issued are difficult to satisfy, the negotiator can stall for time by pointing to the difficulty of locating a

> key decision-maker or some other objective obstacle to meeting the terrorists' deadline.
>
> Further, the negotiator's lack of decision-making authority also allows him or her to effectively disassociate him or herself from the official refusal to comply, while empathetically validating the reasonable component of the demand and promising to keep trying to convince the authorities in favor of its fulfillment. This strategy is useful in stalling for time, decreasing the expectations of the hostage takers, and creating a bond between the negotiator and the suspect.
>
> **(Dolnik and Fitzgerald, 2008, p. 37)**[1]

Similarly, Gary Noesner, former chief of the Crisis Negotiation Unit at the Federal Bureau of Investigation (FBI), notes that the negotiators may give time for the assaulters to prepare:

> Most importantly, there is a strategic benefit to negotiation. Rarely are we sufficiently staffed and equipped with highly trained tactical teams ready to conduct a rescue right away. It typically takes time to assemble these resources. The negotiation process buys time to allow us to assemble the forces necessary, gather the intelligence we need to support their planning (how many terrorist, what do we know about their behavior inside, what weapons have we observed, can we learn anything from speaking to them about their objectives and disposition, have we spoken directly to the hostages and learned anything from them, to name a few). I cannot imagine a competent counter-terrorism force simply sitting outside waiting for our commandos to show up while just sitting on their hands waiting.
>
> Negotiators can use verbal containment skills to stop ongoing violence or prevent it, and we can buy the time needed to get floor plans, architectural drawings, witness information, testimony from released/escaped hostages, and give our teams time to practice their entry plan elsewhere to maximize its success when the time is deemed necessary to pursue that high-risk option. In my judgment, negotiations never fail to be beneficial, it is simply that some perpetrators fail to make good decisions. We would certainly anticipate Jihadist being in that category, yet we still should negotiate as a strategic tool. In my view, anyone who argues against this simply has not worked a major terrorist siege as I have.
>
> **(Noesner, 2016)**

A former member of the FBI's Hostage Rescue Team and commander of the FBI New York Division's special weapons and tactics (SWAT) team (James A. Gagliano) also considered that the negotiator's role with new terrorists should help the assaulter to prepare more than expect to resolve the crisis peacefully:

> Depending on the nature of the case, there is still obviously some potential utility in opening communications with suspects in hostage standoffs. These

[1] However, Dolnik and Fitzgerald, in later writings (2011), do not include negotiation for any other purpose than to negotiate the voluntary release of hostages.

> negotiations—talking it out, stalling for time—can play a role in slowing down their killing to help play for time as more resources can be brought to bear. Islamist terrorists, after all, have an interest in getting their message out, as was seen in the grievances they communicated to negotiators in the Orlando and Paris attacks. Communications with the suspect(s) can also play a role in pinpointing their location as well as provide opportunities to distract the perpetrators just before a planned assault. In the final phase of the Bataclan hostage standoff in Paris, when two of the terrorists had barricaded themselves with hostages in a corridor inside the venue, French RAID commandos placed a call to one of the attackers, as a distraction, moments before the assault. While the hostage-takers were taken down, no one else in that corridor was killed.
>
> **(Cruickshank, 2017)**

Similarly, a law enforcement officer emphasizes the negotiator's role in garnering time for preparations:

> The slow and deliberate method used during a barricade allows the negotiators to potentially develop a rapport with the suspect. During this period, information can be gleaned about the suspect, his/her state of mind, and the overall situation. Research can be done on the suspect's background to enhance the negotiation process. This data would also be useful to the tactical team should they be required to act to resolve the situation.
>
> A well-coordinated law enforcement response to a barricade will involve a cohesive effort between negotiators and the tactical team members, not an adversarial one. Historically, the productive use of time during this process works to the advantage of the police. It levels the playing field, allowing time for planning and deliberation, rather than spontaneous action.
>
> **(Cameron, 2014)**

Simulated Practices

In both of our real-world simulations, the official role-players set out to negotiate for the release of all hostages as their primary objective, but, given the terrorist role-players' intransigence, later decided that an assault was necessary, and dedicated their remaining time for negotiations to deceiving and gathering intelligence. The time allowed for negotiations (in real time, after the periods of planning and orientation) was 2 hours. In both simulations the switch (from negotiating for a peaceful end to negotiating for misinformation of the other side and for information useful to the official side) occurred after around 1 hour.

Our Practical Prescriptions

We recommend that the official side should consider the following seven purposes for negotiations, other than a safe end to the crisis:

1. Gaining intelligence
2. Misleading the other side

3. Stalling for time
4. Wearing down the other side
5. Complying with policy
6. Signaling to other actors
7. Developing a relationship that would be useful in other situations

Given the possibility that some new terrorists may have no intention of releasing any hostages, whatever the negotiator tries, then we must allow the negotiator to prioritize objectives other than the release of hostages by negotiation. If the official side confidently predicts that the hostage-takers will not release any hostages, then the negotiator is useful to the hostage only if he or she helps an official rescue.

These objectives would align if the release of hostages would also release intelligence in the form of the hostages' memories of the hostage situation. However, these same objectives may be antagonistic, where continued negotiation might earn the release of hostages or might just give the hostage-takers more time to harm hostages. In such a case, the official side faces a terrible dilemma under conditions of uncertainty, including the chance of earning the release of hostages eventually (a positive risk), the longer exposure of the hostages to harm by the hostage-takers before assault (a negative risk), and the exposure of hostages to harm pursuant to the assault (another negative risk).

Moreover, any decision to prioritize intelligence collection or any other objective over the safe release of hostages naturally seems heartless to the hostages and their families. Remember that in 2015, Barak Barfi, a former journalist involved with some of the victims of the Islamic State, published criticisms of the U.S. State Department and FBI for apparently prioritizing intelligence collection over the negotiation for the safe release of four Americans held by the Islamic State (Barfi, 2015).

What Is a Good Deal?

Historical Practices

A good deal in classical negotiations literature is one in which both sides get something they want, but this seems particularly difficult in terrorism, given the typical official side's proscription against negotiating with terrorists, the typical terrorist's contempt for opponents, both sides' typical lack of empathy for the other, and the often unearthly demands.

The history of deals between terrorists and officials is difficult to verify, given secrecy on both sides about outcomes that they may not want to admit, such as when negotiating would violate policy or would offend supporters.

From what we know in the public domain about resolutions of past terrorist hostage-taking, we have categorized four types of precedented or prescribed deals:

1. Changed expectations
2. Politically acceptable concessions
3. Safe delivery of hostages
4. Safe passage of terrorists

Changed Expectations

Negotiations in general are easier for the side that persuades the other side to lower its expectations. Given terrorist hostage-takers, William Zartman suggested that the crisis would not be resolved without lowered expectations:

- "As long as the terrorists expect government to give in and government expects terrorists to surrender, no resolution is possible" (Zartman, 1990, p. 171).
- "In hostage negotiations, terrorists need to be taught that their expected demands are not possible and that specific elements among these are not possible for precise reasons" (Zartman, 1990, p. 172).

Zartman advised negotiators:

- To seek to "confirm or revise the parties' purposes, or, alternatively, to find different ways to satisfy goals that cannot be changed" (Zartman, 1990, p. 169)
- To find new terms, including "camouflaged terms of trade," such as paying ransom out of private funds (Zartman, 1990, p. 174)
- To find "creative terms of trade," such as seizing something valued by the other side before trading for it (Zartman, 1990, pp. 177–178)
- To remove something that the other side might want later, in order to trade it later, such as "closing of alternative airports or sanctuaries" (Zartman, 1990, p. 184)

Analysts of new terrorist hostage-taking, while acknowledging that new terrorists are relatively different, advise negotiators to encourage new terrorists to think more like old terrorists:

- Resist or divert any "uncompromising religious rhetoric" (Dolnik and Fitzgerald, 2011, p. 268).
- "Stress the widespread attention [that] the perpetrators' cause had already been achieved...and that killing hostages would only hurt their cause in the eyes of the public." The caveat to this second prescription is to be careful not to challenge their willingness to kill, as previously explained, in the section about the terrorists' suicidal motivations (Dolnik and Fitzgerald, 2011, p. 270).

Politically Acceptable Concessions

Before the new wave of terrorism, the most general objective for the official side was to win concessions without making politically unacceptable concessions in return (Hudson, 1989, p. 335). Alternatively, a realistic deal was termed a "tactical deal":

> A tactical deal should be considered one, such as the case of TWA flight 847 [when Israel, under U.S. pressure, exchanged prisoners for hostage, 1985], that resolves an international HBT incident nonviolently and without making significant concessions other than, at most, allowing the terrorists safe passage or third-country prisoner exchanges, but without absolving them of the legal consequences of their crime.
>
> **(Hudson, 1989, p. 325)**

Ideally, the official side would win the safe delivery of the hostages and the surrender of the terrorists, without giving in to terrorists' demands or their safe conduct (Zartman, 1990, p. 171). Realistically, the official side would win the safe delivery of the hostages in return for the safe conduct of the terrorists to their desired location—essentially an escape from justice (Zartman, 1990, p. 163). These alternatives are explored in the following two sections.

Safe Delivery of Hostages

The common and primary objective in all the prescriptions above is for the release of hostages safely. In the era of new terrorism, the safe delivery of hostages, and official toleration of the escape of the hostage-takers, becomes less likely:

> In incidents encountered by law enforcement offices on day-to-day basis, the main objective is to get everyone out alive, including the hostage-takers. In incidents involving the "new terrorists" however, such an outcome is highly improbable and crisis managers need to understand this in order to avoid panic and the rejection or abandonment of negotiations in case of any unexpected developments.
>
> **(Dolnik and Fitzgerald, 2011, p. 274)**

Safe Passage for Hostage-Takers

Before the new wave of terrorism, analysts suggested that the negotiator should offer safe passage for terrorists, which terrorists rarely think of for themselves (Zartman, 1990, p. 176). Dolnik and Fitzgerald warned that new terrorists' stereotypical "love of death" suggests that "such a proposal will likely be interpreted as an offensive second-guessing of the fighters' commitment to God, possibly only escalating the situation" (Dolnik and Fitzgerald, 2011, p. 271). Dolnik and Fitzgerald conclude with this prescription:

> A preferable course of action is to prolong the incident in order to change the hostage-takers' expectations and to leave it up to the terrorists to initiate debates about their safety. This does not mean that the negotiator always

> wants to avoid drawing the terrorists' attention to their personal safety, but this needs to be done through active listening and subtle communication, as part of an exchange or a conversation about bringing the incident to a negotiated conclusion.
>
> **(Dolnik and Fitzgerald, 2011, p. 275)**

However, when new terrorists are genuinely suicidal—or even if they are simply murderous while understanding that murder of hostages is likely to end in an official assault, then they probably do not expect safe passage. This is more probable if the hostage-takers are under the control of remote controllers who are not exposed to the same risks as the hostage-takers.

Some analysts of old terrorism clarified that while they allowed for safe passage, they did not absolve the hostage-takers of criminal justice, although in practice safe passage has proved to be an escape from justice for most hostage-takers (Hudson, 1989, p. 325). Dolnik and Fitzgerald admitted that safe passage is antithetical to justice, but advised negotiators to "think of achieving these objectives separately—possibly even at different times and in different places" (Dolnik and Fitzgerald, 2011, p. 275).

Simulated Practices

In simulation (2015), the official side, having read the historical prescriptions above, set out to direct the hostage-takers to their political demands (which tend to be more tangible and achievable), rather than their abstract ideological demands or the personal safety of the local hostage-takers.

Meanwhile, the hostage-takers realized that they should have moved away from zero-sum objectives, and allowed for the other side to gain something. The hostage-takers realized that they should have made concessions of the least likely objectives as leverage to achieve other objectives. The hostage-takers realized also that some of their demands could have been more reasonable/achievable. For instance, the hostage-takers initially demanded $2 billion for release of hostages.

In both of our simulations (2015 and 2016), the terrorist sides soon planned on harming hostages as leverage toward their other objectives, and ended up not releasing any safely.

In the first simulation (2015), hostage-takers were prepared to sacrifice their militants from the beginning, and only used safe passage as leverage. Similarly, in the second simulation (2016), the terrorist side initially planned to negotiate for safe passage of the hostage-takers, but soon decided that such a demand would be impossible to achieve, and a distraction from more achievable demands, so planned for the hostage-takers' martyrdom.

Our Practical Prescriptions

We advise negotiators to develop a useful relationship with the other side before suggesting that some of the terrorists' expectations are unrealistic.

The negotiators should be prepared to specify their evidence—an easy claim is to blame an intransigent political, legal, or bureaucratic constraint, but the negotiator should prepare for terrorists to demand a more substantive excuse.

Negotiators should be prepared also to offer alternative objectives that the terrorists could seize on in their disappointment, and that the official side could find easier to grant, such as the delivery of sustenance to hostages and hostage-takers, rather than free passage and immunity from prosecution.

In general, the official side should steer terrorists away from political demands toward politically inconsequential demands, such as official recognition of whatever grievances are already recognized as legitimate by the government.

The safety of hostages is inviolate in any political or legal contexts of which we are aware: thus, the official side should emphasize at all times that the safety of hostages is necessary to any deal.

The official side should consider what it can hold against the other side as leverage, such as the terrorist side's finances, publicity, or route of egress.

We do not allow for any official complicity in the hostage-takers' escape: this would be antithetical to criminal justice, likely encouraging to more hostage-taking, and unlikely to be a priority for new terrorists anyway.

What Are the Practical Difficulties for Executing Any Deal?

Historical Practices

Reaching a deal verbally, or in theory, is not the same as implementing it practically. In the following sections, we consider the implications of international law and new terrorist practices and prescriptions in the past.

International Law

For the process of transferring detainees between terrorist and official sides, the negotiator should find useful the international laws on prisoners of war (POWs), if the negotiator can persuade the other side to honor the provisions of these laws to all detainees.

Part III, Section II, Chapter VIII of the Geneva Convention Relative to the Treatment of Prisoners of War focuses on the transfer of POWs.

Article 46 specifies that

- The detaining power must always make decisions that are in the best interests of the POWs when contemplating their transfer.
- Prior to their departure, the detaining power must compose a list of all POWs who are to be transferred.
- The detaining power must not cause duress or make the process of transfer difficult for POWs.
- All POWs who are transferred must be in good health and capable of transferring to another camp.
- POWs must be transferred to another camp humanely, and the camp to which they are transferred must not be in worse conditions than the camp they vacate.

- The detaining power must transfer POWs in climatic conditions to which POWs are accustomed.
- The conditions under which POWs are transferred must not harm, or be less favorable to, the health of any POW.
- The detaining power must supply all POWs with sufficient food, safe drinking water, weather-appropriate clothing, and medical care throughout the duration of their transfer.
- The detaining power must take all precautionary measures necessary to ensure the safety of POWs during their transfer, especially if they are to be transferred by air or by sea vessels.

Article 47 specifies that

- Sick or wounded POWs may be transferred only if their safety depends on the transfer.
- If the journey will threaten afflicted POWs' recovery, then they should not be transferred.
- If military combat approaches a POW camp, then the POWs within the camp must be evacuated only if they are capable of being transferred safely in "adequate conditions," or if the negative risks of remaining are greater than the negative risks of being transferred.

Article 48 specifies that

- If POWs are to be transferred, then they must be officially notified of their transfer, and they must be notified of the postal address of their new location.
- POWs must be provided adequate time to pack their possessions and to inform their families of their transfer.
- POWs have the right to take all personal items with them, including letters and packages they have received by mail.
- The detaining power has the right to impose limits on how much a POW is allowed to carry, only if the journey of transfer requires such limitations. If POWs must be limited to what they are allowed to carry, then each POW may not carry more than 25 kilograms under any circumstance. The commander of the camp must mail any possessions left behind by POWs to their new location of transfer.
- The detaining power is responsible for all costs related to transfers.

Article 118 of Part IV, Section II of the Convention specifies the conditions for the release and repatriation of POWs upon the end of hostilities:

- POWs must be released and repatriated without delay after violent hostilities cease.

- If parties to a conflict fail to establish agreements that seek to end hostilities, then each of the detaining powers must establish and execute a repatriation plan conforming to the aforementioned rule. The adopted measures will then be brought to the attention of the POWs.
- The costs of POW repatriation must be fairly and equally divided between the detaining power and the power on which the prisoners depend. This allocation will be carried out on the following basis:
    - If the two powers share a border, then the power on which the POWs depend must cover the costs of repatriation from the time the POWs leave the frontiers of the detaining power.
    - If the two powers do not share a border, then the detaining power must cover the costs of POW transport beginning from its own territory, as far as its frontier, or up to the point of departure nearest to the territory of the power on which the POWs depend. The parties concerned must agree as to how costs of repatriation should be divided. All parties to a conflict should not wait until an agreement is settled between them to repatriate POWs.

Article 119 of the convention specifies that POWs must be repatriated and transferred under the conditions of Articles 46 and 48, and 118 in addition to the remainder of this article:

- Any valuable possessions impounded from POWs, as per Article 18, and any foreign currency not yet converted to the currency of the detaining power must be returned to the POWs.
- Valuable possessions and foreign currency not restored to POWs upon repatriation will be given to the information bureau set up under Article 122.
- POWs will be permitted to take their personal effects and any correspondence and parcels that have arrived throughout their time as a POW.
- If the process of repatriation limits baggage, POWs are permitted to carry a weight of at least 25 kilograms up through the limit of what each prisoner can reasonably carry. The remainder of the POWs' belongings will be left in the charge of the detaining power and will be returned upon the conclusion of an agreement with the power on which the prisoner depends relating to the regulation of transport conditions and cost payment.
- POWs already convicted for an indictable offense, and those whose criminal proceedings for such offenses are pending, may be detained until the end of the proceedings or until completion of the punishment, if necessary. "Parties to the conflict" will communicate the names of POWs who will be detained until the end of the

proceedings or completion of the punishment. "Parties to the conflict" will, by agreement, set up commissions to search for dispersed POWs and guarantee as rapid a repatriation as is possible.

Terrorist Practices

We identified four practical difficulties, particular to new terrorist hostage-takers:

1. The terrorists' concerns about counterintelligence
2. Mutual distrust
3. The location of the exchange
4. The travel and transportation to the location of exchange

Terrorist Counterintelligence

If the terrorists consider any release of their detainees, they will be concerned that hostages carry intelligence about the hostage-takers.

This concern will be exacerbated if the terrorists realize that they have not blocked the hostages' observations during the hostage-taking itself. In other words, less-prepared hostage-takers, or hostage-takers who fail to execute their planned counterintelligence, would be more likely to be wary of releasing hostages who carry intelligence. For instance, Al Qa'ida's manual warns that

> When releasing hostages such as women and children, be careful, as they may transfer information that might be helpful to the enemy...Cover the hostage's eyes so that he cannot identify you or any other brothers...Speak in a language or dialect other than your own, in order to prevent revealing your identity.
>
> **(Al Qa'ida, 2004)**

Terrorists will be concerned that any exchanged resources might contain surveillance technologies:

> If the purpose of the kidnapping is to obtain money, you have to ensure that all the money is there, that it is not fake, nor traceable. You must be sure there are no listening or homing devices planting with the money.
>
> **(Al Qa'ida, 2004)**

Mutual Distrust

Both sides will be naturally suspicious about the other side's trustworthiness. Terrorists will be concerned that an exchange will be used by the official side as an opportunity to attack the hostage-takers, as made explicit in Al Qa'ida's manual:

> The brothers must be constantly on alert for possible ambushes...
> You must verify that the food transported to the hostages and kidnappers is safe. This is done by making the delivery person and the hostages taste the food

before you. It is preferable that an elderly person or a child brings in the food, as food delivery could be done by a covert special forces' person.

(Al Qa'ida, 2004)

Location

The official side should expect the hostage-takers to pay particular attention to the place at which the exchange would take place: "In case your demands have been met, releasing the hostages should be made only in a place that is safe to the hostage takers" (Al Qa'ida, 2004).

The official side should expect the hostage-takers to demand an iterated or phased progressive release of the hostages. Al Qa'ida warns that "[during] hostage release, the Brothers should be careful to not release any hostage until they have received their own people…For the withdrawal, some hostages—preferably the most important—must be detained until the Brothers have safely withdrawn" (Al Qa'ida, 2004).

The official side is helped by Al Qa'ida's prescription to the "Brothers" to keep their word (2004), the self-interest for any group to keep their word if they expect to carry out another exchange in the future, and any adherence to the Islamic legal allowance for the fair exchange of prisoners (see Chapter 10).

Transportation

Jihadi terrorists are likely to pay particular attention to the safety of their movements and transportation. One scholar of Medieval Islamic law and practice, of many decades ago, prescribed that any agreement for what we would call today "safe passage" should be honored by both sides:

> It is natural that vehicles employed for the purpose of conveying exchangeable prisoners—cartels as they are called—should be immune during their journey to and fro. It is also obvious that during the time of this journey they should not take part in hostilities on pain or losing their immunity.
>
> **(Hamidullah, 1942, Chapter 15, rule 454)**

Since then, Al Qa'ida gave advice on "transporting the target to a safe place," which is concerned mostly with safety and counterintelligence: "Getting rid of the target after the demands have been met by transporting him to a safe place out of which he can be freely released. The hostage should not be able to identify the place of his detention" (Al Qa'ida, 2004).

Simulated Practices

In the preceding section, we observed that new terrorists are suspicious of the ulterior motives of officials who try to make a deal.

This expectation was proven in simulation (2016), when the terrorist side was suspicious of attempted agreements that were not verified:

> [W]e also faced the problem of compliance. It would have been quite difficult for the other team to prove [to] us that they would effectively meet our demands

> that they would not make empty promises. At one point, they agreed to publish a public statement that would end the American support for the Iraqi Shia government, but as we did not see any proof that this would be done, we did not believe them.
>
> **(Estelle Zielinski)**

In neither simulation did the two sides reach a deal.

Our Practical Prescriptions

We conclude that the negotiator should not make any promises or agreements that the official side cannot tangibly validate to the other side.

If the terrorists consider any release of their detainees, they will be concerned that hostages carry intelligence about the hostage-takers. If the official side prioritizes the eventual voluntary release of the hostages, he or she should remind the other side early and often to block the hostages' observations of the hostage-takers. If the official side prioritizes intelligence, then the negotiator should not remind the other side: we are aware of the ethical concerns about the latter option, even though we choose not to go into them here.

If the terrorists consider any receipt or exchange of resources, such as sustenance, they will be concerned about the official side secretly inserting surveillance technologies, or sending official assaulters in the same transportation, or tracking the terrorists' movements in order to discover their origin or destination.

The official side should prepare measures to persuade the other side that no ulterior actions are planned (even if they are)—probably a third-party intermediary is the best starting condition; a mutually agreeable neutral or safe location for the exchange is probably necessary; an iterated process of exchange is useful.

International law can be used as the foundation for any agreement on the process of transfer, which, if mutually agreed, should help to mitigate mutual distrust, especially if a third party is involved.

12

Should the Official Side Consider Violence?

In this chapter, we focus on the official switch from nonviolent responses to violent responses (the "use of force"; an "assault").

We consider arguments about whether the official side should use violence against the attackers, and when violence should be considered:

1. Should the official side assault?
2. When should force be considered?

Should the Official Side Assault?

The question of whether to assault is related to the question of whether to negotiate, which we reviewed extensively in Chapter 4. In the following sections, we focus on the main sides of the argument:

1. No: negotiating is less risky than assaulting.
2. Yes: violence is sometimes the least risky response.

No: Negotiating Is Less Risky Than Assaulting

As noted in Chapter 4, the immediate reaction to the surge in terrorist hostage-taking in the 1960s was to negotiate toward some convergent deal, primarily on the grounds that terrorists had made rescue practically impossible, and that governments at the times lacked the capacity to rescue the hostages practically.

However, concessions encouraged more hostage-taking. Thus, by the mid-1970s, governments were preparing counterterrorist military units and using more military options. The advantages of these preparations were epitomized by the assault by the British Army's Special Air Service on the Iranian Embassy in 1980, after a siege lasting 6 days and the killing of a hostage, which prompted the assault: 25 of the 26 hostages were rescued; one hostage was shot to death by the takers during the assault (Bolz et al., 2011, p. 106).

When officials chose to use force, force was often used too early, too late, or in unnecessarily risky situations, as epitomized in 1972 by the West German police's attempts to shoot to death Palestinian terrorists during their transfer of their hostages from the Olympic Village in Munich to an airfield, as agreed by the West Germans themselves, less than 24 hours into the crisis, as an opportunity to kill the hostage-takers: all 11 hostages, 10 terrorists, and 1 policeman were killed (Grubb, 2010, p. 342).

For domestic police in America, a formative incident occurred in 1973, when four armed men (all Sunni Muslim Americans seeking firearms for Jihad) took hostages during a botched robbery at a gun store in Williamsburg, in the borough of Brooklyn, New York. Several hostages and two police officers were wounded, and a police officer was shot to death during the initial police response. Police then called in psychologists and clerics to help resolve the crisis, which ended without further violence after 47 hours:

> The Williamsburg incident was a key incident in the development of hostage negotiations. It proved the effectiveness of the "slow things down and talk things out" approach, even in the face of shots having been fired and officers having been wounded and killed. In place of the usual action-oriented approach to an incident in which emotions run high on both sides, the more controlled, slower, and less reactive approach proved successful in the sense that no other people were killed or wounded.
>
> **(McMains and Mullins, 2015, p. 5)**

Immediately, some analysts criticized zealous pursuit of violent responses to terrorist hostage-taking:

> I believe that nonviolent...solutions to inevitable conflicts must and can be found and that in the overwhelming majority of cases, recourse to violence represents only self-serving moral cowardice, lack of imagination, and a failure of knowledge and spirit.
>
> **(Hacker, 1976, p. xvi)**

In the 1980s, inspired by the British precedent particularly, many governments had acquired new military or police units specializing in counterterrorist assaults, but some proved less capable—epitomized by the Egyptian assault on an Egypt Air Boeing 737 (November 23, 1985), in which most passengers died. Meanwhile, terrorists learned how to defend themselves better, encouraging a return to negotiating (Hudson, 1989, p. 327).

Yes: Violence Is Sometimes the Least Risky Response

Since the 2000s, when many military operations failed in the name of counterterrorism—most notably the formal stabilization operations in Afghanistan (from 2001) and Iraq (from 2003), popular culture and many academic analyses have tended to doubt all military effectiveness. For instance, a professor of history at the University of Michigan published this largely unfounded implication that violence is never the answer:

> In order to improve relations, the United States and NATO must repudiate the Bush doctrine of "preventive war," which appears to Muslims as a warrant for aggression. Washington and its allies must recognize that killing civilians creates terrorists. Above all, basic fairness is crucial. The United States must be as willing to condemn Israel for infractions against international law as it is to castigate Palestinians for violence.
>
> **(Cole, 2009, p. 238)**

However, commentators should not make false analogies. Counterinsurgency and nation building failed in Afghanistan and Iraq, not violent responses to violent attackers.

Others have pretended that no terrorist is beyond de-radicalization or negotiation, and that violent responses always reflect badly on the official side (Stern, 2010; Dolnik and Fitzgerald, 2011, p. 272; Powell, 2014, 2015). Despite fashions for stating that violence is never the solution to terrorism, violence is sometimes the solution, such as when the terrorists are resolved on violence, are irreconcilable, and cannot be disarmed practically any other way. As noted already, sometimes an early official intervention in hostage-taking is contrary to historical norms and public expectations, so an early intervention is more likely to be blamed when an attempted rescue fails, but it is justified if the risks will only increase over time. The negative risks of waiting, and the positive risks of assaulting, seem higher with new than with old terrorists, since new terrorists are more murderous, suicidal, and likely to take hostages to garner publicity ahead of their murders.

A former member of the FBI's Hostage Rescue Team and commander of the FBI New York Division's SWAT team (James A. Gagliano) acknowledges that some terrorists, such as those directed by the Islamic State of Iraq and the Levant (ISIL), are so likely to be irreconcilable (to use our term) that a violent response is the best response:

> Not every hostage or active shooter case is identical. The individual mindset of each ISIS-inspired potential terrorist must carefully be weighed and considered, and tactical resolution elements should forever remain contiguous with negotiator units.
>
> But when it comes to terrorism cases, I don't think it's an exaggeration to say that the era of drawn out, negotiation-heavy hostage standoffs is over. Let me give you a bit of a reflection on hostage rescue history. In the 1970s, 1980s, and 1990s, we witnessed a proliferation of aircraft hijackings, domestic terrorist attacks from radical leftist groups, and bank robberies that resulted in

> hostage-takings. But the emphasis in hostage situations was about "stall, stall, buy time, promise them the world, and for each thing we give them, we have to extract hostage capital from them in return."...
>
> For ISIS and its sympathizers, the purpose of carrying out hostage attacks is to gain global headlines rather than to win concessions or even battlefield victories. They control the narrative, and any publicity for them is good publicity. The Orlando shooter, Omar Mateen, for example, showed no interested in negotiating when the police got through to him in several short calls.
>
> **(Cruickshank, 2017, p. 10)**

We agree that violence is more likely to be the least risky response to new terrorists, and we caution negotiators not to follow fashions or norms framed in terms of the rights and wrongs of violence, but to prefer semantic frames of risk. These choices should follow hard risk assessments. For instance, if the terrorists start harming victims, the official side must choose whether to accept the chance of further harm from the terrorist side, or to prefer the chance of harm to the hostages and official personnel pursuant to a violent assault or rescue by the counterterrorist side.

Every situation will offer peculiar risks. In general, we note that the choice to assault becomes more justifiable with any of the following three trends:

1. The hostages' location is discovered.
2. The risks of assault decline.
3. The risks of not assaulting increase.

The choice to assault becomes less justifiable if

1. The hostage-takers cannot be located accurately.
2. The period between confirming the hostage-takers' locations and the assault lengthens.
3. The hostage-takers become more militarily capable.
4. The official forces become less military capable.
5. The terrorists have more time to prepare to defend themselves.

The choice to assault should not be isolated from the choice to negotiate, which we described in Chapter 4 as a choice generally between the risks of continuing to negotiate versus the risks of assaulting now. The choice has some nuances and potential triggers, separate from the risks, which we review in the next section.

When Should Force Be Considered?

As shown in Figure 12.1, the modal hostage-taking lasts from 1 to 5 days, with a considerable proportion being resolved in less than 24 hours, while some last for years.

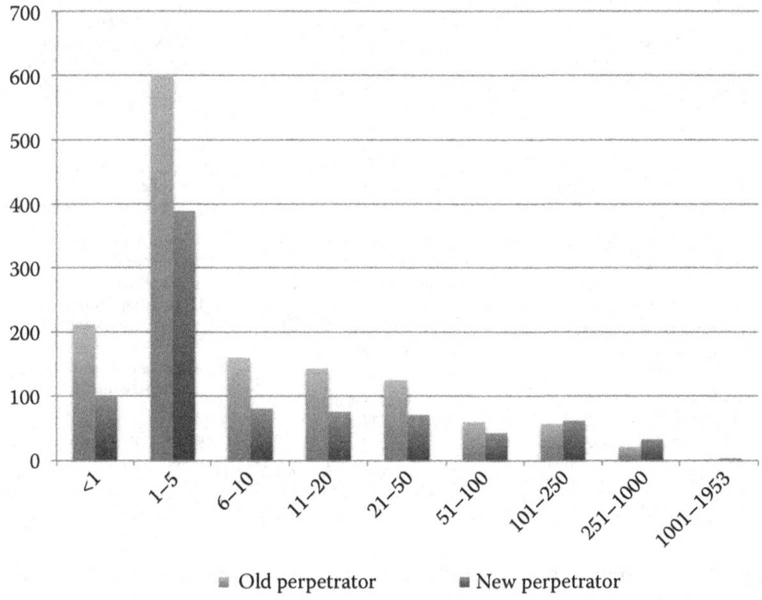

Figure 12.1 Number of hostage-takings by duration (days) and category of terrorist hostage-taker (old terrorist or new terrorist), for 1970 through 2016. (Data from the authors' extension of the GTD.)

Analysis by the Combating Terrorism Center at West Point, New York, of its own data suggests that 70% of executions of Western hostages by Jihadis occurred with the first 30 days of detention. In the subsequent 11 months, the probability of execution dropped to 5%, although after a total of 12 months the probability climbed to 17%. Rescue operations were most successful in the second and third months of detention. Most of the successful operations occurred within the first 6 months (Loertscher and Milton, 2015, p. 51).

In the sections that follow, we review the arguments about when to assault (Figure 12.2). Some of these arguments are contradictory, so we review the conditions under which one or another argument should be preferred. We proceed through the following three sections, in which the arguments are categorized together essentially by timing of the assault:

1. As early as possible, without any necessary negotiations
2. As triggered by certain events
3. As late as possible, only after negotiations have failed

As Early as Possible

In this section, we review reasons to assault as soon as possible, without any necessary negotiations. By contrast, as shown in more detail in the following

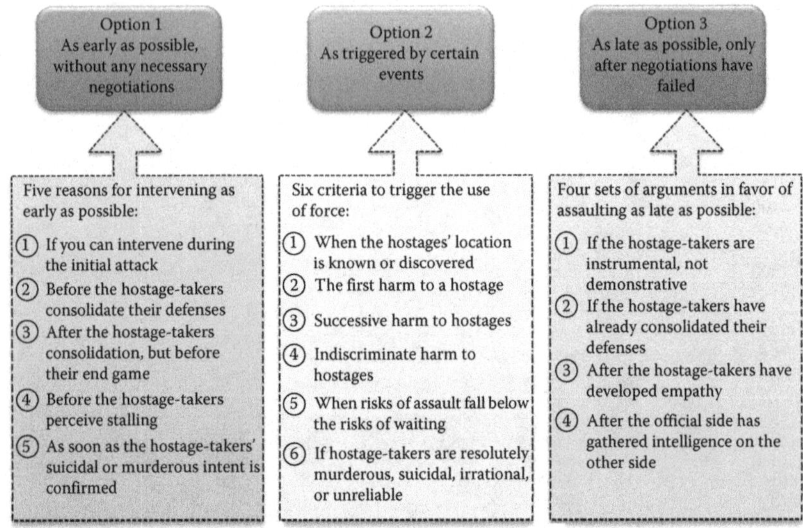

Figure 12.2 The competing arguments about when to assault.

section, under certain conditions—such as an instrumental hostage-taker with reconcilable demands—an assault should be postponed in favor of negotiations.

To give more practical advice, we identified five reasons for intervening as early as possible:

1. If you can intervene during the initial attack
2. Before the hostage-takers consolidate their defenses
3. After the hostage-takers' consolidation, but before their endgame
4. Before the hostage-takers would perceive your stalling
5. As soon as the hostage-takers' suicidal or murderous intent is confirmed

During the Initial Attack

Historical Practices

Some officials point out that legacy responses—setting up a perimeter in order to wait for specialist negotiators or assaulters—just give active or irreconcilable attackers more time to harm people. An important historical event in America occurred at Columbine High School, Colorado, on April 20, 1999, when two high school students shot 13 of their fellow students and teachers, before shooting themselves, while police (from different authorities and jurisdictions) were still securing the perimeter and engaging in other activities outside the school. Gagliano remembers the impact on American law enforcement:

> As a then member of the FBI's Hostage Rescue Team, the lessons learned from Columbine centered on the on-scene law enforcement's "paralysis by analysis." It describes the inherent difficulty in immediately coalescing disparate "parts" of "good guys," upon arrival, into a homogeneous tactical unit prepared to rapidly move toward the sounds of the guns, which in military terms translates to a full-speed, hyper-urgent movement to contact.
>
> **(Cruickshank, 2017, p. 11)**

As described earlier, since September 11, 2001 (9/11), terrorists have taken hostages increasingly often as one step in the process of mass killing. Even if the hostage-takers are not certainly resolved on mass killing, their initial attack is acutely risky and is open to official intervention. Hostage-takers are most likely to brutalize hostages, and to kill perceived threats, during their initial assault—before they have consolidated their hostages, sites, and barricades. For instance, at Beslan in Russia, on September 1, 2004, 33 Chechen-Ingush Jihadi separatists took more than 1,100 hostages in a school, after an active shooting that killed at least one person, perhaps eight persons; between 12 and 24 hostages were shot or blasted to death during consolidation of the hostages in the gym. The victims were selected for noncooperation. Eventually, at least 385 people were killed, mostly during the final official assault.

In subsequent years, we have observed more frequent mass-casualty attacks by terrorists, in which firearms are practically the only weapons, and where mass killing is clearly both the initial and the ultimate objective of hijacking a space and barricading live victims therein, as in the following:

- Mumbai in 2008 (175 killed, including 9 attackers from Lashkar-e-Taiba)
- The Westgate shopping mall in Nairobi in 2013 (71 killed, including 4 attackers from al-Shabaab)
- The murder of 17 people by two gunmen loyal to ISIL, January 7–9, 2015, mostly at the offices of the *Charlie Hebdo* magazine
- The murder of 130 people in Paris overnight November 13–14, 2015, by nine attackers sent by ISIL, operating in three teams, across at least six locations, including the national football station, the Bataclan theater (then hosting a concert), and various cafés
- At a nightclub in Orlando, Florida, on June 12, 2016 (50 killed including the attacker—an American loyal to ISIL)
- At two hotels in Mogadishu, Somalia, on June 26, 2016 (at least 19 killed, including 3 attackers from al-Shabaab)

Official responses to the initial attack tend to vary between effectively immediate assault and a more deliberative process of assessment and preparation of capacity. The current consensually prescribed response to active shooters is to neutralize the active attacker or attackers without waiting for any more deliberative assessment beyond the immediate, on-the-spot, "dynamic" assessments made by personnel as they arrive.

For some analysts, the norm was clear by 2009:

> While the details of active shooter tactical programs may vary somewhat from department to department, the main idea behind them is that the active shooter must be engaged and neutralized as quickly as possible, not allowed to continue on a killing spree unopposed. Depending on the location and situation, this engagement sometimes is accomplished by a single officer or pair of officers with shoulder weapons. Other times, it is accomplished by a group of four or more officers trained to quickly organize and rapidly react as a team to locations where the assailant is firing.
>
> Active shooter programs have proven effective in limiting the damage done by shooters in several cases, including the March 2005 shooting at a high school in Red Lake, Minn. Today, many police departments not only have a policy of confronting active shooters, they also have provided their officers with training courses teaching them how to do so effectively. Such training could make a world of difference in a Mumbai-type attack, where there may not be sufficient time or resources for a specialized tactical team to respond.
>
> **(Burton and Stewart, 2009)**

The normative American response to active shooters became immediate confrontation by the first armed responder:

> We have gone from waiting for SWAT and treating the situation like a barricade (as was the case in the Columbine incident) with disastrous results, to Quick Unit Action Deployment (QUAD) models that involve forming up a four-officer team immediately upon arrival before SWAT gets there, to the current model of "the first guy there with a rifle goes in."
>
> **(Wagner, 2015)**

In November 2015, *The Economist* identified the change in norm:

> The advent of suicidal attackers armed with guns is forcing hostage-rescue teams to throw away their old playbooks. These were premised on the idea that rescue forces could bide their time while building up an intelligence picture of the attackers. In the Iranian Embassy siege in London in 1980, for example, the security forces negotiated over the course of six days before launching a 17-minute assault to rescue hostages.
>
> Yet one key lesson of the attacks in Garissa and Mumbai, in which 166 people died, was that the longer such hostage-takers are left in control, the higher the resulting death toll. In Paris, French security forces could immediately call on elite hostage rescue teams who train intensively for just the sorts of rescue operations that they conducted. But in remoter parts of the world such as Mali, Kenya or Somalia, even the best units will not have the training, equipment or expertise of those in the rich world, and rescue efforts may be riskier and more chaotic.
>
> **(*The Economist*, 2015)**

Inspired particularly by the attacks in Paris in 2015, law enforcement authorities in other cities have enhanced their capacity to neutralize active shooters as soon as possible. For instance, late in 2015, the New York Police Department created the Critical Response Command, which has prepared teams of personnel (525 officers and supervisors, at the time of a public demonstration in July 2016), each located in separate locations across New York City, to respond locally to active shooters within minutes. The dominant prescription in their training is to "move to the shooter" (Wilson, 2016).

Similarly, in January 2016, the Metropolitan Police in London announced that it would increase its qualified armed officers from about 2,200 to 2,800. As of March 2016, English and Welsh police forces counted only 5,639 qualified firearms officers. In April, the national government's Home Office announced that it would resource the training of another 1,500 armed officers, on the grounds of counterterrorism, across police forces in England and Wales—in the hope of deploying most within a year, the rest within another year. In June 2016, Police Scotland announced that it would recruit another 90 armed officers, for a total of 365, and 34 more trainers or specialists. The Metropolitan Police's Specialist Firearms Command (SC&O19) is responsible for preparing 600 Counter-Terrorist Specialist Firearms Officers, some of whom are stationed at landmarks, while some are patrolling in legacy automobiles known as armed response vehicles (three per vehicle) or are standing by with all-terrain motorbikes or are on river boats, ready to respond to active attackers within minutes (BBC, 2016b). Further responders could be mobilized across the Metropolitan Police as a whole—the largest police force in Britain by far, although analysts have warned that more than half of its officers do not live in London; some live in the south of France due to costly housing, crime, and concentrated shift patterns (Gaskarth, 2016).

Germany has instigated new capacity since a spate of Jihadi stabbings and shootings in one week in July 2016, including the shooting to death of nine people by Ali Sonboly on July 22, 2016. The national government's responses included orders by the German defense minister for military forces to make ready to help, despite strong constitutional and conventional objections to military involvement in domestic issues since the Second World War (Bender, 2016).

Legal and Ethical Risks

The legal and ethical risks of this policy include the chance that the attacker or attackers could be treated as active attackers after they have ceased to engage actively in violence and have become open to negotiation. This is a difficult switch to sense or to adjudicate—if a person has illegitimately engaged violently already, remains armed, and does not appear ready to disarm, he or she conventionally would be considered an active threat, which should be neutralized for public safety. However, critics could charge that a response that leads with armed responders rather than negotiators inevitably favors violent over nonviolent resolutions.

Additionally, some official responders still separate traditional reconcilable hostage-takings from irreconcilable active attacks:

> The application of rapid deployment techniques during a barricaded gunman or hostage barricade can have very negative consequences. Officers who receive rapid deployment training should be specifically instructed when these tactics should be applied and concrete examples should be cited. Often the distinction between a barricaded gunman or hostage barricade and an Active Shooter event may not be an easy determination for the initial responding police officers.
>
> For example, if someone who has taken a hostage fires a single shot at police officers on the perimeter and then ceases fire, the event should still be considered to be a barricaded gunman despite the fact that shots have been fired by the suspect. The goal of an Active Shooter is generally to shoot as many victims as possible. Rapid action is essential to mitigate the casualties. Rapid deployment tactics are a necessary reaction to an extreme situation.
>
> Delaying action does not work to law enforcement's advantage; it affords the attacker with more time to inflict harm. Applying rapid deployment tactics to a hostage taker who occasionally fires a shot at police would not be appropriate. Just like every tool in a toolbox has its function, rapid deployment tactics must only be applied during true Active Shooter situations. Misapplication of these tactics will generally lessen the chance of a successful outcome.
>
> **(Cameron, 2014)**

> In traditional barricade or hostage situations, the most common tactical response is for the first officers responding to the scene to establish a perimeter to contain the incident. They then wait for hostage negotiators and SWAT or other hostage rescue teams to arrive to handle the crisis. This response is effective for a prolonged hostage situation. However, in the second type of armed assault, it permits the attackers free rein to find and kill many more victims inside the established perimeter. Many times, the attackers are also suicidal and are not planning on surviving the incident.
>
> **(Stewart, 2015)**

Operational Risks

Irrespective of the legal and ethical risks, the policy of responding with force as soon as possible is challenging in practical or operational terms.

An immediate assault is not possible until the assaulters arrive. An assault is extremely greedy of resources, since armed officers are rare and expensive to select, train, and equip. For instance, the (London) Metropolitan Police's current Counter-Terrorist Specialist Firearms Officers are selected over some weeks, trained in firearms over 9 weeks, and deployed in armed response vehicles on non-counter-terrorist duties for some months, before specialist training of at least 3 months. Once operational, officers are taken away from other policing activities in order to be held on standby to respond to rare terrorist events. Whereas most officers—including most armed officers—are allocated to routine patrolling, with positive externalities for countering other crimes, counterterrorist officers are being held on standby, without liberty to respond to nonterrorist crimes, and with more expensive and exotic equipment, in order to speed up response times to terrorism.

All these resources come to naught unless the response is extremely rapid—within minutes of the attack. For instance, in May 2013, armed police arrived more than 11 minutes after two violent Jihadis had struck an off-duty British soldier (Lee Rigby) with a car, before killing him with knives, on a public street in London, outside a British Army barracks. These particular attackers waited around the scene, waiting for a confrontation with police, while making statements to bystanders, when they could have attacked many others in that time. Reportedly, the Metropolitan Police aims to respond much quicker with its new capabilities (BBC, 2013b, 2016b).

Certainly, a failure to neutralize an active shooter can permit an active shooting to become a protracted hostage crisis. For instance, in Orlando, Florida, some police arrived within around 8 minutes of Omar Mateen's first shootings in a nightclub on June 12, 2016. Ten armed police, some with carbines, one with a shield, entered the nightclub through two different apertures. Some fired on Mateen, when he looked out from the restrooms, to where he had chased his victims, having started firing on the dance floor, but the police chose not to pursue him, leaving him in control of hostages who had barricaded themselves inside the stalls. Three hours later, other police broke into the toilets through the exterior wall to release hostages and ultimately to kill Mateen. Probably at least five people who were alive when Mateen retreated into the restrooms ultimately died there. Later, in an interview with journalists, Orlando Police Chief (John Mina) said that the initial entrants chose not to pursue Mateen into the restrooms because he had stopped shooting there: "He went from an active shooter to a barricaded gunman. If he had continued shooting, our officers would have went in there...Officers followed their training in responding to active-shooter incidents." Concerns about potential explosives were also factors: electrical batteries on the floor were assessed as potential components of bombs, even before Mateen used his telephone to claim to be carrying and to have placed explosives on the site. The Orlando Police Department asked the federal government's Department of Justice to review its response (Goldman and Berman, 2016; Perez-Pena and Robles, 2016; Zapotosky and Berman, 2016).

Even if policies, practices, and resources are optimized for immediate response to active attacks, geographical and other material challenges remain, as simple the great distance over which some first responders are supposed to take responsibility. This is especially true for centralized resources:

> The FBI's Hostage Rescue Team (HRT), the tactical component of its Critical Incident Response Group, is a large, full-time tactical team—a highly capable, Tier One national asset—but its ability to respond effectively to paramilitary terrorism is subject to the tyrannies of time, space, and force. Without specific prior warning of an imminent attack, it would not be deployed forward from its base in Virginia. It could therefore require many hours of air and surface travel to be mission ready at an incident site, particularly one in the central or western United States, even after the processing of a request for assistance and HRT receipt of alert and deployment orders. The HRT lacks sufficient strength and redundancy in both operators and in its command, planning, support, and transportation

> capabilities, to respond to multiple attacks or diversions in dispersed locations, a requirement it might well face in the event of a well-planned terrorist attack.
>
> **(Tallen, 2008)**

New terrorists increasingly seek to confuse and break up the official response by attacking multiple sites at the same time, and by moving on to new targets quickly:

> In Mumbai [2008], transportation infrastructure like the city's main railway station was attacked, and militants detonated explosive devices in taxis and next to gasoline pumps. Meanwhile, roving gunmen attacked other sites around the city. In a country where coordination among first responders is already weak, the way the attackers fanned out across the city caused massive chaos and distracted security forces from the main prize: the hotels. Attacking Cama Hospital also sowed chaos, as the injured from one scene of attack became the targets of another while being rescued.
>
> **(Burton and West, 2008)**

While awaiting dedicated centralized resources, local resources must cover the gap:

> During crisis situations, assault units specializing in terror-event response are activated, especially when hostages are involved. Since these units may require a few hours to organize and deploy, until their arrival the site is usually under the command of local intervention teams for whom fighting terror is only secondary. These teams are responsible for preventing the situation from escalating and collecting intelligence for the assaulting teams.
>
> **(Forest, 2007, p. 471)**

Consequently, local police forces have asserted that they must prepare as the first armed responders, without timely help from centralized armed responders:

> One of the primary reasons that law enforcement officers should be concerned about safety when dealing with extremists is very simple: it is the "street cop" who is most likely to encounter an extremist who has committed a crime or act of terrorism. Elite forces like the Federal Bureau of Investigation's Hostage Rescue Team will never be the first to confront an extremist criminal; they will always arrive on the scene after an encounter has already taken place. In all likelihood, the officer encountering an extremist criminal or fugitive will be a neighborhood patrol officer or a deputy sheriff.
>
> In addition to being most likely to be first on the scene at an event or encounter, law enforcement officers are also most likely to discover the beginning or initial activities of new extremist groups. Local police with limited resources may have to cope for extended periods of time with large, highly motivated and well-organized groups.
>
> **(Burton and Stewart, 2009)**

> The point is this: terrorists have been changing their tactics since the early 1970s and the planners of any future terrorist attack are well aware of NYPD's preparations. They are also aware that they can get the same body count, press coverage, and shock value at any large American mall, college, sporting event or celebration. That means that much of the USA is a soft target and they may just attack a suburban location as well as any major city within the USA, which means you will be the officers responding to it!
>
> **(French, 2011)**

While the policy of using armed responders against attackers as soon as possible can be justified for lowering the risks to unarmed civilians (given an active irreconcilable attacker, at least), the policy may raise the risks to the armed responders, at least because they must respond as soon as possible, perhaps without completing all the preparations that they would prefer:

> One element that is common to almost all hostage-taking situations is the panic reaction, that period early in the incident in which the fight or flight quandary arises in the perpetrators. This panic is dangerous to the hostage-taker, the hostage, and especially to the officers who respond to the incident. More officers are killed during the panic reaction than at any other time during a hostage situation, or other confrontation, for that matter.
>
> **(Bolz et al., 2011, p. 93)**

One simple example of increased risk due to decreased time to prepare is the increased chance of official personnel firing on each other if they were to lack time to coordinate or to adopt distinctive clothing:

> Back when the QUAD model was the primary response methodology, off-duty and plainclothes responses were discouraged due to concerns of blue-on-blue "friendly fire" incidents—and with good reason. However, with the shift to the single-officer emergency response plan of counterattack, an off-duty or plainclothes officer may be the first and only responder available, especially in remote areas. But that doesn't mean that the danger of a blue-on-blue shooting no longer exists. The trend when solo police officers respond to Active Shooter events is clear. Seventy-five percent of the time officers responding alone must take action at Active Shooter events. One third of these officers are wounded during their response.
>
> **(Wagner, 2015)**

Simulated Practices

In our first simulation (2015), the official side wanted to avoid the high costs of assaulting the apparently well-armed and determined Jihadi hostage-takers, so the official side failed to specify when an assault would be justified, and tolerated several rounds of killings by the terrorist side before ordering an assault. As one of the role-players on the official side admitted, "the tactical and the negotiation teams should work closely together and determine at what stage in negotiation the shift to tactical should occur" (Ingrid Munch).

Our Practical Prescriptions

In the 1960s and 1970s, the norm—at least in Western countries—was to negotiate for as long as possible. This fit with good practice when the hostage-takers were mostly old terrorists, but cannot be a rule or law, and is less applicable to new terrorists whose intent is to maximize lethality, or to active shooters who are still killing without intent to negotiate.

If the official side must assault the terrorists at all, the most advantageous time would be after the attackers have acquired the irreconcilable intent and capability to attack, but before the attackers get to their victims. Such an assault would be essentially preventative.

If the attack has started, and the violence continues, then the situation is normatively described—in the American law enforcement community at least, as an "active shooting," although the term "active violence" would be more literal, given that not all attacks rely on firearms.

If the official side is confident that the perpetrators are actively violent and have murderous intent that cannot be dissuaded, then the assault should start as soon as possible, with intent to kill the attackers before they can further perpetrate their murderous intent, without trying to negotiate for the safe release of any hostages. The main advantage of this policy is that it raises the chance of neutralizing the attacker or attackers before they can harm any more people.

We caution officials to have good reasons for choosing to negotiate, not to assume that negotiation is the least risky strategy, just as we caution officials not to assume that negotiation is always a waste of time. (Usually, the choices between negotiation or assault are made by the on-scene incident commander rather than the specialist negotiators.)

We caution officials against assuming that delay is always virtuous. Sometimes delay is the inevitable product of indecisiveness or procrastination about *when* to intervene.

The official side should develop issue clearly observable threshold behaviors and attributes that indicate when the terrorists should be assaulted. All police should be trained as immediate assaulters, pending arrival of more specialized assets.

Before Consolidation of Defenses

Historical Practices

If irreconcilable terrorists are given time to harm hostages or to consolidate their hostages and their defenses, an assault would become riskier for the hostages and the official assaulters. For instance, at Beslan (2004), the 33 hostage-takers wired the buildings with electrically detonated explosive devices, including trip wires and dead-man switches; they smashed windows and carried gas masks as defense against debilitating gases (as used to end the siege of the theater in Moscow in 2002); and they distributed gunmen across groups of hostages, with a threat to kill 50 hostages for every one of their own killed. The assault went on less than 3 days later: it killed at least 385 persons, including at least 10 assaulters:

> One lesson starkly evident in the aftermath of Beslan is that tactical response to such an incident requires discipline, proficiency, and precision. To deny an adversary time to consolidate his position, cause further damage or loss of life, or exploit the propaganda value of his action, the response must also be swift—measured in hours, not days. Rapid deployment of tactical forces capable of resolving the situation is therefore vital.
>
> **(Tallen, 2008)**

Traditionally, negotiators were advised to wear out the hostage-takers by extending the negotiations over time, particularly through the night or any chunk of time in which the hostage-takers would otherwise rest, or by setting up distractions. However, the new terrorists' stronger motivations and their stronger defensive capabilities give them more opportunity to rest or to reassure each other:

> According to the contemporary set of incident assessment criteria, in situations that are deemed as negotiable, hostage takers start bidding high but reduce their demands as the incident progresses, and as their exhaustion triggers a regression to a hierarchically lower (more basic) set of needs such as hunger, thirst, and sleep. If such a process does not occur over a growing period of time, the chances of a negotiated solution allegedly decrease considerably.
>
> At the same time, the presence of multiple hostage takers prolongs this process significantly, as the hostage takers not only have the option of resting some of their crew by working in shifts, but also are able to feed off the energy and determination of their comrades. Particularly when the hostage takers widely publicize their original demands and thus publicly lock themselves into their position, it becomes more difficult to negotiate a peaceful solution, as the one thing the image-conscious and fear-dependent terrorists worry about most is the widespread perception of their weakness and failure.
>
> **(Dolnik and Fitzgerald, 2008, p. 78)**

Our Practical Prescriptions

If irreconcilable attackers get to potential victims, the official side still has an incentive to intervene before the attackers have time to harm hostages or to consolidate their hostages and their defenses, after which an assault would be riskier for the hostages and the official assaulters.

After Their Initial Assault, But Before Their Endgame

Historical Practices

Even if the official side expects the situation to end in assault, some delay may be useful. In the days of old terrorism, before the capacity for hostage rescue was as well developed as today, and after many attempted rescues had failed, experts warned that successful rescue depends on long preparations, and proscribed any attempt for the first 2 or 3 days (Hudson, 1989, pp. 325, 358).

The FBI's training acknowledges that some delay is useful for gathering intelligence. Some delay allows the subject's "stress and anxiety" to decline, and their "basic needs" to accrue—with which the negotiator can bargain.

Some analysts of terrorist hostage-taking observed that delay adds to the hostage-takers' fatigue, so they prescribed an assault when the hostage-takers are most fatigued (Hudson, 1989, p. 335). However, hostage-takers sometimes use drugs to stay alert, while the Al Qa'ida manual urges kidnappers to develop "capability to endure psychological pressure and difficult circumstances" and "capability to take control over the adversary" (2004).

Simulated Practices

In simulation (2015), the terrorist role-players decided to kill hostages as they sensed that they were running out of time—it started toward the end of the third simulated day, of four simulated days, which were modeled within only 3 hours of real time.

Our Practical Prescriptions

While the initial attack is particularly risky for hostages, after which one can expect a lull in the violence, the end of the crisis must be riskier, either because the hostage-takers will seek to put more pressure on the official side by threatening hostages, or because the official side assaults, or because the hostage-takers estimate that an assault or negotiation failure is inevitable, so they should play their "endgame"—their most destructive behavior without concern for the consequences. Jihadis are encouraged to kill as an endgame, ahead of the other side's deadline, or upon their own deadline.

Before the Hostage-Takers Perceive Stalling

Historical Practices

Delay may add to the perception on the hostage-taking side that the official side is stalling for time. This perception would undermine trust in the other side, and could provoke threats to the hostages as punishment for stalling, or to provoke quicker concessions.

The manual produced by Al Qa'ida explicitly warned Jihadis that negotiators would stall, and that the hostage-takers should prefer quicker progress:

> Kidnappers must remain calm at all times, as the enemy negotiator will resort to stalling, in order to give the security forces time to come up with a plan to storm the hostages' location. The duration of the detention should be minimized to reduce the tension on the abducting team. The longer the detention is, the weaker the willpower of the team is, and the more difficult the control over the hostages is.
>
> **(Al Qa'ida, 2004)**

Additionally, Al Qa'ida warned, in the contexts of both site security and negotiations, that "[s]talling by the enemy indicates their intention to storm the location." Therefore, the manual concludes, the hostage-takers should not tolerate delay, but should kill hostages early: "One of the mistakes that the Red Army made in the Japanese Embassy in Lima, Peru—where they detained a large number of diplomats—was to allow the hostage situation to continue for over a month. In the meantime, the storm team excavated tunnels under the Embassy, and was able to liberate the hostages and end the kidnapping" (Al Qa'ida, 2004).

This same manual advises killing as a response to stalled negotiations: "In case of any stalling, starting to execute hostages is necessary. The authorities must realize the seriousness of the kidnappers, and their dedicated resolve and credibility in future operations." The manual repeats the advice under a different section of text, relating to security: "Detention must not be prolonged. In case of stalling, hostages must be gradually executed, so that the enemy knows we are serious." The manual is particularly wary of stalling during final arrangements for a physical exchange: "Stalling by the enemy indicates their intention to storm the location" (Al Qa'ida, 2004).

Simulated Practices

This lesson was borne out in the first simulation (2015), as admitted by two players on the official side:

> I think we tried to buy time in too much of an obvious way to the terrorists, which built their frustration of not being taken seriously and caused them to start killing hostages. Indeed, we waited a long time before answering them, because we were not well coordinated.
>
> **(Emilie Hannezo)**

> Our main negotiation strategy throughout the simulation was to stall time by giving small concessions to the terrorists. By stalling time we wanted the terrorists to loosen up on their main demands, and as the terrorists were barricaded and had a wounded among them, time should be positively correlated with our chance of success. What actually happened in the simulation diverted a lot from our intentions. As we made (small) concessions the terrorists increased and broadened their demands. Ultimately, we tried to stall time by saying that we would try to accommodate these demands, but this only led to the execution of hostages, as the terrorist believed we were bluffing.
>
> **(Esben Mortensen)**

The same lesson was borne out in the second simulation, too (2016), as observed by a player on the terrorist side:

> I think that we were too suspicious of them, because we all knew from the readings that the best strategy to deal with terrorists is to keep them busy by talking to them and pretending to understand their cause while not meeting any of their demands. We soon realized that this was what the other side was trying to do. I also don't think that the telephone conversation was productive, but rather unnecessary.
>
> **(Estelle Zielinski)**

Indeed, the official side always set out to stall:

> We followed the integrative bargaining model and divided our plan into three phases: pre-negotiation, finding a mutually acceptable formula to frame the agreement, and implementing the formula with an agreement on

> details (Zartman, 1990, p. 171). Our reframing of their demands focused on two things: time and understanding. They wanted the U.S. government to admit wrongdoings in Iraq; we established that it would take time for the higher-ups in government to issue a statement. They wanted the withdrawal of U.S. support to the Shia Iraqi government; we countered by assuring them of our neutrality while asking them to consider the time it would take for their demand to be passed by Congress. Yet, for every minute past the deadline in which hostages were spared, we realized that we were in control—inaction was our best friend and their worst enemy. In the end, we acquiesced to their first demand and in return asked them to release a hostage, whereupon they shot and killed him, leading to a forceful infiltration of the site by SWAT.
>
> **(Jonathan Fisher)**

> As a group, we agreed that we would order the SWAT team to infiltrate until a significant number of hostages were killed during the negotiations. In order to convince them to release hostages—threatening hostages first, we wanted to mimic the tone of the terrorist... In addition, we prepared a response for every demand to respond with immediacy. We wanted to prolong the incident as long as possible to change the hostage-takers expectations and leave it up to the terrorists to initiate their demand for safe passage. Essentially we did not want to give them too much control, but enough control that they do not feel backed up in a corner and divert from their original plan... The responses we prepared for their demands did not go well. The terrorist [side] wanted immediate results so our tactic of stalling but expressing their grievances did not work... Instead of giving into their demands, we decided to stall, referring to the bureaucracy of the United States. Stalling irritated the terrorists even more. Instead of stalling, we should have thought of ways to provide them with an alternative demand—one similar to the initial demand.
>
> **(Jason Tran)**

Meanwhile, the terrorist side was stalling for its own advantage, without intent to release hostages:

> The longer they had a channel open with is talking, the less likely it was that they would send SWAT, because they still had the hope of talking us down. This was useful to us, because the longer the hostage situation lasted, the more publicity we received from the press, drawing attention to our organization and our cause.
>
> **(Katrina Oshima)**

Our Practical Prescriptions

In real cases, where both sides are stalling without a mutually acceptable opportunity for the release of hostages, further delay is of no help to the hostages, except to give time for the assaulters to prepare. Otherwise, the assault should go in as soon as ready.

If the Hostage-Takers Are Suicidal or Murderous

Historical Practices

Suicidal intent suggests that the crisis will be short and deadly. The FBI's Hostage Barricade Database System (HOBAS) suggests an average delay between taking hostages and committing suicide by cop is 8 hours (for all events from 1983 to 2009).

If the hostage-takers are resolutely suicidal and murderous, then negotiation would be useless to the official side. Such resolutely suicidal and murderous hostage-taking falls in the category of pseudo-hostage situations—what the FBI terms the "nonhostage" end of the spectrum, in which the hostage-takers have a more "expressive" or "demonstrative" view of hostage-taking, rather than an "instrumental" view, in which hostage-taking serves as an instrument or means toward an end, such as a ransom.

Demonstrative hostage-takers take hostages for demonstrative purposes more than for leverage on external parties, make less tangible demands, and are more likely to victimize the hostages. The FBI induced its "nonhostage" situation category from decades of data on nonterrorist hostage-taking situations, so did not create the category just to rationalize "new terrorism," but clearly "new terrorism" fits the pseudo-hostage-taking end of the spectrum better than the pure hostage-taking end.

While the FBI prescribes "stalling for time" with an instrumental hostage-taker in order to lower the hostage-taker's expectations and sense of power, the FBI prescribes taking time with the expressive/demonstrative hostage-taker for a different purpose: calming down the subject and introducing alternative nonviolent solutions, in the hope of shifting the demonstrative hostage-taker into an instrumental hostage-taker, but if this fails the situation cannot end peacefully.

Given new terrorist trends toward demonstrative hostage-taking, the official side should be ready to assault as soon as it assesses the hostage-takers as demonstrative:

> The authorities must first consider whether the demands are real ones or just measures to stall for time in order to cause greater panic. Then, the authorities must decide if they will enter into negotiations with the terrorists or make an immediate attempt to retake the plan... If the decision is made that the terrorist demands are simply a ruse to gain time, the command must develop a plan to retake the facility very quickly. This plan must be aggressive enough to successfully neutralize the threat to the community, rescue any hostages, and secure the facility—all while sending a strong message to the whole that we are prepared and capable of defeating terrorism decisively.
>
> **(Forest, 2007, p. 267)**

Our Practical Prescriptions

The official side should intervene as soon as it confirms that hostage-takers have definite suicidal and murderous intent that does not allow for the release of hostages.

Triggered by Events

An assault should be triggered by certain events that indicate a change in the risk to the hostages, such that the risks of not assaulting outweigh the risks of assaulting.

We identified six criteria, each of which should add to the movement of the official side toward authorization of an assault:

1. When the hostages' location is known or discovered
2. The first harm to a hostage
3. Successive harm to hostages
4. Indiscriminate harm to hostages
5. When risks of assault fall below the risks of waiting
6. If hostage-takers are resolutely murderous, suicidal, irrational, or unreliable

We prescribe the negotiator to use these criteria collectively in order to assess the relative justification of assaulting, given more case-specific information that we cannot possibly predict in this study. If only one of these criteria is fulfilled, the justification for assault is lower than if all criteria were fulfilled.

When the Hostages' Location Is Known or Discovered

A rescue or assault cannot be considered unless the hostages' location is known or can be discovered. Here we should remember the differences between kidnappings and hostage-takings. A kidnapping of a single person or a few people, in ungoverned spaces—as is prevalent across many parts of the Middle East, Central Asia, South Asia, and South America—leaves the official side with little practical chance of discovering the victims' location. The hostage-takers can make official discovery even more difficult by moving the hostages regularly, communicating infrequently, or threatening harm to hostages in the event of any attempted rescue.

Al Qa'ida prescribes elaborate security measures during transportation and detention:

- The location where the hostage is transferred to must be safe.
- Beware of the police patrol.
- While the hostage is being transported, you must beware of police patrols by identifying their points of presence, to avoid sudden inspection.
- Look for listening or homing devices that VIPs often carry on their watches or with their money. VIPs could have an earpiece microphone that keeps him in touch with his protection detail.
- Everything you take from the enemy must be wrapped in a metal cover and should only be unwrapped in a remote place far from the sheltering group.

- Never make contact from the location where the hostage is detained, and never mention him during phone calls.
- Use an appropriate cover to transport the hostage to and from the location. At some point in time the "Allat" party were drugging the hostage and transporting him in an ambulance.
- It is imperative to not allow the hostage to know where he is.
- In this case, it is preferable to give him an anesthetizing shot or knock him unconscious (Al Qa'ida, 2004).

Discovering the location, or preparing the capacity to assault a remote location, will impose delay, potentially beyond a year. For instance, the first U.S. attempt to rescue the American hostages held by Iran since 1979 was executed after 173 days, in 1980; Iran released the last hostages after 444 days of detention, in January 1981.

Sometimes, a rescue attempt is launched optimistically to save lives, despite inaccurate intelligence, with all commensurate risks. For instance, on November 25, 2014, U.S. and Yemeni personnel rescued eight non-Americans, in an attempt to rescue an American (Luke Somers) who had already been detained by Al Qa'ida of the Arabian Peninsula (AQAP) for 435 days. AQAP had moved him and two other hostages before the rescue attempt. On December 3, AQAP released video threatening to kill him within 3 days. On December 8, a rescue attempt ended in his death and a South African hostage's death.

Depending on intelligence capacity, and the other side's counterintelligence, discovery could take a few days or many months. For instance, on January 25, 2012, United States Navy SEAL Team 6 rescued an American female and Danish male after 93 days of captivity in Somalia. By contrast, on December 8, 2012, United States Navy SEAL Team 6 rescued an American male after just 4 days of captivity—possibly the quicker rescue was due to the hostage-takers' careless betrayal of their location during their quick demand for a ransom of $300,000. (One SEAL was killed during this rescue.)

Upon First Harm to Hostages

Historical Practices

The traditional trigger for violent intervention in any hostage crisis (both terrorist and nonterrorist) has been first harm to hostages, particularly the first killing of a hostage. This policy was demonstrated most dramatically, and thence popularized, on May 5, 1980—the sixth day of a hostage-taking by Iranian minority separatists who had broken into the Iranian Embassy in London, when the hostage-takers brought a hostage to the front of the building, shot him in the head, and rolled his body down the steps. In accordance with policy, the police handed command to the British Army's Special Air Service, which completed an assault within 17 minutes of launch, or within 2 hours of the murder of the hostage. The assaulters killed five terrorists and captured one. The terrorists killed another hostage during the assault.

Similarly, in February 2011, during a hijacking of an American yacht, carrying four American passengers, by 19 Somalis in the Gulf of Aden, the United States Navy personnel on scene, guided by FBI personnel, were prompted to assault when the hijackers fired warning shots toward the United States Navy warship that was shadowing them. Unfortunately, the hijackers killed all the hostages before they could be rescued (FBI, 2013b).

Similarly, early on December 16, 2014, Australian police assaulted the Lindt café, Sydney, after an official sniper/observer saw Han Haron Monis (an Iranian asylum-seeker with allegiance to ISIL) kill a hostage. The assaulters killed Monis, but unfortunately a bullet ricocheted off his body and killed another hostage; the assaulters rescued 11 hostages.

Simulated Practices

The hostage-takers, knowing the norm of assaulting upon first harm, can be expected to exploit the norm by use the threat of harm, or pretense of harm, to influence the negotiator, without harming enough to provoke an official assault. For instance, in simulation (2015), the hostage-takers sought to pressure the official side by pretending to harm, without harm: one of their many schemes with this intent was to release video of mock executions, pretending that they were real executions. In considering the consequences of an actual official assault in response to mock harm to hostages, the terrorists argued that any official assault would look less justified if the hostage-takers had not actually harmed anyone in advance of the assault.

Similarly, in the second simulation (2016) the terrorist side (unfamiliar with anything that happened in the first simulation) also pretended to harm hostages in order to influence the negotiators. In this simulation, their scheme was to record audio of hostages screaming that they would claim was caused by physical violence.

Our Practical Prescriptions

The negotiator is left with a terrible dilemma, between two imperfectly competitive choices:

1. Attempting to negotiate with the hope of achieving the release or liberation of hostages, even though negotiation may only delay the inevitable killing of these hostages or a rescue attempt
2. Eschewing negotiations in favor of an immediate rescue attempt

To resolve this dilemma, the official side must take some time to estimate the hostage-takers' real ultimate intentions, while bearing in mind the urgency of an assault if the hostage-takers have no intent to release hostages unharmed.

The official side is sometimes forced to estimate the intent of the hostage-takers separately from their remote controllers. If the attackers do not represent a group or ideology that gives any preceding clues, then the official side is left to assess the attackers' initial behavior alone: the official side should assess whether the attackers are killing randomly or with clear intent to maximize lethality or public terror, or whether the attackers are killing for purposes that seem instrumental toward taking hostages in an unharmed state. For instance, initial harm to the hostages may have been intended to enforce compliance from the hostages, or to demonstrate to negotiators the capacity for violence if the negotiations fail, rather than to maximize lethality for the sake of lethality.

Successive Harm, Not on First Harm

Historical Practices

Given uncertainties about whether hostages really have been harmed, particularly if terrorists attempt to pretend to harm without actually harming the hostages, the official side might wait for confirmation of the harm. If so, the justification for assault increases with each successive harm to the hostages.

Before the new wave of terrorism, analysts urged reconsideration of the first harm to hostages as to whether it truly indicated intent to further harm or was an artifact of the initial assault or the hostage-takers' own insecurities. The chance of brutalization of hostages is highest in the first few hours, so traditional advice has advised against using force early, in favor of waiting for interpersonal bonds to develop between hostage-takers and hostages, and between hostage-takers and negotiators (Hudson, 1989, p. 335). Dolnik and Fitzgerald referred back to the history of old terrorism in order to prove that killing is less likely in "preplanned" or "premeditated" operations: "The 'new terrorists' tend to kill their hostages mainly in situations where they experienced obstacles to their initial plan (i.e., Egypt Air 648 and Pan Am 73 hijackings) or in cases where they have been pushed too far into a corner and then use threats to the hostages as levers of influence back on the negotiators (i.e., Air France 8969)" (Dolnik and Fitzgerald, 2011, p. 276).

Dolnik and Fitzgerald were on less justifiable ground when they suggested that new terrorist murders are most likely motivated to put pressure on the other side, without intent to kill everybody, and when they suggested that this vague, selectively proven description could be turned into an equally vague, impractical prescription. "So while responders certainly should not give up on the desire to save as many people as possible, they should prepare themselves for the likelihood of violence while still pursuing negotiation" (Dolnik and Fitzgerald, 2011, p. 274).

As we have noted above, we find this advice too general to be practical: the official side needs to assess whether the particular hostage-takers in the particular case are taking hostages with allowance for a peaceful outcome, or are taking hostages just to postpone inevitable murders. If the latter, the assault is justified as soon as it is ready.

Simulated Practices

Dolnik and Fitzgerald's advice was read by all participants of the two simulations, but the results suggest that the advice is not practical on its own. In the first simulation (2015), one part of the official side accepted that new terrorists would probably kill, but still expected to negotiate, while another part of the official side assumed that the hostage-takers' initial lethality and Jihadi motivations suggested no chance of negotiation:

> As we treated the incident as a case of new terrorism we also expected that getting everyone out alive was highly improbable, and thus we mentally settled on that we should not abandon negotiations if unexpected developments, such as the execution of some hostages, occurred.
>
> **(Esben Mortensen)**

> We felt that if we went in hard and fast, we had the best real-world chance of intervening in the middle of executions and stopping the killing. Waiting offered the benefit of what the Zartman and Dolnik [and Fitzgerald] readings identified as the Stockholm Syndrome humanizing hostages and perhaps coming up with some other solution... One of the biggest conflicts came after we devised a strike strategy intended to make the terrorists blind by destroying the security cameras, then moving in. After the terrorists threatened to execute hostages if we cut power, most of our group did not want to execute any kind of plan that tampered with anything for fear of killing hostages.
>
> **(Kurt Wagner)**

In the second simulation (2016), the official side hoped to avoid any harm to the hostages, by building rapport with the terrorist side, but when the terrorist side killed two hostages late in the simulation, then the official side voted for assault rather than further negotiation.

Our Practical Prescriptions

Negotiators cannot be expected to continue negotiating while hostages are being harmed repeatedly, unless the negotiators have other reasons to estimate that breaking off negotiations would be more harmful to the hostages than continuing negotiations. To repeat: in this section we have gathered criteria by which to judge whether an assault is justified—we expect them to be used collectively to assess the justification for assault; we do not expect one to be used alone, but rather relative to each other; if the hostage-takers were to fulfill six of the criteria, an assault is more justified than if the hostage-takers fulfill only one criterion.

Indiscriminate Harm to Hostages

Historical Practices

Dolnik and Fitzgerald suggest not assaulting so long as the hostage-takers are targeting the hostages discriminately, specifically the following discriminate targets:

- Provocative hostages
- Hostages representing the target government
- Threatening hostages

These analysts conclude that the historical record of discriminate targeting "underlines the fact that terrorists' willingness to execute certain hostages does not necessarily translate into a willingness to kill **all** captives indiscriminately" (Dolnik and Fitzgerald, 2011, p. 278, original emphasis).

Simulated Practices

Simulations suggest that the terrorist side's discrimination is not necessarily clear to the other side. In simulation (2015), the hostage-takers recognized in advance that they should victimize representatives of the other side, the troublesome, or the threatening hostages, but in this simulation the hostage-takers did not want harm anybody initially. When they did decide to kill, they chose to kill the low-value hostages, who had no links with the official side and whose killings would thus be less provocative. The official side did not realize such discrimination.

Our Practical Prescriptions

We confirm our earlier advice to assault based on our comparison of the risks of assaulting versus nonassaulting, and do not consider as practical any estimate of whether the terrorists are harming discriminately or not. The official side is unlikely to be able to confirm any ethical or legal difference between indiscriminate or discriminate targeting of hostages: the hostage-takers are still harming hostages. Moreover, harm to discriminate targets may be a gateway to harm to indiscriminate targets. Whether or not the harm is discriminatory, the risk assessment upon first harm generally justifies an assault (where the risks of not assaulting outweigh the risks of assaulting).

When Risks of Assault Are Lower Than Risks of Waiting

Historical Practices

Analysts of old terrorism prescribed official assault under three necessary conditions: when hostages are harmed, a peaceful solution seems unlikely, and a successful rescue seems likely (Hudson, 1989, p. 325).

Roy Ramm has urged continual assessment of these risks:

> I think the crucial word in relation to the use of force is "considered." Insomuch as an incident commander should be considering the use force from the very outset and continually consolidating resources and reassessing the risk of intervention against continuing to negotiate. Pretty much what is being postulated at 3.4 above. Intelligence from within the stronghold will be critical in helping the IC make that decision. But I must stress the need for continued risk assessment. If a hostage taker harms or even kills a hostage, the incident commander should still only consider intervention if he/she has effective resources available to launch an assault on a stronghold that is more likely than not to secure the hostages. The most successful assaults on strongholds have been carried out when the SWAT/Special Forces have had time to thoroughly plan and choreograph the attack.
>
> **(Ramm, 2016)**

Similarly, Gary Noesner urges a continual comparison of risks of waiting versus risks of assaulting:

> I think the decision as to whether or not to attempt a tactical rescue should be driven almost exclusively by the behavior of the terrorists, and nothing else. We should not use force because we can, rather we should use it when we are left with no other choice and we have come to the conclusion (supported by facts) that our failure to make a rescue attempt will likely result in further loss of life. Typically, when hostage takers begin to kill hostage, we are left with little choice but to go in. Otherwise, our assessment will be undertaken based on what has happened so far, what is this groups track record and MO, and what are they saying they plan to do. Have they killed anyone already? Much of this has to be developed at the scene and cannot normally be done in advance. Every situation is different. Everyone wants to see terrorists punished for their terrible deeds, but we have to be smart and not make the situation worse, for when men with guns go up against other men with guns and explosives, bad things are always going to happen. With that in mind, it needs to be absolutely necessary.
>
> **(Noesner, 2016)**

A former SWAT operator has made the risk balance explicit:

> Continual re-evaluation must be conducted to ensure that the proper tactics are applied to the specific incident at hand. Delaying action during an Active Shooter event will most likely increase the amount of harm that the attacker can inflict, while taking spontaneous action to resolve a barricaded subject with or without hostages, unless the hostages are being actively harmed, will generally increase the risk of injury to the hostage, the police and the suspect.
>
> **(Cameron, 2014)**

An overlapping point is made by a former member of the United States Army's Delta Force: "The definition of a decisive point is a point in time or location where the success or failure of your actions will ultimately predicate the success or failure of the entire mission" (Blaber, 2008, p. 57).

Recent events suggest that official tolerance for the risks of assault has increased (meaning officials are less risk averse, more risk seeking, in the assault). In recent years, the United States has launched attempts to rescue hostages in highly hostile environments in the Middle East. Following the deaths of Luke Somers and a South African hostage during a U.S.-Yemeni rescue attempt on December 6, 2014, U.S. President Barack Obama stated: "It is my highest responsibility to do everything possible to protect American citizens. As this and previous hostage rescue operations demonstrate, the United States will spare no effort to use all of its military, intelligence and diplomatic capabilities to bring Americans home safely, wherever they are located" (United States, White House, 2014).

The U.S. government's tolerance for the risks of rescue are probably increased by the accidental killing of two hostages (one American, one Italian) during a U.S. air strike by an unmanned aerial vehicle (UAV) in Pakistan against an Al Qa'ida target in January 2015 (for which the White House admitted U.S. responsibility on April 23, 2015).

Our Practical Prescriptions

Officials could use a risk assessment to decide when to assault. The assault becomes more attractive as the risks of assault fall lower than the risks of waiting.

If Attackers Are Resolutely Murderous, Suicidal, Irrational, or Unreliable

Historical Practices

If the hostage-takers appear resolutely murderous, suicidal, irrational, or unreliable, then a negotiated agreement would be untrustworthy, suggesting that an assault becomes more justifiable. For instance, on the second day of the Beslan siege (2004), hostage-takers were jumpy enough—on a hot day in crowded rooms with a self-imposed shortage of food and water, while taking narcotics and stimulants—to fire on police several times, apparently unprovoked. This siege ended in an official assault the next day. Clearly, the hostage-takers at Beslan were not reliably peaceful enough to expect a peaceful outcome.

Simulated Practices

In both simulations, the official role-players explicitly sought to identify when the terrorist role-players were murderous enough to justify an assault, and generally reacted cautiously to uncertainty.

In the first simulation (2015), the official side misinterpreted the terrorist side's multiple users of the commander's e-mail account, which suggested to the official side that the hostage-takers were not rational or in control. At the same time, the official side allowed multiple people to use one e-mail account, which agitated the hostage-takers:

> Using our clandestine agent Mel, we had direct contact via email with the head of the scheme, but not with the hostage-takers themselves. Our method of communicating with him was itself technically disorganized—our designated negotiators were also using Mel's email contact to contact Abdul. Conflicting messages were sent to the hostage-takers, consequently agitating them and breeding mistrust.
>
> **(Ryley Simcox)**

Our Practical Prescriptions

If the attackers are resolutely murderous—particularly if they are also suicidal—then the crisis is practically impossible to resolve peaceably, and the official side should use force as soon as possible to interrupt further murder. In theory, the attackers could be restrained by force without death, but this is practically impossible without exposing the official responders to unacceptable risks.

Unprovoked aggression against the official side seems like a justifiable cause for an official assault. However, we should be careful not to misinterpret the other side's understandably confused or indecisive behavior as irrational or unreliable.

As Late as Possible, But Before the Negative Risks Increase

Some prescriptions are contradictory: in the previous sections, the prescriptions are for an assault as early as possible under some conditions, but under other conditions, as discussed in this section, it should be as late as possible.

Here we consider four sets of arguments in favor of assaulting as late as possible:

1. If the hostage-takers are instrumental, not demonstrative
2. If the hostage-takers have already consolidated their defenses
3. After the hostage-takers have developed empathy
4. After the official side has gathered intelligence on the other side

If the Hostage-Taker Is "Instrumental," Not Demonstrative

The FBI broadly categorizes hostage-takers as either "instrumental" or "demonstrative." An "instrumental" hostage-taker is using the crime as an instrument or means toward some objective, such as ransom. A "demonstrative" hostage-taker is demonstrating his or her capacity for violence or desperation. The FBI's current course on "basic crisis negotiation training" advises negotiators to "stall for time" with an instrumental hostage-taker; time gives the subject time to lower expectations and perceptions of power. "[A] basic premise of negotiation…is that time can be a tool that allows anger to dissipate and better options to enter into the mind of the subject" (Noesner, 2011, p. 76). By contrast, a demonstrative hostage-taker needs time to calm down or consider nonviolent solutions, but if the demonstrative hostage-taker cannot be shifted into an instrumental hostage-taker, then the situation cannot end peacefully.

If the Hostage-Takers Had Time to Consolidate Their Defenses

If terrorists have time to consolidate their defenses, or if the official side is too late to intervene in the terrorists' initial assault, then the chances of a successful assault rapidly decline, suggesting that the assaulters should wait and hope for negotiations to resolve the crisis peacefully, hope for the hostage-takers' defensive capacities to decline, or stand by to assault if the assault capabilities improve.

Give Time for the Hostage-Takers to Empathize

In the days of old terrorism, analysts noted that terrorists deliberately brutalized hostages early (in the first hours) as defense against empathy or sympathy for the hostages. Consequently, one prescription to the official side was to wait, in order to give more time for the brutality to abate, and for empathy or sympathy to develop, which would lower the chance of further violence (Hudson, 1989, p. 335).

Some analysts think that this principle still applies to new terrorists:

> Experience shows that the vast majority of hostage casualties in barricade incidents occur in the opening moments of the siege, when the hostage-takers are aroused and highly nervous as they are trying to establish control over the panicking crowd… There are only 14 barricade-hostage crises in history where terrorists demonstrated a willingness to execute hostages in order to create pressure on the government to concede to their demands.
>
> **(Dolnik and Fitzgerald, 2011, p. 277)**

These same analysts expect longer stability in "preplanned incidents involving multiple attackers working in shifts." They listed the following five cases of preplanned hostage-takings, at the end of each of which the official side assaulted, after days to weeks, "despite many promising indicators of a positive progression in most of these incidents":

1. Beslan school, 2004: 52 hours
2. Moscow theater, 2002: 58 hours
3. Mumbai, 2008: 60 hours
4. Red mosque, Islamabad, 2007: 11 days
5. Japanese ambassador's residence, 1996–1997: 126 days (Dolnik and Fitzgerald, 2011, p. 275)

However, these cases are unrepresentative; Dolnik and Fitzgerald do not justify their selection of these particular cases. As Figure 12.1 shows, most hostage-takings end within 5 days.

Worse, Dolnik and Fitzgerald's vicarious observations of "many promising indicators of a positive progression" are so vague as to be unfalsifiable. In any case, these analysts contradict themselves by noting the tendency for the dehumanizing of hostages to become self-reinforcing over time: "Consequently, executions of some hostages throughout the course of barricade hostage crises involving the 'new terrorists' constitute a likely development" (Dolnik and Fitzgerald, 2011, p. 271). Moreover, terrorists prepare against empathy. For instance, Al Qa'ida's manual advises: "Do not be emotionally affected by the distress of your captives… Do not approach the hostages. In case you must, you need to have protection, and keep a minimum distance of one and a half meters from them" (Al Qa'ida, 2004).

We do not agree with Dolnik and Fitzgerald's implication that the assaults went in too early in their selected five cases, or that the official side must be certain that further negotiations will fail.

The choice between continued negotiation and immediate assault is always inherently risky—a choice between the risks of continued negotiation versus the risks of immediate assault. Crises cannot last indefinitely; otherwise, the official side would be tolerating the indefinite illegal detention of innocent persons. What the official side needs are practical prescriptions for when to assault, not vague advisories against going in too early given five ambiguous cases.

As found earlier, some hostage-takers are taking hostages with intent to harm them all eventually, after garnering maximum publicity. In these cases, the assault should go in as soon as possible. If the official side cannot be sure that the hostage-takers are intent on harming the hostages eventually, then the official side is under conditions of uncertainty and so must make the comparative risk assessment prescribed above, under the section on assaulting when triggered by events: if the risks of the continued hostage crisis outweigh the risks of an assault, then the assault should be executed.

After Gathering Intelligence

Even if the official side is certain that the other side cannot be dissuaded from detaining or murdering the hostages, the official side is still incentivized to continue negotiating (or at least communicating) if in the process it is gaining intelligence on the other side, or gaining time to prepare the assault.

The FBI's training manual acknowledges that some delay is useful for gathering intelligence. Roy Ramm, the former director of Negotiation Training at the Metropolitan Police in London, focuses on these benefits:

> Negotiation offers a path to non-violent incident resolution that presents the least risk of harm to hostages, hostage takers and intervention agents. Negotiation provides both time and opportunity. It provides the time to gather law enforcement resources and to develop and refine intervention options. It provides the opportunity to gather intelligence about the hostage takers, their motivation, intention, mental capacity and weaponry; about the location and resilience of the stronghold and about the hostages; their numbers, vulnerability, physical condition and locations within the stronghold.
>
> Unless the life of hostages is at immediate risk and any delay in a tactical intervention for which resources are immediately available will increase that risk, negotiation should be attempted as part of a developed strategic approach. Intervention without relevant tactical intelligence or adequate resource will result in a sub-optimal outcome.
>
> **(Ramm, 2016)**

13

Assaulting

In this chapter, we consider the practical challenges facing the assaulters, and the principles, processes, and tactics of the assault (Figure 13.1). Thus, the following sections review two main questions:

1. What are the practical challenges for the assaulters?
2. How should you assault?

What Are the Practical Challenges for the Assaulters?

Plenty of armed responders have identified new terrorists as the most challenging human threats. For instance, a retired leader of a special weapons and tactics (SWAT) team, in a police department in Michigan, identified the following 13 expectations:

1. The terrorist will be well armed.
2. The terrorist may have body armor.
3. Explosives and improvised explosive devices (IEDs) are common.
4. Planning and training will be extensive.
5. Terrorists will know the target locations better than most responding officers.
6. Terrorists fight like soldiers and not common criminals.
7. Terrorists will blend in with the landscape.
8. SWAT teams must be aware of the constitutional rights of our citizens.

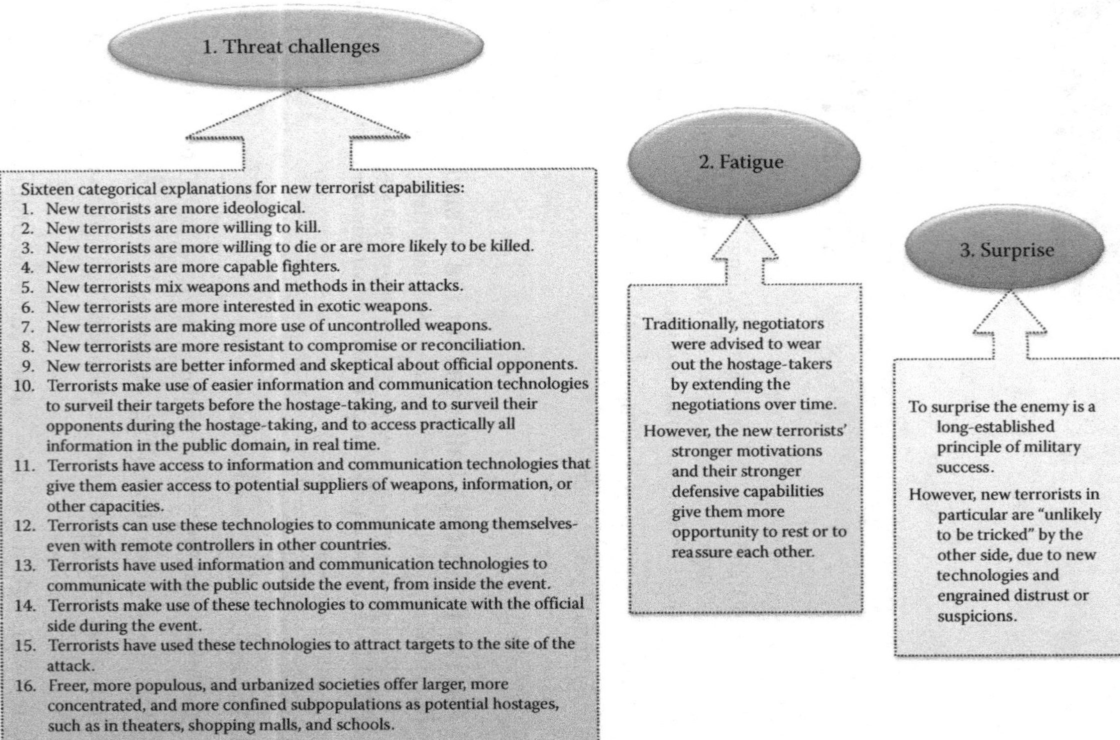

What are the practical challenges for the assaulters?
1. Threat challenges
Sixteen categorical explanations for new terrorist capabilities:
1. New terrorists are more ideological.
2. New terrorists are more willing to kill.
3. New terrorists are more willing to die or are more likely to be killed.
4. New terrorists are more capable fighters.
5. New terrorists mix weapons and methods in their attacks.
6. New terrorists are more interested in exotic weapons.
7. New terrorists are making more use of uncontrolled weapons.
8. New terrorists are more resistant to compromise or reconciliation.
9. New terrorists are better informed and skeptical about official opponents.
10. Terrorists make use of easier information and communication technologies to surveil their targets before the hostage-taking, and to surveil their opponents during the hostage-taking, and to access practically all information in the public domain, in real time.
11. Terrorists have access to information and communication technologies that give them easier access to potential suppliers of weapons, information, or other capacities.
12. Terrorists can use these technologies to communicate among themselves- even with remote controllers in other countries.
13. Terrorists have used information and communication technologies to communicate with the public outside the event, from inside the event.
14. Terrorists make use of these technologies to communicate with the official side during the event.
15. Terrorists have used these technologies to attract targets to the site of the attack.
16. Freer, more populous, and urbanized societies offer larger, more concentrated, and more confined subpopulations as potential hostages, such as in theaters, shopping malls, and schools.
2. Fatigue
Traditionally, negotiators were advised to wear out the hostage-takers by extending the negotiations over time.
However, the new terrorists' stronger motivations and their stronger defensive capabilities give them more opportunity to rest or to reassure each other.
3. Surprise
To surprise the enemy is a long-established principle of military success.
However, new terrorists in particular are "unlikely to be tricked" by the other side, due to new technologies and engrained distrust or suspicions.

Figure 13.1 A summary of the challenges for the assaulters facing new terrorists.

9. SWAT teams must be aware of the search and seizure laws and regulations.
10. Terrorists will engage law enforcement in open combat, preferably in populated areas.
11. Unity of command will be a challenge.
12. Communications with assisting tactical teams may be difficult for smaller agencies.
13. Tactical teams will not have enough medics available to triage everybody (French, 2013).

As previewed in Chapter 3, new terrorists are more challenging threats. Consider the early Jihadi hostage crises at the Dubrovka Theater in Moscow (2002), Beslan (2004), and Mumbai (2008), where the hostage-takers were abnormally well armed, well prepared, murderous, and suicidal. In Beslan (2004) the attackers accessed about 1,100 victims or hostages immediately (most of them children). The attackers kept hundreds of hostages alive, but wired them with explosives in a crowded gymnasium, and kept them under the muzzles of small arms carried by around a dozen men at a time. The official assault could not realistically expect to avoid the deaths of hostages: in the end, at least 385 people died.

We identified 16 categorical explanations:

1. New terrorists are more ideological, which is associated with more murderousness, more willingness to die, and more intransigence.

2. New terrorists are more willing to kill. As shown in Table 3.2, twice as many people die during new terrorist hostage-takings than old terrorist hostage-takings, and less than half as many hostages are released by new terrorists than old terrorists. As shown in Table 3.3, twice as many hostages die per hostage-taking under new terrorists than old terrorists. As shown in Table 3.6, new terrorist hostage-takings end in the death of at least some hostages 60% of the time, while old terrorist hostage-takings end in at least some hostage deaths less than 40% of the time.

3. As Table 3.3 summarizes, our analysis suggests that new terrorists are more willing to die or are more likely to be killed: more than twice as many new terrorists die per hostage-taking event than old terrorists die. Moreover, almost all the explicit suicidal hostage-taking events are new terrorist events. (These are undercounted due to the coding difficulties.)

4. New terrorists are more capable fighters. Given wider political instability and state failure in the 2000s, the opportunities to acquire weapons and to prepare in ungoverned spaces have increased. New terrorists tend to kill more people, even though they deploy fewer hostage-takers per event and per hostage. As shown in Table 3.4, new terrorists deploy more hostage-takers per event and hold more hostages per hostage-taker.

5. New terrorists mix weapons and methods in their attacks.
6. New terrorists are more interested in exotic weapons, in pursuit of increased lethality or terror, including chemical, biological, radiological, and nuclear weapons.
7. New terrorists are encouraging more use of uncontrolled weapons, such as knives and automobiles, rather than procurement of more lethal weapons that would draw official attention.
8. New terrorists, being more religious, lethal, and suicidal in motivations, are more resistant to compromise or reconciliation. Certainly, new terrorists are less likely to release hostages, at least in most cases—in which a ransom has not been demanded. As shown in Table 3.6, new terrorist hostage-takings end in the release of the hostages only 31% of the time, whereas old terrorist hostage-takings end in the release of the hostages 51% of the time.
9. New terrorists are better informed and skeptical about official opponents. As shown in Chapter 3, new terrorists are better read on the other side's armed capacities and procedures, thanks in part to the readier availability and accessibility of official information, and the easier travel associated with globalization, with one notable effect being wider diffusion of terrorist skills and knowledge.
10. Terrorists make use of easier information and communication technologies to surveil their targets before the hostage-taking, to surveil their opponents during the hostage-taking, and to access practically all information in the public domain, in real time.
11. New information and communication technologies give new terrorists easier access to potential suppliers of weapons, information, or other capacities.
12. Terrorists can use these technologies to communicate among themselves—even with remote controllers in other countries.
13. Terrorists have used information and communication technologies to communicate with the public outside the event, from inside the event.
14. Terrorists make use of these technologies to communicate with the official side during the event.
15. Terrorists have used these technologies to attract targets to the site of the attack.
16. Freer, more populous, and urbanized societies offer larger, more concentrated, and more confined subpopulations as potential targets, such as in theaters, shopping malls, and schools.

How Should You Assault Tactically?

In this section, we review the principles and processes of assault—focusing on speed, surprise, and violence of action, and competing tactics for assaulters.

Principles and Processes

In the SWAT community, three principles are fundamental:

1. Speed
2. Surprise
3. Violence of action

A former member of the Federal Bureau of Investigation's (FBI) Hostage Rescue Team and commander of the FBI New York Division's SWAT team (James A. Gagliano) has stated that four principles are fundamental for effective assaults:

1. Speed
2. Surprise
3. Violence of action
4. A fail-safe breach (Cruickshank, 2017)

The last of his principles might be considered more technological and tactical than the other three, so we consider it in the following section (on tactics). The first three principles have been described in the public domain as originating with the U.S. Army's Delta Force, which is known to have shared lessons with civilian law enforcers (*Newsweek*, 2015). One former member of Delta Force has written this personal advice:

> The key to success on all battlefields—past, present, and future—has very little to do with electronic whiz-bang gadgets and top-secret technologies; instead, it's all about how you think, how you make decisions, and how you execute those decisions... For it's not the action—the blinding flash of a concussion grenade, or the stealthy approach of the night vision-clad commando, but the interaction, in the form of the way we think, the way we make decisions, and the way we operationalize our decisions that matter most.
>
> **(Blaber, 2008, p. 7)**

A military training services provider ("D-Company," formed by former members of Delta Force) issues the following nine "principles":

1. Objective
2. Offense
3. Maneuver

4. Economy of force
5. Mass
6. Unity of command
7. Simplicity
8. Surprise
9. Security

D-Company prescribes the following process for tactical leaders:

1. Receive the mission
2. Issue a warning order
3. Make a tentative plan
4. Move to assembly area or observation area
5. Conduct reconnaissance
6. Complete the plan
7. Issue the orders commensurate with the final plan
8. Rehearse and refine the plan

In the following sections, we focus on the top three consensual principles:

1. Speed
2. Surprise
3. Violence of action

Speed

Historical Practices

Generally, one principle of the assault, if it must be launched, is speed, to minimize the opportunities for the other side to respond. The director of training at the school for the FBI's Hostage Rescue Team (Special Agent John Piser) has said, "How quickly we can secure a house with a credible threat inside might mean the difference between a hostage living or dying" (FBI, 2013a).

Gagliano has added, "It's all about momentum in this business. Every second counts." Gagliano went on to emphasize the special cognition and psychology:

> Keeping calm is critical. As an operator, it's about controlling your own fears. Fear is a natural emotion. And while it is to be acknowledged and respected, it must be controlled and channeled properly. Left unchecked, it has a deleterious effect on the effectiveness of a unit. At the FBI Swat Team in New York and at the Hostage Rescue Team in Quantico, we weren't interested in bringing on people who said they'd never been scared. Fear is a rational response to impending

danger, and those who sense it are more prone to make sensible decisions to protect themselves, their teammates, and the hostages they are trying to save.

Being able to adapt and improvise in a kinetic situation is a necessary trait for counterterror operators and SWAT operators. They must be able to adapt to fluid circumstances against an unconventional enemy. Therefore, split-second reaction to an adversary's unanticipated action is a critical skillset for new team members. The countless hours spent training together as a tactical response team are vital because they allow individuals to react with muscle memory, on auto-pilot, which frees the mind to have a capacity to improvise in fluid and dangerous situations. This tactical choreography is what sets team members apart from their less skilled adversaries who don't have the same familiarity with each other.

(Cruickshank, 2017)

Similarly, the British Metropolitan Police emphasize speed in rescuing hostages, as during the following rescue in south London in 2006:

There was no luxury of time, as the unit strongly believed the hostage's life was in imminent danger. The gang would have no qualms about murdering their hostage if they believed the police were involved...On a given signal, Hatton rounds fired from a shotgun were used to disrupt the front door lock. Once entry was made, the team fanned out into the rooms of the flat. Distraction stun grenades were deployed creating noise and smoke, giving the entry team the time to move in and dominate each room and everyone inside. As the smoke cleared, the hostage was located tied up on a bed.

(Smith, 2013, p. 210)

An Israeli school teaches shooting to incapacitate the threat before moving as fast as possible toward the attacker for the final kill.

This is the Israeli technique of "sprinting" with the weapon one-handed (weapon hand pumping just like free hand) as fast as we can toward the target. If the instructor yelled "target up," we'd have to come to an Israeli-style shuffle stop with our feet evenly spread, quickly reacquire the Israeli point-shooting stance, and fire at the target until the instructor yelled "target down." We then sprinted to the target again to continue to close the distance. Unless the instructor yelled, "target up" again, we closed to contact distance and fired a neutralization shot into the target's/terrorist's head (anchor shot).

This sprint-to-the-target, stop, shoot, and sprint again technique is very different from the American shooting-while-moving technique. The Israelis believe they can close to the threat faster, shoot from a more stable platform, and maintain a better total situational awareness and target focus with this method. In Israel, CT operators train to always attack forward immediately...

In this situation, sprinting with the weapon held one-handed allows you to physically shove or strike innocent people out of the way as necessary. Sometimes, innocent bystanders might freeze out of fear or actively try to impede you if they don't know who you are, so you have to be prepared and able to deal with this obstacle quickly and decisively.

(Crane, 2007)

Simulated Practices

In both our simulations (2015 and 2016), all sides considered violence early (within the first 30 minutes) and were mindful of the advantages of acting quicker than the other side might expect. These outcomes are hypothetical, given the simulated scenario, so the same persons might have behaved differently in a real-world equivalent—theoretically, we expect people to be more cautious and deliberative in the real-world than the simulated scenario. However, at least the simulations provide evidence of the general awareness of the advantages of acting quicker than the opponent, even though the achievement of acting quicker is practically more challenging.

Our Practical Prescriptions

The main trade-off in emphasizing speed is accuracy in decision making. When an actor is emphasizing speed, the actor is foregoing more time to deliberate before making decisions. If the actor takes time to deliberate, he or she presumably hopes to improve the accuracy of the decision, but might wait longer than the decision is useful, or may become mired in indecision or procrastination. In assaulting terrorists, the assaulter wants to make decisions quicker than the terrorist about when to fire on each other, but does not want to be hasty with another human being who turns out to be a hostage, not a terrorist. With training, the actor can learn techniques that are both faster and more accurate—techniques such as recognition-primed decision making, in which the user is trained to respond to certain cues without deliberation. For instance, law enforcement officers are conventionally practiced to shoot targets representing armed threats, but not to shoot targets representing unarmed hostages. Eventually, with practice, the decisions can be made without deliberation, automatically (Newsome, 2007, pp. 78–83).

Surprise

Historical Practices

To surprise the enemy is a long-established principle of military success.

This principle becomes necessary if the assaulters want to overcome the other side so quickly as to catch the other side unprepared, thence to avoid effective resistance. For instance, from December 1995, the North Atlantic Treaty Organization (NATO) took over from the United Nations the military command of the peacekeeping mission in Bosnia and Herzegovina, in the former Yugoslavia. NATO's local force (the Implementation Force, which became the Stabilization Force in December 1996) took over authority and responsibility for capturing and detaining persons indicted as war criminals by the International Criminal Tribune for the former Yugoslavia (PIFWCs). U.S. and other national special operations forces led the search for PIFWCs, including the United States Army's Delta Force. In the 1990s, a team from Delta Force received intelligence from a local Bosnian human source (code-named "4AZ") about a PIFWC:

> This particular mission had an additional complication: 4AZ mentioned that the PIFWC might be traveling with his daughter. This meant at least two things. First, whatever concept we came up with to capture the PIFWC would have to depend on nonlethal force to ensure we didn't inadvertently endanger the life of his daughter. Second, to ensure that we didn't initiate an uncontrollable gunfight with PIFWC's security detail, we needed to achieve total surprise...As a matter of principle our goal was to conduct all capture operations without firing a shot.
>
> **(Blaber, 2008, p. 47)**

Traditionally, negotiators were advised to distract the hostage-takers, particularly closer to any official assault. However, some analysts have warned that new terrorists in particular are "unlikely to be tricked" by the other side, due to their use of information communication technologies to access real-time news or coconspirators on the outside (Dolnik and Fitzgerald, 2011, p. 268).

Evidence comes from one of the manuals issued by Al Qa'ida, which warned hostage-takers that negotiators arrange for diversions away from an official assault: "The authorities often attempt to create diversions and attack the kidnappers." The manual made the same point in the context of security for the site: "Beware of sudden attacks as they may be trying to create a diversion which could allow them to seize control of the situation. Combating teams will use two attacks: a secondary one just to attract attention, and a main attack elsewhere" (Al Qa'ida, 2004).

Al Qa'ida has urged hostage-takers to pay attention to apertures: "Watch out for the ventilation or other openings as they could be used to plant surveillance devices through which the number of kidnappers could be counted and gases could be used." The manual prescribed attention to the perimeter: "Wire the perimeter of the hostage location to deny access to the enemy" (Al Qa'ida, 2004).

The Al Qa'ida manual prescribes also the distribution of defenders in five groups:

> The execution team must be formed of five groups: The alarming group that reports the movements of the target; the protection group that protects the kidnappers from any external intervention; the kidnapping group which kidnaps the target and delivers him to a sheltering group; the sheltering group whose role is to keep an eye on the hostage until it is time for exchange or get rid of them; the pursuit deterring group which will ensure the shelter group is not followed or watched.
>
> **(Al Qa'ida, 2004)**

While acknowledging the increasing difficulties of deceiving new terrorists, this acknowledgment does not preclude the possibilities. For instance, in November 2015, French assaulters telephoned one of the two terrorists who had barricaded themselves with hostages in a corridor inside the Bataclan theater in Paris, as a distraction before the assault; both terrorists, but no hostages, died in that particular corridor; 89 hostages died elsewhere in the theater (Cruickshank, 2017).

Simulated Practices

In simulation (2015), the terrorist side interpreted the accelerated frequency of messages from the official side as a deliberate attempt to delay or distract, and as an indicator that the official side was preparing to assault, which caused the hostage-takers to kill more rapidly.

In the second simulation (2016), the official role-players eventually decided to use a ransom as cover for an assault—a ruse that the terrorist role-players realized and preempted by killing hostages.

Our Practical Prescriptions

If the official side decides to assault, it should try to surprise the terrorists, but surprise will be difficult to achieve against new terrorists. The official side should not rely on ruses well known to history or popular culture, and should not slide into an assault through deteriorating negotiations, or clumsy attempts at deception. Surprise is most likely when the terrorists are actively engaged in a negotiation that they perceive as genuine.

Violence of Action

In addition to assaulting as quickly and with as much surprise as possible, assaulters are advised to act violently, which is not necessarily obvious or natural, particularly for communities brought up on norms of cooperation, negotiation, empathy, and so on, but is prescribed with irreconcilable new terrorists at least.

Historical Practices

Gagliano has stated that his four principles (speed, surprise, violence of action, and a fail-safe breach) are "inter-related," and that a synergistic combination can leave the opponent hapless:

> Let me provide you with an example from early in my career. In June 1993, I was a young shooter on the FBI SWAT team that moved in to arrest five terrorists who were part of a group linked to the "Blind Sheikh" Omar Abdel Rahman, which was planning to bomb the Holland Tunnel, Lincoln Tunnel, the FBI's New York office building, the United Nations, the George Washington Bridge, and the St. Regis Hotel. We effected entry into their "bomb factory" in a Brooklyn warehouse as they were literally stirring their "witch's brew"—as it was later described in media accounts—a drum of diesel fuel and fertilizer. One of the terrorists exited a side room and immediately confronted the entry team, with a SWAT operator immediately shouting, "Gun!" The bewildered bomb-builder wisely chose to hand the Kalashnikov-style assault rifle he was holding to our Number One man who was armed with a ballistic shield and a handgun.
>
> **(Cruickshank, 2017)**

Gagliano emphasizes the synergy of prior intelligence (useful information), although this is not one of his explicit principles:

> In the Blind Sheikh case, we had several advantages as we knew who we were dealing with—the case squad had completed an exhaustive workup on the subjects—and we had time to painstakingly prepare in advance. We also had the warehouse wired up with audio and video feeds because we had a solid cooperating witness. The CCTV video feed accurately showed us in real time where people were positioned and where weapons were emplaced in the room, so we were able to make the entry with informational superiority. Knowledge, or intelligence, is power and a force multiplier. In situations where you are responding to an active shooter or a hostage standoff, you have much less time to appraise a kinetic situation. In those instances, rehearsals, standard operating procedures, and experience are what you rely on to augment the momentum necessary to effect a successful rescue.
>
> As a responding tactical unit, the success of your action is always going to depend on your evaluation of the situation before going in, reducing as many variables as conceivably possible. The key here is to obtain what we call "speculative intelligence"—a profile assessment, if you will—to figure out how likely it is the hostage-taker(s) are going to kill the hostage(s). You need to understand the mindset, desperation level, and motivation of the attacker(s). In all cases, you need to come up with a "hasty assault plan" basically right away. That then forms the genesis of your "deliberate assault plan" as intelligence improves and more resources are assembled.
>
> **(Cruickshank, 2017)**

Such prior intelligence and decisiveness are not easy practically. The counterterrorist side wants to be prepared to be reliably better informed, quicker, more surprising, and more violent than opponents.

Superiority of training is necessary, but most law enforcement agents do not receive any training in the particular skills of assaulting (even their handling of firearms might be limited to a single day's requalification once per year), while new terrorists are known to emphasize equivalent training, and to claim superior motivations or even divine help than even specialist assaulters can offer. Moreover, we have heard complaints from SWAT operators about the advantages that the terrorists carry, having already decided to act illegitimately, compared to the ethical and judicial constraints on the counterterrorist operator, especially given increasing public and judicial attention, in recent years, to the legitimacy of killings by law enforcement operatives.

Consequently, some on the counterterrorist side emphasize more violence of action in public and personal expectations. For instance, a counterterrorist manual has urged a new "mindset" in assaulters confronted by new terrorists:

> In preparing officers to respond to terrorist incidents, it appears that DHS has realized that we cannot hope to defeat a determined terror attack using traditional police tactics. The local SWAT officer must adopt the mindset that we are in a state of war and must act more along the lines of a soldier than a police officer...
>
> Training and equipment are far less valuable if the team doesn't have the correct mindset, one that says, "I will put my life on the line to prevent these terrorists from killing large numbers of Americans; I am prepared to sacrifice myself to accomplish this mission." In many departments, the SOP [standard operating procedure]

> is to withdraw if the team takes casualties... In a terrorist incident, withdrawal is simply not an option; the team must maximize surprise, speed, and violence of action and aggressively continue the operation in the face of casualties because once the assault has begun, the terrorists must not be given a chance to regroup.
>
> **(Forest, 2007, pp. 260, 267)**

Simulated Practices

In our simulations, all sides considered violence early, although the terrorist role-players were more demonstrative in their intentions. We did not observe explicit awareness of the principle of "violence of action" in the unofficial participants, and the principle did not arise explicitly except from the certified SWAT advisers, who struggled to generalize awareness across their respective sides. We can imagine the same problem in real-world scenarios, where even incident commanders are unlikely to be as mindful of the principle as their SWAT advisers.

In any case, awareness of the principle is not sufficient for practical execution of the principle in ways superior to the opponent, which our simulations did not test.

Our Practical Prescriptions

We agree that the counterterrorist side should be prepared to synergize speed, surprise, and violence in ways that leave their opponents hapless in the brief moment of ultimate confrontation.

We agree also that the violence of action needs to be emphasized more given that new terrorists are aware of the principle and aim to achieve superiority of violence of action.

We foresee that the assaulters can achieve superiority of violence of action if given prior confidence in

1. The legitimacy and urgency of unlimited lethal force against such terrorists, following authorization of the assault
2. Their automaticity of decision making in using such lethal force, given sufficient training and routine recalibration in shoot/don't-shoot decisions
3. The received intelligence on the location, intents, and capabilities of the opponents

Tactics

We identified four broad approaches for armed personnel to neutralize the threats:

1. The official assaulters can contain the threats.
2. Official snipers can shoot the terrorists from outside the containment area.
3. The official assaulters can approach the threats.
4. The official assaulters can encourage the threats to approach.

Containment

Containment is a conventional strategy for restricting the spread of a threat, or for separating a threat from its targets to the extent that it is reduced to a hazard (Newsome, 2014, pp. 60, 184–195). This chapter focuses on assaults, rather than nonviolent resolutions to the crisis, such as a negotiated peaceful outcome, in which the active role for armed personnel is mostly to hold the perimeter defensively (Figure 13.2). Such nonviolent resolutions are the foci of earlier chapters. In Chapter 12, we described the shift in the 2000s from containment of active shooters to confrontation. Thus, for brevity and to avoid redundancy, we refer readers to Chapter 12 for consideration of the tactics of containment.

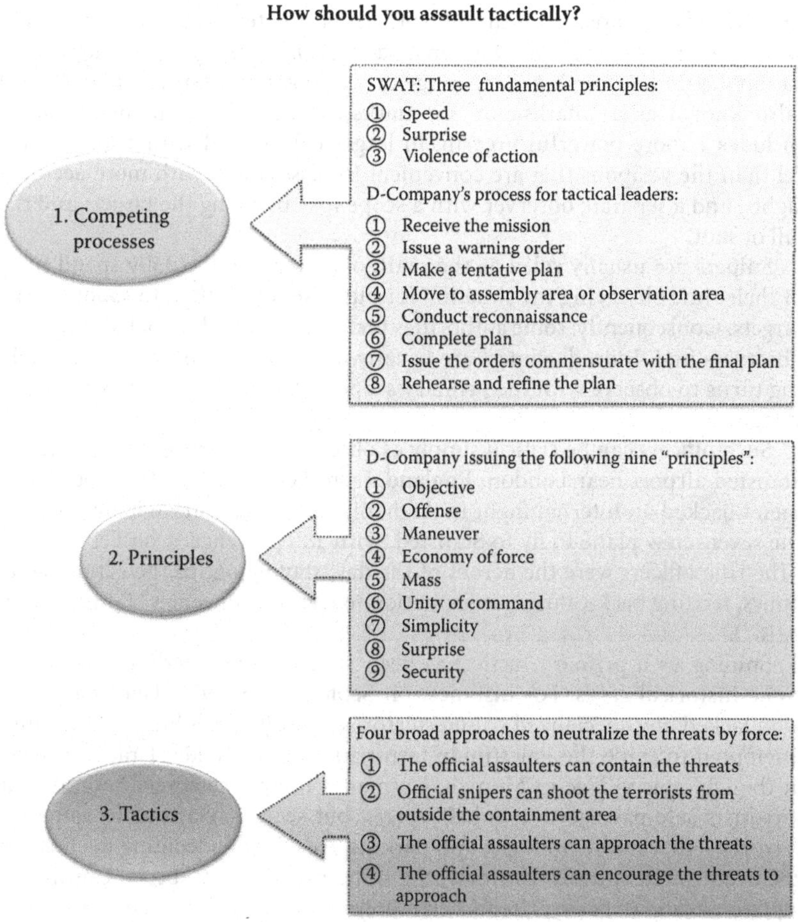

How should you assault tactically?

1. Competing processes

SWAT: Three fundamental principles:
① Speed
② Surprise
③ Violence of action

D-Company's process for tactical leaders:
① Receive the mission
② Issue a warning order
③ Make a tentative plan
④ Move to assembly area or observation area
⑤ Conduct reconnaissance
⑥ Complete plan
⑦ Issue the orders commensurate with the final plan
⑧ Rehearse and refine the plan

2. Principles

D-Company issuing the following nine "principles":
① Objective
② Offense
③ Maneuver
④ Economy of force
⑤ Mass
⑥ Unity of command
⑦ Simplicity
⑧ Surprise
⑨ Security

3. Tactics

Four broad approaches to neutralize the threats by force:
① The official assaulters can contain the threats
② Official snipers can shoot the terrorists from outside the containment area
③ The official assaulters can approach the threats
④ The official assaulters can encourage the threats to approach

Figure 13.2 A summary of the processes, principles, and tactics of assaulting terrorists.

A former SWAT operator prescribes the containment of the hostage-takers, although he prescribes approaching their space, although not yet closing the final gap:

> The hostage-taker should be confined to the smallest possible area, preferably without a face-to-face confrontation. If possible, the perpetrator should be locked in, i.e., by chocking the door or blocking it with a desk or other heavy, but movable, object.
>
> **(French, 2013)**

Sniping

The official side could prepare snipers to shoot the terrorists from outside the containment area, with the advantage that the terrorists' capacity would shrink before or without need for an assault. A *sniper* is equipped and trained to shoot a target from a greater range or with greater accuracy than normal (also known as a "marksman" or markswoman). The equipment usually includes a more powerful firearm, in larger caliber and with a longer barrel than the weapons that are convenient for assaulting, with more accurate sights, and a separate observer with a scope for observing the targets and the fall of shot.

Snipers are usually roled as the main observers, and usually spend most of their time observing the situation for purposes other than to shoot on any targets. Consequently, some authorities prefer to refer to designated snipers as observers first. Indeed, snipers are usually in teams of two, each person taking turns to observe with the primary scope or to stand by with the primary weapon.

Such officers can be critical simply as observers, as during the hijacking at Stansted airport near London, England, from February 6 to 10, 2000. (Nine men hijacked an internal flight in Afghanistan on February 6 before forcing the seven-crew plane to fly to Stansted, with 180 passengers, on February 7.) "The rifle officers were the heroes of the day, staying out in their hides at all hours, feeding back valuable information to the control center" (Smith, 2013, p. 167).

Sniping as a primary tactic has been shown to be overly optimistic in some historical cases. For instance, on September 6, 1972, German police, who lacked any specialized counterterrorist assault capabilities at that time, attempted to snipe the Palestinian terrorists who had taken Israeli hostages at the Olympic village in Munich, Germany. The police agreed to grant the terrorists safe passage to two helicopters, but secretly planned to snipe the terrorists, first in the underground parking area, before deciding to shoot on the overground runway. However, the snipers lacked any special training or equipment and were surprised when more hostage-takers showed up than had been counted by observers at the Olympic village. The sniping was indecisive and left most of the terrorists with capacity to shoot back at the police and their hostages, leading to the deaths of nine hostages (on top of the two hostages killed during the initial taking), one policeman, and five of the eight terrorists.

By contrast, British sniper-observers proved more useful during a hostage-taking in Islington, London, on October 30, 2000, when, after 11 hours of containment and negotiation, a sniper was able to observe the imminent threat to one of the two hostages, and to shoot the perpetrator (Kieran O'Donnell):

> Local police attended and it soon became apparent that a man was holding two women inside the premises against their will and had armed himself with two knives and possibly other weapons. The duty officer contacted SO19 [the Metropolitan Police's specialist firearms command] and requested urgent armed assistance. Armed response vehicles attended and soon contained the flat. Officers began evacuating other residents within the building and an SFO [specialist firearms officer] team was scrambled out from Old Street. Local enquiries were made and it [intelligence] was soon established... By 11:55 a.m. the SFO team were kitted up and ready to carry out an intervention as an emergency response if required...An SFO team sniper had found a suitable position in an adjoining flat overlooking the room where most of the activity was occurring. He was able to give a commentary of movement within the flat...They advised the scene commander that they would continue to negotiate until they felt the situation had deteriorated beyond repair...Using their scopes, the SO19 sniper and his observer could see O'Donnell and his hostage clearly... At 6:06 p.m., police saw O'Donnell climb on top of Nadia and begin stabbing her in the head with the corkscrew. Stun grenades were thrown into the flat and the teams began making their entries. The sniper, however, knew he had to act immediately if he was to stop O'Donnell killing his hostage. Although the distance was relatively small, he was firing through two windows and he knew the slightest contact could deflect a bullet...The action taken by the officer in identifying the threat to life undoubtedly saved the hostage from even more serious injury or death.
>
> **(Smith, 2013, pp. 172–174)**

Sniping is rarely used. The threshold seems to depend on whether the risks of not incapacitating the hostage-taker rise ahead of the risks to the hostage of leaving the hostage with the hostage-taker. For instance, in April 1988, during a self-barricade by an armed man with his estranged partner and their son, the woman shouted to Gary Noesner, "Can't you get us out of here?" The hostage-taker leapt on this plural idea, in the hope that it would keep them together as a family. Noesner was doubtful about keeping the hostage-taker stable, so he talked to the incident commander: "I then did something that is extremely rare in the negotiation business. I recommended that I be given permission to lure Charlie out of the house by negotiating with him for access to the helicopter, and that we prepare to have a sniper take him out as he left the house" (Noesner, 2011, p. 17). Charlie was indeed shot to death, and both hostages were freed.

In most cases, sniping is not an option, because of the superior chances of a peaceful resolution, or the risks to innocent parties near the threat, or the difficulties of confirming the threat. For instance, on October 31, 2006, during an armed robbery of a van delivering cash to automated teller machines in New Romney, Kent, the sniper-observers decided that sniping would be too risky:

> There was no clear shot from the rifle position, so all the officers in the observation point could do was to continue their commentary as the guard passed over the money cassettes containing £105,000...Up until this point, police could not intervene because of the risk of the custodian becoming a hostage or being shot by [Robert] Haines, so they had no option but to call the attack when he left the building society.
>
> **(Smith, 2013, pp. 214–215)**

Instead, other officers shot to death Haines when he fired on them during his escape. The other three members of the gang were arrested and convicted.

Approach the Attacker

In order to incapacitate the opponent without anybody else reliable, one usually needs to approach the opponent, and to approach the opponent one usually needs to breach some barricade into a confined space occupied by the opponent. This is why Gagliano emphasizes "a fail-safe breach" as his fourth principle of successful assaults, but warns that the emphasis and the capabilities are lacking elsewhere, due to want of authorizations or awareness:

> If and when you need to "go in," a failsafe breach is absolutely key. There are a number of techniques for this, including mechanical breaching, which we employed in the Blind Sheikh case, and may involve implementation of a hydraulic or pneumatic device to separate a door from its jamb and shotgun breaching, which involves the use of a short-barreled shotgun to blast open the lock on a door with a round comprised of dental plaster. But the most reliable way to enter is to apply a suitable amount of explosives. Explosive breaching is one of the key domain capabilities of the FBI's Hostage Rescue Team (HRT) at Quantico, Virginia, a team I was proud to be a member of once. It is also a capability that has been developed by a small number of police departments across the country, as illustrated in the response by the Orlando Police Department to the nightclub attack. But many local police forces and municipalities do not have explosive breaching capabilities in their department's tactical arsenal. Many are only armed with simple and rudimentary sledge hammers, crowbars, heavy battering rams, "Halligan Tools," and maybe a "rabbit"—pneumatic door-jamb spreaders—if they're lucky. All of these breaching accoutrements are similar to what most fire departments and emergency rescue units have in stock.
>
> Neither the NYPD's Emergency Services Unit (ESU) nor the FBI tactical response teams in New York City have an explosive breaching capability. If and when a hostage situation were to occur in New York, on-scene command authorities would need to wait for the arrival of the FBI Hostage Rescue Team from Quantico to bring this capability to bear. That would likely take more than an hour or two, under the best set of circumstances. While there are reservations in some quarters about arming police departments and part-time SWAT teams with explosives, in my view the current terrorist threat, and ISIS's calls for attacks against soft targets all across the United States rather than just against high-profile, more traditionally hardened targets, means there are strong arguments for police forces around the country developing and maintaining this capability. As the current FBI director has repeatedly stated, the FBI has open cases against ISIS subjects in all 50 states. That's a lot of territory

> for law enforcement to cover and maintain a posture so that immediate entries into barricaded locations can be effected safely and expeditiously. Minutes, and seconds, in this business absolutely matter.
>
> **(Cruickshank, 2017, p. 9)**

The dominant tactics in the New York Police Department's Critical Response Command training are to move silently, as quickly as possible, and to execute a "dynamic entry" into each contested space without hesitation and with all forces, in order to give the opponents little opportunity to respond.

> To demonstrate, the Command later allowed journalists to stand in an empty room and wait for the team to enter.
>
> The silence was startling, unnerving. The officers did not speak as they snaked toward the room. They communicated in pats on the back and hand signals. There was no warning of their arrival.
>
> One moment, the room was empty. A heartbeat later, it was filled with the six men and their guns. Traditionally, when officers stormed a room, the first one was known as the "rabbit," likely drawing the fire of the gunman inside while the second officer took aim at him. With this team, it was as if there were no rabbit—the entire team seemed to swarm the room at once.
>
> **(Wilson, 2016)**

An Israeli school teaches two operators to enter the room together:

> If you're approaching a doorway at the corner of a room, the procedure is slightly different. You handle it just like the corner of a structure, accept once you pop the doorway to clear 90 degrees and thus address any threats immediately visible in the room (muzzle not breaking the plane of entry into the room), you have to then address the blind corner inside the room.
>
> So, once you clear the immediately visible area from the doorway, you have to handle the blind corner by inching around until you can pop it as well. Again, you're shuffling the whole time and popping the blind corner with a fast step, lean and point. If you have two operators, you can employ a two-man pop technique where one takes high position and the other takes low position.
>
> If you have a doorway in the center of the room, you want at least two operators to handle the room. In this scenario, you initially approach the doorway from one side just like you would a corner doorway, and clear the main section of the room from the one side (to 90 degrees).
>
> To clear both blind corners inside the room, the rear operator now has to get to the safe area on the other side of the door. He does this by smacking the point man on the back hard enough to get his attention and let him know he's moving, and then running past the opening as fast as he can. Once he makes it to the other side, both men pop both corners simultaneously.
>
> **(Crane, 2007)**

Encourage the Attacker to Approach

Rather than approach the attackers, the official assaulters could encourage the attackers to exit. Traditionally, assaulters have acquired technologies and techniques useful to encourage such an exit, even by deception or violence, although the necessary intelligence and material context is difficult to achieve:

> During the negotiation process, various surveillance tools such as cameras and robots can be employed to acquire information about the structure involved and specifically about where the suspect is located within the building. Family members or friends can be consulted regarding access to weapons and asked about the floor plan of the building. Tactical teams can utilize a variety of less-lethal options, such as tear gas, to attempt to compel the suspect to exit the location and surrender.
>
> **(Cameron, 2014)**

With suicidal and murderous subjects, whose intent to kill is clear whatever alternatives are offered to them, the official side could try to encourage the subjects to choose suicide over murder.

Some analysts have suggested that if terrorists are intent on dying, the negotiator can negotiate an honorable death against combatants (without involving hostages) or discuss the handling of their bodies (Dolnik and Fitzgerald, 2011, p. 282).

This is practical if the assaulters can persuade willingly suicidal hostage-takers of a mutually exclusive choice between harming hostages or martyring themselves. Some terrorist behavior suggests that the compulsion for a glorious martyrdom can trump the immediate opportunities for murder or safety. For instance, in May 2013, two violent Jihadis struck an off-duty British soldier (Lee Rigby) with a car, before killing him with kitchen knives. These particular attackers waited around the scene, while making statements to bystanders, and showing their bloody knives and an unloaded revolver, until police arrived, when they rushed to attack, as they had agreed in advance. Although they had planned to die as martyrs, both were injured, arrested, and convicted (BBC, 2013b, 2016b).

Similarly, the two perpetrators (brothers Chérif and Said Kouachi) of the attacks on the office of the magazine "Charlie Hebdo" (January 7, 2015), having killed 11 people inside the office and a policeman outside the office, escaped Paris, exchanged gunfire with police, and took one hostage in a small town on January 9, but preferred to charge to their deaths against the police, without harming the hostage, perhaps because the brothers were fatalistic (one had a minor injury, and they were facing their fourth firefight).

Whatever their motivations, the Islamic State's interpretation of their final suicidalism includes their intents to martyr themselves and to surprise their enemies—presumably on the off-chance of causing further harm to their enemies:

> The phone signals in the locality of the building were cut off so the boys could not communicate with any other person they knew. Finally, a negotiator from the French phoned them and asked them what their demands were, they replied they would die as martyrs...But suddenly to the Western Special Forces' surprise, the brothers jumped out from their hiding places and began to shoot at

> the Special Forces. A huge barricade of fire was shot back and even explosions took place! Two mujahideen vs [versus] thousands of French security forces gained the martyrdom which they were seeking.
>
> **(Islamic State of Iraq and Levant, 2015, p. 57)**

Similarly, on the same day (January 9, 2015), a friend (Ahmed Coulibaly) of the Kouachi brothers charged police during their assault of the kosher supermarket, without harming any more hostages, having killed a policewoman the day before his assault on the supermarket, and another four people during his initial assault on the supermarket. Again, the Islamic State tells the story of Coulibaly's inevitable, pious, and glorious martyrdom:

> Meanwhile in the Jewish grocery store, Ahmed (also called: Amedy) Coulibaly received a call from the negotiator. He had replied that he would only free the Jewish hostages if the Kouachi brothers were allowed to escape. The negotiation discussion had now ended, but for some reason Ahmed had forgot to shut his phone off. Then, to the negotiators' surprise, Ahmed Cloulibaly started to pray his Maghrib salaah (sunset prayer). Suddenly there were explosions outside the building by the special forces which led to the release of the hostages. The last action of this Islamic State martyr was his prayer, less than 20 minutes after the martyrdom of the Kouachi brothers. His wife, Hayat Boumeddiene had escaped a few days before into the Islamic State for refuge via Turkey (and she is still safe there right now).
>
> **(Islamic State of Iraq and Levant, 2015, p. 57)**

These narratives might not be accurate of past behaviors, but they must encourage future emulations.

Similarly, toward the end of the crisis in Orlando, Florida, in June 2016, Omar Mateen (who pledged allegiance to the Islamic State of Iraq and the Levant [ISIL]) approached assaulters through a hole in the wall that assaulters themselves had made to help hostages escape out of a tightly bound area of toilets: as Mateen exposed himself by climbing through this hole, assaulters were able to shoot him to death, 3 hours after police had first exchanged fire with Mateen, without harming him, or discouraging his shooting to death of 49 people (Zapotosky and Berman, 2016).

On the official side, the negotiators can encourage the hostage-takers to choose martyrdom over murder by reminding the hostage-takers of the precedents above, while the assaulters should look for opportunities to assault in time and space so that the hostage-takers are closer to the assaulters than the hostages.

Appendix A: The Sects of Islam

Table A.1 The Sects of Islam, by Founders, Loci, and Primary Beliefs or Precepts

School of Thought	Denomination: School of Thought: Subsect	Foundation (Founder, Date of Foundation, Place of Foundation)	Loci of Adherents (Total Muslim Population, Majority Governments That Identify with Sect; Other Locations Where Sect Is Found)	General Beliefs and Precepts
Sunni	Sunni	No single founder; see following for greater detail	Global Population ~85%–90% (Esposito, 2011) Sunni Governments: Saudi Arabia, Qatar, Dubai, United Arab Emirates (UAE), Pakistan, Oman, Bahrain, Tunisia, Malaysia, Algeria, Egypt, Morocco, Somalia, Kuwait, Mauritania, Comoros, Brunei Darussalam, Maldives Jordan, Libya, Yemen, Afghanistan (U.S. State Department, 2015; CFR, 2014; Pew Research Center, 2009) Other Locations: Europe, Middle East, South-East Asia, South Asia, North Africa, East Africa, North America (Pew Research Center, 2009)	1. Four *Rahshidun* (righteously guided) caliphs elected to succeed Prophet Mohammed's caliphate: Abu Bakr ibn Abi Quhafa, Ummar ibn al-Khatab, Uthman ibn Affan, and Ali ibn Abi Talib (Urban, 2016). 2. Follow the Prophet's *sunna* (his behavior and beliefs) as taught by the first four caliphs (Syed, 2013, p. 535). 3. Do not recognize later caliphs as being righteously guided (Syed, 2013, p. 535). 4. Only members of Prophet's tribe (Quraish) were qualified for political leadership (Syed, 2013, p. 535). 5. Believe that resistance to injustice should be "passive, rather than armed"; martyrdom (being killed) by unjust leaders is preferred to committing violence in self-defense (Syed, 2013, p. 535).

(*Continued*)

Table A.1 (*Continued*) The Sects of Islam, by Founders, Loci, and Primary Beliefs or Precepts

School of Thought	Denomination: School of Thought: Subsect	Foundation (Founder, Date of Foundation, Place of Foundation)	Loci of Adherents (Total Muslim Population, Majority Governments That Identify with Sect; Other Locations Where Sect Is Found)	General Beliefs and Precepts
				6. Qur'an and Hadith as sole authoritative source of Islamic legal practice (*sharia*) (Syed, 2013, p. 535). 7. Messianism: Final Imam (Mahdi) not yet born; Sunnis await his arrival (Syed, 2013, p. 535).
Hanafi	Sunni: Hanafi	Abu Hanifa (699–767 CE) (Safrir, 2013)	Hanafi Governments: None found Other Locations: Afghanistan, Syria, India, Pakistan, Egypt (Heffening and Schacht, 2012; CFR, 2014)	Built on the traditions of Iraqi towns of Basrah and Kufah. School was favored by early Abbasid caliphs and became well established in Syria and Iraq. Places emphasis on individual legal judgment (Safrir, 2013, p. 14).
Hanbali	Sunni: Hanbali	Ahmad bin Hanbal (780–855 CE) (Melchert, 2013, p. 25)	Hanbali Governments: Saudi Arabia, Qatar, UAE (Melton, n.d.; CFR, 2014) Other Locations: North Africa, East Africa, Iraq, Syria, South Asia, Southeast Asia (CFR, 2014)	One of the four main schools of law in Sunni Islam. Generally regarded as the most stringent, a reputation enhanced by its adoption, in modified form, by the Wahhabis as the official school of law in Saudi Arabia (Newby, 2002, p. 75).

(*Continued*)

Table A.1 (*Continued*) The Sects of Islam, by Founders, Loci, and Primary Beliefs or Precepts

School of Thought	Denomination: School of Thought: Subsect	Foundation (Founder, Date of Foundation, Place of Foundation)	Loci of Adherents (Total Muslim Population, Majority Governments That Identify with Sect; Other Locations Where Sect Is Found)	General Beliefs and Precepts
Salafi	Sunni: Hanbali: Salafi	Ibn Taymiyya (1263–1328 CE) (Michot, 2012, pp. 238–241)	Salafi Governments: None found Other Locations: North Africa (esp. Egypt, Tunisia, Algeria, to a lesser extent Morocco), Syria (Shinar and Ende, 2012)	1. Literalist interpretation of One-ness of God (*tawhid*); reject allegorical interpretations of faith and reason-based arguments (Michot, 2012, pp. 238–241). 2. Claim to adhere to Hanbalism (Michot, 2012, pp. 238–241). 3. Rejection of superstitious beliefs and intercessory practice (Michot, 2012, pp. 238–241). 4. Regard Shi'ites and Sufis as unbelievers (Michot, 2012, pp. 238–241). 5. *Takfiri*: Reserve the right to deem others as infidels (Michot, 2012, pp. 238–241). 6. *Hadith* as supreme authority; Islam as implemented by Prophet Mohammad as model for governing society (Michot, 2012, pp. 238–241). 7. Those who do not follow Sharia as accepted by the Salafist tradition are apostates who are deserving of death (Michot, 2012, pp. 238–241).

(*Continued*)

Table A.1 (*Continued*) The Sects of Islam, by Founders, Loci, and Primary Beliefs or Precepts

School of Thought	Denomination: School of Thought: Subsect	Foundation (Founder, Date of Foundation, Place of Foundation)	Loci of Adherents (Total Muslim Population, Majority Governments That Identify with Sect; Other Locations Where Sect Is Found)	General Beliefs and Precepts
Wahhabi	Sunni: Hanbali: Wahhabi	Muhammad Ibn 'Abd al-Wahhab (1703–1792 CE) (Haykel, 2013, pp. 231–232)	Wahhabi Government: Saudi Arabia (Haykel, 2013, pp. 231–232) Other Locations: Tunisia, Qatar, UAE, North Africa, Algeria, Syria	1. Strict interpretation of One-ness of God; association of divinity with any entity other than God constitutes unbelief (*kufr*) (Haykel, 2013, pp. 231–232). 2. Quran and Hadith as authoritative sources; writings of Ibn Taymiyya as influential source (Haykel, 2013, pp. 231–232). 3. Follow Hanbali legal tradition (Haykel, 2013, pp. 231–232). 4. Revivalist; Islam as Prophet Muhammad practiced as only way (Haykel, 2013, pp. 231–232). 5. To be Muslim, one must believe in the declaration of faith and reject all perceived forms of polytheistic worship (Haykel, 2013, pp. 231–232).

(*Continued*)

Table A.1 (*Continued*) The Sects of Islam, by Founders, Loci, and Primary Beliefs or Precepts

School of Thought	Denomination: School of Thought: Subsect	Foundation (Founder, Date of Foundation, Place of Foundation)	Loci of Adherents (Total Muslim Population, Majority Governments That Identify with Sect; Other Locations Where Sect Is Found)	General Beliefs and Precepts
Maliki	Sunni: Maliki	Malik bin Anas (712–795 CE) (Blankminship, 2013, p. 326)	Maliki Governments: None found Other Locations: Morocco, Algeria, Tunisia, Libya, Senegal, Mali, Niger, Togo, Chad, and Nigeria (Cottart, 2012)	Based on legal practices developed in the city of Madinah, a Sunni school of law regarded as somewhat conservative and dependent on tradition. Remains neutral on legitimacy of 'Ali bin Abi Talib' and adds consensus of Madinah to that of Muslims in general. Particularly hard on schismatics, Sufis and Shi'i which made it a powerful tool for the Abbasid dynasty (Blankminship, 2013, p. 326).
Shafi'i	Sunni: Shafi'i	Mohammad bin Idris al-Shafi'i (767–820 CE) (Lowry, 2013, p. 492)	Shafi'i Governments: None found Other Locations: Yemen, Southern India, Malaysia, Indonesia, East African Coast (Melton, n.d.)	1. In contrast to the customary usages (Sunnah) of the Medinah community upon which Malik Ibn Anas drew to amplify the law and against the deductions and interpretations of the Hanafi school, Idris Al Shafi'i promoted the Hadith and Sunnah of the Prophet as being the primary authority as the interpretation of the Quranic injunctions (Glassé, 1989, p. 359).

(*Continued*)

Table A.1 (*Continued*) The Sects of Islam, by Founders, Loci, and Primary Beliefs or Precepts

School of Thought	Denomination: School of Thought: Subsect	Foundation (Founder, Date of Foundation, Place of Foundation)	Loci of Adherents (Total Muslim Population, Majority Governments That Identify with Sect; Other Locations Where Sect Is Found)	General Beliefs and Precepts
				2. These are considered more important than *Qiyas* (analogy), and are followed in degree of importance by *ijma* (consensus) as the legitimizing basis of law (Glassé, 1989, p. 359). 3. Quran, Hadith, and Sunnah, *qiyas* and *ijma* thus became jointly *usul al-fiqh* (roots of jurisprudence) or the systematic basis of law (Glassé, 1989, p. 359).
Khariji	Sunni Breakaway: Khawarij	Battle of Siffin: 657 CE (Levi Della Vida, 2012)	See following for greater details	1. Do not recognize Uthman bin Affan and Ali ibn Abi Talib as legitimate caliphs (Glassé, 1989, p. 359). 2. Imamate granted on the basis of merit, not descent. Use of violence and militancy to remove "sinful" leaders is justified (Lewinstein, 2013a, pp. 294–294). 3. Practice *takfir*: Deem ordinary Muslims to be "infidels" and enslavement, seizure of property, and indiscriminate killing of them during battle is acceptable (Lewinstein, 2013a, pp. 294–295).

(*Continued*)

Table A.1 (*Continued*) The Sects of Islam, by Founders, Loci, and Primary Beliefs or Precepts

School of Thought	Denomination: School of Thought: Subsect	Foundation (Founder, Date of Foundation, Place of Foundation)	Loci of Adherents (Total Muslim Population, Majority Governments That Identify with Sect; Other Locations Where Sect Is Found)	General Beliefs and Precepts
Ibadi	Sunni Breakaway: Khawarij: Ibadi	'Abd Allāh bin Ibāḍ al-Murrī al-Tamīmī, (founded ~684–685 CE) (Lewicki, 2012)	Ibadi Governments: Oman Other Locations: Sporadic distribution in East Africa, southern Algeria (Lewicki, 2012)	1. Softer view of "ordinary Muslims" (non-Ibadi/ non-Khawarij Muslims) as "hypocrites," not "infidels" (Lewinstein, 2013b, pp. 230–231). 2. Intermarriage between "ordinary Muslims" and Ibadis is acceptable (Lewinstein, 2013b, pp. 230–231). 3. Indiscriminate killings of "ordinary Muslims" during battle is unacceptable (Lewinstein, 2013b, pp. 230–231).
Azraqi	Sunni Breakaway: Khawarij: Azraqi	693 (Glassé, 1989, p. 222)	Extinct	1. Puritanism; nostalgia for the Islam of the Caliphate of 'Umar (Glassé, 1989, p. 222). 2. Their doctrine of "sin" was defined as a "fall from a state of perfection" (logically so, since they considered the upheavals that befell the Muslim polity a fall from a state of perfection) (Glassé, 1989, p. 222).

(*Continued*)

Table A.1 (*Continued*) The Sects of Islam, by Founders, Loci, and Primary Beliefs or Precepts

School of Thought	Denomination: School of Thought: Subsect	Foundation (Founder, Date of Foundation, Place of Foundation)	Loci of Adherents (Total Muslim Population, Majority Governments That Identify with Sect; Other Locations Where Sect Is Found)	General Beliefs and Precepts
Haruriyah	Sunni Breakaway: Khawarij: Haruriyah	Unknown	Extinct	Unknown
Sufri	Sunni Breakaway: Khawarij: Sufri	Unknown	Extinct	1. Sufri was the general name used to describe those belonging to Kharijite sects. Derived from the word *surf* meaning "yellow-faced" because of pious adherence to ritualistic devotion (Madelung and Lewinstein, 2012). 2. Ardently venerated the causes of the earlier Kharijites and rejected those who broke away and developed theologies and set legal principles (Madelung and Lewinstein, 2012).
Shi'a	Shi'a	No one founder See the following for details	Global Population ~13.8% (Momen, 2016) Majority Shi'a Governments: Iran, Iraq, Syria	1. Ali bin Abi Talib as Mohammed's rightful heir (Gleave, 2013, pp. 510–512).

(*Continued*)

Table A.1 (*Continued*) The Sects of Islam, by Founders, Loci, and Primary Beliefs or Precepts

School of Thought	Denomination: School of Thought: Subsect	Foundation (Founder, Date of Foundation, Place of Foundation)	Loci of Adherents (Total Muslim Population, Majority Governments That Identify with Sect; Other Locations Where Sect Is Found)	General Beliefs and Precepts
			Other Locations: Pakistan, Azerbaijan, Afghanistan, Saudi Arabia, Lebanon, Jordan, Kuwait, India, Turkey, Yemen, Nigeria, Tanzania, Germany, Bahrain, Tajikstan, UAE, United States, Oman, United Kingdom, Bulgaria, Qatar (Pew Research Center, 2009)	2. Only spiritual leaders (Imams) accepted as legitimate political leaders under the belief that they are granted with a divine right to govern (Gleave, 2013, pp. 510–512). 3. Only the Prophet's *ahl al-bayt* (Prophet's descendants) had divine right to govern (Gleave, 2013, pp. 510–512). 4. Messianism: Last Imam (Mahdi) to reappear as a sign of end of times.
Ismai'li	Shi'a: Ismai'li	Named after Isma'il bin Jafar al-Sadiq in ~765 CE (Madelung, 2012a)	Ismai'li Governments: None found Other Locations: India, Central Asia, Iran, Syria, and East Africa (Glassé, 1989, p. 365)	1. Major branch of the Shi'a with many subsects (*see the following*). Also known as the "sevener" tradition (Madelung, 2012a). 2. Accept the main beliefs of orthodox Shi'a Islam (see *Shia: Beliefs* above) (Madelung, 2012a).

(*Continued*)

Table A.1 (*Continued*) The Sects of Islam, by Founders, Loci, and Primary Beliefs or Precepts

School of Thought	Denomination: School of Thought: Subsect	Foundation (Founder, Date of Foundation, Place of Foundation)	Loci of Adherents (Total Muslim Population, Majority Governments That Identify with Sect; Other Locations Where Sect Is Found)	General Beliefs and Precepts
				3. However, they only accept the legitimacy of the first six imams of the dominant (*Ithna'shari*) tradition and view the sixth imam Jafar al-Sadiq's eldest son, Isma'il, to be the legitimate seventh imam, hence the name "sevener" (Madelung, 2012a). 4. Isma'il passed away, but, according to Isma'ili tradition, he did not really die, but went into occultation and will return when the time is right (Madelung, 2012a).
Nizari (Ismai'li)	Shi'a Breakaway: Ismai'li: Nizari	Nizar bin al-Mustansir (1045–1095 CE) (Daftary, 2013a, p. 395)	Nizari Governments: None found Other Locations: India, Pakistan, Syria, Central Asia, Iran (Glassé, 1989, p. 199)	"Gnosticism-Dualism"; integral part of Nizari belief. As documented by Pir Sadr ad-din's conversions in twelfth or thirteenth century Sind "to take any religious form as its starting point and then to lead the novice through it to the hidden and secret knowledge" (Glassé, 1989, p. 198).

(*Continued*)

Table A.1 (*Continued*) The Sects of Islam, by Founders, Loci, and Primary Beliefs or Precepts

School of Thought	Denomination: School of Thought: Subsect	Foundation (Founder, Date of Foundation, Place of Foundation)	Loci of Adherents (Total Muslim Population, Majority Governments That Identify with Sect; Other Locations Where Sect Is Found)	General Beliefs and Precepts
Musta'li (Ismai'li)	Shi'a Breakaway: Ismai'li: Musta'li	Ahmad bin Mustansir (1074–1101 CE) (Daftary, 2013a, p. 295)	Musta'li Governments: None found Other Locations: India, Pakistan, Yemen (Glassé, 1989, p. 199)	"Concealment"; holds belief that a descendant of at-Tayyib subsists somewhere in secret and fulfills the function of Imam. Others believe that, as with the *Ghaybah* of the Hidden Imam for the Twelvers, and al-Hakim of the Druzes, this concealment is supernatural and the function is still held by at-Tayyib himself in the invisible world (Glassé, 1989, p. 197).
Qaramita (Ismai'li)	Shi'a: Ismai'li: Qaramita	Hamdan Qarmat bin Al As'at (321–933 CE) (Daftary, 2013b, pp. 445–446)	Unknown	An offshoot of the early Ismaili Shi'a, their doctrine show a mixture of extreme Shi'a thought, Gnosticism, and other philosophical systems. With the rise of Fatimids, the main thrust of their movement was absorbed into the mainstream of Ismaili Shi'a (Newby, 2002, p. 176).

(*Continued*)

Table A.1 (*Continued*) The Sects of Islam, by Founders, Loci, and Primary Beliefs or Precepts

School of Thought	Denomination: School of Thought: Subsect	Foundation (Founder, Date of Foundation, Place of Foundation)	Loci of Adherents (Total Muslim Population, Majority Governments That Identify with Sect; Other Locations Where Sect Is Found)	General Beliefs and Precepts
Druze	Shi'a: Ismai'li: Druze	Mohammad bin Isma'il al-Darazi (Date of Life: 1017 CE) (Bar-Asher, 2013, p. 139)	Druze Governments: None found Other Locations: Syria, Lebanon (Hodgson et al., 2012), Palestine (Sourdel and Minganti, 2012)	1. Originated as an offshoot of Ismaili Shi'ism, but broke away upon the recognition of the sixth Fatimid caliph as a divine ruler. Druze profess to be monotheist, although many of their religious practices are unknown. 2. *Kitabl-al-Hikma,* the Book of Wisdom, is the Druze canonical scripture. It consists of the New Testament, the Quran, and works from ancient philosophers. 3. A religion distinct from traditional Islamic theology; esoteric, and it allows its members to practice Taqiyyah or religious dissimulation, giving the impression that they are Muslims or of any other religion in circumstances in which it would be dangerous to reveal their religion (Newby, 2002, p. 54).

(*Continued*)

Table A.1 (*Continued*) The Sects of Islam, by Founders, Loci, and Primary Beliefs or Precepts

School of Thought	Denomination: School of Thought: Subsect	Foundation (Founder, Date of Foundation, Place of Foundation)	Loci of Adherents (Total Muslim Population, Majority Governments That Identify with Sect; Other Locations Where Sect Is Found)	General Beliefs and Precepts
Tayyabi (Isma'ili)	Shi'a: Ismai'li: Tayyabi	al-Amir bi-Ahkam Allah's son, al-Tayyib; ~1130 CE (Daftary, 2012)	Tayyabi Governments: None found Other Locations: Western India (Daftary, 2012)	A branch of Ismaili Shi'a that preserves a large part of the extensive Fatimid literature and beliefs (Daftary, 2012).
Bohra (Isma'ili)	Shi'a: Ismai'li: Bohra	(See Isma'ili section)	Bohra Governments: None found Other Locations: India (Daftary, 2012)	1. "Bohra" is applied to Ismaili Muslims, Sunni Muslims, and some Hindus and Jains in Western India; it generally refers to a merchant class of people in India (Fyzee, 2012). When used for Ismaili Muslims, it refers to those who do not follow Agha Khan. A greater portion of this sect is made up of Ismailis who are governed by their own officials and customs (Newby, 2002, p. 54). 2. Treats ritual principles of orthodox Islam in a symbolic or allegorical fashion (Glassé, 1989, p. 199).

(*Continued*)

Table A.1 (*Continued*) The Sects of Islam, by Founders, Loci, and Primary Beliefs or Precepts

School of Thought	Denomination: School of Thought: Subsect	Foundation (Founder, Date of Foundation, Place of Foundation)	Loci of Adherents (Total Muslim Population, Majority Governments That Identify with Sect; Other Locations Where Sect Is Found)	General Beliefs and Precepts
Dawoodi Bohra (Isma'ili)	Shi'a: Ismai'li: Dawoodi Bohra	Dawood Burhan al-Din bin Kutbshah Founded ~1591 CE (Daftary, 2012)	Dawoodi Bohra Governments: None found Other Locations: India (Glassé, 1989, p. 77)	Follows branch of Musta'li Isma'lism known as Daudi (or Dawoodi); the Da'i Mutlaq of the Daudi branch is called the Mulla-Ji and is resident in Bombay (Mumbai) (Glassé, 1989, p. 77).
Jafan Bohra (Isma'ili)	Shi'a: Ismai'li: Jafan Bohra	Unknown	Unknown	Unknown
Suleimani Bohra (Isma'ili)	Shi'a: Ismai'li: Suleimani Bohra	Suleiman bin Hasan Founded ~1591 CE (Daftary, 2012)	Suleimani Bohra Governments: None found Other Locations: India (Mumbai and Gujarat) and parts of East Africa (Glassé, 1989, p. 78) North Yemen (Daftary, 2012)	A minority sect whose leader formerly resided in Yemen, but in this century transferred his seat to Baroda, India, which was the seat of his Indian *Mansub* (representative) (Glassé, 1989, p. 78).
Alavi Bohra (Isma'ili)	Shi'a: Ismai'li: Alavi Bohra	Ali bin Ibrahim (Sikand, 2003) Founded ~1621 CE (Fyzee, 1934)	Alavi Bohra Governments: None found Other Locations: India (Fyzee, 1934)	Separate leadership. For beliefs refer to *Dawoodi Bohra* (Glassé, 1989, p. 199). Branched off from the Dawoodi Bohra after death of 28th Dawoodi *da'i* (or imam) (Sikand, 2003).

(*Continued*)

Table A.1 (*Continued*) The Sects of Islam, by Founders, Loci, and Primary Beliefs or Precepts

School of Thought	Denomination: School of Thought: Subsect	Foundation (Founder, Date of Foundation, Place of Foundation)	Loci of Adherents (Total Muslim Population, Majority Governments That Identify with Sect; Other Locations Where Sect Is Found)	General Beliefs and Precepts
Hebitahs Bohra (Isma'ili)	Shi'a: Ismai'li Hebitahs Bohra	Sayyedna Ibrahim Vajihuddin Founded ~1754 CE (Sikand, 2003)	Hebitahs Bohra Governments: None found Other Locations: India (Sikand, 2003)	Separate leadership. For beliefs refer to *Shi'a: Ismai'li: Bohra* (Newby, 2002, p. 54).
Atb'l Malak Bohra (Isma'ili)	Shi'a: Ismai'li: Atb'l Malak Bohra	Sayyedna Muhammad Badruddin (Sikand, 2003)	Atb'l Malak Governments: None found Other Locations: India (Sikand, 2003)	Separate leadership. For beliefs refer to *Ismai'li: Musta'li* (Glassé, 1989, p. 197).
Progressive Dawoodi Bohra (Isma'ili)	Shi'a: Ismai'li: Progressive Dawoodi Bohra	See Dawoodi Bohra	See Dawoodi Bohra	Separate leadership. For beliefs refer to *Suleimani Bohra* (Glassé, 1989, p. 78).
Jafri	Shi'a: Jafri	Named after sixth imam of the Ithna'ashari tradition: Ja'far al-Sadiq (Tucker, 1994, p. 164)	See *Ithna'ashari*	1. Shi'i legal school (or *madhhab*) that is influenced by the legal thoughts of Ja'far al-Sadiq (Tucker, 1994, p. 164). Widely known to refer to the *Ithna'ashiri* (Tucker, 1994, p. 164). Some adherents are *akhbari* (see *Akhbari*) and others are *shaykhi* (see *Shaykhi*).

(*Continued*)

Table A.1 (*Continued*) The Sects of Islam, by Founders, Loci, and Primary Beliefs or Precepts

School of Thought	Denomination: School of Thought: Subsect	Foundation (Founder, Date of Foundation, Place of Foundation)	Loci of Adherents (Total Muslim Population, Majority Governments That Identify with Sect; Other Locations Where Sect Is Found)	General Beliefs and Precepts
				2. Encompasses heterodox doctrines of the Seveners into Islam and what later becomes known as Ismai'lism (Glassé, 1989, p. 203).
Ithna'ashari	Shi'a: Jafri: Ithna'ashari	No one founder, developed over an extensive period of time	Ithna'ashari Governments: Iran, Iraq Other Locations: Syria, Lebanon, Pakistan, some Gulf states and Eastern Province of Saudi Arabia (Glassé, 1989, p. 202)	The "twelve-Imam" branch; so-called because they hold belief that there were 12 imams, the last of whom is still mysteriously alive since his occultation in the third or ninth century, and will return as the Mahdi (Glassé, 1989, p. 202).
Akhbari	Shi'a: Jafri: Akhbari	Mulla Muhammad Amin Astarabadi (Momen, 1985, p. 222)	Unknown	School among the Shi'a theologians that correspond to the acts and sayings of the Prophet among Sunnis—that is, traditionalists who eschew speculation. Restricts the authority and prerogatives of the *Ulama*, in the belief that jurisprudence should be limited to the application of existing tradition. They do admit the existence of rational institution in the solution of questions.

(*Continued*)

Table A.1 (*Continued*) The Sects of Islam, by Founders, Loci, and Primary Beliefs or Precepts

School of Thought	Denomination: School of Thought: Subsect	Foundation (Founder, Date of Foundation, Place of Foundation)	Loci of Adherents (Total Muslim Population, Majority Governments That Identify with Sect; Other Locations Where Sect Is Found)	General Beliefs and Precepts
				They restrict the sources of religious authority to Quran and Sunnah and insist on its interpretation through the inspired traditions of the Imams. They do not accept "consensus" and "intellect." They reject *Ijtihad*, or the coming to original and unprecedented conclusions as a result of the investigation of sources, reasoning, and endeavouring to understand (Glassé, 1989, pp. 29–30).
Shaykhi	Shi'a: Jafri: Shaykhi	Ahmad ibn Zayn ad-Din al-Ahsai (Glassé, 1989, p. 363)	Unknown	Doctrine exalts the Imams and their role in creation beyond the claims of ordinary Shi'ism to the point of polytheism. Incorporates modernist elements such as equality of women and abrogation of the Quran, advocates removal of the Ka'bah and tomb of the Prophet and proposes a set of pseudo-mystical practices centering on the numbers 19 (lunatic metonic cycle) and 28 (another lunar cycle) (Glassé, 1989, pp. 363–364).

(*Continued*)

Table A.1 (*Continued*) The Sects of Islam, by Founders, Loci, and Primary Beliefs or Precepts

School of Thought	Denomination: School of Thought: Subsect	Foundation (Founder, Date of Foundation, Place of Foundation)	Loci of Adherents (Total Muslim Population, Majority Governments That Identify with Sect; Other Locations Where Sect Is Found)	General Beliefs and Precepts
Usuli	Shi'a: Jafri: Usuli	Unknown	Unknown	Favors speculation and extrapolation on the basis of principles (Usul). Maintains that competence to arrive at original decisions and interpretations of the religious law resides in living authorities entitled the *marja' at-taqlid* ("exemplars for emulation"). Every Usuli who is therefore not an emulator must adhere to a Mujtahid (emulator), to whom he must pay a religious tax and *Khums*, thus to follow a Mujtahid brings a heavenly reward even if their views are erroneous. It is forbidden to follow a dead Mujtahid (Glassé, 1989, p. 411).
Alawi/ Nusayri	Shi'a: Alawi/ Nusayriyya	Muḥammad bin Nuṣayr al-Namīri Founded mid-ninth century (Halm, 2012)	Alawi Governments: Syria Other Locations: Lebanon (Glassé, 1989, p. 30)	1. Possibly relic of the Sevener movement, or simply of pre-Islamic Christian Gnosticism and closely related to the Syrian branch of the revolutionary Qarmatian (Carmathians) of the fourth or tenth century (Glassé, 1989, p. 31).

(*Continued*)

Table A.1 (*Continued*) The Sects of Islam, by Founders, Loci, and Primary Beliefs or Precepts

School of Thought	Denomination: School of Thought: Subsect	Foundation (Founder, Date of Foundation, Place of Foundation)	Loci of Adherents (Total Muslim Population, Majority Governments That Identify with Sect; Other Locations Where Sect Is Found)	General Beliefs and Precepts
				2. Often called Shi'ites but despite the reference to Ali in their preferred name today, their doctrines do not correspond in any way to Shi'ism as such. Instead bears an unmissable resemblance to Isma'ili teachings with their characteristic Gnostic or dualistic ideas (Glassé, 1989, p. 31). 3. Beliefs and practices are extremely heteroclite and therefore vary from group to group (Glassé, 1989, p. 31). 4. Their collection of writings called *Kitab-al Majmu* (The Book of the Collection), which constitutes their holy book, and this contains among other things, it is said, scraps of the corrupt version of the Nicomachean Ethics of Aristotle and doctrine includes elements of astral religion which are ultimately of Babylonian origin (Glassé, 1989, p. 31).

(*Continued*)

Table A.1 (*Continued*) The Sects of Islam, by Founders, Loci, and Primary Beliefs or Precepts

School of Thought	Denomination: School of Thought: Subsect	Foundation (Founder, Date of Foundation, Place of Foundation)	Loci of Adherents (Total Muslim Population, Majority Governments That Identify with Sect; Other Locations Where Sect Is Found)	General Beliefs and Precepts
				5. Possess elements of Christianity such as use of certain Christian names and mark, in their own way, certain Christian holidays (Glassé, 1989, p. 31). 6. Religious practices are carried out in secret, in their own places of congregation, which are not open to outsiders. 7. Believes women to not possess souls which runs contrary to Islamic doctrine (Glassé, 1989, p. 31).
Alevi; Nusayri	Shi'a: Alevi, Nusayri	Muḥammad bin Nuṣayr al-Namīri Founded mid-ninth century (Halm, 2012)	Alevi Governments: None found Other Locations: Turkey (Glassé, 1989, p. 30)	Same as Alawi; only referred to as *Alevi* in Turkey (Glassé, 1989, p. 30).
Ahl-i Haqq	Shi'a: Ahl-i Haqq	Unknown	Ahl-i; Haqq Governments: None found	1. Trace their religious history back to the development of the Alawites (Minorsky, 2012).

(*Continued*)

Table A.1 (*Continued*) The Sects of Islam, by Founders, Loci, and Primary Beliefs or Precepts

School of Thought	Denomination: School of Thought: Subsect	Foundation (Founder, Date of Foundation, Place of Foundation)	Loci of Adherents (Total Muslim Population, Majority Governments That Identify with Sect; Other Locations Where Sect Is Found)	General Beliefs and Precepts
			Other Locations: Iran (Luristan), parts of Kurdistan (Guran), Azerbaijan, some in Kirkuk, Iraq (Minorsky, 2012)	2. Believe in seven successive manifestations of divinity, which are compared to garments worn by the divinity (Minorsky, 2012). 3. Divinity is usually accompanied by four or five angels (Minorsky, 2012). 4. Believe in the transmigration of the soul; people will pass through 1,001 soul migrations, during which people receive reward for their actions, but are limited by nature of their beings (Minorsky, 2012). 5. Those made of yellow clay are good and have more possibilities for reward than those made of black clay, who are bad (Minorsky, 2012). 6. People are awaiting the coming of the Lord of Time, who will bring justice to the universe (Minorsky, 2012).

(*Continued*)

Table A.1 (*Continued*) The Sects of Islam, by Founders, Loci, and Primary Beliefs or Precepts

School of Thought	Denomination: School of Thought: Subsect	Foundation (Founder, Date of Foundation, Place of Foundation)	Loci of Adherents (Total Muslim Population, Majority Governments That Identify with Sect; Other Locations Where Sect Is Found)	General Beliefs and Precepts
Zaidi	Shi'a: Zaidi	Zayd ibn Ali b Husayn (Glassé, 1989, p. 336) (694–740 CE) (Madelung, 2012b)	Zaidi Governments: None found Other Locations: Yemen, Syria (Glassé, 1989, p. 364)	1. Accept the first four imams of the main Ithna Ashri' tradition but deviate at the fifth imam, and claim Zayd bin Ali to be the fifth imam (Momen, 1985, p. 221). 2. Observes in the Imamate—a function that may or may not be exercised at a particular time by a descendant of the Prophet, and which does not necessarily include a claim to sanctity (Glassé, 1989, p. 366).
Tasawwuf (or Sufism) (Massington et al., 2012)	Tasawwuf (or Sufism)	Unknown	See following for greater details	1. Understood to be the mystical dimension within Islam (Massington et al., 2012). 2. Believe in the idea of the Perfect Man, in which there exists on Earth a human being who is the essential channel through which the grace of God is expressed; this person is called a *qutb* (or axis) (Momen, 1985, p. 208).

(*Continued*)

Table A.1 (*Continued*) The Sects of Islam, by Founders, Loci, and Primary Beliefs or Precepts

School of Thought	Denomination: School of Thought: Subsect	Foundation (Founder, Date of Foundation, Place of Foundation)	Loci of Adherents (Total Muslim Population, Majority Governments That Identify with Sect; Other Locations Where Sect Is Found)	General Beliefs and Precepts
				3. There can only be one *qutb* at any given time on the Earth, and only recognition of the *qutb* confers true belief (Momen, 1985, pp. 208–209). 4. Believe in the total renunciation of the self and the world, and the complete absorption of one's existence to coincide with God's; this doctrine is known as annihilation or *fanaa'* (Massington et al., 2012). 5. Generally accept one of the four legal schools of (Sunni) Islam as well as the Quran, and Sunna and *ahadith* so as to aid the Sufi student in better being able to devote oneself entirely to God and renounce the material world, along with their own practices of *dhikr*, or remembrance of God, so as to cultivate knowledge of the "inner self" (Massington et al., 2012).

(*Continued*)

Table A.1 (*Continued*) The Sects of Islam, by Founders, Loci, and Primary Beliefs or Precepts

School of Thought	Denomination: School of Thought: Subsect	Foundation (Founder, Date of Foundation, Place of Foundation)	Loci of Adherents (Total Muslim Population, Majority Governments That Identify with Sect; Other Locations Where Sect Is Found)	General Beliefs and Precepts
Qadiri	Sufi: Qadiriyya	‘Abd al-Qadir al-Jilani (died 1166 CE) (Margoliouth, 2012)	Qadiri Governments: None found Other Locations: North Africa, Nigeria, India, Sub-Saharan Africa, Pakistan (Margoliouth, 2012)	1. Practice the general Sufi tenants but also have adopted the Hanbali legal tradition. Encourage both fasting and retreating (*khalwa*) from society (generally for 40 days) (Margoliouth, 2012). 2. Despite the strict traditionalism of Hanbali thought, are said to be more tolerant of difference and charitable to others (Margoliouth, 2012).
Jilalism	Sufi: Qadiriyya: Jilalism	Unknown	Jilalism Governments: None found Other Locations: North Africa (Margoliouth, 2012)	1. This form of Qadiri Sufism emphasizes the veneration of founder of the Qadiriyya. 2. Are thought to apply Sufi mystical principles and rituals to pre-Islamic regional tribal practices (Margoliouth, 2012). *Khalwa* is thought to refer to “a heap of stones where women attach rags to reeds planted between the stones and where they burn benzoin and styrax in potsherds” and not to a mystical retreat from society (Margoliouth, 2012).

(*Continued*)

Table A.1 (*Continued*) The Sects of Islam, by Founders, Loci, and Primary Beliefs or Precepts

School of Thought	Denomination: School of Thought: Subsect	Foundation (Founder, Date of Foundation, Place of Foundation)	Loci of Adherents (Total Muslim Population, Majority Governments That Identify with Sect; Other Locations Where Sect Is Found)	General Beliefs and Precepts
Kubrawi	Sufi: Kubrawiyya	Shaykh Abu 'l-Jannab Ahmad bin 'Umar Nadjm al-Din (1145–1220 CE) (Algar, 2012a)	Kubrawi Governments: None found Other Locations: Mainly in Iran and Baltistan (Algar, 2012a)	1. Began as a Sunni order; had marked Shi'a sympathies (Adel, 2012). 2. Believed that the station of divine guardianship (*wilaya*) belonged to members of the house of the Prophet, specifically 12 of them. And the last Wali (guardian) is known as the Mehdi (Adel, 2012).
Nurbakhsi	Sufi: Kubrawiyya: Nurbakhshiyya	Muhammad Nurbakhsh (1392–1464 CE) (Algar, 2012b)	Nurbakhsi Governments: None found Other Locations: Baltistan Province in Pakistan (Algar, 2012c)	Offshoot of the Kubrawi Sufi order, maintained distinct Shi'i identity. Founder claimed to be *mahdi* (Algar, 2012a,b,c). (See Kubrawiyya for beliefs.)
Dhahabi	Sufi: Kubrawiyya: Dhahabiyya	Uncertain; however some sources point to 'Abdu'llah Barzishabadi (Momen, 1985, pp. 210–212)	Dhahabi Governments: None found Other Locations: Iran (Shiraz, some in Tehran, and Tabriz) (Momen, 1985, p. 212)	Persian name of the Kubrawiyyah. General beliefs are the same. Adopted a distinct Shi'i identity. Also sometimes known as *Ightishashiyya* (Momen, 1985, p. 212).

(*Continued*)

Table A.1 (*Continued*) The Sects of Islam, by Founders, Loci, and Primary Beliefs or Precepts

School of Thought	Denomination: School of Thought: Subsect	Foundation (Founder, Date of Foundation, Place of Foundation)	Loci of Adherents (Total Muslim Population, Majority Governments That Identify with Sect; Other Locations Where Sect Is Found)	General Beliefs and Precepts
Naqshbandi	Sufi: Naqshbandiyya	Khwaja Baha' al-Din Muḥammad bin Muḥammad (1318–1389 CE) (Algar, 2012a,b,c)	Naqshbandi Governments: None found Other Locations: Northern India, Pakistan, Afghanistan (Momen, 1985), Daghistan (Barthold and Bennigsen, 2012)	1. Early period of Naqshbandi belief stressed somberness in ritual remembrance, with no use of music or singing, preferred silent remembrance of God, and stressed temporal awareness (the persistent examination of one's spiritual state); numerical awareness (the enumerating the amount of times *dhikr* is performed to limit distracting thoughts); and awareness of the heart (direction the attention of one's physical heart so as to make it synchronize with *dhikr* ritual) (Algar, 2012a,b,c). 2. Later developments tended to include visceral disdain for Shi'i sects and eschewing seclusion and preferring pious company, instead, and remaining duty-bound to sharia/legal traditions in both private and political spheres of life (Algar, 2012a,b,c).

(*Continued*)

Table A.1 (*Continued*) The Sects of Islam, by Founders, Loci, and Primary Beliefs or Precepts

School of Thought	Denomination: School of Thought: Subsect	Foundation (Founder, Date of Foundation, Place of Foundation)	Loci of Adherents (Total Muslim Population, Majority Governments That Identify with Sect; Other Locations Where Sect Is Found)	General Beliefs and Precepts
Mujaddidi	Sufi: Naqshbandiyya: Mujaddidiyya	Sheikh Ahmed Sirhindi (aka Mujaddid Alf Thani. Sirhindi) (1564–1624 CE) (Inayatullah, 2012)	Mujaddidi Governments: None found Other Locations: India, Turkey, Syria (Algar and Nizami, 2012), Pakistan, Afghanistan (Haroon, 2008)	1. Break away from earlier Sufi Naqshbandi belief in pantheism (*wahdat-al -wujud*) and supported the idea of *wahdat al-shuhud* (the unity of the phenomenal world) (Algar and Nizami, 2012). 2. Developed an active and assertive outlook that encouraged political engagement (Algar and Nizami, 2012). 3. Closed possibility of interfaith dialogue and drawing similarities with other religions. No mixing ideologies of a different faith with ideologies of Islam (Haroon, 2008). 4. These beliefs were further developed by future adherent and influential thinker Shah Wali Ullah who encouraged the re-introduction of Qur'an and *ahadith* into the Sufi path (Haroon, 2008).

(*Continued*)

Table A.1 (*Continued*) The Sects of Islam, by Founders, Loci, and Primary Beliefs or Precepts

School of Thought	Denomination: School of Thought: Subsect	Foundation (Founder, Date of Foundation, Place of Foundation)	Loci of Adherents (Total Muslim Population, Majority Governments That Identify with Sect; Other Locations Where Sect Is Found)	General Beliefs and Precepts
Brelwi	Sufi: Naqshbandiyya: Brelwi	Sayyid Ahmad Brelwi (1786–1831 CE) (Inayatullah, 2012)	Brelwi Governments: None found Other Locations: India, Pakistan, Afghanistan, Kashmir (Inayatullah, 2012)	1. Adopted many of the main Mujaddidiyya beliefs but was changed by Sayyid Ahmad to focus more on Quran and *ahadith* (Inayatullah, 2012). 2. Adopted many purist notions of Islam, unadulterated by excessive veneration of Prophets and God as propounded by Wahhabi ideology (Inayatullah, 2012). 3. Militantly reformist, and encourages political engagement as well as picking up arms (Inayatullah, 2012).
Khalwati	Sufi: Khalwatiyya	Often attributed to ‘Umar al-Khalwati (d. 1397 CE) (Jong, 2012)	Khalwati Governments: None found Other Locations: Egypt, Syria, Lebanon, Turkey, Ethiopia, Tunisia (Jong, 2012)	1. Place an emphasis on periodic retreats (or *khalwa* seclusion) (Jong, 2012). 2. The soul must progress through seven stages (*maqam)* for it to reach the level of a *qutb* (Jong, 2012).
Shadili	Sufi: Shadiliyya	Abu ’l-Ḥasan al-Shadhili (1196–1258 CE) (Lory, 2012)	Shadili Governments: none found Other Locations: Egypt, Sudan, Indonesia (Lory, 2012)	1. Place a greater emphasis on practice than on doctrine, so there is a strong emphasis on observing sharia/Islamic jurisprudence as observed by the head *shaykh* (the *qutb*) (Lory, 2012).

(*Continued*)

Table A.1 (*Continued*) The Sects of Islam, by Founders, Loci, and Primary Beliefs or Precepts

School of Thought	Denomination: School of Thought: Subsect	Foundation (Founder, Date of Foundation, Place of Foundation)	Loci of Adherents (Total Muslim Population, Majority Governments That Identify with Sect; Other Locations Where Sect Is Found)	General Beliefs and Precepts
				2. There is general acceptance of music and dance in *dhikr* practices; however, it must not be excessive. Spirituality is mainly expressed through reading chants out loud (if Shadili literature is accessible to a practitioner) (Lory, 2012).
Mevlevi/ Mawlawi/ Mewlewi	Sufi: Mawlawiyya	Named after Jalal al Din al Rumi (1207–1273 CE) (Ritter and Bausani, 2012)	Mevlevi Governments: None found Other Locations: Turkey (Ritter and Bausani, 2012)	1. Places particular emphasis on *sama'* musical ceremony, which is central to *dhikr* practice. It is performed in a circular motion in a room dedicated for the *sama'* ceremony (Yazıcı et al., 2012). 2. Places emphasis on a trial period, which focuses on 1,001 days of service in the kitchen (Yazıcı et al., 2012). 3. Show extreme love and respect for anything that is useful to human beings (Yazıcı et al., 2012).

(*Continued*)

Table A.1 (*Continued*) The Sects of Islam, by Founders, Loci, and Primary Beliefs or Precepts

School of Thought	Denomination: School of Thought: Subsect	Foundation (Founder, Date of Foundation, Place of Foundation)	Loci of Adherents (Total Muslim Population, Majority Governments That Identify with Sect; Other Locations Where Sect Is Found)	General Beliefs and Precepts
Bektashi	Sufi: Bektashiyya	Hajji Bektashi Wali (founded beginning of the fifteenth century) (Tschudi, 2012)	Bektashi Governments: None found Other Locations: Balkan peninsula, Albania (Tschudi, 2012)	Sufi dervish order that started in Turkey which subscribes to many Shi'i doctrines. 1. They believe in 12 imams, beginning with Ali, hold Jafar al-Sadiq, the sixth imam of the *ithna'ashri* tradition in high esteem (Tschudi, 2012). 2. The center of their worship is Ali, and unite Ali, Muhammad, and Allah to form their own trinity (Tschudi, 2012). 3. Take part in mourning rituals during the month of Muharram from the 1st to 10th of the month (Tschudi, 2012). 4. Believe in the transmigration of the soul (Tschudi, 2012). 5. Generally disregard orthodox form of ritualistic worship, but incorporate Christian traditions, including confession of sins, consuming bread, wine, and cheese, to new members. Some take a vow of celibacy (Tschudi, 2012).

References

Adel, G. H. 2012. *Sufism: An Entry from Encyclopaedia of the World of Islam*. N.p.: EWI, pp. 53–54.

Algar, H. 2012a. "Kubrā," in: P. Bearman, Th. Bianquis, C. E. Bosworth, E. van Donzel, W. P. Heinrichs (Eds.), *Encyclopaedia of Islam*, 2nd edition. Available at: http://dx.doi.org/10.1163/1573-3912_islam_SIM_4470. Accessed on October 16, 2016.

Algar, H. 2012b. "Naḳshband," in: P. Bearman, Th. Bianquis, C. E. Bosworth, E. van Donzel, W. P. Heinrichs (Eds.), *Encyclopaedia of Islam*, 2nd edition. Available at: http://dx.doi.org/10.1163/1573-3912_islam_SIM_5781. Accessed on October 16, 2016.

Algar, H. 2012c. "Nūrbakhshiyya," in: P. Bearman, Th. Bianquis, C. E. Bosworth, E. van Donzel, W. P. Heinrichs (Eds.), *Encyclopaedia of Islam*, 2nd edition. Available at: http://dx.doi.org/10.1163/1573-3912_islam_SIM_5992. Accessed on October 16, 2016.

Algar, H. and K. A. Nizami. 2012. "Naḳshbandiyya," in: P. Bearman, Th. Bianquis, C. E. Bosworth, E. van Donzel, W. P. Heinrichs (Eds.), *Encyclopaedia of Islam*, 2nd edition. Available at: http://dx.doi.org/10.1163/1573-3912_islam_COM_0843. Accessed on October 19, 2016.

Bar-Asher, M. M. 2013. "Druze," in: *The Princeton Encyclopedia of Islamic Political Thought*. Princeton, NJ: Princeton University Press, p. 139.

Barthold, W. and A. Bennigsen. 2012. "Dāghistān," in: P. Bearman, Th. Bianquis, C. E. Bosworth, E. van Donzel, W. P. Heinrichs (Eds.), *Encyclopaedia of Islam*, 2nd edition. Available at: http://dx.doi.org/10.1163/1573-3912_islam_COM_0147. Accessed on October 24, 2016.

Blankminship, K. Y. 2013. "Malik bin Anasm," in: *The Princeton Encyclopedia of Islamic Political Thought*. Princeton, NJ: Princeton University Press, p. 326.

Cottart, N. 2012. "Mālikiyya," in: P. Bearman, Th. Bianquis, C. E. Bosworth, E. van Donzel, W. P. Heinrichs (Eds.), *Encyclopaedia of Islam*, 2nd edition. Available at: http://dx.doi.org/10.1163/1573-3912_islam_COM_0652. Accessed on October 24, 2016.

Daftary, F. 2012. "al-Ṭayyibiyya," in: P. Bearman, Th. Bianquis, C. E. Bosworth, E. van Donzel, W. P. Heinrichs (Eds.), *Encyclopaedia of Islam*, 2nd edition. Available at: http://dx.doi.org/10.1163/1573-3912_islam_SIM_7472. Accessed on October 24, 2016.

Daftary, F. 2013a. "Nizaris," in: G. Bowering (Ed.), *The Princeton Encyclopedia of Islamic Political Thought*. Princeton, NJ: Princeton University Press, p. 395.

Daftary, F. 2013b. "Qarmatians," in: G. Bowering (Ed.), *The Princeton Encyclopedia of Islamic Political Thought*. Princeton, NJ: Princeton University Press, p. 445.

Esposito, J. L. 2011. *What Everyone Needs to Know about Islam (2)*. Cary, GB: Oxford University Press. Accessed on August 19, 2016. ProQuest ebrary.

Fyzee, A. 1934. "A Chronological List of the Imams and Dais of the Mustàlian Ismailia." *Journal of the Royal Asiatic Society*, 10, 8–16. South Asia Archive. Accessed on October 23, 2016.

Fyzee, A. A. A. 2012. "Bohorās," in: P. Bearman, Th. Bianquis, C. E. Bosworth, E. van Donzel, W. P. Heinrichs (Eds.), *Encyclopaedia of Islam*, 2nd edition. Available at: http://dx.doi.org/10.1163/1573-3912_islam_SIM_1468. Accessed on October 24, 2016.

Glassé, C. 1989. *The Concise Encyclopedia of Islam*. San Francisco, CA: Harper & Row.

Gleave, R. 2013. "Shi'ism," in: G. Bowering (Ed.), *The Princeton Encyclopedia of Islamic Political Thought*. Princeton, NJ: Princeton University Press, pp. 510–512.

Halm, H. 2012. "Nuṣayriyya," in: P. Bearman, Th. Bianquis, C. E. Bosworth, E. van Donzel, W. P. Heinrichs (Eds.), *Encyclopaedia of Islam*, 2nd edition. Available at: http://referenceworks.brillonline.com/entries/encyclopaedia-of-islam-2/nusayriyya-COM_0876?s.num=0&s.f.s2_parent=s.f.book.encyclopaediaof-islam-2&s.q=Nu%E1%B9%A3ayriyya. Accessed on October 24, 2016.

Haroon, S. 2008. "The Rise of Deobandi Islam in the North-West Frontier Province and Its Implications in Colonial India and Pakistan 1914–1996." *Journal of the Royal Asiatic Society*, 18(1), 47–70. http://www.jstor.org/stable/27755911

Haykel, B. 2013. "Ibn 'Abd al-Wahhab, Muhammad (1703–1792)," in: G. Bowering (Ed.), *The Princeton Encyclopedia of Islamic Political Thought*. Princeton, NJ: Princeton University Press, pp. 231–232.

Heffening, W. and J. Schacht. 2012. "Ḥanafiyya," in: P. Bearman, Th. Bianquis, C. E. Bosworth, E. van Donzel, W. P. Heinrichs (Eds.), *Encyclopaedia of Islam*, 2nd edition. Available at: http://dx.doi.org/10.1163/1573-3912_islam_SIM_2703. Accessed on October 23, 2016.

Hodgson, M. G. S., M. C. Şehabeddin Tekindağ, and M. Tayyib Gökbilgin. 2012. "Durūz," in: P. Bearman, Th. Bianquis, C. E. Bosworth, E. van Donzel, W. P. Heinrichs (Eds.), *Encyclopaedia of Islam*, 2nd edition. Available at: http://dx.doi.org/10.1163/1573-3912_islam_COM_0198. Accessed on October 24, 2016.

Inayatullah, Sh. 2012. "Sayyid Aḥmad Brēlwī," in: P. Bearman, Th. Bianquis, C. E. Bosworth, E. van Donzel, W. P. Heinrichs (Eds.), *Encyclopaedia of Islam*, 2nd edition. Available at: http://dx.doi.org/10.1163/1573-3912_islam_SIM_0404. Accessed on October 22, 2016.

International Religious Freedom Report for 2015. 2015. Report. United States Department of State, Available at: http://www.state.gov/j/drl/rls/irf/religiousfreedom/index.htm#wrapper.

Jong, F. de. 2012. "Khalwatiyya," in: P. Bearman, Th. Bianquis, C. E. Bosworth, E. van Donzel, W. P. Heinrichs (Eds.), *Encyclopaedia of Islam*, 2nd edition. Available at: http://dx.doi.org/10.1163/1573-3912_islam_COM_0489. Accessed on October 22, 2016.

Levi Della Vida, G. 2012. "Khāridjites," in: P. Bearman, Th. Bianquis, C. E. Bosworth, E. van Donzel, W. P. Heinrichs (Eds.), *Encyclopaedia of Islam*, 2nd edition. Available at: http://dx.doi.org/10.1163/1573-3912_islam_COM_0497. Accessed on October 29, 2016.

Lewicki, T. 2012. "al-Ibāḍiyya," in: P. Bearman, Th. Bianquis, C. E. Bosworth, E. van Donzel, W. P. Heinrichs (Eds.), *Encyclopaedia of Islam*, 2nd edition. Available at: http://dx.doi.org/10.1163/1573-3912_islam_COM_0307. Accessed on October 24, 2016.

Lewinstein, K. 2013a. "Ibadis," in: G. Bowering (Ed.), *The Princeton Encyclopedia of Islamic Political Thought*. Princeton, NJ: Princeton University Press, pp. 294–295.

Lewinstein, K. 2013b. "Kharijis," in: G. Bowering (Ed.), *The Princeton Encyclopedia of Islamic Political Thought*. Princeton, NJ: Princeton University Press, pp. 230–231.

Lory, P. 2012. "al-Shādhilī," in: P. Bearman, Th. Bianquis, C. E. Bosworth, E. van Donzel, W. P. Heinrichs (Eds.), *Encyclopaedia of Islam*, 2nd edition. Available at: http://dx.doi.org/10.1163/1573-3912_islam_SIM_673. Accessed on October 16, 2016.

Lowry, J. E. 2013. "al-Shafi'i, Mohammad b. Idris (767–820)," in: G. Bowering (Ed.), *The Princeton Encyclopedia of Islamic Political Thought*. Princeton, NJ: Princeton University Press, pp. 491–492.

Madelung, W. 2012a. "Ismāʿīliyya," in: P. Bearman, Th. Bianquis, C. E. Bosworth, E. van Donzel, W. P. Heinrichs (Eds.), *Encyclopaedia of Islam*, 2nd edition. Available at: http://dx.doi.org/10.1163/1573-3912_islam_COM_0390. Accessed on October 23, 2016.

Madelung, W. 2012b. "Zayd b. ʿAlī b. al-Ḥusayn," in: P. Bearman, Th. Bianquis, C. E. Bosworth, E. van Donzel, W. P. Heinrichs (Eds.), *Encyclopaedia of Islam*, 2nd edition. Available at: http://dx.doi.org/10.1163/1573-3912_islam_SIM_8137. Accessed on October 23, 2016.

Madelung, W. and K. Lewinstein. 2012. "Ṣufriyya," in: P. Bearman, Th. Bianquis, C. E. Bosworth, E. van Donzel, W. P. Heinrichs (Eds.), *Encyclopaedia of Islam*, 2nd edition. Available at: http://dx.doi.org/10.1163/1573-3912_islam_COM_1105. Accessed on October 24, 2016.

Mapping the Global Muslim Population. 2009. Pew Research Center: Religion and Public Life. Available at: http://www.pewforum.org/2009/10/07/mapping-the-global-muslim-population/. Accessed on October 23, 2016.

Margoliouth, D. S. 2012. "Ḳādiriyya," in: P. Bearman, Th. Bianquis, C. E. Bosworth, E. van Donzel, W. P. Heinrichs (Eds.), *Encyclopaedia of Islam*, 2nd edition. Available at: http://dx.doi.org/10.1163/1573-3912_islam_COM_0411. Accessed on October 16, 2016.

Massington, L., B. Radtke, W. C. Chittick, F. de Jong, L. Lewisohn, Th. Zarcone, C. Ernst, F. Aubin, and J. O. Hunwick. 2012. "Taṣawwuf," in: P. Bearman, Th. Bianquis, C. E. Bosworth, E. van Donzel, W. P. Heinrichs (Eds.), *Encyclopaedia of Islam*, 2nd edition. Available at: http://dx.doi.org/10.1163/1573-3912_islam_COM_1188. Accessed on October 16, 2016.

Melchert, C. 2013. "Ahmad b. Hanbal (780–855)," in: G. Bowering (Ed.), *The Princeton Encyclopedia of Islamic Political Thought*. Princeton, NJ: Princeton University Press, pp. 24–25.

Melton, J. G. n.d. "Religion Family Trees: Islam," in: *The Association of Religion Data Archives*. The Association of Religion. Available at: http://www.thearda.com/denoms/families/trees/familytree_islam.asp. Accessed on October 23, 2016.

Michot, Y. M. 2012. "Ibn Taymiyya," in: G. Bowering (Ed.), *The Princeton Encyclopedia of Islamic Political Thought*. Princeton, NJ: Princeton University Press, pp. 238–241.

Minorsky, V. 2012. "Ahl-i Ḥaḳḳ," in: P. Bearman, Th. Bianquis, C. E. Bosworth, E. van Donzel, W. P. Heinrichs (Eds.), *Encyclopaedia of Islam*, 2nd edition. Available at: http://dx.doi.org/10.1163/1573-3912_islam_COM_0026. Accessed on October 24, 2016.

Momen, M. 1985. *An Introduction to Shi'i Islam: The History and Doctrines of Twelver Shi'ism*. New Haven, CT: Yale University Press.

Momen, M. 2016. *Shi'i Islam: A Beginner's Guide*. London, UK: OneWorld Publications.

Newby, G. D. 2002. *A Concise Encyclopedia of Islam*. London, UK: OneWorld Publications.

Ritter, H. and V. Bausani. 2012. "Dj̲alāl al-Dīn Rūmī," in: P. Bearman, Th. Bianquis, C. E. Bosworth, E. van Donzel, W. P. Heinrichs (Eds.), *Encyclopaedia of Islam*, 2nd edition. Available at: http://dx.doi.org/10.1163/1573-3912_islam_COM_0177. Accessed on October 22, 2016.

Safrir, N. 2013. "Abu Hanifa," in: G. Bowering (Ed.), *The Princeton Encyclopedia of Islamic Political Thought*. Princeton, NJ: Princeton University Press, pp. 14–15.

Shinar, P. and W. Ende. 2012. "Salafiyya," in: P. Bearman, Th. Bianquis, C. E. Bosworth, E. van Donzel, W. P. Heinrichs (Eds.), *Encyclopaedia of Islam*, 2nd edition. Available at: http://dx.doi.org/10.1163/1573-3912_islam_COM_0982. Accessed on October 24, 2016.

Sikand, Y. 2003. "Shi'ism in Contemporary India: The Badri-Vakili Controversy Among Indian Isma'ilis." *Muslim World*, 93(1), 99. Academic Search Complete, EBSCOhost. Accessed on October 23, 2016.

Sourdel, E. D. and P. Minganti. 2012. "Filasṭīn," in: P. Bearman, Th. Bianquis, C. E. Bosworth, E. van Donzel, W. P. Heinrichs (Eds.), *Encyclopaedia of Islam*, 2nd edition. Available at: http://dx.doi.org/10.1163/1573-3912_islam_COM_0223. Accessed on October 24, 2016.

Syed, M. J. 2013. "Sunnism," in: G. Bowering (Ed.), *The Princeton Encyclopedia of Islamic Political Thought*. Princeton, NJ: Princeton University Press, pp. 535–536.

"The Sunni-Shi'a Divide 2014". Council on Foreign Relations. Available at: http://www.cfr.org/peace-conflict-and-human-rights/sunni-shia-divide/p33176#!/?cid=otr-marketing_url-sunni_shia_infoguide. Accessed on October 23, 2016.

Tschudi, R. 2012. "Bektās͟hiyya," in: P. Bearman, Th. Bianquis, C. E. Bosworth, E. van Donzel, W. P. Heinrichs (Eds.), *Encyclopaedia of Islam*, 2nd edition. Available at: http://dx.doi.org/10.1163/1573-3912_islam_SIM_1359. Accessed on October 24, 2016.

Tucker, E. 1994. "Nadir Shah and the Ja 'fari Madhhab Reconsidered." *Iranian Studies*, 27(1/4), 163–179. http://www.jstor.org/stable/4310891. Accessed on October 30, 2016.

Urban, E. 2016. *Rashidun Caliphate*. Wiley Online Library. Available at: http://onlinelibrary.wiley.com/doi/10.1002/9781118455074.wbeoe277/full. Accessed on August 19, 2016.

Yazıcı, T., D. S. Margoliouth, and F. de Jong. 2012. "Mawlawiyya," in: P. Bearman, Th. Bianquis, C. E. Bosworth, E. van Donzel, W. P. Heinrichs (Eds.), *Encyclopaedia of Islam*, 2nd edition. Available at: http://dx.doi.org/10.1163/1573-3912_islam_COM_0715. Accessed on October 22, 2016.

Appendix B: Public Responses to Active Attacks

The first responders to a terrorist attack are almost always unsuspecting members of the public, even though conventionally we refer to "first responders" as the first official responders—primarily local police and medical personnel.

Terrorism is still extremely rare compared to other crimes, but terrorism risk is increasing, and terrorism tends to be more consequential than other crimes, particularly "new terrorism." Moreover, public exposure is widening under the pressures of globalization—more open borders, easier travel, urbanization, more connectivity, and the diffusion of technologies, ideologies, and malicious skills. We are all exposed, so we should not reproach ourselves for thinking of sensible precautions, most of which are applicable in any emergency, not just terrorism.

In America, official advice has focused on the following three steps:

1. Run
2. Hide
3. Fight

This official advice prioritizes running away from the threats, if possible; if escape is not possible—say if the victims are confined in a built structure—then victims should try to hide from the threats, or self-barricade against the threats; if running and hiding are not possible, then their last resort is to fight back.

Bruce Oliver Newsome (2015) published the following 10 steps to surviving terrorist attacks (Figure B.1):

1. Reduce exposure
2. Identify your exits
3. Practice your escape
4. Escape, acting decisively
5. Shield yourself materially
6. Hide
7. Respond to opportunities
8. Separate from the threats
9. Remain safe
10. Fight

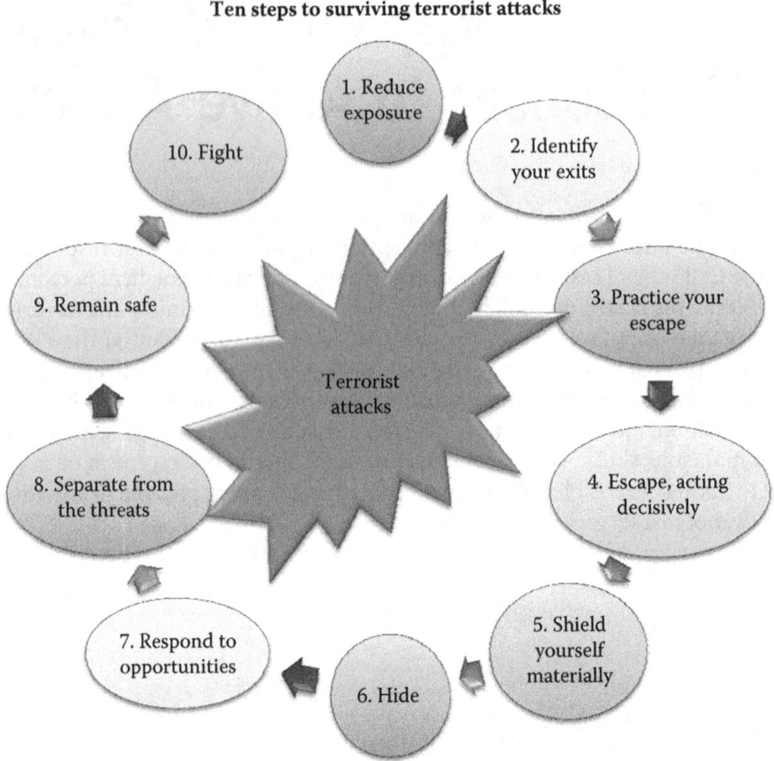

Figure B.1 A graphical representation of Bruce Newsome's recommended process for surviving active attacks.

Reduce Exposure

Chances are that you are not important enough for a terrorist to target you personally, or that you will ever coincide with a terrorist target, but if you still worry about your exposure, then avoid poorly protected, crowded sites with political, economic, or religious significance. New terrorists are seeking to maximize lethality inside the most significant sites, in order to terrorize people where they feel most comfortable. At the same time, the most significant sites tend to be well protected, such as a parliament, a financial institution, an international sports game, or a national concert hall. Terrorists adapt by targeting sites of medium value—those that are not as well protected, but still with capacity for hundreds of people, and with some local political or economic significance, such as local judicial buildings, town halls, schools, theaters, or shopping and dining centers. You can minimize your exposure by spending less time in significant sites, just the same as you can minimize your exposure to road traffic accidents by spending less time on the roads.

Identify Your Exits

As you enter crowded spaces, identify your exits, particularly the nearest, quickest, widest, nonelectrical exits. Identify these exits as you enter, so that you do not need to search for them during any emergency. Do not use the elevator or escalator, which tends to be a chokepoint, and may lose electrical power. Use fixed steps. If you have a choice of stairs, use the building's main staircase, rather than the narrower stairways that are more frequently and conveniently located.

Practice Your Escape

If you visit a site repeatedly, practice entering and exiting by the safest route, so that you train yourself to it. If you must flee, do not get sucked into fleeing the way you came in just because it is the way you came in, or get sucked in the direction that the crowd is moving—comply with your prior evaluation of the safest exit, unless a threat gets in the way.

Escape, Decisively

Once you have identified a threat, flee immediately, and do not consider any other action. In other words, do not think about it, just react; do not take time to consider what happened. Some people will do nothing—they may be cognitively overloaded. Some people will question what is happening. Some people will panic without completing a single choice. If you are confident of an emergency, act immediately, stick to your emergency plan, and get out via the best exit as soon as possible. You are helping everybody else by removing your body from the crowded space, after which you can consider helping others.

Shield Yourself Materially

If you cannot flee, then lay down behind the hardest cover available—ideally reinforced concrete or masonry. Forget everything you have seen in the movies. Do not rely on tables, cars, chipboard/pasteboard walls, appliances, or furniture—except to hide from view or to shield yourself from falling objects. Bulletproof walls are 7–8 inches (15–20 cm) of reinforced masonry or concrete; most load-bearing walls in that material are only 6 inches thick; most non-load-bearing walls are of thinner, inferior materials.

Do not err toward metals: most metals in buildings and automobiles are thin sheets of soft aluminum or mild steel, which are easily perforated by bullets and blown into secondary projectiles by blast.

Get out of the way of windows, which are easily blown into hundreds of projectiles.

Be aware that even if the material is bulletproof, bullets can flow through joints in masonry or paneling, bounce around corners, and even bounce backward with enough energy to kill, while objects overhead can be dislodged by blast, so do not be complacent about the many directions in which you need protection.

Stay prone on the ground: a standing target offers more surface area to projectiles traveling horizontally; blast tends to travel upward; and collapsing structures can be held up by objects around you.

Hide

If you cannot find hard cover, at least hide from the attackers' line of sight. If you find a good hiding place, barricade yourself in, wirelessly communicate with officials if safe to do so, be patient in waiting for official help, and be wary of threats that pretend to be official helpers. Popular culture tends to describe modern multimethod attacks as "simultaneous" or "coordinated," as if they finish in seconds to minutes, but in fact they are consecutive over minutes to hours, as terrorists strike at different responders in the same location or move to different locations. At the Stade de France, the second bomber blew up around 20 minutes after the first; the third bomber blew up nearly 60 minutes after the first; the gunmen in central Paris were still fighting about 200 minutes after the first bomber; accomplices escaped overnight; and some remained at large days later.

Respond to Opportunities

If, while hiding, you realize an exit, take it as soon as the threats are distracted or reloading. To be discovered or taken hostage by a new terrorist is usually fatal. If you are confronted by official personnel as they approach to rescue you or to confront the threats, keep your hands open, up, and away from your body. If you can, point out the threats with an open hand and verbally identify the threats. Obey official instructions to get out of the way and exit.

Separate from the Threats

Once you have exited, follow any official instructions to a safe area, or keep putting distance between you and the threats, or put taller buildings between you and the threats. Do not just stop in the open. Blast, blown objects, and bullets can travel more than a kilometer (1,000 yards) with enough energy to kill. Be mindful that terrorists sometimes prepare a second attack on the route by which survivors are likely to flee the first attack. Get away from any further chokepoints or confined spaces until you find official help, then calmly describe to the officials what you observed—your accurate observations could save lives. Do not embellish, assume, exaggerate, conflate, or imagine—inaccurate observations could waste time or misdirect resources.

Remain Safe

Do not be tempted to leave a safe area in order to see what is happening at the attack site, and do not go back to help unless you are sure that security personnel have made the site safe and will not mistake you for a threat.

Fight

If you are confronted with an unavoidable threat without an exit or cover, fight with everything available, and encourage the crowd to overwhelm the attackers—some may die, but eventually the majority must triumph.

References

Acosta, B. T., and K. Ramos. 2016. Introducing the 1993 terrorism and political violence dataset, *Studies in Conflict and Terrorism*, 2016, 1–34. Available at: http://www.tandfonline.com/doi/abs/10.1080/1057610X.2016.1184061

Al-Adm, A. U. A. 2010. *Safety and Security Guidelines for Lone Wolf Mujahideen and Small Cells*, summarized and translated by al-Fajr Media Center. Available at: https://cryptome.org/2016/01/lone-wolf-safe-sec.pdf

Al-Adnani, A. M. 2015. ISIL issued warning to "Filthy French": Video message encouraged attacks "Wherever You May Be." Available at: http://www.politico.eu/article/paris-terrorist-attacks-isil-issued-warning-to-filthy-french/

Al-Dawoody, A. 2015. Al-Sarakhsī's contribution to the Islamic Law of War, *UCLA Journal of Islamic and Near Eastern Law*, 14(1), 29–44. Available at: http://escholarship.org/uc/item/2mz9k4q1

Al-Jazeera. 2016a. Saudi-led coalition announces Yemen prisoner swap. Available at: http://www.aljazeera.com/news/2016/03/saudi-led-coalition-announces-yemen-prisoner-swap-160328063102436.html

Al-Jazeera. 2016b. Libyan plane hijack ends peacefully in Malta. Available at: http://www.aljazeera.com/news/2016/12/libyan-plane-hijack-ends-peacefully-malta-161223145040091.html

Al-Najdi, A. 2006. How to kill a crusader in the Arabian Peninsula. Available at: http://worldanalysis.net/smf/index.php?topic=222.0

Al Qa'ida. 1990. *Declaration of Jihad against the Country's Tyrants, Military Series*. Available at: http://fas.org/irp/world/para/aqmanual.pdf

Al Qa'ida [al Muqrin]. 2004. *Al-Battar [manual], Number 10, Kidnapping*. Available at: http://netwar04.blogspot.com/2004/09/al-battar-al-qaeda-manual-on.html

Ali, A. Y. 1934. *The Holy Qur-an: Text, Translation, and Commentary*, Lahore, Pakistan. Available at: http://www.sacred-texts.com/isl/quran/index.htm

Ali, M. M. 2015. *A Handbook of Islam: An Abridged Edition of "The Religion of Islam,"* Wembley, UK: Ahmadiyya Anjuman Lahore Publications. Available at: http://ahmadiyya.org/bookspdf/hb-islam.pdf

Anti-Defamation League. 2012. Officer safety and extremists: An overview for law enforcement officers. Available at: https://www.adl.org/sites/default/files/documents/assets/pdf/combating-hate/Officer-Safety-and-Extremists-An-Overview.pdf

Arena, M. P., and B. A. Arrigo. 2006. *The Terrorist Identity: Explaining the Terrorist Threat*, New York, NY: New York University Press.

Associated Press. 2016. Hostage crisis leaves 28 dead in Bangladesh diplomatic zone, *New York Times*, July 11. Available at: http://www.nytimes.com/aponline/2016/07/02/world/asia/ap-as-bangladesh-attack.html

Baker, A. 2014. Taliban commander: More kidnappings to come after Bergdahl deal, *Time*, Available at: http://time.com/2826442/taliban-kidnappings-bergdahl/

Bakker, E. 2012. Forecasting terrorism: The need for a more systematic approach, *Journal of Strategic Security*, 5(4), 69–84.

Barclay, J. 2011. Allah's law interpreted to justify jihad, *Jane's Islamic Affairs Analyst*, March 21.

Barfi, B. 2015. How the White House abandoned American hostages, *Foreign Policy*. Available at: https://foreignpolicy.com/2015/06/23/how-the-white-house-abandoned-american-hostages-foley-sotloff-mueller/

References

Baruch, M., and N. Zarse. 2012. Components in a hostage negotiation training curriculum, *Journal of Police Crisis Negotiations*, 12(1), 39–50.

BBC. 2006. Reid loses Afghan hijack ruling. Available at: http://news.bbc.co.uk/2/hi/uk_news/5244936.stm

BBC. 2012a. Pakistan's Shias fear sectarian attacks. Available at: http://www.bbc.co.uk/news/world-asia-17936651

BBC. 2012b. Pakistan Shias killed in Gilgit sectarian attack. Available at: http://www.bbc.co.uk/news/world-asia-19280339

BBC. 2013a. Pakistan violence: Gunman storm Quetta hospital. Available at: http://www.bbc.co.uk/news/world-asia-22920542

BBC. 2013b. Two guilty of Lee Rigby murder. Available at: http://www.bbc.co.uk/news/uk-25450555

BBC. 2014. Serge Lazarevic: Mali confirms militants freed for French hostage. Available at: http://www.bbc.com/news/world-africa-30450092

BBC. 2015. Attacks continue in Jerusalem despite new checkpoints. Available at: http://www.bbc.com/news/world-middle-east-34535573

BBC. 2016a. Islamic State "releases Assyrian Christian hostages." Available at: http://www.bbc.com/news/world-middle-east-35630196

BBC. 2016b. More armed police set to protect London, say Met chief and mayor. Available at: http://www.bbc.co.uk/news/uk-36961338

Beaumont, P. 2009. Kidnapped U.S. reporter makes dramatic escape from Taliban, *The Guardian*. Available at: https://www.theguardian.com/world/2009/jun/21/new-york-times-reporter-taliban

Bender, R. 2016. Germany discusses enlisting military help at home to fight terrorism, *Wall Street Journal*. Available at: http://www.wsj.com/articles/germany-discusses-enlisting-military-help-at-home-to-fight-terrorism-1470243199

Berman, M. 2015. FBI says UC Merced attacker appeared to be "self-radicalized" and inspired by the Islamic State, *Washington Post*. Available at: https://www.washingtonpost.com/news/post-nation/wp/2016/03/17/fbi-says-uc-merced-attacker-was-self-radicalized-and-inspired-by-the-islamic-state/

Binali, T. 2015. *Course in Monotheism*, Islamic State training camp textbook, translated by Aymenn Jawad Al-Tamimi. Available at: http://www.aymennjawad.org/17633/islamic-state-training-camp-textbook-course-in

Blaber, P. 2008. *The Mission, The Men, and Me: Lessons from a Former Delta Force Commander*, New York, NY: Penguin Group.

Bolz, F., K. Dudonis, and D. Schulz. 2011. *The Counterterrorism Handbook: Tactics, Procedures, and Techniques*, 4th edition, Boca Raton, FL: CRC Press.

Boutilier, A. 2016. Toronto man kidnapped in Afghanistan freed after 5-year ordeal, *The Toronto Staff*. Available at: http://www.thestar.com/news/canada/2016/01/11/toronto-man-freed-by-taliban-after-5-year-ordeal.html.

Bryan, D. 2012. A landscape of meaning: Constructing understandings of political violence from the broken paradigm of "terrorism," in: R. Jackson and S. J. Sinclair (Eds.), *Contemporary Debates on Terrorism*, London, UK: Routledge, pp. 17–25.

Burns, J. F. 1994. Indian police free 3 Britons held hostage, *New York Times*. Available at: http://www.nytimes.com/1994/11/02/world/indian-police-free-3-britons-held-hostage.html

Burton, F., and S. Stewart. 2009. Mitigating Mumbai. Available at: https://www.stratfor.com/weekly/20090114_mitigating_mumbai

Burton, F., and B. West. 2008. From the New York Landmarks plot to the Mumbai attack. Available at: https://www.stratfor.com/weekly/20081203_new_york_landmarks_plot_mumbai_attack

Butlangan, N. 2016. Norwegian says his Philippine kidnapping was "devastating", *Associated Press*. Available at: http://bigstory.ap.org/article/97bfef9fb3194ef1add8279be94a2056/freed-norwegian-3-indonesian-hostages-handed-philippines

Cafarella, J. 2015. *Backgrounder: Syrian Jihadists Signal Intent for Lebanon*. PDF. Institute for the Study of War. Available at: http://www.understandingwar.org/sites/default/files/Syrian_Backgrounder_approved_0.pdf

Cajee, N. A. 2012. Oral hygiene in the Shari'ah: A thousand-year-old conversation between Islam's schools of legal thought, *Journal of the History of Dentistry*, 60(3), 148–157. Available at: http://europepmc.org/abstract/med/23409533

Callimachi, R. 2014. Paying ransoms, Europe bankrolls Qaeda terror, *New York Times*. Available at: http://www.nytimes.com/2014/07/30/world/africa/ransoming-citizens-europe-becomes-al-qaedas-patron.html

Callimachi, R. July 13, 2015. ISIS enshrines a theology of rape, *New York Times*, Available at: http://www.nytimes.com/2015/08/14/world/middleeast/isis-enshrines-a-theology-of-rape.html

Callimachi, R., and E. Schmitt. 2015. Iran released top members of al Qaeda in a trade, *New York Times*, September 17. Available at: http://www.nytimes.com/2015/09/18/world/middleeast/iran-released-top-members-of-al-qaeda-in-a-trade.html

Cameron, S. 2014. Applying the right tactic, *Law and Order*. Available at: http://www.hendonpub.com/resources/article_archive/results/details?id=5083

Cantey, S. 2017. Beyond the pale? Exploring prospects for negotiations with al Qaeda and the Islamic State, *Studies in Conflict and Terrorism*. Available at: http://www.tandfonline.com/doi/full/10.1080/1057610X.2017.1348096

Chalk, P., B. Hoffman, R. Reville, and A.-B. Kasupski. 2005. *Trends in Terrorism: Threats to the United States and the Future of the Terrorism Risk Reinsurance Act*, Santa Monica, CA: RAND.

Chan, S., and S. Sengupta. 2016. Nadia Murad, Yazidi woman who survived ISIS captivity, wins Human Rights Prize, *New York Times*, October 10. Available at: http://www.nytimes.com/2016/10/11/world/middleeast/yazidis-isis-nadia-murad.html

Chapman, C. B., and S. C. Ward. 2003. *Project Risk Management: Processes, Techniques and Insights*, 2nd edition, Chichester, England: John Wiley.

Chaudhry, M. S. 2003. Dynamics of Islamic jihad, Pakistan: Burhan Education and Welfare Trust. Available at: http://www.muslimtents.com/shaufi/b17/b177.htm

CNN. 2016. Bowe Bergdahl fast facts. Available at: http://www.cnn.com/2014/01/19/us/bowe-bergdahl-fast-facts/

Cole, J. 2009. *Engaging the Muslim World*, New York, NY: Palgrave Macmillan.

Combs, C. C. 1997. *Terrorism in the Twenty-First Century*, Upper Saddle River, NJ: Prentice-Hall.

Corsi, J. R. 1981. Terrorism as a desperate game: Fear, bargaining, and communication in the terrorist event, *Journal of Conflict Resolution*, 25(1), 47–81.

Cragin, R. K., and P. Padilla. 2017. Old becomes new again: Kidnappings by Daesh and other Salafi-Jihadists in the twenty-first century, *Studies in Conflict & Terrorism*, 40(8), 665–683.

Craig, T., and H. N. Khan. 2014. Bicyclist from China kidnapped in Pakistan, *Washington Post*. Available at: https://www.washingtonpost.com/world/asia_pacific/bicyclist-from-china-kidnapped-in-pakistan/2014/05/20/26293422-e01c-11e3-8dcc-d6b7fede081a_story.html

References

Crane, D. 2007. Israeli anti-terrorist SWAT school, *Tactical Response*. Available at: http://www.hendonpub.com/resources/article_archive/results/details?id=3331

Cratty, C. 2013. Anwar al-Awlaki visited prostitutes, FBI documents say. Available at: http://www.cnn.com/2013/07/03/us/fbi-al-awlaki-prostitution/

Cruickshank, P. 2017. A view from the CT foxhole: James A. Gagliano, former FBI hostage rescue team counterterrorist operator, *CTC Sentinel*, 10(5), 8–12. Available at: https://www.ctc.usma.edu/posts/a-view-from-the-ct-foxhole-james-a-gagliano-former-fbi-hostage-rescue-team-counterterrorist-operator

Davies, W. A. 2017. Counterterrorism effectiveness to Jihadists in Western Europe and the United States: We are losing the war on terror, *Studies in Conflict and Terrorism*. Available at: http://www.tandfonline.com/doi/full/10.1080/10576 10X.2017.1284447

DeYoung, K. 2011. U.S. trucking funds reach Taliban, military-led investigation concludes, *Washington Post*. Accessed on July 25, 2011.

Dolnik, A., and K. M. Fitzgerald. 2008. *Negotiating Crises with the New Terrorists*, Santa Barbara, CA: Praeger Security International.

Dolnik, A., and K. M. Fitzgerald. 2011. Negotiating hostage crises with the new terrorists, *Studies in Conflict and Terrorism*, 34(4), 267–294.

Dörmann, K. 2003. The legal situation of "unlawful/unprivileged combatants", *International Review of the Red Cross*, 85(849), 45–73. Available at: https://www.icrc.org/eng/assets/files/other/irrc_849_dorman.pdf

Dovere, E.-I. 2016. Trump pledges to pull back in Middle East, lean in against ISIS, *Politico.com*. Available at: http://www.politico.com/story/2016/12/trump-middle-east-isis-232291

Economist, The. 2015. How to respond to the new tactics of terrorism. Available at: http://www.economist.com/news/middle-east-and-africa/21678907-deadly-style-suicidal-gun-assault-has-spread-across-globe-how-respond

El-Dakkak, S. 1990. International humanitarian law lies between the Islamic concept and positive international law, *International Review of the Red Cross*, 275, 101–114. Available at: https://www.loc.gov/rr/frd/Military_Law/pdf/RC_Mar-Apr-1990.pdf

El Fadl, K. A. 1999. The rules of killing at war: An inquiry into classical sources, *The Muslim World*, 89(2), 144–157. Available at: http://onlinelibrary.wiley.com/doi/10.1111/j.1478-1913.1999.tb03675.x/epdf

Entous, A., and D. Barrett. 2015. FBI helped facilitate ransom for hostage killed in drone strike, *Wall Street Journal*. Available at: http://www.wsj.com/articles/fbi-helped-facilitate-ransom-for-u-s-hostage-killed-in-drone-strike-1430328084

Entous, A., and G. Zampano. 2015. U.S. says militants demanded ransom for hostage bodies in Pakistan, *Wall Street Journal*. Available at: http://www.wsj.com/articles/u-s-says-militants-demanded-ransom-for-hostage-bodies-in-pakistan-1440112045

Faulconbridge, G. 2016. British spy chief says Islamic State plotting attacks as Russia makes desert of Syria, *Reuters*. Available at: http://www.reuters.com/article/us-britain-security-idUSKBN13X1CX

Faure, G., and I. W. Zartman. 2011. *Negotiating with Terrorists: Strategy, Tactics, and Politics, Cass Series on Political Violence*, London: Routledge.

FBI (United States, Federal Bureau of Investigations). 2013a. The Hostage Rescue Team, Part 3, Training for every contingency. Available at: https://www.fbi.gov/news/stories/hostage-rescue-team-training-for-every-contingency

FBI (United States, Federal Bureau of Investigations). 2013b. The Hostage Rescue Team, Part 6, Mission in the Gulf of Aden. Available at: https://www.fbi.gov/news/stories/hostage-rescue-team-mission-in-the-gulf-of-aden

FBI (United States, Federal Bureau of Investigations). 2014. 2014: The FBI story, FBI. Available at: https://www.fbi.gov/stats-services/publications/fbi-story/the-fbi-story-2014

FBI (United States, Federal Bureau of Investigations). 2016a. Active shooter incidents, FBI. Available at: https://www.fbi.gov/about/partnerships/office-of-partner-engagement/active-shooter-incidents

FBI (United States, Federal Bureau of Investigations). 2016b. Crime in the United States, 2015, FBI. Available at: https://ucr.fbi.gov/crime-in-the-u.s/2015/crime-in-the-u.s.-2015/offenses-known-to-law-enforcement/murder

Fearon, J. 1995. Rationalist explanations for war, *International Organization*, 49(3), 379–414.

Fitsanakis, J. 2016. Comment: Far-right militancy just as dangerous as Islamist extremism. Intelnews.org. Available at: https://intelnews.org/author/intelnewsjoe/

Flynn, A. 2016. U.K. cop warns of gun-linked terror plots, *Wall Street Journal*. Available at: http://www.wsj.com/articles/u-k-cop-warns-of-gun-linked-terror-plots-1477935957

Forest, J. J. F. 2007. *Countering Terrorism and Insurgency in the 21st Century: International Perspectives*, Westport, CT: Praeger.

French, G. 2011. Is your SWAT team ready for rampaging jihadis? *Police One*. Available at: https://www.policeone.com/swat/articles/3261180-Is-your-SWAT-team-ready-for-rampaging-Jihadis/

French, G. 2013. Active terrorist response: Tactical considerations for SWAT teams. Available at: https://www.policeone.com/swat/articles/6222800-Active-terrorist-response-Tacticalconsiderations-for-SWAT-teams/

Gannon, K. 2013. Taliban offer to free U.S. soldier Bowe Bergdahl, *Idaho State Journal*. Available at http://www.idahostatejournal.com/news/national/article_d8d8c366-d9b6-11e2-9db6001a4bcf887a.html

Gaskarth, G. 2016. *Commuter Cops: Helping Our Police to Live in the City They Serve*, London, UK: Policy Exchange, Capital City Foundation. Available at: http://policyexchange.org.uk/images/publications/commuter%20cops%20-%20august%2016.pdf

Geneva Convention. 1949. Available at: http://www.un.org/en/preventgenocide/rwanda/text-images/Geneva_POW.pdf

Global Terrorism Database (GTD). 2009–2017, University of Maryland. Available at www.start.umd.edu/gtd

Goldaber, I. 1979. A typology of hostage-takers, *The Police Chief*, 46(6), 21–23.

Goldman, A. 2016. In a shift, U.S. includes families in hostage rescue efforts, *New York Times*. Available at: http://www.nytimes.com/2016/09/12/us/politics/in-policy-shift-us-includes-families-in-hostage-rescue-efforts.html

Goldman, A., and M. Berman. 2016. "They took too damn long": Inside the police response to the Orlando shooting, *Washington Post*. Available at: https://www.washingtonpost.com/world/national-security/they-took-too-damn-long-inside-the-police-response-to-the-orlando-shooting/2016/08/01/67a66130-5447-11e6-88eb-7dda4e2f2aec_story.html

Gomez, J. 2016. Abu Sayyaf got $7.3 million from kidnappings, *Associated Press*. Available at: http://bigstory.ap.org/296ebfddbd324236a840301a46b8bc6e

References

Grubb, A. R. 2010. Modern day hostage (crisis) negotiation: The evolution of an art form within the policing arena, *Aggression and Violent Behavior*, 15(5), 341–348.

Hacker, F. J. 1976. *Crusaders, Criminals, Crazies: Terror and Terrorism in Our Time*, New York, NY: W.W. Norton.

Hamidullah, M. 1942. The Muslim conduct of state. Available at: http://muslimcanada.org/conductofstate.html

Hassan, F., and T. Arango. 2016. Bombing kills more than 140 in Baghdad, *New York Times*, July 3. Available at: http://www.nytimes.com/2016/07/04/world/middleeast/baghdad-bombings.html?_r=0

Hassan, M. H. 2013. Rethinking classical Jihad ideas, *Counterterrorist Trends and Analysis*, 5(3), 2–7.

Hassel, C. 1975. The hostage situation: Exploring motivation and cause, *The Police Chief*, 42(9), 55–58.

Hassner, R. E. 2010. Debating the role of religion in war, *International Security*, 35(1), 201–208.

Heincke, D. H. 2017. German foreign fighters in Syria and Iraq: The updated data and its implications, *CTC Sentinel*, 10(3), 17–22.

Henckaerts, J.-M., and L. Doswald-Beck. 2005. *Customary International Humanitarian Law: Volume 1: Rules*, vol. 1, Cambridge, UK: Cambridge University Press.

Hensley, N. 2015. American contractor dies in Yemen … , *New York Daily News*. Available at http://www.nydailynews.com/news/world/american-dies-yemen-detained-shiite-rebels-article-1.2430568

Hoffman, B. 2001. Change and continuity in terrorism. *Studies in Conflict and Terrorism*, 24(5), 417–428.

Hoffman, B. 2006. *Inside Terrorism*, New York, NY: Columbia University Press.

Holmwood, L. 2008. Channel 4 paid my captors, says kidnapped documentary maker Sean Langan. Available at: https://www.theguardian.com/media/2008/jul/01/channel4.television

Horowitz, M. C. 2009. Long time going: Religion and the duration of crusading, *International Security*, 34(2), 162–193.

Hudson, Rex A. 1989. Dealing with international hostage-taking: Alternatives to reactive counterterrorist assaults, *Terrorism*, 12(5), 321–378.

Hughes, S., and A. Meleagrou-Hitchens. 2017. The threat to the United States from the Islamic State's virtual entrepreneurs, *CTC Sentinel*, 10(3), 1–8.

Humanitarian Practice Network. 2010. *Operational Security Management in Violent Environments*, Number 8 (new edition), London, UK: Overseas Development Institute.

Human Rights Watch. 2014. Those terrible weeks in their camp, Human Rights Watch. Available at: http://features.hrw.org/features/HRW_2014_report/Those_Terrible_Weeks_in_Their_Camp/

Hunzai, I. 2013. *United States Institute of Peace Special Report: Conflict Dynamics in Gilgit-Baltistan*. Report no. 321. Available at: http://www-origin.usip.org/sites/default/files/SR321.pdf

Hussein, A., A. Sheikh, and F. Omar. 2016. Al Shabaab car bomber strikes hotel in Somalia capital, at least 15 dead, *Reuters*. Available at: http://www.reuters.com/article/us-somalia-security-idUSKCN0YN4TF

Ibrahim, Y. 2010. The ultimate mowing machine, *Inspire*. Available at: https://azelin.files.wordpress.com/2010/10/inspire-magazine-2.pdf

Institute for Economics and Peace. 2012. Global Terrorism Index Report 2012. Available at: http://economicsandpeace.org/publications

Institute for Economics and Peace. 2014. Global Terrorism Index 2014. Available at: http://economicsandpeace.org/publications

Institute for Economics and Peace. 2016. Global Terrorism Index 2016. Available at: http://www.visionofhumanity.org/sites/default/files/Global%20Terrorism%20Index%202016_0.pdf

International Committee of the Red Cross. 2016. Rule 5. Definition of civilians. Available at: https://ihl-databases.icrc.org/customary-ihl/eng/docs/v1_cha_chapter1_rule5

Islam, M. S. 2015. Fundamental human rights towards childhood: Islamic guidelines are unique to protect the child, *Journal of Asia Pacific Studies*, 4(2), 177–202.

Islamic Emirate of Afghanistan, The. 2009. The Layha [code of conduct] for Mujahids, *International Review of the Red Cross*, 93(881), 103–120. Available at: https://www.icrc.org/eng/assets/files/review/2011/irrc-881-munir-annex.pdf

Islamic State of Iraq and the Levant (ISIL). 2014a. *Su'al wa-Jawab fi al-Sabi wa-Riqab ("Questions and Answers on Taking Captives and Slaves")*. Available at: http://www.memrijttm.org/islamic-state-isis-releases-pamphlet-on-female-slaves.html

Islamic State of Iraq and the Levant (ISIL). 2014b. Reflections on the crusade, Dabiq, No. 4. Available at: http://media.clarionproject.org/files/islamic-state/islamic-state-isis-magazine-Issue-4-the-failed-crusade.pdf

Islamic State of Iraq and the Levant (ISIL). 2015. How to survive in the West: A Mujahid guide. Available at: http://www.investigativeproject.org/documents/misc/863.pdf

Jaffe, G., and D. Makamura. 2016. Obama defends his wartime strategy and laments Trump's likely change of course, *Washington Post*. Available at: https://www.washingtonpost.com/politics/obama-to-defend-his-terror-strategy-as-trump-names-prepares-to-alter-it/2016/12/05/a585f9de-bb1c-11e6-91ee-1adddfe36cbe_story.html

Johnson, T. H., and M. C. DuPee. 2012. Analysing the new Taliban code of conduct (Layeha): An assessment of changing perspectives and strategies of the Afghan Taliban, *Central Asian Survey*, 31(1), 77–91.

Joscelyn, T. 2015. Senior al Qaeda leaders reportedly released from custody in Iran, *The Long War Journal*. Available at: http://www.longwarjournal.org/archives/2015/09/senior-al-qaeda-leaders-reportedly-released-from-iran.php

Juergensmeyer, M. 2001. *Terror in the Mind of God: The Global Rise of Religious Violence*, Berkeley, CA: University of California Press.

Kearney, V. 2017. Christine Connor: Swedish model to "lone wolf dissident". Available at: http://www.bbc.com/news/uk-northern-ireland-40330784

Khurasani, M. 2008. Military lessons for a better preparation of Mujahideen. Available at: https://thejihadproject.files.wordpress.com/2011/03/mujahideen-handbook.pdf

Kirkpatrick, D. 2017. Why negotiate when you can criminalize? Lessons for conflict transformation from Northern Ireland and South Africa, *Studies in Conflict and Terrorism (Online)*. Available at: http://www.tandfonline.com/doi/full/10.1080/1057610X.2017.1338055

Kurzman, C. 2016. *Muslim-American Involvement with Violent Extremis, 2015*, Chapel Hill, NC: Triangle Center. Available at: https://kurzman.unc.edu/files/2016/02/Kurzman_Muslim-American_Involvement_in_Violent_Extremism_2015.pdf

Lanceley, F. J. 2003. *On-Scene Guide for Crisis Negotiators*, 2nd edition, Boca Raton, FL: CRC Press.

References

Landau-Tasseron, E. 2006. *"Non-Combatants" in Muslim Legal Thought*, Washington, DC: Hudson Institute. Available at: http://www.hudson.org/content/researchattachments/attachment/1136/20061226_noncombatantsfinal.pdf

Lappin, Y., and E. Lefkovits. 2011. Background: Ramming terror attacks in recent years, *Jerusalem Post*. Available at: http://www.jpost.com/printarticle.aspx?id=235810

Laqueur, W. 1977. *Terrorism*, Boston, MA: Little, Brown.

Leetaru, K. 2015. Why we can't just read English newspapers to understand terrorism: And how big data can help. *Foreign Policy*. Available at: http://foreignpolicy.com/2015/04/15/why-we-cant-just-read-english-newspapers-to-understand-terrorism-big-data/

Levie, H. S. 1961. Prisoners of war and the protecting power, *American Journal of International Law*, 55(2), 374–397.

Lewis, J. W. 2013. The human use of human beings: A brief history of suicide bombing, *Origins: Current Events in Historical Perspective*, 6(7). Available at: http://origins.osu.edu/article/human-use-human-beings-brief-history-suicide-bombing

Loertscher, S., and D. Milton. 2015. *Held Hostage: Analyses of Kidnapping Across Time and among Jihadist Organizations*, Combating Terrorism Center at West Point, the United States Military Academy. Available at: https://www.ctc.usma.edu/v2/wp-content/uploads/2015/12/Held-Hostagereportc2.pdf

Maclean, R., and E. Akinwotu. 2016. Nigeria ready to swap Boko Haram prisoners for Chibok girls, *The Guardian*. Available at: https://www.theguardian.com/world/2016/sep/16/nigerias-president-muhammadu-buhari-says-he-will-trade-boko-haram-prisoners-for-chibok-girls

Maher, G. F. 1979. *Hostage: A Police Approach to a Contemporary Crisis*, Springfield, IL: Charles C. Thomas.

Mair, D. 2016. #Westgate: A case study: How al-Shabaab used Twitter during an ongoing attack, *Studies in Conflict and Terrorism*, 40(1), 24–43.

Malami, H. U. 1994. Financing Islamic education in Muslim minority states: The case of Nigeria, *Journal Institute of Muslim Minority Affairs*, 14(1&2), 46–52. Available at: http://www.tandfonline.com/doi/pdf/10.1080/13602009308716276.

Malik, (Brigadier) S. K. 1979. *The Quranic Concept of War*, Lahore, Pakistan: Associated Printers.

Manik, J. A., G. Anand, and E. Barry. 2016. Bangladesh attack is new evidence that ISIS has shifted its focus beyond the Mideast, *New York Times*. Available at: http://www.nytimes.com/2016/07/03/world/asia/bangladesh-hostage-standoff.html

March, A. F., and M. Revkin. 2015. Caliphate of law: ISIS' ground rules, *Foreign Affairs*. Available at: http://www.foreignaffairs.com/articles/143679/andrew-f-march-and-mara-revkin/caliphate-of-law

Masood, S., and M. Mashal. 2016. Ali Haider Gilani, ex-Pakistan leader's son, is rescued after 3 years, *New York Times*. Available at: http://www.nytimes.com/2016/05/11/world/asia/pakistan-ali-haider-gilani.html

McGowan, H. M. 2007. A prediction model for incident resolution, *Journal of Police Crisis Negotiations*, 7(2), 53–83.

McMains, M. J., and W. C. Mullins. 2015. *Crisis Negotiations: Managing Critical Incidents and Hostage Situations in Law Enforcement and Corrections*. London, UK: Routledge.

Meek, J. G., and B. Ross. 2016. American hostage of Taliban appears in new video, *ABC News*. Available at: http://abcnews.go.com/US/american-hostage-taliban-appears-video/story?id=41753327

Miller, C. 2011. Is it possible and preferable to negotiate with terrorists? *Defence Studies*, 11(1), 145–185.

Miller, G., and G. Jaffe. 2016. U.S. agrees to pay nearly $3 million to family of Italian killed in CIA strike, *Washington Post*. Available at: https://www.washingtonpost.com/world/national-security/us-agrees-to-pay-nearly-3-million-to-family-of-italian-killed-in-cia-strike/2016/09/16/5c213af6-7c1a-11e6-bd86-b7bbd53d2b5d_story.html

Miller, L. 2005. Hostage negotiation: Psychological principles and practices, *International Journal of Emergency Mental Health*, 7(44), 277–298.

Mockaitis, T. R. 2011. Terrorism, insurgency, and organized crime, in: P. Shemella (Ed.), *Fighting Back: What Governments Can Do About Terrorism*, Stanford, CA: Stanford Security Studies, pp. 11–26.

Morello, C. 2016a. Money paid to Iran was "leverage" not ransom, State Department says, *Washington Post*. Available at: https://www.washingtonpost.com/world/national-security/money-paid-to-iran-was-leverage-not-ransom-state-department-says/2016/08/18/4c1040b7-8ea0-40bd-b7cd-8629dc16c036_story.html

Morello, C. 2016b. American held in Yemen for over a year released, *Washington Post*. Available at: https://www.washingtonpost.com/world/middle_east/american-held-in-yemen-for-over-a-year-released/2016/11/06/4edb5961-6078-4c4d-9348-f420e9edda26_story.html

al-Munajjid, M. S. 2009. Islamic punishment for rape. Archive Islam Online. Available at: http://archive.islamonline.net/?p=646

Munir, M. 2010. Debates on the rights of prisoners of war in Islamic law, *Islamic Studies*, 49(4), 463–492. Available at: http://www.jstor.org/stable/41581120

Munir, M. 2011. The Layha for the Mujahideen: An analysis of the code of conduct for the Taliban fighters under Islamic law, *International Review of the Red Cross*, 93(881), 81–102.

Musharraf, P. 2006. *In the Line of Fire: A Memoir*, New York, NY: Free Press.

Nacos, B. 2009. The next terror attack: The centrality of media and public information in preparedness planning, in: C. Beyer and M. Bauer (Eds.), *Effectively Countering Terrorism: The Challenges of Prevention, Preparedness and Response*, Eastbourne, England: Sussex Academic Press, pp. 208–229.

Naji, A. B. 2006. *The Management of Savagery: The Most Critical Stage through which the Umma Will Pass*. Translated by William McCants, John M. Olin Institute for Strategic Studies at Harvard University. Available at: https://azelin.files.wordpress.com/2010/08/abu-bakr-naji-the-management-of-savagery-the-most-critical-stage-through-which-the-umma-will-pass.pdf

Naqvi, A. R. 1974. Laws of war in Islam, *Islamic Studies*, 13(1), 25–43. Available at: http://irigs.iiu.edu.pk:64447/gsdl/collect/islamics/index/assoc/HASHd0df.dir/doc.pdf

National Counterterrorism Center (NCTC). 2016–2017, United States: http://www.nctc.gov/

National Institute of Justice. 2017. Terrorism. Available at: https://www.nij.gov/topics/crime/terrorism/Pages/welcome.aspx

Nazir, S. 2011. Faithless warriors, *The Express Tribune*. Available at: http://tribune.com.pk/story/157813/faithless-warriors/

Nelson, R., and T. M. Sanderson. 2011. *Confronting an Uncertain Threat: The Future of al-Qaida and Associated Movements*, Washington, DC: Center for Strategic and International Studies.

References

Newsome, B. O. 2006. Expatriate games: Inter-organizational coordination and international counterterrorism, *Studies in Conflict and Terrorism*, 29(1), 75–89.

Newsome, B. O. 2007. *Made, Not Born: Why Some Soldiers Are Better than Others*, Westport, CT: Praeger Security International.

Newsome, B. O. 2014. *A Practical Introduction to Security and Risk Management*, Thousand Oaks, CA: Sage.

Newsome, B. O. 2015. Surviving new terrorist attacks in ten steps, *Berkeley Blogs*. Available at: http://blogs.berkeley.edu/2015/11/18/surviving-new-terrorism-in-10-steps/

Newsome, B. O. 2016. *An Introduction to Research, Analysis, and Writing: Practical Skills for Social Science Students*, Thousand Oaks, CA: Sage.

Newsome, B. O., and J. Jarmon. 2016. *A Practical Introduction to Homeland Security and Emergency Management from Home to Abroad*, Thousand Oaks, CA: Sage.

Newsweek. 2015. Delta force: Speed, surprise, and violence of action. Available at: http://www.newsweek.com/us-military-special-forces-veterans-delta-force-detachment-delta-vietnam-390666

New York Times. 1995a. Fifth tourist kidnapped in Kashmir, *New York Times*. Available at: http://www.nytimes.com/1995/07/09/world/fifth-tourist-kidnapped-in-kashmir.html

New York Times. 1995b. Kashmiri rebels decapitate captive Norwegian tourist, *New York Times*. http://www.nytimes.com/1995/08/14/world/kashmiri-rebels-decapitate-captive-norwegian-tourist.html

New York Times. 2015. What investigators know about the San Bernardino shooting, *New York Times*. Available at: http://www.nytimes.com/interactive/2015/12/02/us/california-mass-shooting-san-bernardino.html

Noesner, G. 2011. *Stalling for Time: My Life as an FBI Hostage Negotiator*, New York, NY: Random House.

Noesner, G. 2013. Negotiating with terrorists, *Negotiator Magazine*, April. Available at: http://negotiatormagazine.com/openarticle.php?art=AR201304198.php

Noesner, G. 2016. Interview by Bruce Oliver Newsome, by e-mail.

Organization of Islamic Cooperation (OIC). 1990. Cairo Declaration on Human Rights. Available at: http://hrlibrary.umn.edu/instree/cairodeclaration.html

Organization of Islamic Cooperation. 2004. Covenant on the Rights of the Child in Islam. Available at: http://www.oic-iphrc.org/en/data/docs/legal_instruments/OIC Instruments/OIC Covenant on the Right of the Child/OIC Convention-Rights of the Child In Islam - EV.pdf

Organization of Islamic Cooperation. 2008. OIC Plan of Action for the Advancement of Women. Available at: http://www.oic-iphrc.org/en/data/docs/legal_instruments/OIC%20Instruments/OPAAW/OPAAW%20-%20EV.pdf

O'Toole, M. 2016. Family of U.S. hostage killed in botched strike blasts the White House. Available at: http://foreignpolicy.com/2016/04/22/family-of-u-s-hostage-killed-in-botched-strike-blasts-the-white-house/

Paoli, G. P., J. Aldridge, N. Ryan, and R. Warnes. 2017. *Behind the Curtain: The Illicit Trade of Firearms, Explosives, and Ammunition on the Dark Web*, Santa Monica, CA: RAND.

Paul, M. V., O. Fahmy, and S. White. 2016. Three Spanish journalists kidnapped in Syria freed. Available at: http://www.reuters.com/article/us-mideast-crisis-spain-journalists-idUSKCN0XY0O0

Pellegrini, F. 2002. Daniel Pearl: 1963–2002, *TIME*. Available at: http://content.time.com/time/nation/article/0,8599,212284,00.html

Perez-Pena, R., and F. Robles. 2016. Gunfire and panicked calls on police log of Orlando shooting, *New York Times*. Available at: http://www.nytimes.com/2016/06/29/us/orlando-shooting-documents.html

Peritz, A., and J. W. Walker. 2015. The Islamic State may have derailed Japan's foreign policy outreach. Available at: http://thediplomat.com/2015/02/the-islamic-state-may-have-derailed-japans-foreign-policy-outreach/

Perry, T., and L. Bassam. 2015. Prisoner swap frees Lebanese soldiers and IS leader's ex-wife, *Reuters*. Available at: http://www.reuters.com/article/2015/12/01/us-lebanon-security-idUSKBN0TK3JA20151201#L6qdAkMW4cF3ufe2.97

Pitt, C. 2015. Fair trade: The president's power to recover captured U.S. service members and the recent prisoner exchange with the Taliban, *Fordham Law Review*, 83(83), 2837–2885. Available at: http://ir.lawnet.fordham.edu/flr/vol83/iss5/22

Post, J. M. 2005. When hatred is bred in the bone: Psycho-cultural foundations of contemporary terrorism, *Political Psychology*, 26(4), 615–636.

Powell, J. 2014. *Talking to Terrorists: How to End Armed Conflicts*, London: Random House.

Powell, J. 2015. *Terrorists at the Table: Why Negotiating Is the Only Way to Peace*, New York: Palgrave Macmillan.

Ramm, R. 2016. Interview by Bruce Oliver Newsome, by e-mail.

Rapoport, D. 2004. Four waves of modern terrorism, in: A. K. Cronin and J. S. Ludes (Eds.), *Attacking Terrorism: Elements of Grand Strategy*, Washington, DC: Georgetown University Press, pp. 46–73.

Revo, R. 2016. Why militancy has failed in Kashmir. Available at: http://www.dailyo.in/politics/jammu-and-kashmir-militancy-azadi-pakistan-handwara-indian-army-isis-hurriyat/story/1/10298.html

RFI. 2013. Millions paid to free French AQIM hostages. Available at: http://en.rfi.fr/africa/20131030-millions-paid-free-french-aqim-hostages-report

Richardson, L. 2006. *What Terrorists Want: Understanding the Enemy, Containing the Threat*, New York, NY: Random House.

Roberts, D. 2015. Obama administration clears way for hostages' families to pay ransom, *The Guardian*. Available at: http://www.theguardian.com/us-news/2015/jun/24/obama-administration-hostages-families-ransom

Roberts, K. 2017. Should we negotiate with terrorist hostage-takers? Available at: https://theconversation.com/should-we-negotiate-with-terrorist-hostage-takers-78390

Rogan, R. G., and F. J. Lanceley. 2010. *Contemporary Theory, Research, and Practice of Crisis and Hostage Negotiation*, New York, NY: Hampton Press.

Roggio, B. 2009. Taliban exchange Swat official for prisoners, *The Long War Journal*. Available at: http://www.longwarjournal.org/archives/2009/02/taliban_exchange_swa.php

Roggio, B. 2012. AQAP demands prisoner exchange for 73 captured Yemeni soldiers, *The Long War Journal*. Available at: http://www.longwarjournal.org/archives/2012/03/aqap_demands_prisoner_exchange.php

Roggio, B. 2013. Lashkar-e-Jhangvi launches suicide assault at hospital in Quetta, *The Long War Journal*. Available at: http://www.longwarjournal.org/archives/2013/06/lashkar-e-jhangvi_la.php

Rosemain, M., and S. Carraud. 2016. Man stabs Paris police commander to death, *Reuters*. Available at: http://www.reuters.com/article/us-france-crime-idUSKCN0YZ2KA

Rosenberg, M. March 24, 2014. CIA cash ended up in coffers of al Qaeda, *New York Times*. Available at: http://www.nytimes.com/2015/03/15/world/asia/cia-funds-found-their-way-into-al-qaeda-coffers.htm

Rosenberg, M., and K. Fahim. 2015. Americans among 6 hostages freed in Yemen after months of captivity, *New York Times*, September 20. Available at: http://www.nytimes.com/2015/09/21/international-home/2-american-hostages-freed-in-yemen-after-months-of-captivity.html

Rushd, I., I. A. K. Nyazee, and M. A. Rauf. 1999. *The Distinguished Jurist's Primer*, Reading, England: Garnet.

Sageman, M. 2004. *Understanding Terror Networks*, Philadelphia, PA: University of Pennsylvania.

Salaymeh, L. 2008. Early Islamic legal-historical precedents: Prisoners of war, *Law and History Review*, 26(3), 521–544. Available at: https://www.cambridge.org/core/journals/law-and-history-review/article/div-classtitleearly-islamic-legal-historical-precedents-prisoners-of-wardiv/700D90E1074E9E3C58A8BC6666F2177A

Saleem, S. 2002. Jihad: Some important questions, Ghamidi: Javed Ahmad Ghamidi. Available at: http://www.javedahmadghamidi.com/renaissance/view/jihad-some-important-questions

Sandler, T., and J. Scott. 1987. Terrorist success in hostage-taking incidents: An empirical study, *Journal of Conflict Resolution*, 31(1), 35–53.

Sawer, P. 2010. British film-maker tells of Jihadist kidnap ordeal, *The Daily Telegraph*. Available at: http://www.telegraph.co.uk/news/worldnews/asia/pakistan/8024970/British-film-maker-tells-of-jihadist-kidnap-ordeal.html

Schmid, A. P., and A. J. Jongman. 1988. *Political Terrorism: A New Guide to Actors, Authors, Concepts, Databases, Theories and Literature*, Amsterdam: North-Holland.

Schmitt, E. 2016. ISIS used chemical arms at least 52 times in Syria and Iraq, report says, *New York Times*. Available at: http://www.nytimes.com/2016/11/21/world/middleeast/isis-chemical-weapons-syria-iraq-mosul.html

Shahabuddin, S., K. Johnson, and D. Evans. 2015. Chinese cyclist kidnapped in Pakistan freed after a year. Available at: http://www.reuters.com/article/us-pakistan-china-kidnap-idUSKCN0QS0LF20150823

Sharma, M. 2009. The hijacking of Indian Airlines Flight IC-814, *NDTV*. Available at: http://www.ndtv.com/india-news/the-hijacking-of-indian-airlines-flight-ic-814-400555

Shear, M. D. 2016. $400 million cash payment to Iran fuels latest campaign dispute, *New York Times*. Available at: http://www.nytimes.com/2016/08/04/world/middleeast/400-million-cash-payment-to-iran-fuels-latest-campaign-dispute.html

Sheehan, I. S. 2012. Assessing and comparing data sources for terrorism research, in: C. Lum and L. W. Kennedy (Eds.), *Evidence-Based Counterterrorism Policy*, New York, NY: Springer, pp. 13–40.

Sherazi, Z. S. 2014. TTP splinter group claims abduction of Chinese tourist, *Dawn*. Available at: http://www.dawn.com/news/1107511

Shimbun, Y. 2015a. ISIL sent memento of Yukawa. Available at: http://www.yomiuri.co.jp/feature/TO000679/20150223-OYT1T50106.html

Shimbun, Y. 2015b. Prime Minister Abe laments the difficult situation. Available at: http://www.yomiuri.co.jp/feature/yokoku/20150220-OYT8T50064.html

Shimbun, Y. 2015c. Hostage exchange demanded. Available at: http://www.yomiuri.co.jp/feature/yokoku/20150220-OYT8T50062.html

Sidahmed, M. 2016. Kayla Mueller abduction: MSF withheld key information from us, parents say, *The Guardian*. Available at: https://www.theguardian.com/world/2016/aug/27/kayla-mueller-isis-kidnapping-parents-medecins-sans-frontieres

Silverman, R. 2015. ISIS's newest issue of their English-language magazine justifies the enslavement of women, Center for Security Policy. Available at: http://www.centerforsecuritypolicy.org/2015/05/28/isiss-newest-issue-of-their-english-language-magazine-justifies-the-enslavement-of-women/

Simon, U. 2010. Sunni concepts of ritual purity in a contemporary diaspora context, in: U. Hüsken and C. Brosius (Eds.), *Ritual Matters: Dynamic Dimensions in Practice*, Oxford, UK: Routledge, pp. 124–143.

al-Sistani, S. A. A.-H. 2010. Ayatollah Al-Sistani prohibits the enslavement and rape of women during a military campaign, and forbids sex with non-Muslim concubines, *Islamopedia Online*, April 4. Available at: http://www.islamopedia-online.org/fatwa/ayatollah-al-sistani-prohibits-enslavement-and-rape-women-during-military-campaign-and-forbids

al-Sistani, S. A. A.-H. 2015. Advice and guidance to the fighters on the battlefields, *Sistani.org*, February 15. Available at: http://www.sistani.org/downloads/Advice.pdf

Sister Al. 2005. *A Sister's Role in Jihad*. Available at: https://ia800809.us.archive.org/16/items/SistersRoleInJihad/78644461-Sister-s-Role-in-Jihad.pdf

Smith, S. 2013. *Stop! Armed Police! Inside the Met's Firearms Unit*, London, UK: Robert Hale.

Soskis, D. A., and C. R. Van Zandt. 1986. Hostage negotiation: Law enforcement's most effective nonlethal weapon, *Behavioral Sciences and the Law*, 4(4), 423–435.

Soufan Group. 2016. America in the age of active shooters. Available at: http://soufangroup.com/tsg-intelbrief-america-in-the-age-of-active-shooters/

South Asia Terrorism Portal. 2013a. Incidents and statements involving Hizb-ul-Mujahideen: 2005–2012, South Asia Terrorism Portal. Available at: http://www.satp.org/satporgtp/countries/india/states/jandk/terrorist_outfits/hizb_ul_mujahideen_tl.htm

South Asia Terrorism Portal. 2013b. Incidents and statements involving TTP: 2011–2012. South Asia Terrorism Portal. Available at: http://www.satp.org/satporgtp/countries/pakistan/terroristoutfits/ttp_tl.htm

Spencer, A. 2014. The "new terrorism" of al-Qaeda is not so new, in: S. Gottlieb (Ed.), *Debating Terrorism and Counterterrorism: Conflicting Perspectives on Causes, Contexts, and Responses*, 2nd edition, Los Angeles, CA: Sage, pp. 1–15.

Sproat, P. A. 1991. Can the state be terrorist? *Terrorism*, 14(1), 19–30.

Stanford University. 2012. Lashkar-e-Islam. Available at: http://web.stanford.edu/group/mappingmilitants/cgi-bin/groups/view/445

START (National Consortium for the Study of Terrorism and Responses to Terrorism). 2016. *Codebook: Inclusion Criteria and Variables*. Available at: http://www.start.umd.edu/gtd/downloads/Codebook.pdf

Stern, J. 2010. Mind over martyr: How to deradicalize Islamist extremists, *Foreign Affairs*, 89(1), 95–108. Available at: https://www.foreignaffairs.com/articles/saudi-arabia/2009-12-21/mind-over-martyr

Stewart, S. 2015. How to counter armed assaults, *Stratfor*. Available at: https://www.stratfor.com/weekly/how-counter-armed-assaults

Stohl, M. 2012. State terror: The theoretical and practical utilities and implications of a contested concept, in: R. Jackson and S. J. Sinclair (Eds.), *Contemporary Debates on Terrorism*, London, UK: Routledge, pp. 43–50.

References

Stohl, M., and G. A. Lopez. (Eds.). 1984. *The State as Terrorist: The Dynamics of Governmental Violence and Repression*, London, UK: Aldwych.

Stratton, J. G. 1978. The terrorist act of hostage taking: A view of violence and the perpetrators, *Police Science and Administration*, 6(1), 1–9.

Strobel, W., P. Stewart, and M. Hosenball. March 1, 2016. New bin Laden documents show a suspicious al Qaeda, *Reuters*. Available at: http://www.reuters.com/article/us-usa-binladen-documents-idUSKCN0W348A

Suleiman, O. 2016. Slavery and rape in Islamic law Q&A, Lecture. Available at: https://www.youtube.com/watch?v=4sVo_-j2THE

Suttmoeller, M., S. Chermak, J. D. Freilich, and S. Fitzgerald. 2011. Radicalization and risk assessment, in: L. W. Kennedy and E. F. McGarrell (Eds.), *Crime and Terrorism Risk: Studies in Criminology and Criminal Justice*, New York, NY: Routledge, pp. 81–96.

Tadros, S., H. Haqqani, T. Ahmad, F. Ispahani, J. Zenn, and A. U. Noi. 2013. Current trends in Islamist ideology, *Hudson Institute*, 15, 5–115. Available at: http://www.hudson.org/content/researchattachments/attachment/1367/20140110_current_trends_vol15.pdf

Taliban, A. 2009. Rules and regulations booklet, captured on July 15, 2009, in Ivo Sangin Valley, Afghanistan. Translated document. Available at: http://wwwtc.pbs.org/wgbh/pages/frontline/obamaswar/etc/mullahomar.pdf

Taliban, A. 2010. The code of conduct for Mujahids. Available at: https://www.icrc.org/eng/assets/files/review/2011/irrc-881-munir-annex.pdf

Tallen, B. 2008. Paramilitary terrorism: A neglected threat, *Homeland Security Affairs*, 4, Article 6. Available at: https://www.hsaj.org/articles/123

Tawfeeq, M., J. Sterling, T. Ap, and H. Alkhshali. 2016. Bombing that killed more than 200 deadliest attack in Baghdad in years, *CNN*, July 4. Available at: http://www.cnn.com/2016/07/04/middleeast/baghdad-car-bombs/index.html

Thundercloud, M. 2016. Interview by Bruce Oliver Newsome, by e-mail.

Toft, M. D. 2010. *Securing the Peace: The Durable Settlement of Civil Wars*, Princeton, NJ: Princeton University Press.

United Nations. 1948. *Convention on the Prevention and the Punishment of the Crime of Genocide*. Available at: https://treaties.un.org/doc/publication/unts/volume%2078/volume-78-i-1021-english.pdf

United Nations. 1979a. *International Convention against the Taking of Hostages* (December 17, 1979), New York, NY: United Nations. Available at: http://www.un.org/en/sc/ctc/docs/conventions/Conv5.pdf

United Nations. 1979b. *Convention on the Elimination of All Forms of Discrimination against Women*. New York, NY: United Nations. Available at: http://www.ohchr.org/Documents/ProfessionalInterest/cedaw.pdf

United Nations. 1984. Convention against torture and other cruel, inhuman or degrading treatment or punishment. Adapted by the General Assembly of the United Nations on 10 December 1984, United Nations Treaty Collection. Available at: https://treaties.un.org/doc/Publication/UNTS/Volume1465/volume-1465-I-24841-English.pdf

United Nations. 1993. *Declaration on the Elimination of Violence against Women*, New York, NY: United Nations. Available at: http://www.ohchr.org/Documents/ProfessionalInterest/eliminationvaw.pdf

United Nations. 1998. *International Criminal Tribunal for Rwanda*. Available at: http://unictr.unmict.org/sites/unictr.org/files/case-documents/ictr-96-4/trial-judgements/en/980902.pdf

United Nations. 2014. After CIA torture revelations, U.S. must now recover moral high ground, UN News Centre. Available at: http://www.un.org/apps/news/story.asp?NewsID=49578#.WA41v-grKhc

United States, Department of Homeland Security. 2010. Terrorist use of vehicle ramming tactics, *Roll Call Release*. Available at: https://info.publicintelligence.net/DHS-TerroristRamming.pdf

United States, White House. 2014. Statement about the death of Luke Somers. Available at: http://www.whitehouse.gov/the-press-office/2014/12/06/statement-president-death-luke-somers

United States, White House. 2015. Statement by the President on the U.S. Government's Hostage Policy Review. Available at: https://www.whitehouse.gov/the-press-office/2015/06/24/statement-president-us-governments-hostage-policy-review

UNOHCHR (United Nations Office of the High Commissioner for Human Rights). 1989. Convention on the Rights of the Child. Available at: http://www.ohchr.org/en/professionalinterest/pages/crc.aspx

UNOHCHR (United Nations Office of the High Commissioner for Human Rights). 2016. "It's Not Just About Closing Guantánamo, but Also Ensuring Accountability," UN Rights Experts Say. Available at: http://www.ohchr.org/en/NewsEvents/Pages/DisplayNews.aspx?NewsID=17097&LangID=E

Van Hasselt, V. B., S. J. Romano, and G. M. Vecchi. 2008. Role-playing: Applications in hostage and crisis negotiation skills training, *Behavior Modification*, 32, 248–263.

Vecchi, G. M., V. B. Van Hasselt, and S. J. Romano. 2005. Crisis (hostage) negotiation current strategies and issues in high-risk conflict resolution, *Aggression and Violent Behavior: A Review Journal*, 10, 533–551.

Wagner, S. 2015. Street smarts: Active shooter takedowns and tactics. Available at: http://www.tactical-life.com/tactics/active-shooter-takedowns

Walsh, D. 2011. Pakistan's godfather of the Taliban dies, *The Guardian*. Available at: https://www.theguardian.com/world/2011/jan/23/pakistan-godfather-taliban-dies

Wardlaw, G. 1989. *Political Terrorism: Theory, Tactics, and Counter-Measures*, 2nd edition, Cambridge, UK: Cambridge University Press.

Watson, D. L. 2002. Testimony. Available at: https://archives.fbi.gov/archives/news/testimony/the-terrorist-threat-confronting-the-united-states

Watts, C. 2015. Should the United States negotiate with terrorists? *Lawfare* (blog). Retrieved from: https://www.lawfareblog.com/should-united-states-negotiate-terrorists

Weinberg, L., and A. Pedahzur. 2003. *Political Parties and Terrorist Groups*, London, UK: Routledge.

Weinberg, L., A. Pedahzur, and S. Hirsch-Hoefler. 2004. The challenges of conceptualizing terrorism, *Terrorism and Political Violence*, 16(4), 777–794.

Wilkinson, P. 1977. *Terrorism and the Liberal State*, London, UK: Macmillan.

Wilkinson, P. 2010. Terrorism, in: V. Mauer and M. D. Cavelty (Eds.), *The Routledge Handbook of Security Studies*, London, UK: Routledge, pp. 129–138.

Wilkinson, P. 2012. The utility of the concept of terrorism, in: R. Jackson and S. J. Sinclair (Eds.), *Contemporary Debates on Terrorism*, London, UK: Routledge, pp. 11–16.

Wilson, M. 2016. How an elite New York Police unit rehearses for a terrorist attack, *New York Times*. Available at: http://www.nytimes.com/2016/08/01/nyregion/new-york-police-prepare-terrorist-attack.html

References

World Bank, S. Devarajan, L. Mottaghi, Q.-T. Do, A. Brockmeyer, C. Joubert, K. Bhatia, and M. A. Jelil. 2016. *Economic and Social Inclusion to Prevent Violent Extremism*, Washington, DC: World Bank. Available at: http://documents.worldbank.org/curated/en/409591474983005625/pdf/108525-REVISED-PUBLIC.pdf

Yeginsu, C., and R. Callimachi. 2016. Turkey says airport bombers were from Kyrgyzstan, Russia and Uzbekistan, *New York Times*, June 30. Available at: http://www.nytimes.com/2016/07/01/world/europe/istanbul-airport-attack-turkey.html

Yehoshua, Y., R. Green, and A. Agron. 2015. Sex slavery in the Islamic State—Practices, social media discourse, and justifications; Jabhat Al-Nusra: ISIS is taking our women as sex slaves too, *MEMRI: The Middle East Media Research Institute*, Inquiry & Analysis Series, 1181. Available at: https://www.memri.org/reports/sex-slavery-islamic-state-%E2%80%93-practices-social-media-discourse-and-justifications-jabhat-al

Yousufzai, M. 2010. Taliban to execute U.S. soldier if Aafia not released, *The News*. Available at: http://www.webcitation.org/5nLKvx1mG

Yusufzai, R. 2010. The kidnapping and execution of Khalid Khwaja in Pakistan, combating terrorism center at West Point. Available at: https://www.ctc.usma.edu/posts/the-kidnapping-and-execution-of-khalid-khwaja-in-pakistan

Zaheer, K. 2004. Human Rights Law and Islamic Shari'ah: Areas of compatibility and conflict, Ghamidi: Javed Ahmad Ghamadi. Available at: http://www.javedahmadghamidi.com/renaissance/view/humans-rights-law-and-islamic-shariah-areas-of-compatibility-and-conflict

Zapotosky, M., and M. Berman. 2016. What the Orlando gunman told the police during his rampage, *Washington Post*. Available at: https://www.washingtonpost.com/news/post-nation/wp/2016/06/20/what-the-orlando-gunman-told-hostage-negotiators-and-dispatchers-during-his-rampage/

Zartman, I. W. 1990. Negotiating effectively with terrorists, in: B. Rubin (Ed.), *The Politics of Counterterrorism: The Ordeal of Democratic States*, Washington, DC: Johns Hopkins Foreign Policy Institute, pp. 163–188.

Zartman, I. W. 2008. *Negotiation and Conflict Management: Essays on Theory and Practice*, New York, NY: Routledge.

Zartman, I. W. (Ed.). 2011. *Engaging Extremists: Trade-offs, Timing, and Diplomacy*, Washington, DC: United States Institute of Peace.

al-Zuhili, W. 2005. Islam and International Law, *International Review of the Red Cross*, 87(858), 269–283. Available at: https://www.icrc.org/eng/assets/files/other/irrc_858_zuhili.pdf

Index

Note: Page numbers followed by "*n*" with numbers indicate notes.

Index

B

C

D

Index

I

J

K

L

M

N

O

P

Q

R

U

V

W

Y

Printed in the United States
by Baker & Taylor Publisher Services